A Partnership for Disorder examines American–Chinese foreign policy planning during World War II for decolonizing the Japanese Empire and controlling Japan after the war. This study unravels some of the complex origins of the postwar upheavals in Asia by demonstrating how the disagreements between the United States and China on many concrete issues prevented their governments from forging an effective partnership. The disagreements stemmed from the two countries' different geostrategic positions, power status, domestic conditions, and historical experiences in international affairs; the results were divergent policies concerning the disposition of Japan. The two powers' quest for a long-term partnership was further complicated by Moscow's eleventh-hour involvement in the Pacific war.

By the war's end, a triangular relationship among Washington, Moscow, and Chongqing surfaced from secret negotiations at Yalta and Moscow. Yet the Yalta–Moscow system in Asia proved too ambiguous and fragile to be useful even for the purpose of defining a new balance of power among the Allies. The conclusion of World War II found the victorious Allies neither in cooperation among themselves nor in a position to cope with the turmoil in Asia.

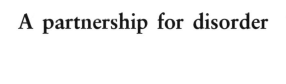

A partnership for disorder

A partnership for disorder

China, the United States, and their policies for the postwar disposition of the Japanese Empire, 1941–1945

XIAOYUAN LIU

Potsdam College of the State University of New York

CAMBRIDGE
UNIVERSITY PRESS

Published by the Press Syndicate of the University of Cambridge
The Pitt Building, Trumpington Street, Cambridge CB2 1RP
40 West 20th Street, New York, NY 10011–4211, USA
10 Stamford Road, Oakleigh, Melbourne 3166, Australia

© Cambridge University Press 1996

First published 1996

Printed in the United States of America

Library of Congress cataloging-in-publication data applied for.

A catalog record for this book is available from the British Library.

ISBN 0–521–55099–8 Hardback

1000849883

For My Parents

Contents

Acknowledgments

The publication of this book gives me the opportunity to express my gratitude to those individuals and institutes that assisted me in writing it. The book is the result of many years of graduate work at the University of Iowa. The first note of appreciation is therefore addressed to Professors R. David Arkush, Ellis W. Hawley, Lawrence E. Gelfand, Allan Megill, and Alan B. Spitzer of the Department of History. These distinguished historians served diligently on my dissertation committee, and their constructive questions and remarks helped keep my research on the right track. As teachers and scholars, these individuals are models for me to emulate. I am deeply grateful to Professor Lawrence E. Gelfand, my dissertation supervisor, intellectual mentor, and dear friend. About a decade ago, he suggested that I investigate American–Chinese foreign policy planning in World War II. Since then, I have completed my graduate work and have started my teaching career. Throughout these years, Professor Gelfand has always been a source of scholarly wisdom, moral support, and warm friendship from which I draw strength. I would have never been able to write this book without taking advantage of Professor Gelfand's knowledge in international relations and his generosity in sharing his mind and energy with students. I present this volume to him as evidence that I am trying to meet his high standards.

I am indebted to Drs. Akira Iriye and Michael H. Hunt. During my research for the dissertation, Dr. Iriye enlightened me on some important sources on Chinese diplomacy. The title of this book is due to my correspondence with Dr. Hunt. Both professors read the manuscript in its early stages and offered many suggestions and criticisms. I also wish to thank the two anonymous readers who evaluated my work for Cambridge University Press. Their remarks helped me perform the final restructuring of the manuscript. At Cambridge University Press, Mr. Frank Smith, the Executive Editor for Social Sciences, and his staff wisely and patiently

ix

x   *Acknowledgments*

guided the production of the book. Dr. Victoria Levitt at Potsdam College
did a marvelous job of editing the manuscript and thus spared the readers
many awkward sentences. Although all of these individuals contributed to
the making of *A Partnership for Disorder*, I alone, of course, am responsible for its mistakes and flaws.

Most of the research for the book was financed by the Laurence D.
Lafore Dissertation Fellowship of the Department of History, the University of Iowa. Two research grants from the Research and Creative Endeavors
Committee, the State University College of New York at Potsdam, enabled
me to engage in further archival research. My colleagues in the Department of History, Potsdam College, provided me with a congenial environment in which I was able to finish the revision of the book. The research
was facilitated by the assistance of the efficient and friendly staffs of the
Diplomatic Branch of the National Archives; the National Archives and
Federal Records Center at Suitland, Maryland; the Manuscript Division of
the Library of Congress; the Hoover Institution on War, Revolution and
Peace; the Rare Book and Manuscript Library of Columbia University; the
Franklin D. Roosevelt Presidential Library; and the Second Historical
Archives, Nanjing, China.

During the lengthy writing period, Hongxing Ma, my wife, was the one
person who shared with me the emotions caused by the ups and downs of
the project. Her love, understanding, encouragement, and constant interest
in the project were indispensable. Our two daughters, Ying Ying and
Tanni, have grown with the book. To them, father is someone who sits in
front of the computer day and night. Fortunately, they have never accepted
such a conception of fatherhood and kept rescuing me from piles of notes
and documents. My parents, who have personal experiences in China's
war, revolution, and foreign affairs during the period described in this
study, have encouraged my interest in international relations. I dedicate
this book to them.

Parts of Chapters 4 and 8 first appeared in a different form in *The
Journal of American–East Asia Relations*, vol. 1 (Summer 1992), no. 2. I
acknowledge the journal's permission to use these materials here.

Note on romanization

In this study, I use *pinyin* to romanize Chinese names and titles of Chinese materials. But there are exceptions: (1) some Chinese names, such as Sun Yat-sen, Chiang Kai-shek, T. V. Soong, and Wellington Koo, have already become part of the historical literature in Western languages, and thus their Wade–Giles forms are kept here as well; (2) Chinese sources cited in this study that are housed in institutions in the United States are listed in Wade–Giles as they are by their depositories; and (3) geographical names of historical places that no longer exist appear in their original forms (for instance, Jehol but not Rehe). Otherwise, names of places on the Chinese mainland are in *pinyin*, but those in Taiwan in Wade–Giles.

Abbreviations

CCP	Chinese Communist Party
CPPC	*Complete Presidential Press Conferences of Franklin D. Roosevelt, 1933–1945*
CSYZ	*Xian Zongtong Chiang Gong Sixiang Yanlun Zongji* (Complete Works of the Late President Chiang)
CZM	*Chiang Zongtong Milu* (Secret Records of President Chiang)
DELD	Zhongguo Di Er Lishi Dang'anguan (Second Historical Archives of China, Nanjing, China)
FRUS	*Foreign Relations of the United States: Diplomatic Papers*
GRCE	General Records of Chungking [Chongqing] Embassy, China, 1943–1945
GW	*Geming Wenxian* (Revolutionary Documents)
HDYS	*Guomin Zhengfu yu Hanguo Duli Yundong Shiliao* (Historical Records on the Nationalist Government and the Korean Independence Movement)
HHP	Harry L. Hopkins Papers
HSD	Henry L. Stimson Diaries
HSP	Hsiung Shih-hui (Xiong Shihui) Papers
JCS	Joint Chiefs of Staff (United States)
JSP	Joseph W. Stilwell Papers
KMT	Kuomintang (National People's Party)
KPG	Korean Provisional Government
LCP	Lauchlin Currie Papers
OJ	*The Occupation of Japan: U.S. Planning Documents, 1942–1945*
OSSR	O.S.S./State Department Intelligence and Research Reports
PRC	Institute of Pacific Relations Collections
RC	Research Committee on Postwar International Peace Organization (China)

RCT	Records of the China Theatre of Operations, United States Army (CT): Records of the Office of the Commanding General (Albert C. Wedemeyer)
RDCA	Records of Division of China Affairs, U.S. Department of State
RHN	Records of Harley A. Notter
RJCS	Records of the Joint Chiefs of Staff
RLP	Records of the Special Assistant to the Secretary of State (Leo Pasvolsky)
RPMF	Franklin D. Roosevelt Papers: Map Room File
RPOF	Franklin D. Roosevelt Papers: Official File
RPPF	Franklin D. Roosevelt Papers: President's Personal File
RPSF	Franklin D. Roosevelt Papers: President's Secretary's File
RWK	Reminiscences of V. K. Wellington Koo (Gu Weijun)
SAI	*Studies of American Interests in War and Peace* (Memoranda of the Council on Foreign Relations)
SHP	Stanley Hornbeck Papers
SWNCC	State–War–Navy Coordinating Committee
SWNCCF	State–War–Navy Coordinating Committee Policy Files, 1944–1947
TG	*Taiwan Guangfu he Guangfu hou Wu Nian Shengqing* (Restoration of Taiwan and the Situation in the Province During the first Five Years)
TRA	Taiwanese Revolutionary Alliance
TSGR	Top Secret General Records of the Chongqing Embassy, China, 1945
TSP	T. V. Soong (Song Ziwen) Papers
VHP	Victor Chi-ts'ai Hoo (Hu Shize) Papers
WKP	V. K. Wellington Koo (Gu Weijun) Papers
ZRWJ	*Zhong Ri Waijiao Shiliao Congbian* (Historical Records on Sino–Japanese Diplomatic Relations)
ZZSC	*Zhonghua Minguo Zhongyao Shiliao Chubian – Dui Ri Kangzhan Shiqi* (Preliminary Compilation of Important Historical Records of the Republic of China: The Period of the War of Resistance against Japan)
ZW	*Zhuanji Wenxue* (Biographical Literature)

A partnership for disorder

Introduction

The Asian–Pacific dimension of World War II is an extremely complicated and significant aspect in the international history of this century. This is so not only because the Asian–Pacific conflict encompassed the largest geographic theater of the war, but also because the war fought against Imperial Japan involved forces that combined political, racial, ideological, and cultural differences. If one can liken the military dimension of the war to a two-sided chess game, on the political–diplomatic front the belligerents were playing a Chinese checker game that almost continuously redivided them into many sides. This study examines one aspect of the wartime American–Chinese relationship that has been largely overlooked by the existing historiography of World War II: the American and Chinese governments' wartime cooperation in conceiving of a new international order for postwar East Asia. Focusing on this one subject, the study cannot avoid being cursory on certain other important issues regarding the Asian dimension of World War II.

By tracing those paths in which the American and Chinese war and peace aims for East Asia were constructed and then exploring the two governments' efforts to coordinate their postwar programs, this inquiry bears some resemblance to three groups of scholarly works pertinent to the international relations of World War II. The first is the literature on the wartime inter-Allied diplomacy for reorganizing peace. In these studies, China's role is usually minute. Since China was the only Asian member of the so-called Big Four in the United Nations coalition, the exclusion of China by these studies from the inter-Allied consultation for the postwar settlement is a noteworthy omission. This omission has created an impression that in World War II, Asian peoples were largely passive spectators of the diplomatic maneuvering among the Anglo–American–Soviet powers.[1]

---

[1] It is impossible to list here all the important studies of inter-Allied diplomacy, but my point can be verified by the *Guide to American Foreign Relations since 1700* (Santa Barbara, CA:

Considering the fact that in World War I Japan had participated in the secret diplomacy among the allied powers only for the purpose of taking advantage of China's weakness, one wonders whether World War II saw an even less active and accountable Asia in international politics than did the earlier world war.

This study offers a different picture. Without question, China was the weakest among the Big Four, and its foreign policy initiatives more often foundered than succeeded. But it is also true that the war years saw an unprecedented activism in Chinese diplomacy. This activism was reflected not only in the Chinese government's routine diplomatic activities but also in its part in important consultations taking place at the highest level in association with the Allied governments. Although China's dire military situation mandated Chongqing's frantic search for assistance from the Western Allies, this was not the only concern of China's wartime diplomacy. The Chinese government also participated in the inter-Allied maneuvering for organizing peace and was resolved not to be excluded from the process, especially where Asia was concerned. The two-way personal diplomacy between Chiang Kai-shek and President Franklin D. Roosevelt, the Chinese government's participation in international conferences bearing on issues of the postwar world, and Kuomintang (KMT, or the National People's Party) leaders' often erratic bargaining with the Americans at Cairo in 1943 and then with the Russians at Moscow in 1945 all indicated significant escalations of China's importance in international politics. Until the Asian war of 1937–1945, foreign powers never accepted China as a worthy participant in important diplomatic undertakings.

The second category of scholarship that facilitated this inquiry includes studies concerning wartime American–Chinese relations. During the past forty years, steady scholarly interest in the wartime encounters between the United States and China has produced many important works. In the process, a conventional approach to investigation, which I call the "America-in-China approach," has been perfected. Typically, many books in this area include "in China" in their titles. This approach usually depicts the wartime American–Chinese relationship as a shabby structure at the beginning that was eventually torn apart by its own built-in time bombs, such as incoordinate military strategies, disputes over American aid to China, mutual misgivings about reforms in China, diverging orientations on the Chinese Communists, and feuds between personalities. In this picture, what has been left out or only sketched in passing is the American–Chinese relations over issues *external* to China. Although principal research interests have sought to analyze America's foreign policy in China, in these studies China's domestic conditions have received far more attention than

ABC-Clio, Inc., 1983), published by the Society for Historians of American Foreign Relations. The section on inter-Allied diplomacy is entitled "Anglo–American–Soviet Diplomacy for the Postwar World, 1941–1945," and China is not included.

its foreign policies.[2] The America in China approach to the study of wartime American–Chinese relations and the "China exclusion" tendency in the study of inter-Allied diplomacy have had the same effect: both imply that during World War II, "China affairs" remained basically unchanged. Foreign powers might view China as a problem, an arena, a prize, a geographic name, or, at most, a lesser adjunct to their strategies in the power politics of the world, but not as a force in its own right in international relations.

A careful examination of the wartime American–Chinese relationship with regard to a peace settlement in Asia indicates that this old image of China affairs was no longer held by either American or Chinese policymakers. That relationship itself affords a salient indication that during World War II the international politics of East Asia underwent a profound change. At the core of the revolution was China's entry into world affairs with new credentials. These credentials arose partly from China's own tenacious resistance against Japan and partly from Washington's promotion. Once nationalism became a potent force behind China's foreign policy in the early twentieth century, Chinese diplomacy was never again content to function only by adjusting to the prevailing international system as defined by the Western powers. But China's chance to redefine its international posture came only during World War II at a time when China's principal suppressor, Japan, was defeated and when China was brought into an alliance with the United States.[3]

[2] For instance, Herbert Feis, *The China Tangle: The American Effort in China from Pearl Harbor to the Marshall Mission* (Princeton, NJ: Princeton University Press, 1953); Tang Tsou, *America's Failure in China, 1941–1950* (Chicago: University of Chicago Press, 1963); Wilma Fairbank, *America's Cultural Experiment in China, 1942–1949* (Washington, DC: G.P.O., 1976); Liang Jingtong, *General Stilwell in China, 1942–1944: The Full Story* (Jamaica, NY: St. John's University Press, 1972); Michael Schaller, *The U.S. Crusade in China, 1938–1945* (New York: Columbia University Press, 1979); and Barbara W. Tuchman, *Stilwell and the American Experience in China, 1911–1945* (New York: Macmillan, 1970). A noteworthy exception to the conventional line of inquiry is Kenneth E. Shewmaker, *Americans and Chinese Communists, 1927–1945: A Persuading Encounter* (Ithaca, NY: Cornell University Press, 1971), which is about a nonofficial aspect of the wartime Sino–American relationship. Anthony Kubek's *How the Far East Was Lost: American Policy and the Creation of Communist China, 1941–1949* (Chicago: Regnery, 1951); Joseph W. Esherick, ed., *Lost Chance in China: The World War II Despatches of John S. Service* (New York: Random House, 1974); and Dorothy Borg and Waldo Heinrichs, ed., *Uncertain Years: Chinese–American Relations, 1947–1950* (New York: Columbia University Press, 1980), are useful studies showing some of the ongoing debates in the field.

[3] Before dealing with Japan's aggression, Chinese diplomacy in the 1920s had a broad agenda: to reform China's foreign affairs. Akira Iriye's *After Imperialism: The Search for a New Order in the Far East, 1921–1931* (Cambridge, MA: Harvard University Press, 1965) offers a classic treatment of the subject. Edmund S. K. Fung's *The Diplomacy of Imperial Retreat: Britain's South China Policy, 1924–1931* (Hong Kong: Oxford University Press, 1991) and Zhang Yongjin's *China in the International System, 1918–1920: The Middle Kingdom at the Periphery* (New York: St. Martin's Press, 1991) are two noteworthy new studies.

In the war years, to empower the new China state and restructure the
international relations of East Asia, policymakers in Chongqing and Washington agreed that China should recover its lost territories from Japan,
maintain a preeminent interest in Korea's postwar settlement, share the
responsibility for postwar control of Japan, and participate in consultations among the world's leading powers. Yet, wartime American–Chinese
cooperation in designing peace for Asia is easy to forget. The principal
reason is that in the immediate postwar years, China's withdrawal into
another civil war and Soviet Russia's ascendance in Asian politics prevented the Chinese government from participating effectively in Allied
actions to restore peace in Asia. But these developments should not prevent us from observing the new vigor of Chinese nationalism driving toward substantial renovation of China's foreign affairs and the initiative in
U.S. foreign policy for fostering its first Asian client state.

Here an explanation should be given with regard to the geographical
range of this inquiry. The study examines closely American and Chinese
policies on postwar settlement in Korea, Manchuria (to the Chinese, Dongbei
or the Northeast), the Ryukyu Islands, Taiwan, and Japan proper but only
mentions in passing Japan's other imperial territories. The reason is that
the latter group of territories had only marginal significance to the wartime
American–Chinese relationship.[4] Territories in Southeast Asia are also not
treated in detail. In the war years, despite Japan's occupation or indirect
control over territories in this area, the American and Chinese governments continued to view them as European colonies and hence as part of
the European problem. Although there are some valuable studies of wartime
Anglo–American diplomacy surrounding these issues, a study of wartime
American–Chinese encounters pertinent to Southeast Asia remains to be
written. That subject deserves a separate treatment.[5]

My inquiry also benefits from a third category of scholarship that has

[4] For discussions of the conceptions of Japan's "formal" and "informal" empires, see Mark
R. Peattie's introduction to Ramon H. Myers and Mark R. Peattie, ed., *The Japanese
Colonial Empire, 1895–1945* (Princeton, NJ: Princeton University Press, 1984), 3–52, and
Peter Duus's introduction to Peter Duus et al., ed., *The Japanese Informal Empire in China,
1895–1937* (Princeton, NJ: Princeton University Press, 1989), xi–xxix.
[5] The best studies of the Anglo–American relationship over postwar settlement in Asia are
Wm. Roger Louis, *Imperialism at Bay: The United States and the Decolonization of the
British Empire, 1941–1945* (New York: Oxford University Press, 1978), and Christopher
Thorne, *Allies of a Kind: The United States, Britain, and the War Against Japan, 1941–
1945* (Oxford: Oxford University Press, 1978). Also noteworthy is John Sbrega, *Anglo–
American Relations and Colonialism in East Asia, 1941–1945* (New York: Garland, 1983).
King C. Chen's *Vietnam and China, 1938–1954* (Princeton, NJ: Princeton University Press,
1969) presents the problematic theory that during World War II the Chinese government
did not have a policy toward Vietnam. This theme is continued in a recent study by Stein
Tonnesson, *The Vietnamese Revolution of 1945: Roosevelt, Ho Chi Minh and de Gaulle
in a World at War* (London: Sage Publications, 1992), 57.

helped recast an understanding of the Chinese foreign relations in the Republican period.[6] Students of Chinese diplomacy of this period cannot avoid confronting a question of immense importance: given China's fragmentary political condition at home and especially the existence of a vigorous Communist regime in Yan'an, to what extent can the official foreign policy of the KMT regime be interpreted as China's national foreign policy? Researchers who see continuity in the evolution of modern China's foreign policy and those who see aberrations and interruptions will likely have different answers. This study argues that the wartime foreign policies of the KMT and the Chinese Communist Party (CCP) converged in important aspects. It points to continuity in China's international orientation between World War II and the ensuing periods. Important studies in both Chinese and Western languages of the CCP's foreign policy in World War II agree that the war years constituted a formative period for the CCP's international behavior. In other words, the foreign policy of the People's Republic of China had its origins in the caves of Yan'an.[7]

The coexistence of the KMT and the CCP regimes in wartime China, however, should not lead to a conclusion that in wartime China there were two or more partisan foreign policies but none that can be named as "national." It is undeniable that both the KMT and the CCP utilized foreign policy as an instrument in their struggle for power in China. Yet, a fundamental fact is that unlike Chinese warlords in the early 1920s, the KMT and the CCP were not struggling merely for *dipan* (territory) but mainly for *zhengquan* (state power). In the long run, their success or failure would have to rely on the extent to which their domestic and foreign policy programs were compatible with the prevailing national aspirations in China.

A prominent phenomenon in wartime China is that while upholding conflicting prescriptions for China's domestic problems, the KMT and the CCP embraced many of the same goals in China's foreign affairs. In the war years, the KMT's execution of China's foreign policy did not necessarily make the policy a partisan pet on all occasions and in all issues. As

[6] In terms of the genre of investigation, three works are particularly relevant to this study: William C. Kirby, *Germany and Republican China* (Stanford, CA: Stanford University Press, 1984); John W. Garver, *Chinese-Soviet Relations, 1937–1945: The Diplomacy of Chinese Nationalism* (New York: Oxford University Press, 1988); and Youli Sun, *China and the Origins of the Pacific War, 1931–1941* (New York: St. Martin's Press, 1993).

[7] Garver, *Chinese-Soviet Relations*, 123–152, 237–270; James Reardon-Anderson, *Yenan and the Great Power: The Origins of Chinese Communist Foreign Policy, 1944–1946* (New York: Columbia University Press, 1980); Steven M. Goldstein, "The CCP's Foreign Policy of Opposition, 1937–1945," in James C. Hsung and Steven I. Levine, ed., *China's Bitter Victory: The War with Japan, 1937–1945* (Armonk, NY: M. E. Sharpe, 1992), 107–129; Niu Jun, *Cong Yan'an Zouxiang Shijie–Zhongguo Gongchandang Duiwai Guanxi de Qiyuan* (Approach the World from Yan'an: The Origins of the Foreign Relations of the Chinese Communist Party) (Fuchou: Fujian Renmin Chubanshe, 1992).

a party in power, the KMT had to consider its foreign policy from the perspective of a national government, though from time to time it was also forced to choose between its partisan interests and the nation's broader interests. In fact, as Japan's aggression inflicted unprecedented crises on China, the popular will in China for national salvation and future development more than ever manifested itself in a clear and unanimous voice. To this will, both the KMT and the CCP felt obliged to subscribe. Therefore, although focusing on the KMT regime's foreign policy, which is inevitable due to the KMT's direct participation in the wartime diplomacy among the leading Allies, this study reveals not a mere partisan undertaking disguised as a national policy, but a foreign policy that, despite interference from partisan spirit, reflected a genuine national essence transcending the KMT–CCP conflict.

The comparative approach of this study is based on the conviction that by juxtaposing the stands of the United States and China on the same set of postwar issues in Asia, new insights can be brought to both the American and Chinese experiences. In his study *Power and Culture: The Japanese–American War, 1941–1945*, Akira Iriye views international relations as both power-level interactions and cultural-level interchanges. His finding about wartime Japanese–American relations is thought-provoking: although Japan and America were involved in a struggle for power, their views on a peaceful structure in postwar Asia were basically in agreement. The reason for this paradox, Iriye argues, is that "the two governments included leaders with a shared past who had once worked together for similar goals and in accordance with the same principles, but who had gone separate ways to experiment with alternative solutions to global and domestic problems."[8]

Iriye's two-level view of international politics can also be applied to the wartime American–Chinese relationship, which presents a different paradox. Namely, although the United States and China fought on the same side during the war, the two governments were driving toward different directions in their political schemes on the future of East Asia. When contemplating the same complex of subjects on postwar international relations in Asia, leaders of the two governments tended to encounter rather different problems with their foreign policies. Nor did they subscribe to the same set of principles when looking for solutions. China and the United States certainly did not have a shared past. Furthermore, unlike Japan and other counterparts of America's wartime diplomacy, China did not operate at the same power level as the United States. During the war years, even when Western and Chinese leaders managed to tailor a garment of legal

---

[8] Akira Iriye, *Power and Culture: The Japanese–American War, 1941–1945* (Cambridge, MA: Harvard University Press, 1981), vii, 265.

equality for their relationship, they could not bridge the chasm created by the difference in power and status between China and the other leading Allied powers. Historical, cultural, and status differences existent in the wartime American–Chinese relationship tended to generate disagreements more enduring and profound than those caused by strategies, personalities, and political orientations. Briefly, Chinese officials often contemplated China's postwar foreign relations with a spirit of absolute nationalism, an Asia-centered calculation, and a confrontational perception of international politics, whereas American leaders approached the issue of postwar international order from an inclusive and world-systemic view.

Therefore, although Japan was the enemy, in the long run China the partner posed a greater challenge to U.S. foreign policy. During World War II, the United States was on its way to becoming the hegemon of the world. But in Asia, Western influence was receding. To maintain the momentum of America's leadership in Asian affairs, policymakers in Washington were compelled to seek new pivots for their Asian policy and to look for new partners. With its newly achieved yet confusing international identity – a great power without substance – China became associated closely with the United States. American leaders treated China as the representative of the emerging new Asia and at the same time ignored completely other Asian nationalist movements. In a sense, America's ill-conceived encounter with China in the war years was responsible for the American government's unpreparedness to cope with Asian nationalist movements after the war. In dealing with the Chinese government, American policymakers also often misconstrued Chongqing's foreign policy intentions and underestimated the difficulty of enlisting the Chinese in America's foreign policy agenda. The Chinese government established its war aims in Asia as absolute conditions for both achieving fundamental improvement in China's international environment and winning popular support for its leadership in China. But leaders in Washington tended to view China's new international role and solutions in Asian territories as building blocks that could be arranged in different ways to underpin a world peace system according to the American vision.

To Chinese diplomacy, the wartime partnership with the United States was transcendent but hazardous. The practice surpassed the ancient Chinese statecraft of "using barbarians to curb barbarians," which since the mid-nineteenth century had been used repeatedly by Chinese rulers without effect. Also, unlike the Chinese government's prewar cooperation with Germany and the Soviet Union, which were useful for China's resistance against Japan but had no direct impact on the general conditions of China's foreign affairs, China's wartime partnership with the Western Allies marked the *lawful* (in contrast to Japan's unilateralism) conclusion of the old relations between China and the treaty powers and, consequently, promised to renovate drastically China's foreign affairs.[9] In other words, during the war years, the American alliance enabled Chinese foreign policy to shift from its single-minded anti-Japanese effort to a comprehensive program for enhancing China's international stature. Yet, although the KMT regime sought in earnest a long-term alliance with the United States, its officials were apprehensive about the price they would have to pay for relying on a Western power to solve their domestic and foreign policy problems. Like the South Korean and South Vietnamese regimes in the postwar years, the wartime Chinese government wanted in its American ally a generous patron, not a dictating superintendent, of its own policies. Among KMT officials, suspicions and bitterness toward the United States were accentuated when they discovered that America's postwar objectives in Asia were not congruent with theirs.

Eventually, American–Chinese cooperation in searching for peace culminated in failure. When World War II ended, a fragile configuration of international forces emerged in East Asia that consisted principally of stopgap compromises and improvised arrangements among China, the Soviet Union, and the United States. An effective American–Chinese partnership was not an element in the new status quo. Nor did the new status quo promise a lasting peace. Although the American–Chinese collaboration in war succeeded in crushing the Japanese Empire, in an American–Chinese– Soviet political triangular relationship for a postwar settlement in East Asia, the link between America and China proved weak and ineffectual. Indeed, although the main target of the American and Chinese foreign policy planning was the Japanese Empire, it was the Soviet Union that posed a more troublesome problem to the American–Chinese partnership. During the first half of the Pacific war, the official mind set in both Washington and Chongqing was focused on the historical job of dismantling the Japanese Empire. When the Soviet issue did emerge in their bilateral discussions, it was either evaded or postponed.

Although both the American and Chinese governments had concerns about Soviet intentions in the postwar years, each preferred a different approach. During the second half of the Pacific war, when the Soviet Union began to engage actively in inter-Allied discussions of postwar issues in Asia, the American–Chinese alliance based on their common interest for dealing with the Japanese Empire began to erode. In 1945, inter-Allied diplomacy became highly political and volatile. The two-stage diplomacy proceeding from Yalta to Moscow in that year, during which the Americans and Chinese negotiated with the Russians separately, offered only the most conspicuous indication of the bankruptcy of the American–Chinese partnership for peace. The ascendance of Soviet power in Northeast Asia

[9] See Kirby, *Germany and Republican China* and Garver, *Chinese–Soviet Relations* for Chinese–German and Chinese–Soviet cooperation in the 1930s.

at the very end of the war changed the whole context of American–Chinese foreign policy planning and rendered certain earlier plans irrelevant. Under the circumstances, then, leaders in the two countries improvised. As a result, in contrast to the negotiated balance of power in postwar Europe, in which the Big Three fully participated, the peace structure in East Asia was based on temporary arrangements and incomplete deals for which no collective responsibility ever existed. If the situation in postwar Europe was an "armed truce," the postwar international relations in the Asian–Pacific region were even less organized and constituted but a disorder heading toward new wars.[10]

The narrative in this book generally follows the chronological order of events. Chapter 1 comments on some features of the wartime Sino–American alliance that had roots in the two countries' prewar relations. Chapters 2 to 6 examine the two governments' policy planning operations and their diplomatic maneuvers with regard to East Asian territories as of the Cairo Conference. Chapter 7 discusses the Chinese Communist leaders' intentions in postwar East Asia in comparison with the KMT foreign policy. Chapters 8 and 9 trace the post-Cairo developments in Chongqing's and Washington's search for a peace settlement in East Asia, indicating signs of erosion in the Sino–American alliance. Chapters 10 and 11 shed light on the course and causes of the emergence of an American–Chinese–Soviet triangular relationship by the end of the Pacific war. And Chapter 12, the Epilogue, attempts to establish the relevance, or lack of relevance, of the wartime strategic planning of the Allied governments to postwar developments in East Asia.

[10] Hugh Thomas's *Armed Truce: The Beginnings of the Cold War, 1945–1946* (London: Hodder and Stoughton, 1988), 11, quotes Dean Acheson's and the Soviet diplomat Maxim Litvinov's similar opinions, expressed during the initial months of the postwar period, that the Soviet–Western relationship in Europe was an armed truce.

1

The making of an alliance

A "matter not of principle but of expediency," alliance making in the history of international relations often encompasses strange bed fellows.[1] The American–Chinese alliance during World War II represented an unprecedented degree of cooperation between two very different countries. Until the war, the only parallel between American and Chinese histories took place in the mid-1860s, when both countries emerged from their civil wars. In China a peasants' "Heavenly Kingdom of Grand Peace" was suppressed, and in the United States the southern Confederacy was defeated. But the connotations of the two events cannot plausibly stand comparison. The rest of the nineteenth century found the United States and China moving in opposite directions. At a time when the United States was emerging as one of the dominant powers of the world, the Chinese Empire was suffering from political erosion and was on the brink of collapse. During the first few decades of the twentieth century, the Chinese–American relationship was cemented by the old "treaty system" in China and its recent corollaries that indicated the gap rather than the common interests of the two nations. Then, between 1937 and 1941, Japan's aggressive policy to seal the Asian–Pacific region for itself unwittingly helped bridge the distance between China and the United States. After the militarists in Tokyo masterminded the Pearl Harbor attack, leaders in Washington and Chongqing forged an alliance. The war in the Pacific revolutionized the international relations of East Asia, but it could not change the fundamental characteristics of the nations involved. Although both were determined to undo Japan's Great East Asia Co-Prosperity Sphere, the Chinese and American governments harbored divergent perceptions of the alternative. Simply put, whereas Chinese leaders contemplated their

[1] Hans J. Morgenthau, *Politics among Nations: The Struggle for Power and Peace* (New York: Knopf, 1967), 175.

postwar foreign policies to meet China's developing regional and nationalistic needs, leaders on the other side of the Pacific considered Asia's
position in their design for a more stable global system in economic and
security terms. The differences between the two sides resulted in a tortuous
experience for both in their separate or common search for peace.

China's search for allies

During the first half of the twentieth century, China, striving to shake itself
loose from the burdens and humiliations that it had suffered in foreign
affairs since the mid-nineteenth century, had nationalism as a most potent
driving force behind its foreign policies. It is only partially true to suggest
that, due to a lingering traditional view among Chinese leaders of the
"Chinese world order," modern China has constantly experienced difficulties in adjusting to the prevailing international order based on the European tradition of equality among nation-states.[2] At least for the period in
question, equality, which characterized the relations among the industrialized powers of the world, did not exist between the Western powers and
most of the Asian nations. The truth is that, when extended to Asia, the
European type of international relations was supplemented by the advanced powers' imperial domination over underdeveloped Asian nations.
The international order was at once enlightening and suppressive to China
but also served to generate a modern Chinese diplomacy of dual nature:
to become a full-fledged member of the modern international community,
China had to struggle to overcome both its own past of a China-centric
"cultural empire" and the Western presence of colonial empires. In other
words, modern China could not simply adjust itself to the existing international system; its foreign policy tended to assume the transformation of
China and of the modern international order in East Asia to be the same
process.

At the conclusion of World War I, due to initiatives taken by the
principal participants, the international system in East Asia indeed underwent changes. But the changes took place more slowly than Chinese nationalists had hoped for and in directions not always compatible with the goals
of Chinese diplomacy.[3] Before being engulfed by a new national crisis in
the 1930s, China was able to achieve mere piecemeal improvements of its
external conditions. In two of the most important international undertakings
in the interwar years that concerned China, the Paris Peace Conference of
1919 and the Washington Conference of 1921–1922, China had to settle

---

[2] John K. Fairbank, ed., *The Chinese World Order: Traditional China's Foreign Relations*
(Cambridge, MA: Harvard University Press, 1968), 4.

[3] For a thoughtful study of the evolving international system in East Asia in the interwar
years, see Akira Iriye, *After Imperialism: The Search for a New Order in the Far East,
1921–1931* (Cambridge, MA: Harvard University Press, 1965).

for a course of change charted by the treaty powers. Fragmentary conditions in China in the 1920s never allowed Chinese diplomacy to break the grasp of the treaty powers, but when the treaty-power unity started to collapse in the 1930s, the consequence was at first disastrous rather than a blessing for China.

It was China's misfortune that Japanese expansionism would prove a more vigorous and unscrupulous force for change during the interwar years. Yet there were positive consequences of China's suffering from Japanese aggression. Japan's intrusion into northeastern China in the early 1930s and the ensuing Sino–Japanese war in 1937 eroded the treaty system and also, for the time being at least, helped break a tradition of Chinese politics that tended to put the domestic power struggle ahead of resistance against foreign encroachment. For about a century, China had failed to resist the foreign powers' encroachment on its territories and their diminishing definition of China's international position. Now China at last fought as a nation against foreign imperialism. Although China's war with Japan after 1937 was marred by military disasters, Chinese foreign policy reached a turning point. Differing from earlier diplomatic efforts that had had only limited objectives, the official Chinese foreign policy between 1937 and 1945 embarked on an ambitious undertaking for renovating the international order in Asia. Significantly, in the war years, despite continued civil frictions and anticipation of a new round of power struggles in China after the war, the Chinese Nationalists and the Chinese Communists had no fundamental disagreement on China's international rehabilitation.

During the early decades of the twentieth century, the obsession of the Chinese populace with national revival demonstrated the maturity of modern nationalism in China. Yet Chinese nationalists were faced with a serious challenge in defining their tasks. It has been suggested that after the overthrow of the Manchu rule in China, Chinese nationalism embarked upon two tasks – "to reclaim everything imperial China had ever lost to foreign powers" and to organize a "modern, centralized nation-state, capable both of forcing back the imperialists and of forwarding the country's new aspirations in political, social, economic, and cultural life."[4] Clearly, the immediate difficulty was how a modern nation-state could be formed on the foundation of imperial China. When Sun Yat-sen, founder of the Kuomintang (KMT, National People's Party), sought to articulate the ideology of Chinese nationalism in the 1920s, he attempted without much success to find a blend of China's imperial glory in the past and its nation-state destiny in the future.[5] Setting the restoration of China's "lost national

---

[4] Mary C. Wright, ed., *China in Revolution: The First Phase, 1900–1913* (New Haven, CT: Yale University Press, 1968), 3–4.

[5] The following discussion is based on Sun Yat-sen, "The Principle of Nationalism," part 1 of *San Min Chu I: The Three Principles of the People* (Chongqing: Ministry of Information of the Republic of China, 1943), 3–148.

standing" as the ultimate goal of Chinese nationalism, Sun tried to conceptualize a new international identity for China. A national standing for modern China could not be simply construed from the past, when the country had only had an imperial standing. Nor did it merely mean independence from foreign powers' control, which was only the initial step for achieving that standing. What Sun wanted for China was a new but ill defined great-power status. For Sun, consistency and clarity in theory were less important than the practical need to revive his compatriots' self-confidence and to guide the nationalist revolution in a progressive direction. Consequently, Sun's nationalist foreign policy embraced both the traditional sense of China's cultural superiority and modern conceptions of international relations.[6]

Sun argued that, having a *wangdao* (kingly way or way of right) tradition and being spiritually superior to all existing great powers, China deserved to recover its role as provider of world order. Yet, aside from stressing China as a peace-loving model, Sun was unable to pinpoint other qualities of China that could lead to its great-power status in the modern world. Sun's discussion of recovery by China of its lost territories also failed to make a distinction between the boundaries of imperial China in the past and those of a Chinese nation-state advancing into the future. When praising the *wangdao* tradition of the Chinese Empire, Sun described how China had related to neighboring areas like Annam (Vietnam), Burma, Korea, and Siam (Thailand) as independent states. But when counting China's territorial losses, Sun included not only these areas and foreign concessions inside China, but also a vast ocean crescent running from the Ryukyu Islands in the western Pacific to Borneo and the Java islands in the southern Pacific and then to Ceylon (Sri Lanka) in the Indian Ocean. In both the spiritual and physical senses, Sun Yat-sen aimed at reclaiming everything imperial China had ever lost to foreign powers, but at the same time, he failed to bequeath to his successors a clear conception of the Chinese nation-state.

The reason for Sun's ambivalence about China as a nation-state was neither his cultural conservatism nor his lack of vision. The reason was rooted in Chinese historical experience. As in other Asian countries, nationalism in China arose as a reaction to the impact of Western imperialism. But, differing from other Asian countries, China could claim an imperial past. Although the Western and especially the Japanese experience of modernization became relevant to China's internal development, in external affairs China could neither be just one of the Asian nations struggling for independence nor follow Japan's path by imitating Western imperialism.

---

[6] John K. Fairbank and Edwin O. Reischauer, *China: Tradition and Transformation* (Boston: Houghton Mifflin, 1989), 178–179, use "Chinese culturalism" to indicate an unfailing sense of cultural superiority that was not suppressed even during China's political subjugation by foreign powers and a constant evocation of China's glorious past for inspirations for the present.

Chinese nationalism faced a historical dilemma: a complete rollback of foreign encroachment might lead to the restoration of China's own ancient imperialism, but less than that would mean a compromise with modern imperialism. During World War II, therefore, when Chinese leaders contemplated programs for reestablishing China's national standing, they showed a natural interest in Asianwide anticolonialism but were often bewildered by the question of what new relationship should be formed between China and other Asian countries.

In the war years, officials in Chongqing envisaged a new Asia in which China would again become a leading influence. In their view, this would necessitate the removal of all the unequal treaties between China and foreign powers and the reestablishment of Chinese sovereignty over territories that were then directly or indirectly controlled by Japan, Britain, and Russia. But China's leadership in Asia would be manifested principally through its relations with those states that had formerly been tributaries to the ancient Chinese Empire. These included Korea, Burma, Thailand, Indochina (Vietnam, Laos, and Cambodia), some areas in the southern Pacific, and, to a certain degree, even Japan. Although leaders in Chongqing did not want to revive the tributary system, and although their intentions were more strategic and economic than cultural, they hoped to use devices compatible with modern international relations to reclaim Chinese influence over these countries. Chinese officials summarized this policy in an ancient Chinese saying: *"cunwang jijue jiruo fuqing"* ("rescue the subjugated, revive the extinct, assist the feeble, and sustain the collapsing"). Thus Chinese leaders' support of the anticolonial struggles of other Asian peoples also implied a recurrence of Chinese patronage. Where Sun Yat-sen had been ambiguous, leaders in wartime China set definite policy objectives. These objectives did not revive the traditional view of a China-centric world, but they likely pointed to a China-centric Asia.[7]

Such an ambitious program needed international support. In his political alliance with Soviet Russia during the early 1920s, Sun Yat-sen had shown a way for the wartime KMT leaders to use a bilateral alliance in order to achieve their goals at home and in foreign affairs. Sun had also predicted that China's regeneration would take place only when another world war led to a universal realignment among world powers. The Armageddon clash between the "white and yellow defenders of right" and the "white and yellow defenders of might" would make the whole world over, and only then would China have a chance of rebirth.[8]

---

[7] Waijiaobu memorandum, "Taipingyang shang zhimindi wenti yu yiban anquan wenti" (The Colonial and General Security Problems in the Pacific), 7 June 1944, *VHP*, box 3; Waijiaobu memorandum, "Zhuxi duiyu waijiao fangmian zhishi" (Chairman's [Chiang's] Instructions on Diplomacy), n.d., ibid.

[8] Sun Yat-sen, *San Min Chu I*, 20–21, 109.

China's conflict with Japan in the 1930s at first generated a two-pronged foreign policy of the KMT regime: one was to retreat temporarily from its "treaty abrogation" stand and to seek legal protection from the treaty system in China and the general interwar peace systems of the world; and the other was to seek foreign alliances outside the treaty system. Except for morally aligning China with the West, the former proved futile in checking Japan's advance in China. At the same time, the latter brought beneficial cooperation with Germany and the Soviet Union.[9] Although these diplomatic successes indicated a new level of flexibility and initiative in Chinese diplomacy, what they achieved fell far short of the universal realignment that Sun Yat-sen longed for. Instead, the lessons of the 1930s taught Chinese leaders to trust bilateral cooperation and power-political approaches more than any grand international coalition.

When the world was engulfed by another world war, China's foreign policy also became increasingly anchored to an alliance with the United States. Controlling China's foreign affairs closely, Chiang Kai-shek at first did not perceive the United States to be an ideal ally. Chiang's association with the formidable Song family through his marriage with the American-educated Song Meiling did not help much in fostering Chiang's affection for things American. To Chiang, if there was anything worth learning from the West, it was the German spirit and way of doing things. Once he told his son, Weiguo: "We have nothing to learn from the Japanese – their goods are too cheaply made. The Americans are too fancy, the British too slow. Germany is the only country from which we can learn something. They can give us the base from which to develop our own style: firm and solid."[10]

In the late 1930s and early 1940s, however, when deserted by "solid Germany" and troubled by the ambivalent Soviet policy in East Asia, the Chinese government looked more and more in the direction of "fancy America" for help. After Moscow and Tokyo concluded a neutrality treaty in April 1940, Chiang told his officials that from now on, China would pay special attention to the direction of Washington's policy. Until Japan attacked America's Pacific fleet at Pearl Harbor in December 1941, however, the Chinese government's search for an alliance with the United States accomplished little except obtaining piecemeal aid from America. At one point, Chiang even thought gloomily that the "best" course for China's foreign policy was probably to fight Japan "independently."[11]

---

[9] See John W. Garver, *Chinese–Soviet Relations, 1937–1945: The Diplomacy of Chinese Nationalism* (New York: Oxford University Press, 1988); and William C. Kirby, *Germany and Republican China* (Stanford, CA: Stanford University Press, 1984).

[10] Quoted in Kirby, *Germany and Republican China*, 147.

[11] Chiang to Soong, 1 November 1940, ZZSC, vol. 3 (book 1), 107–108; Chiang to Soong, 9 November 1940, ibid., 111–112; Chiang to Soong, 21 November 1940, ibid., 119–120; CZM, 12: 17–19, 61–62, 65, 133–136; Garver, *Chinese–Soviet Relations*, 91–93.

Despite the slow progress of Chinese–American cooperation prior to Pearl Harbor, KMT leaders entertained broad expectations about the United States. Paradoxically, China's difficult war with Japan helped stimulate optimism among Chinese officials about China's international rehabilitation. The war terminated hesitant diplomacy and justified a thorough rectification of all the historical wrongs that Japan had inflicted on China. Before Pearl Harbor, China's role as the only country resisting Japanese aggression also helped inflate the positive self-image of the Chinese government. Some KMT officials were so exhilarated that at times they even spoke about China's "great mission" for making the world "one great Commonwealth." Although continuing to court Western support, the Chinese government presented itself to other powers no longer merely as a victim of aggression pleading for sympathy, but also as the defender of peace and humanity and, as such, justifying proper recognition.[12]

When the crises in Europe and Asia escalated in the second half of 1940, Chiang Kai-shek advised the American and British governments that in order to achieve China's full cooperation in the war, they must abandon their century-old conception of China as a semicolony and begin to treat it as an equal. Chiang tactfully threw his sharpest words only at the British; at the same time, he promised the Americans that in future international struggles China would follow American leadership and cooperate closely with the Western powers.[13] The idea of a Sino–American partnership or special relationship in both war and peace was advanced early in 1941, when President Franklin D. Roosevelt sent Lauchlin Currie to China as his personal envoy. Currie was impressed by Chiang's confidence in President Roosevelt and by his determination to form a long-term cooperative understanding between the two governments. In his conversations with Currie, Chiang spoke of China as a place that had almost unlimited capacity to absorb America's industrial surplus after the war. He also pleaded for Washington's support for his economic and political policies at home and his foreign policy programs for recovering China's national standing in Asia.[14] Having been slow in warming up to the United States, Chiang Kai-shek now invested great hope in President Roosevelt. After receiving Currie, he felt that personal rapport was growing between himself and Roosevelt. In the last few months of 1941, Chiang convinced

---

[12] *GW*, 76: 370; Chinese Ministry of Information, *The Collected Wartime Messages of Generalissimo Chiang Kai-shek, 1937–1945* (New York: John Day, 1946; reprint, New York: Kraus Reprint, 1969), 118–119 (hereafter cited as *Messages of Chiang*); Chiang to Roosevelt, 24 December 1937, *FRUS, 1937*, 3: 832–833.

[13] Minutes of a conversation between Chiang and British Ambassador Clark Kerr, 14 October 1940, ZZSC, 3(2): 39–40; minutes of a conversation between Chiang and U.S. Ambassador Nelson T. Johnson, 18 October 1940, ibid., 3(1): 100–102.

[14] Minutes of the Chiang-Currie conversations on 8 and 26 February 1941, ZZSC, 3(1): 542–545, 591–595.

himself that his "honorable and trustworthy" diplomacy with the Americans had enhanced his stature in the eyes of President Roosevelt and influenced the Roosevelt administration to adopt more determined measures to check Japanese expansion. Chiang expected that Roosevelt's respect and trust in him would continue to grow in the future.[15]

What sealed the understanding between Chongqing and Washington was Japan's attack on Pearl Harbor. Chongqing immediately benefited from a U.S. loan of $500 million without any strings attached. That fateful December, an Allied military conference convened in Chongqing, and President Roosevelt nominated Chiang Kai-shek as Supreme Commander of the Allied forces in the China theater. In early January 1942, the two governments' appearance among the signatories of the United Nations Declaration joined them in a common front against the Axis powers, something close to Sun Yat-sen's coalition of "white and yellow defenders of right." In May 1942, an agreement between the two governments included China among those countries that received American lend-lease assistance. However, the Chinese government was not satisfied with these wartime expediencies. Recalling China's diplomatic isolation vis-à-vis foreign powers' collective imperialism in the past, KMT leaders wanted the Americans and the British to commit themselves unequivocally to the complete defeat of Japan and to a long-term alliance with China.[16]

Yet, they were disappointed by the American leaders' unwillingness to commit to a bilateral Sino–American alliance. Also, Chinese officials soon discovered that instead of enhancing China's position in the eyes of the Western Allies, the Pacific war deprived China of its prominent role as Japan's principal adversary. Now receiving more American aid than before, they began to worry about losing independence. For instance, when Washington adopted a policy of promoting China as a great power, Chiang was chilled rather than exhilarated by, in his own words, the "misfortune of undeserved reputation."[17] KMT leaders recognized that although China's military situation was improved by the Pacific war, its diplomatic position remained questionable after it entered the patron–beneficiary relationship with the United States. In terms of their dream for restoring China's splendor, the American connection was construed at best as a mixed blessing. KMT leaders' anxieties would increase during the war when, from time to time, Washington attempted to influence the direction of Chongqing's internal and foreign policies.

[15] CZM, 12: 30, 63, 138–139, 144–145, 164.
[16] Gauss to Hull, 8 December 1941, *FRUS, 1941*, 4: 736; Robert E. Sherwood, *Roosevelt and Hopkins: An Intimate History* (New York: Harper, 1948), 448; Soong to Chiang, 27 May 1942, ZZSC, 3(1): 501–503; minutes of a conversation between Chiang and General John Magruder, 18 May 1942, ibid., 3(3): 142–147.
[17] CZM, 12: 197–198, 200; 13: 2–3, 15.

America's response to China

Only slowly did American officials accept the idea that their country and China could become partners in war or peace. Soon after Japan occupied Manchuria, the U.S. minister in China, Nelson T. Johnson, reported to Washington that the Chinese were cultivating an "improbable" idea of China and the United States being "natural allies." Then in late 1935, to set the tone for the forthcoming London Naval Conference, Secretary of State Cordell Hull issued a statement on behalf of the U.S. government that "in relations with China and in China, the treaty rights and the treaty obligations of the treaty powers are in general identical." Although Hull meant to show America's concern about Japan's unilateral actions in China, this statement also indicated that despite its erosion, the treaty system would continue to serve as the basis of U.S. policy in China.[18] In the following years, when the Chinese–Japanese confrontation became heated, Washington's detached attitude toward the Chinese–Japanese conflict was especially disappointing to the Chinese. Some editorial opinion complained that "it is simply a dream if we expect the United States to help China to resist Japan." But the Chinese government kept the dream alive. As expressed laconically by Hu Shi, the Chinese ambassador to the United States between 1938 and 1942, in these years Chongqing's policy was *"kucheng daibian"* ("to persist arduously [in the war] with an ardent desire for changes [in the international situation]").[19]

In fact, in these years there were people in the United States who argued for a more positive China policy. When making such arguments, they were not advocating aid to China just to defend the American rights and interests listed by Secretary Hull. They were redefining U.S. policy in East Asia. After the Sino–Japanese war commenced, Admiral Harry E. Yarnell, Commander in Chief of the U.S. Asiatic Fleet, suggested to officials in Washington that "a free, stable, democratic government in China is essential to the peace of eastern Asia and our own welfare." He also believed that the emergence of a new China would depend not only on the result of China's resistance against Japan, but also on all other treaty powers' willingness to abandon their old privileges in China, such as extraterritoriality.[20] Lauchlin Currie emerged from his 1941 trip to Chongqing as a self-appointed expert on China. Back in Washington, he challenged in public certain ideas

---

[18] Johnson to Hull, 24 May 1932, *FRUS, 1932*, 4: 36–40; Cordell Hull, *Memoirs of Cordell Hull* (New York: Macmillan, 1948), 1: 445–446.

[19] Lai Guanglin, *Qishi Nian Zhongguo Baoye Shi* (Seventy Years of the Chinese Press) (Taipei: Zhongyang Ribao, 1981), 131; Hu Songping, *Hu Shizhi Xiansheng Nianpu Changbian Chugao* (The Primary Draft of the Chronicle of Mr. Hu Shi's Life) (Taipei: Lianjing Chuban Shiye Gongsi, 1984), 1640; *ZRWJ*, 4: 343.

[20] Johnson to Hull, 3 November 1937, *FRUS, 1937*, 3: 654–655; Hornbeck to Hull, 16 September 1939, *FRUS, 1939*, 3: 250–251.

held by those China hands in the State Department who, in Currie's opinion, took the Chinese to be an exotic people. Currie argued that the Chinese and American nations had more similarities than differences, and that they must work together in both the current crisis and beyond in the postwar years. He also urged President Roosevelt that the United States "guide China in her development as a great power in the postwar period." Currie was probably echoing Chiang Kai-shek's rhetoric, but he also brought to Roosevelt's attention a fresh conception of American–Chinese relations.[21]

A concrete result of the Currie mission was to have President Roosevelt recommend an American political adviser to Chiang Kai-shek in mid-1941. The position fell to Owen Lattimore, a journalist turned scholar from Johns Hopkins University known for his specialty in Asian history and geopolitics.[22] Before Pearl Harbor, Lattimore was one of the few Americans who subscribed to a "Chinese new order" as the preferred solution to the Asian crisis. In a position paper prepared for a war and peace studies program of the Council on Foreign Relations, Lattimore outlined how a Chinese new order in Asia could be achieved. The steps included Japan's withdrawal from China (including Manchuria); the treaty powers' abrogation of extraterritoriality and other privileged statuses in Chinese–foreign relations; and negotiations between China and the Soviet Union leading to settlement of their bilateral disagreements. With these accomplished, "complete Chinese independence and freedom in foreign relations" would be achieved. The U.S. government, Lattimore stated, should use its economic strength to assist China in stabilizing its internal conditions and its new international status in Asia. A similar opinion was held by a semiofficial discussion group called the Andover Study Group, which communicated regularly with the State Department.[23] Lattimore's brief sojourn in Chongqing would prove to be unproductive in enhancing Chinese–American cooperation. Yet, his appointment in 1941 was evidence that American policy in China was beginning to slide slowly out of its old tracks.

Even after the United States joined China in the war against Japan,

[21] Chinese version of a public speech by Currie on 16 April 1941, ZZSC, 3(1): 608–617; Currie to Roosevelt, 15 March 1941, FRUS, 1941, 4: 81–95; Michael Schaller, *The U.S. Crusade in China, 1938–1945* (New York: Columbia University Press, 1979), 48–51.

[22] Currie to Chiang, 25 June 1941, ZZSC, 3(1): 622–623; Schaller, *U.S. Crusade in China*, 53–54.

[23] Owen Lattimore, "Alternatives of United States Policy in the Western Pacific," 5 October 1940, SAI, T-B17; Blakeslee to Hornbeck, 20 May 1940, SHP, box 29. An important difference between Lattimore and the Andover group is that the latter could not decide whether Manchuria should be returned to China. Members of the group included Admiral Harry Yarnell, Major Evans Carlson, George H. Blakeslee, Kurt Bloch, Harvey H. Bundy, Leonard W. Cronkhite, John K. Fairbank, Albert E. Hindmarsh, Arthur N. Holcombe, Eldon R. James, S. Shepard Jones, A. Lawrence Lowell, Denys P. Myers, Norman J. Padelford, and George N. Steiger.

American officials did not attach much value to the ally in Chongqing. In March 1942, U.S. Ambassador Clarence E. Gauss reported from Chongqing that since Pearl Harbor the Chinese leadership had had a "passive attitude of wait and see," and that China was at best a "minor asset" to the Allies.[24] From the very beginning of the Pacific war, "passivity" became a stigma of China in the military planning of the U.S. government. In America's military strategy in the Pacific, China was often treated in symbolic, even negative, terms. True, the Chinese example of resistance countered Japan's propaganda that its war was designed to liberate the Asian people from white imperialism. China's resistance was also useful for trapping more than a half million Japanese troops and for denying Japan a free hand in deploying China's enormous manpower and rich natural resources. Yet, China was not an ally capable of contributing decisively to the defeat of Japan. American strategists believed that even with the Western Allies' assistance, the KMT regime would not be able to improve fundamentally the poor conditions of its military forces and the feeble economy of China. Within the U.S. government, this judgment was not disputed even by usually staunch supporters of Chongqing, such as Stanley Hornbeck and Lauchlin Currie.[25] The judgment would be vindicated in 1944, when, despite American assistance to it throughout the war years, Chinese government forces suffered new setbacks under Japan's military offensive in eastern China.

Paradoxically, the consensus among American officials on China's military weakness helped create the wartime myth of the great-power China. Washington's Europe-first strategy meant that the United States could divert only limited resources to assist Chongqing's war effort. To supplement U.S. lend-lease materials to Chongqing, American policymakers decided to keep China in the war by working on the Chinese mind. The result, in Hornbeck's words, was an "expedient ad hoc" policy of treating China as a great power. The rationale and steps of the policy were spelled out by the Joint Psychological Warfare Committee of the Joint Chiefs of Staff in early 1942:

> [The] present difficulties of supplying material aid [to China] make it apparent that the existing means of influencing the course of the war in China is through the use of psychological warfare.... [The] modern Chinese

[24] Grace P. Hayes, *The History of the Joint Chiefs of Staff in World War II: The War against Japan* (Annapolis, MD: Naval Institute Press, 1982), 71; JCS 21, "U.S. Relations with China," 11 March 1942, *RJCS*, reel 13.

[25] Memorandum no. 14, "Chinese Capacities," 4 July 1942, *RJCS*, reel 13; memorandum no. 43, "Value of China to the Allied War Effort," 2 January 1943, ibid.; Hornbeck, "U.S. Policy and the Far East: Problem of Attitude toward China and Expression thereof in Relations with China," 31 August 1943, *SHP*, box 114; Currie to Roosevelt, 9 June 1942, *LCP*, box 5.

represent almost [a] virgin territory for skillful psychological manipulation from the United States. . . . Since a propaganda plan includes diplomatic issues necessary to its execution, a forecast should be made of China's post-war role by exploratory comments and consultations which will enable the present Chinese government to make realistic promises to its citizens of national dignity, prosperity, and stability for the postwar period.[26]

Thus Lattimore's prewar argument for a long-term political settlement in East Asia was both reinforced and confused by a wartime policy based on military expedience. A common premise underlying Lattimore's Chinese new order and the psychological warfare strategy aimed at China was that U.S. diplomacy in East Asia should endorse, in practice or in theory, the national aspirations of China. But neither was prepared to endorse a China-centric Asia. Lattimore's new order emphasized China's freedom from foreign powers' control as the basis for Asia's regional stability. But beyond that, he did not contemplate a rapid ascendancy of China to a great-power status. American psychological warriors were more willing to flirt with Chongqing's ambitions, but they only wanted to encourage Chinese leaders up to a "realistic" limit. Thus, it took a third and stronger motive to make the policy of treating China as a great power a trademark of Washington's wartime policy toward China.

It was President Roosevelt's expectation that after the war China would play an important role in his "grand design" for a new international order. Not long before Pearl Harbor, Roosevelt asserted that a vital condition for peace in the Far East was to get China out of the status quo.[27] Then, during the war years, the president became a decisive supporter for the policy of treating China as a great power. In the spring of 1942 and then in March 1943, Roosevelt outlined separately for the Soviet Foreign Minister and the British Foreign Secretary his idea about America, Britain, the Soviet Union, and China acting as "four policemen" at the end of the war to enforce the postwar settlement. The president expected that in the postwar years China would act as a policeman in the Pacific and also help strengthen America's hand in world politics.[28] The origins of his famous four police-men formula had much to do with America's own activist tradition in the Western Hemisphere and Roosevelt's reservations about Wilsonian universalism. But as far as China's inclusion was concerned, the formula was not based on any precedent of Chinese–foreign cooperation or on China's active role in modern Asian politics. Instead, behind it was an assumption that after the war China would fill in the power vacuum in Asia relinquished by Japan and would follow Washington's leadership in world affairs.

[26] "Autobiography [of Stanley Hornbeck], 1942–1944," n.d., *SHP*, box 497; JPWC 3, "Suggested China Plan," 16 March 1942, *RJCS*, reel 13.
[27] *CPPC*, 18: 325.
[28] Sherwood, *Roosevelt and Hopkins*, 572–573, 716–718.

This policy was conceived in a global context and with a geopolitical strategic perception. Since it was based on speculation, not realistic judgments, about the character of Chinese foreign policy and strength, the policy was bound to run into difficulties. In the war years the Chinese government was quite in tune with the idea about unity among the big powers. It had actually used such rhetoric earlier than Washington. Before Pearl Harbor, Chiang Kai-shek had advocated that in their struggle against the Axis powers, the so-called "five great democracies," including America, Britain, China, the Netherlands, and the Soviet Union, must act as one.[29] There were two important differences between Roosevelt's and Chiang's ideas about the big powers' cooperation. First, whereas Chiang was principally interested in the benefits of obtaining the Western Allies' assistance and recognition of China's status as an equal, Roosevelt wanted China to assume the responsibilities and prescribed actions of a great power. Second, Chiang used the "big five" concept only for the purpose of depicting figuratively the division of the world at war; his practical policy was to achieve a bilateral alliance with the United States. The KMT leadership needed American support to achieve China's international rehabilitation, which was at first aimed at rolling back Japanese imperialism but would also lead to China's friction with British, Soviet, and other Western countries' interests in Asia. In contrast, President Roosevelt made the Grand Alliance the cornerstone of his new international order. Two cardinal conditions for a lasting peace, according to the Roosevelt formula, were readjustment of interests and division of responsibilities among the leading members of the United Nations.

Given their consensus on China's military weakness, American policymakers were conscious that they were speculating in expecting China to function as a policeman in postwar Asia. Secretary of State Hull predicted that "China has only a fifty-fifty chance to re-establish itself as a great power."[30] Yet, American leaders obviously based their China policy on the favorable "fifty." As defined by a wartime study by the Council on Foreign Relations, a great power was one that had a "general international interest" and the "widest international obligations." The study made a careful distinction between "power status," which separated states into classes according to their capacities to exercise political rights and perform military–political duties on the international scene, and "legal equality," which should be a principle for all interstate relationships.[31] Obviously, diplomacy could implement the latter but not change the former. Yet, Washington's wartime policy of treating China as a great power attempted to alter that country's power status mainly through diplomacy.

[29] CSYZ, 18: 410.
[30] Hull, *Memoirs*, 2: 1586–1587.
[31] Arthur Sweetser et al., "The 'Grading' of States," 4 January 1943, SAI, P-B 57.

President Roosevelt realized that a great power created merely by diplomacy would lack substance. He declared: "I want to put China in the sun even before she has the economic power."[32] The president was eager to see China become a political great power. Yet the political situation of China in the war years was no more promising than its economic condition. In the war years, no serious observer of China could afford to discount the possibility of resumed civil strife in China after the defeat of Japan. By the same token, there were unpleasant indications in Chongqing's foreign policy orientation that a nationalist China "in the sun" might not be quite so benign as President Roosevelt expected. In 1943, after Chiang Kai-shek published his book *China's Destiny*, Stanley Hornbeck, political adviser to the Secretary of State on Far Eastern Affairs, observed that the spirit of nationalism was rampant in high quarters in Chongqing because China was "still in the throes of revolution." To gain China's trust and cooperation in the long run, in his opinion, the United States must tolerate the "disagreeable and unfortunate follies and excesses" of the Chinese revolution. Not many of Hornbeck's colleagues in the State Department were as tolerant, and they did not think Chongqing's "reactionary type of nationalism" was suitable to the Grand Alliance.[33]

A final aspect of Washington's "make China a great power" formula dealt with its racial concerns about postwar Asian affairs. This was derived from the current struggle in the Pacific, which, "to scores of millions of participants, . . . was also a race war."[34] To American leaders, the ideological struggle with Japan on the racial front had to be won with the help of China, which was the only "Oriental" or "Asiatic" member of the Grand Alliance. China's presence among the Big Four would in the postwar years automatically bring the largest Asian nation and its enormous population into a coalition with the West. Other Asiatic peoples were expected to follow the Chinese.[35] As in their approach, which treated China as a "great" rather than a "nationalist" power, the general perspective of the American government on Asian affairs paid lip service but gave

[32] "Record of conversation with the President and Mr. Hopkins," 16 July 1943, *TSP*, box 32.

[33] Hornbeck to Hull, 8 July 1942, *SHP*, box 377; Hornbeck to Welles, 20 August 1942, ibid., box 440; note by Hornbeck, 24 June 1943, ibid., box 114; Hornbeck to Berle, 20 February 1943, ibid., box 367; Hornbeck to Hull, 29 January 1943, ibid., box 378; note by Hornbeck (unofficial and impersonal), 25 September 1943, ibid., box 425; Salisbury, Bishop, and others to the Secretary of State, 2 September 1943, ibid., box 70.

[34] John W. Dower, *War without Mercy: Race and Power in the Pacific War* (New York: Pantheon, 1986), 4.

[35] Memorandum by Maxwell Hamilton, 27 February 1943, *FRUS, 1943: China*, 14–15; Hull, *Memoirs*, 2: 1586–1587; memorandum by Hornbeck on a conversation with President Roosevelt, 20 November 1944, *SHP*, box 367; Thomas M. Campbell and George C. Herring, Jr., ed., *The Diaries of Edward R. Stettinius, Jr., 1943–1946* (New York: New Viewpoints, 1975), 210, 215.

little weight to nationalist dynamics in the region. The "racial war" with Japan and the "racial cooperation" with China reflected the same narrow focus on big powers alone. During the war, the U.S. government developed a formula known as "trusteeship," assigning to the great powers in the UN coalition responsibilities for helping "dependent areas" of Asia. At the same time, American policymakers made no attempt to envision how to establish meaningful contacts with nationalist movements in Asia. In this sense, the great-power China policy also failed to prepare American leaders to deal with Asian nationalism in the postwar years. In the war years, they believed they had found in China the missing piece of the jigsaw puzzle of new global peace order. Yet, at the end of the war, China itself would prove a puzzle for which Washington had no ready solution.

Partnership for waging peace

The cooperation between Chongqing and Washington for redesigning the international order in East Asia was only one of the stranger and less well known aspects of the difficult, contradictory Chinese–American alliance in World War II. Although the concept seemed historically phenomenal, the practical enterprise suffered from the same drawbacks that characterized the Sino–American collaboration for prosecuting the war. In other words, the so-called common efforts between the two governments consisted mainly of separate, hidden agendas that often led to mutually distasteful operations. Although consultations between the two sides continued, they were never systematic and regular. The two governments' alliance in war was sustained by mutual needs but not guided by a common strategy. Likewise, the Sino–American association for eventual peace was generated by mutual, but often unrealistic, expectations; it was not founded on a solid common understanding of policy objectives and was not well nurtured by close teamwork.

Chiang Kai-shek's interest in foreign policy planning had begun long before the Pacific war commenced in December 1941. A year after Japan turned China's northeastern provinces into "Manchukuo," Chiang ordered the establishment of a "planning committee." Its purpose was to put together a group of Western-trained scholars to serve as Chiang's think tank on important foreign and domestic policy issues. But, according to Chen Bulei, head of the committee and one of Chiang's most trusted advisers, this effort was a total failure. The reason was that "there are only a limited number of people in China who have specialized knowledge. But even more difficult to find are experts who are devoted to public interests and devoid of factional bias and pretentious tendency." In 1935, the committee had to be dissolved and its members integrated into Chiang's Office of Aides.[36]

[36] Chen Bulei, *Chen Bulei Huiyilu* (Memoir of Chen Bulei) (Taipei: Zhuanji Wenxue Chubanshe, 1967), 98, 127.

Chiang, however, did not give up. A few months after the undeclared Sino–Japanese war began, he asked Zhu Jiahua, then head of the Organization Department of the KMT, to organize an Office of Councilors. At the beginning, this agency involved "councilors" of academic and official backgrounds in informal discussions of current international events. Then the discussions evolved into regular meetings once a week in Chiang Kai-shek's official residence. Later, Zhu was replaced by Wang Shijie, who was then also the Minister of Information. An offshoot of the Office of Councilors was a Research Institute of International Problems, which paid special attention to collecting and analyzing intelligence information on Japan.[37]

But it was after Pearl Harbor that the Chinese government became seriously involved in what can be called "victory planning." With America and Britain fighting on its side, Chongqing could contemplate its war and peace aims in terms more positive and definite than before. The advisory network around Chiang became further complicated. During the first half of 1942, a "Research Committee on Postwar International Peace Organization (RC)" was established. Its director was Wang Chonghui. Wang was an established scholar of international law, but more important was his wartime position as secretary-general of the Supreme Council of National Defense, Chiang Kai-shek's top decision-making body in the war years. Members of the committee were chosen from three departments of the government: the Supreme Council of National Defense, the National Military Council, and the *Waijiaobu* (the Ministry of Foreign Affairs). Chiang Kai-shek himself chaired the first two and T. V. Soong, Chiang's brother-in-law, was in charge of the third.[38] In theory, the RC was the only official agency designated especially to make plans for China's postwar foreign policy issues. In practice, however, its position in the labyrinth of the KMT policymaking structure was ambiguous. As with many other wartime agencies of the KMT government, the importance of the RC

[37] Hu Songping, *Zhu Jiahua Nianpu* (A Chronicle of Zhu Jiahua's Life) (Taipei: Zhuanji Wenxue Chubanshe, 1969), 44–45; Zhang Zhongfu, *Miwang Ji* (Perplexed Reminiscences) (Taipei: Wenhai Chubanshe, 1978), 129–131; Shao Yulin et al., *Wang Pengsheng Xiansheng Jinian Ji* (Mr. Wang Pengsheng Memorialized) (Taipei: Wenhai Chubanshe, n.d.), 3–4. The Research Institute of International Problems was headed by Wang Pengsheng and during the war developed into a body of more than 200 members, some of whom were Koreans and Taiwanese.

[38] Zhang Zhongfu, *Miwang Ji*, 152–153; Pu Xuefeng, "Wo guo dangnian duiyu zhanhou Riben tianhuang zhidu zhi lichang" (Wartime Policy of Our Government toward the Postwar Status of the Japanese Imperial Institution), *ZW*, 28 (1976): 6: 51–53; Pu Xuefeng, *Taixukong Li Yi Youchen* (A Drifting Grain of Dust in the Universe) (Taipei: Taiwan Shangwu Yinshuguan, 1979), 187–188. There are different opinions about the time when the RC was established. According to the date of a letter by Wang Chonghui on an RC matter, the committee existed as early as March 1942. See Wang Chonghui, *Wang Chonghui Xiansheng Wenji* (Writings by Mr. Wang Chonghui) (Taipei: Zhongyang Wenwu Gongyingshe, 1981), 658.

depended on the closeness of its director to Chiang Kai-shek. Wang Chonghui had to compete with his rivals for Chiang's attention in order to ensure the relevance of the RC. T. V. Soong's Waijiaobu, the Office of Aides under Chen Bulei, and the Office of Councilors under Wang Shijie were strong rivals of the RC in foreign policy planning, and the latter two officers gained a special advantage from being on Chiang's personal staff.[39]

During its two-year existence, the RC tasted both the thrill of being at the center of events and the chagrin of being ignored. Its finest moment occurred during the Cairo Conference in late 1943. Chiang Kai-shek chose Wang Chonghui to accompany him to Cairo. There, Wang worked closely with Chiang in presenting China's postwar foreign policy to the Western Allies. After Cairo, the responsibility for sorting out the proceedings of the conference was also delegated to the RC staff.[40] But, on another occasion, the Dumbarton Oaks Conference in 1944, the role of the RC proved inconsequential. Although Wang Chonghui's committee had studied problems of postwar international organization for more than two years, its policy recommendations were not adopted as the official program of the Chinese delegation to Dumbarton Oaks. Wellington Koo (Gu Weijun), China's wartime ambassador in London, was appointed to head the Chinese delegation only after tense competition for the position among several high officials in Chongqing. The Chinese delegation arrived in Washington with no definite program: five draft plans for a new international organization had been drawn up by different agencies of the government. Four plans had been produced separately by the Waijiaobu, the RC, the Office of Councilors, and a semiofficial Association of People's Diplomacy. None of these was eventually adopted as China's official policy. A fifth plan, drafted in haste and on the spot at the conference by two or three members of the Chinese delegation, was sent to the American and British delegations. This was done without authorization from Chongqing, behind the backs of the other members of the Chinese delegation, including Ambassador Koo himself. It turned out to be a "masterpiece" formulated under the direction of H. H. Kung (Kong Xiangxi), another brother-in-law of Chiang Kai-shek and the president of the Executive Yuan. Kung had failed to get the appointment as head of the Chinese delegation, but he nevertheless went to Washington in a special capacity and there outmaneuvered all his rivals by improvising the "Chinese" program.[41]

[39] For these two offices' positions within the KMT power structure, see Ch'ien Tuan-sheng (Qian Duansheng), *The Government and Politics of China, 1912–1949* (Stanford, CA: Stanford University Press, 1950), 187, and Shao Yulin, *Shi Han Huiyilu* (My Mission to Korea) (Taipei: Zhuanji Wenxue Chubanshe, 1980), 41–42.

[40] Three plans by the secretariat of the Supreme Council of National Defense for Chiang to use at the Cairo Conference, November 1943 (n.d.), ZZSC, 3(3): 503–506; Pu Xuefeng, "Wo guo."

[41] *RWK*, 5(A): 619–620; Zhang Zhongfu, *Miwang Ji*, 153, 163–164.

The weakness of the RC also lay in its inability to form a working relationship with the Waijiaobu. During the war, the Waijiaobu often functioned to clarify for the Allied governments the war and peace aims of the Chinese government. But there were no arrangements for regular communication or effective liaison between the RC and the Waijiaobu. During the Cairo Conference, the RC overshadowed the Waijiaobu. T. V. Soong had to accept the arrangement because Chiang Kai-shek decided to direct Chinese diplomacy at the summit personally. In view of Soong's familiarity with the American and British leaders, his presence at Cairo would almost certainly have outshone Chiang's own.[42] Nevertheless, the Waijiaobu had one great advantage with which the RC could not compete: its direct contact with the other Allied governments. Soong and other spokesmen for the Foreign Ministry could legitimately express to the outside world their opinions on wartime and postwar issues. These views were usually interpreted by the Allies as representative of China's official position. At the same time, the RC staff could only distill their ideas behind closed doors and await their chance to be heard. In fact, what the Waijiaobu officials said to the other Allied governments was not always in concert with what was being considered by the RC planners.

Aside from its organizational shortcomings, the RC suffered from the lack of a clearly defined mission. When the RC was founded, four categories of issues were included in its agenda: (1) a new international peace and security organization; (2) postwar economic adjustments within China and in the world; (3) China's postwar relations with Japan and the other states of East Asia; and (4) the issue of abrogating the privileged positions of foreign powers in China. When approached by U.S. Ambassador Clarence Gauss with regard to the purposes of the RC, Wang Chonghui informed him of only the first three, lest the last one disturb China's wartime relations with the Western Allies.[43] In fact, only the first of these issues became the abiding central interest of RC planning. This seemed to indicate that, in spite of its frustration with the League of Nations in the 1930s, the Chinese government did not completely lose faith in the "world government" approach. Wang Chonghui's own legalist interest may also help explain the RC's focus.

[42] Chiang had no choice but to rely on T. V. Soong and his younger sister, Meiling (Mrs. Chiang), in communicating with the Western Allies. The family tie and T. V.'s alleged ability to convince Washington to give China more aid were important reasons for his appointment to the post of Foreign Minister. But the personal relationship between Chiang and Soong was often rough. In the early winter of 1943, the two in-laws had some violent quarrels and thus started one of the cold intervals in their political relationship. This may be another reason that Chiang bypassed the Waijiaobu when preparing for the Cairo Conference. For an interesting contemporary observation by an American diplomat, see Joseph W. Esherick, ed., *Lost Chance in China: The World War II Despatches of John S. Service* (New York: Random House, 1974), 78–80.

[43] Wang Chonghui, *Wenji*, 658–660; Gauss to Hull, 3 August 1942, *FRUS, 1942: China*, 735–737.

This is not to say that the RC devoted most of its time to contemplating a world organization, thereby contradicting Chiang Kai-shek's own intention of pursuing a bilateral alliance with the United States. Instead, the divergence between the RC's postwar planning and the bilateral orientation of Chongqing's wartime foreign policy reflected a bewildering question facing the Chinese government during the war: what international identity should be sought by China after the war? In other words, should China stand with small and weak states of the world and seek a new world organization that would be able to represent and protect their interests as equal member states, or should China join the big powers' club that would make the rules for the rest of the world? The dilemma of the Chinese government was best summarized by a member of the Chinese delegation to the Dumbarton Oaks Conference: "We stand in the position of a great power but entertain the anxiety of a small state."[44]

The consequence of the RC's indulgence in the subject of world peace organization was to delay systematic considerations of other important issues that would affect China at the end of the war. For instance, the issue of postwar treatment of Japan was supposedly one of the most important subjects for Chongqing's foreign policy planners to consider. But during the two years before the Cairo Conference, the RC was unable to make any well-considered policy recommendation in this regard. For the Chinese policy at the Cairo Conference, the planning staff of the RC could only suggest certain obvious retributive measures against Japan. They failed to provide long-range plans regarding Japan's postwar treatment. The Cairo Conference proved to be the only opportunity for the Chinese government to exert any influence on the reconfiguration of international relations in East Asia. It was also the only chance for the RC to make a contribution to Chinese foreign policy. But in the planning agenda of the RC, the issues discussed at Cairo assumed only minor importance. The RC continued its deliberation on world peace organization until the Dumbarton Oaks Conference in the fall of 1944. After that, the mission of the committee was concluded.[45]

During the last two years of the war, Chongqing's foreign policy planning was mainly carried out by the Waijiaobu. Concrete postwar issues in East Asia also became the central interests of Chinese planning. Soon after Chiang Kai-shek published *China's Destiny* in 1943, the Waijiaobu began to study China's postwar foreign relations in light of the ideas laid out in Chiang's book. In late 1944, the effort resulted in several concrete plans for a peace settlement in Asia.[46] Yet Chinese postwar planning never kept

---

[44] Minutes of a meeting of the Chinese delegation at Dumbarton Oaks, 9 September 1944, *WKP*, box 75.

[45] Zhang Zhongfu, *Miwang Ji*, 152.

[46] Waijiaobu memorandum, "Zhuxi duiyu waijiao fangmian zhishi," n.d., *VHP*, box 3.

abreast of the trends in inter-Allied diplomacy. During the first two years of the Pacific war, when the Western Allies were still interested in discussing Asian problems with China, Chinese postwar planning turned to the problem of international organization more than anything else. But when the Waijiaobu came up with a cluster of plans for postwar Asia, the Chinese government had to bring them to the attention of the Western Allies during the inter-Allied conference on the United Nations in San Francisco in the spring of 1945.

With Chiang Kai-shek's approval, the Chinese delegation carried these plans to San Francisco, hoping to discuss them with the American and British delegations outside the formal conference. The topics covered by these plans included (1) an "advisory council for the Far East," (2) administration of liberated Chinese territories, (3) terms for the Japanese surrender, (4) independence of Korea, (5) an American–British–Chinese military agreement regarding Thailand, (6) the postwar status of Indochina, (7) Sino–Soviet relations, and (8) repatriation of overseas Chinese to the areas where they had resided before the war.[47] This time T. V. Soong headed the Chinese delegation, and he was able to exchange opinions with American leaders on certain issues. But generally, the Allied powers were not prepared to conduct serious negotiations with Chongqing on these subjects. At the time, KMT leaders did not know that earlier, at Yalta, without the knowledge of the Chinese government, American and British leaders had already reached a secret agreement on Asia with the Soviet government. In the summer, the Chinese government felt seriously handicapped in its own negotiations with Moscow because of its lack of understandings with the Western Allies.

In 1945, as a late participant in the war in Asia and the Pacific, the Soviet Union had a sudden military impact on the region. In terms of diplomacy, however, Moscow was never really absent from the inter-Allied discussions of postwar East Asian affairs. Still, Soviet ascension in the inter-Allied consultation about Asia in 1945 reflected a weakness in the Chongqing–Washington bond that had been present for years. The truth was that despite all their planning operations and mutual consultations with regard to postwar East Asia in the war years, no effective working relationship between Chongqing's and Washington's planning agencies ever existed. Similarly, in these years, the two governments were able to reach tentative agreements on postwar issues in Asia, but these were by no means definite.

The organizational evolution of the U.S. government's foreign policy preparations for postwar settlement in East Asia has been chronicled by

---

[47] Waijiaobu memorandum, "Ni ju Jiujinshan huiyi huiwai ying yu Mei Ying Su shangtan zhi gexiang fang'an qingshiyou" (Draft Plans to be Discussed with America, Britain, and the Soviets Outside the San Francisco Conference), 25 March 1945, *WKP*, box 81.

Harley Notter and Hugh Borton, two participants in these planning operations. After a moderate beginning in the summer of 1942, the State Department's East Asian policy preparation eventually created an impressive record of intensive activities involving more than 200 committee meetings and a large number of position papers. By contrast, during World War I, America's official preparatory operations produced only 48 reports on the Far East.[48]

Early in 1942, the Special Research Division of the U.S. Department of State suggested that certain informal arrangements be made with Chongqing for a "continuous exchange of views and information on the subject of existing facilities and postwar plans." Specifically, the Chinese government should be asked to send "qualified and trained technicians with official status and with access to official Chinese information" to Washington, where they could either serve as liaisons between the two governments' planning agencies, or engage in independent studies, or work closely with experts in the U.S. government on postwar East Asian problems. Soon the Chinese, on their own initiative, expressed the same interest in establishing a working relationship between the two sides for foreign policy planning.[49]

For some reason, these notions never resulted in concrete collaboration. In view of Chongqing's strong desire to forge a long-term partnership with the United States, it is likely that the U.S. government was the reluctant partner. During the war, the State Department was merely engaged in investigating Chongqing's intentions on postwar issues through its embassy. The impressions of Chongqing's foreign policy planning obtained in this manner were not favorable. One report received by the State Department from China observed: "Kuomintang postwar planning is generally impractical, assuming as it does that implementation of the plans evolved will be effected, apparently gratis, by the victorious United Nations, especially the United States."[50] Whatever the reason, the fact remained that at the planning level, the postwar foreign policy preparations of the Chinese and American governments never made direct contact.

At the level of wartime foreign policy execution, there was still a chance

---

[48] The U.S. government's postwar planning in World War I is the subject of Lawrence E. Gelfand's classic study, *The Inquiry: American Preparations for Peace, 1917–1919* (New Haven, CT: Yale University Press, 1963), which discusses the Far East on pp. 227–228. For the organizational evolution of the State Department's postwar planning in World War II, see Harley Notter, *Postwar Foreign Policy Preparation, 1939–1945* (Washington, DC: G.P.O., 1949), and Hugh Borton, *American Presurrender Planning for Postwar Japan* (New York: Columbia University Press, 1967).

[49] Memorandum, "Comments and Suggestions on the Orientation of Our Postwar Work Relating to the Far East," n.d. (1942), *RLP*, box 2; memorandum of conversations with Chinese officials by Vincent, 29 July 1942, *FRUS, 1942: China*, 733–735.

[50] Memorandum of conversations with Chinese officials by Vincent, 29 July 1942, *FRUS, 1942: China*, 733–735; Gauss to Hull, 29 September 1943, *FRUS, 1943: China*, 869–870.

for Chongqing and Washington to coordinate their postwar intentions in Asia. Although diplomatic activities for that purpose did occur between the two sides, the role of the State Department was marginal. The reason was President Roosevelt's penchant for conducting personal diplomacy through informal channels. After "heartily" authorizing the State Department to initiate postwar foreign policy planning, President Roosevelt ignored the State Department for the better part of the war. According to Harley Notter, Roosevelt's interest in the department's planning was "to be able later to reach in his basket and to find there whatever he needed in regard to postwar foreign policy and meanwhile wished to devote himself wholly to ways and means of winning the war."[51] Yet, when the time came for the president to discuss postwar problems with other Allied governments, he proved unwilling to reach into the basket for ideas.

During the war, President Roosevelt held an ambivalent attitude toward postwar foreign policy preparation. He was responsible for important Allied proclamations such as the Atlantic Charter and the unconditional surrender principle. Although these had a profound impact on the course of the war and on the conditions of peace, they were too general and vague to guide concrete foreign policy planning.[52] In fact, the Allies did not even have common interpretations of these principles. President Roosevelt himself had no illusions about the practical value of the Atlantic Charter. Once he compared it with the Ten Commandments, which, in his opinion, had set cardinal goals for human life but after many centuries still remained ambiguous.[53] By the same token, the president believed it sufficient to announce the principle of unconditional surrender without explaining its concrete policy connotations. He feared that while the war was still in progress, premature meddling with detailed and definite conditions of peace would amount to a "loss of energy" and would disturb the Allied war effort.[54] In addition, he did not want to be bound by any fixed definition of unconditional surrender lest such a commitment fail to meet different contingencies that might emerge in different areas of the world at the end of the war.[55]

Aloof from the policy planning in the State Department and reluctant to get into details and specifics about postwar issues, President Roosevelt was nevertheless committed to the idea that the foundation of peace must

[51] Notter, *Postwar Foreign Policy Preparation*, 63–64, 79.

[52] See Leon V. Sigal, *Fighting to a Finish: The Politics of War Termination in the United States and Japan, 1945* (Ithaca, NY: Cornell University Press, 1989), for the impact of the unconditional surrender policy on the conclusion of the Pacific war.

[53] CPPC, 24: 276.

[54] CPPC, 21: 254; Samnel I. Rosenman, *Working with Roosevelt* (New York: Harper, 1952), 373.

[55] Warren F. Kimbell, ed., *Churchill and Roosevelt: The Complete Correspondence* (Princeton, NJ: Princeton University Press, 1984), 2: 652; Elliott Roosevelt, ed., *F.D.R.: His Personal Letters, 1928–1945* (New York: Duell, Sloan & Pearce, 1950), 4: 1485–1486.

be laid during the war. The Pacific War Council, located in Washington, seemed a logical place for the president to consult with other Allied leaders systematically in respect to Asian–Pacific affairs. But the council never really assumed such a function. Its first meeting was held on 1 April 1942, and in the succeeding years of the war the council met frequently. President Roosevelt always presided over the discussions; other governments represented were Britain, China, the Netherlands, New Zealand, Australia, and Canada. Chinese foreign minister T. V. Soong participated in most of the meetings.

From the outset, the purpose of the council was ambiguous. Roosevelt wanted to keep the meetings as informal as possible in order to facilitate discussion of whatever problems of general significance a participating government wanted to bring to the council's attention. During the first two years of its existence, topics brought up to the council included both military developments and certain postwar issues in Asia and the Pacific. Yet insofar as the U.S. War Department and the Joint Chiefs of Staff were concerned, the discussions at the council were of a political nature and therefore had nothing to do with themselves. Not until the council's thirty-sixth meeting, on 12 January 1944, did President Roosevelt tell the others present that he thought the council was "the body that should work out preliminary studies about the final solution of the Pacific problems."[56] These words never led to effective action. At most, the council served as a place for the president, and occasionally others, to throw out some general thoughts on postwar issues. Exchange of opinions rarely happened. Privately, President Roosevelt regarded the council as a body serving "primarily to disseminate information as to the progress of operations in the Pacific – and, secondly, to give me a chance to keep everybody happy by telling stories and doing most of the talking"![57]

Roosevelt preferred to test his thoughts about the postwar world with other Allied leaders through personal diplomacy. He sent Lauchlin Currie, Wendell Willkie, and Henry Wallace as his personal envoys to Chongqing, and in Washington he also received Chiang Kai-shek's representatives, including Chiang's wife, Song Meiling, and his two brothers-in-law, T. V. Soong and H. H. Kung. There were also those inter-Allied summit meetings, in which the role of the State Department proved minimal.[58] The

[56] Memorandum by J. L. McCrea on the first meeting of the Pacific War Council, 3 April 1942, *RPMF*, box 168; memorandum by Wilson Brown on the thirty-sixth meeting of the Pacific War Council, 12 January 1944, ibid.; B. W. Davenport to Rumelt (first name or initial unknown), 5 May 1944, *RPOF* 4875.

[57] E. Roosevelt, *F.D.R: His Personal Letters*, 2: 1329–1330.

[58] Notter, *Postwar Foreign Policy Preparation*, 187–189, 194–199, 200–202, 294–300; Borton, *American Presurrender Planning*, 19, 26; F. S. Dunn, *Peace-Making and the Settlement with Japan* (Princeton, NJ: Princeton University Press, 1963), 19; James F. Byrnes, *Speaking Frankly* (New York: Harper, 1947), 23.

Cairo Conference of 1943 and the Yalta Conference of 1945 were two
landmarks in inter-Allied diplomacy in East Asian affairs. When conducting his summit diplomacy, President Roosevelt purposely sought to avoid
America's failed peacemaking experience in Paris in 1919. On that occasion, in Roosevelt's words, "everybody who had a 'happy thought', or
who thought he was an expert got a free ride" to Versailles. Such bedlam
at the end of *this* war could be averted through wartime consultations
among the Allies. In Roosevelt's opinion, by discussing postwar issues in
an exploratory way, the leaders of the principal Allied powers would
become familiar with one another's postwar intentions. Then they would
not be caught by surprise if the war came to a sudden conclusion. In
Roosevelt's view, it was important that these consultations not be aimed
at producing signed agreements, but rather at finding out how closely the
leading Allies could bring their minds together.[59] Although Chiang Kai-
shek was at first flattered by the intimacy of his personal contact with the
American president, eventually he could not fail to realize that Roosevelt's
informal approach worked to Chongqing's disadvantage. The weakest
among the Big Four, the KMT regime could not afford to play the game
of uncertainty with many wild cards. At Yalta in early 1945, President
Roosevelt's effort to reduce surprises with the Russians in Asian affairs
turned out to be a bombshell to Chongqing.

   This is not to say that Chongqing–Washington diplomacy over postwar
issues would have fared differently had President Roosevelt worked closely
with the State Department. In the case of the Cairo Conference, although
officials of the State Department were unhappy about being ignored in the
inter-Allied consultation, they also admitted that the Cairo communiqué
did not contradict their own policy suggestions in any serious way. A few
months after the Yalta Conference, there were indeed suggestions in the
State Department for reconsidering the secret Yalta accord about the Far
East. But the proposed amendments did not alter the Yalta agreement
substantially.[60] Despite President Roosevelt's reluctance to carry out his
foreign policies through the State Department, he did not necessarily dis-
agree with the State Department on important policies. Inadequate and
irregular as they might be, communication and mutual influence between
the president and the State Department did exist. For instance, between
1942 and 1943 Roosevelt held a series of meetings with a small circle
called the Informal Agenda Group, which included Secretary Hull, Under-
Secretary Sumner Welles, and some senior members of the departmental
research staff. Originally the group intended to meet with the president on

[59] CPPC, 21: 248, 254.
[60] Borton, *American Presurrender Planning*, 12–13, 20; Joseph C. Grew, *Turbulent Era: A
    Diplomatic Record of Forty Years, 1904–1945* (Boston: Houghton Mifflin, 1952), 2:
    1455–1457.

a weekly basis, but actual consultation was less frequent. These meetings covered a wide range of topics, including postwar territorial settlement in Europe and Asia, postwar treatment of Germany, disarmament, trusteeship, and a new international peace organization. But discussions on these occasions tended to be superficial. Some in the State Department attributed this to the participants' reluctance to become involved in too many premature speculations on postwar policies. Some also noted the awkward atmosphere caused by the mutual antipathy between Hull and Welles.[61]

Although it is true that President Roosevelt had his own trusted policy advisers outside the State Department, such as Harry Hopkins, Henry Morgenthau, and Lauchlin Currie, these people did not function in a political vacuum. They mingled and exchanged opinions with State Department officials. For instance, between 1941 and 1943, when he frequently advised Roosevelt on China policy, Currie also maintained contact with foreign service officers such as John P. Davies and John C. Vincent, whose knowledge of China was respected. Hopkins was especially uncomfortable with the lack of cooperation between the White House and the State Department. After Edward R. Stettinius succeeded Cordell Hull as Secretary of State in November 1944, Hopkins made serious efforts to improve relations between the two offices.[62] Although hard to pinpoint, there should be no question about the existence of the mutual influence between the two groups of advisers. The agreement between President Roosevelt's policy at the Cairo Conference and the East Asian planning operations in the State Department was not accidental. It was a result of the "interflow of influence on thinking" between the planning officers of the State Department and the White House staff.[63] In his study of the Allied trusteeship policy during World War II, historian William Roger Louis suggests that "there was a continuity of official thought" about postwar issues in American government. This continuity was reflected not only in the agreement without prior consultation between the Roosevelt administration and the State Department during most of the war, but also in the improved cooperation between the Truman administration and the State Department in the final months of the war.[64] The implication of

---

[61] Memorandum, "Indications of Contact with President on Postwar Matters," n.d., *RHN*, box 54; Notter, *Postwar Foreign Policy Preparation*, 169–172.

[62] John P. Davies, Jr., *Dragon by the Tail: American, British, Japanese, and Russian Encounters with China and One Another* (New York: W. W. Norton, 1972), 212, 226, 250–254; Gary May, *China Scapegoat: The Diplomatic Ordeal of John Carter Vincent* (Washington, DC: New Republic Books, 1979), 75, 91, 218; George T. McJimsey, *Hopkins: Ally of the Poor and Defender of Democracy* (Cambridge, MA: Harvard University Press, 1987), 346–353.

[63] Borton, *American Presurrender Planning*, 12–13; Notter, *Postwar Foreign Policy Preparation*, 107.

[64] Louis, *Imperialism at Bay*, 70; Borton, *American Presurrender Planning*, 19, 22.

"continuity" to the American–Chinese relationship is that, viewed from the American side, the conditions of the relationship were not created by personal and accidental reasons but had deep roots in the two governments' perceptions of their nations' objectives and interests.

In other words, although President Roosevelt and Chiang Kai-shek were two dominant figures in the relationship between Washington and Chongqing, in the long run, American policy was better institutionalized and Chongqing's foreign policy was more personalized around Chiang Kai-shek. In China, Chiang Kai-shek held a tight rein on foreign policy making and planning. The hesitant course followed by Chongqing's postwar planning reflected to a large degree Chiang's own wavering attitude toward China's foreign policy issues. During World War II, Chiang's responsibility in foreign affairs was more complicated than any of his predecessors' in modern times. Until World War II, Chinese diplomacy had been limited geographically to China itself and functioned mainly to accept or contradict foreign powers' conduct of their "China affairs." The war changed the character of East Asian international politics to such an extent that the old China affairs almost disappeared, and the Chinese government and the Allies no longer dealt with one another only within and about China. While the Allied powers adopted new perspectives about China's role in the international politics of Asia, Chongqing also went beyond Chinese boundaries to cultivate new relations with the other powers on a wide range of international problems.

The extremely complicated and volatile international situation in the war years tended to render Chiang's control over Chinese foreign policy hollow. His limited international experience was overtaxed by the enormous task of China's wartime diplomacy. Chiang had to seek assistance from his advisers, especially his wife and two brothers-in-law, when conducting relations with other Allied governments. Yet, as the following chapters will show, although often inviting suggestions from experienced Chinese diplomats, Chiang hardly changed his own view about how Chinese foreign relations should be managed. Although constantly emphasizing the importance of diplomacy for resolving China's predicament, Chiang rarely allowed his foreign policy planners at home and diplomats abroad to take initiative on their own. This situation guaranteed an inflexible and almost one-dimensional foreign policy based on an alliance with the United States, even though Chongqing was constantly dissatisfied with the evolution of the alliance.

The Sino–American relationship was also affected by the two governments' confidence in their own ability to implement their foreign policies. In this regard, Chongqing and Washington did not belong in the same league. The wartime reliance of Chongqing on American aid to a large extent set a cardinal proviso for Chinese postwar planning – Washington's endorsement. Chiang Kai-shek had learned from China's dealings with foreign powers in the past that reliance on foreign support might be futile and dangerous. In the postwar years, he asserted, "If I should make a few requests or show a little dependence on other nations or foreigners, no matter how good and friendly their national character, I would necessarily become their slave and what is called equality, freedom and justice [in international relations] would disappear."[65] In view of the wartime Chinese–American relationship, this can be read as an expression of Chiang's ultimate bitterness, after the war, toward his government's reliance on the United States during World War II. The fundamental weakness of the Chongqing regime in foreign and domestic affairs left the KMT leaders reluctant to challenge the United States in any explicit manner when they disagreed with Washington on postwar Asian policies. The KMT regime could only resort to passive and ineffectual resistance against those American policies in Asia that it deemed undesirable.

In contrast, American policymakers had few, if any, concerns about their country's ability to pursue its postwar aspirations. Although trying from time to time to obtain support from other Allied governments for its policy objectives, the American government was determined to reshape the world according to its own perspectives. As the following chapters will show, because of America's overriding military responsibility in the Asian–Pacific region, American policymakers tended to view the region as one in which the United States must achieve predominance in the postwar years. Although treating China as America's principal ally in the Pacific war, American officials formulated their policy for postwar Asia despite Chongqing's intentions. They considered China's postwar aspirations only in terms of how these could be accommodated to America's own postwar plans, or whether or not they should be altered or simply ignored.

[65] Tang Tsou, *America's Failure in China, 1941–1950* (Chicago: University of Chicago Press, 1963), 105.

2

The issue of postwar Japan

Twenty days before the Pearl Harbor attack, Chiang Kai-shek delivered a speech to the People's Political Council (a body established in 1938 by the KMT government to symbolize national unity), asserting that it was time for the world to "settle the Japanese problem." Chiang broached this theme to the world as an antithesis to the Japanese propaganda that the conflict in East Asia was caused by a "China incident." He contended that to achieve lasting peace in Asia, Japan must be forced to relinquish its ambition for hegemony in the region, to withdraw its troops from all overseas territories acquired by force, and to readjust its international alignment by shifting to the side of the democracies.[1] What Chiang hoped to achieve was nothing less than the dissolution of the Japanese Empire. When the Chinese government began its "victory planning" after Pearl Harbor, the subject of the postwar treatment of Japan and its empire was formally listed in Chongqing's postwar agenda. Meanwhile, across the Pacific, the U.S. government also quietly launched its postwar planning for Japan. During the first two years of the Pacific war, although Chongqing and Washington became allies in the hostilities, the two governments were slow to forge a working relationship with regard to the postwar disposition of Japan. Actually, in this period, Chongqing's and Washington's postwar planning for Japan followed their own paths, and consultations between them on the subject rarely occurred.

Chongqing: revenge or reconciliation?

In the spring of 1942, Wang Chonghui's RC responded to Chiang's summons by contemplating a study guide on postwar readjustment of Sino–Japanese relations. The committee proposed to consider five aspects of the

[1] CSYZ, 18: 409–419.

issue: (1) recovery of China's territorial and administrative integrity; (2) Japan's war guilt; (3) Japanese indemnity for China's losses in the war and return to China of Chinese properties seized by Japan before the war; (4) Japanese compensation for foreign nationals' property losses in China; and (5) confiscation of Japanese enterprises in China.[2] It would take some time for the RC and other planning agencies of the Chinese government to fill in this agenda with concrete details.

From the onset of their consideration of the Japanese issue, however, officials in Chongqing sought to correct two fundamental conditions in prewar East Asian international relations involving Japan. One was to change the allegedly pro-Japanese attitude in the Western powers' Asian policies; the other was to establish genuine racial equality between Eastern peoples and Western states, not merely power equity between Japan and Western powers. For these purposes, Chinese officials were not satisfied with the Anglo–American formula in the Atlantic Charter. In July 1942, in a memorandum to Chiang Kai-shek, Wang Chonghui suggested that the Chinese government take the initiative with the Allies to amend the Atlantic Charter. Wang saw two principal defects in the charter: (1) although the colonial issues in the Pacific would need *positive* readjustment at the end of the war, the Atlantic Charter included only a *passive* statement calling for self-government; and (2) the goal of destruction of Japan was not mentioned in the charter. To make the Atlantic Charter a truly universal document, Wang proposed to supplement it with three new features: destruction of Japan, positive national self-government, and the principle of racial equality. To create a new world security system, Wang and his group also proposed to use a "mutual assistance treaty of the Pacific states" to replace the prewar "Washington treaty system." In the eyes of many Chinese officials, the Washington system had been a "spiritual humiliation" to China and a "glorious obligation" to Japan. Although these suggestions did not prod Chiang Kai-shek into immediate action, they would linger in Chinese diplomacy throughout the war.[3]

In the war years, KMT leaders had a curious apprehension about both a compromise between the Western Allies and Japan in war and a total removal of Japan from Asia's political scene in peace. When recommending the amending of the Atlantic Charter with a clause calling for the thorough defeat of Japan, the RC by no means argued for any postwar

---

[2] Wang Chonghui, *Wang Chonghui Xiansheng Wenji* (Writings by Mr. Wang Chonghui) (Taipei: Zhongyang Wenwu Gongyingshe, 1981), 658–660.

[3] Wang Chonghui to Chiang, 7 July 1942, ZZSC, 3(3): 796–798; Jiang Fangzhen, *Riben Ren –Yige Waiguoren de Yanjiu* (The Japanese: A Study by a Foreigner) (n.p., n.d. [1938?]), 39; Wang Chonghui, *Wenji*, 661–662; "Mutual Assistance Treaty of the Pacific States," 7 May 1942, WKP, box 54. By "positive national self-government" Wang meant voluntary relinquishment by the Allied powers of their own colonies, as well as depriving the enemies of their colonial possessions.

security arrangement in the Pacific to treat Japan as an international out-law. To leaders in Chongqing, the Western Allies' agreement favoring the destruction of Japan was more important than the actual destruction. In their view, since Japanese expansionism historically had been fostered and encouraged by Western powers, it was actually an extension of Western imperialism. If in the 1930s Japan's aggression toward China dismayed Western powers due to its deviation from international cooperation, KMT leaders had long felt frustrated by Japan's refusal to join China's efforts against Western imperialism. When the war between Japan and the West-ern powers began in the Pacific, KMT leaders were inclined to view the struggle in Asia and the Pacific as a second chance for the Japanese to abandon their imperialism learned from the West and revert to some sem-blance of pan-Asianism. According to Owen Lattimore's observation, "China is inclined to put faith in a new liberalism in Japan, and would be against a drastic peace." He predicted: "A clash between American and Chinese policies on this point is possible."[4]

Yet, "pan-Asianism" was a confusing concept in the KMT ideology. Although it was regarded within the KMT as a legacy from Sun Yat-sen, the doctrine was too ambiguous to serve the KMT's policy toward Japan. During the Sino–Japanese conflict in the 1930s, KMT officials became divided in their policies toward Japan, yet all claimed that they themselves were following Sun's teachings. For instance, between 1931 and 1936, Hu Hanmin, a senior right-wing leader of the KMT, attacked Chiang Kai-shek's Japan policy as a violation of Sun Yat-sen's pan-Asianism. In Hu's opinion, the government's policies of seeking a negotiated settlement with Japan and of asking for financial aid from Western powers both betrayed Sun's doctrine, which was aimed at unifying Asian peoples on the basis of Asia's own "kingly way" culture and ridding Asia of Western powers' exploitation. The government's negotiation with Japan was tantamount to capitulation to Japan's "Monroe Doctrine for Asia," and the search for Western help was no better than a repetition of the old self-destructive practice of "using barbarians against barbarians."[5] To Chiang's govern-ment, however, Hu's orientation would only lead to China's isolation. The difficulty for KMT orthodoxy was that after Japan invaded China and offended Western powers' interests, Sun Yat-sen's old question for the Japanese – "Will you act as the falcons and hounds of the Western way of might or serve as the weapon and shield of the Eastern way of right?" – could no longer be posed properly. It was only to China's disadvantage

[4] Zhang Qun, *Wo yu Riben Qishi Nian* (I and Japan for Seventy Years) (Taipei: Zhong Ri Guanxi Yanjiuhui, 1980), 1, 91; T documents-44, "Principal Points of a Report by Owen Lattimore on China and Chinese Opinion on Postwar Problems," 21 August 1942, *RHN*, box 60.

[5] See Hu Hanmin, *Yuandong Wenti yu Dayaxiya Zhuyi* (The Far Eastern Problem and Pan-Asianism) (Guangzhou: Zhongxing Xuehui, 1935).

to continue to view the Asia problem as one between an exploited East
and an imperialist West. Now, as Akira Iriye points out, "the Chinese view
was to contradict Japanese particularism and present the East Asian crisis
as a common problem of the world."[6]

In view of their desire for long-term postwar cooperation with the
United States, KMT leaders in World War II certainly did not want to go
back to Sun's anti-Western pan-Asianism. On the other hand, neither did
China's wartime alliance with the West convince them that from now on
the Western powers would become trustworthy friends of China. Chiang
always believed that "in the relationship between two countries, there is
no enmity that will last forever."[7] Hu Hanmin's prewar aversion to the
Western powers and the RC's wartime recommendation for racial equality
reflected the same deep suspicion of "white imperialism," to which Chiang
himself was not immune. Although a Chinese–Japanese rapprochement for
some anti-Western purpose was not sought by Chongqing's wartime foreign policy planning, Chinese officials nevertheless hoped that Japan's lingering role in postwar international politics would be useful to China's
dealing with the Western powers.

After the Pacific war began, a sense of responsibility for bringing Japan
back to the right track began to develop among KMT officials. Wang
Pengsheng, a leading expert on Japan for the KMT regime and a member
of the RC, stated in public that China must help Japan achieve "spiritual
liberation" and assist Japanese revolutionaries to accomplish a psychological reconstruction. To assume such a role, Chinese revolutionaries themselves must be equipped with "an outlook of the world centered on Chinese
history" and a "Sino-centric" view of Japan. To Wang, China's wartime
cooperation with the West by no means reduced the importance of Japan
in China's foreign policy. In his opinion, due to China's geopolitical position, Japan and the Soviet Union were the two most important countries
to Chinese diplomacy: "China's destiny and these two nations' fate affect
each other and such a relationship has not changed and will not change
for thousands of years."[8] Therefore, China must help bring about a new
Japan through this war. The first step was necessarily the destruction of
Japanese militarism. In 1942 and 1943, Wang Pengsheng and some other
KMT officials publicly propagated the view that, although the Allied naval
and air forces might be powerful enough to force Japan to its knees,
nothing short of total destruction of the Japanese Army on the Asian

[6] Akira Iriye, *Across the Pacific: An Inner History of American–East Asian Relations* (Chicago: Imprint Publications, 1992), 189.
[7] Chiang's speech to the fifth national assembly of the KMT, 19 November 1935, ZZSC,
1(3): 657–658.
[8] Quoted in Shao Yulin et al., *Wang Pengsheng Xiansheng Jinian Ji* (Mr. Wang Pengsheng
Memorialized) (Taipei: Wenhai Chubanshe, n.d.), 43–44, 48.

mainland could thoroughly eradicate the militarist foundation of the aggressive Japanese Empire.[9]

Arguments like this in Chongqing during the first two years of the Pacific war did not merely reflect a postwar policy for a thorough demilitarization of Japan. They also expressed a fear shared by Chiang Kai-shek and his advisers that the Americans and the British might want to conduct an inexpensive war in the Pacific and opt for an easy settlement with Japan. If this was the real intention of the Anglo–American powers, the bulk of the Japanese Army in Asia, mainly in China, would remain intact at the war's end, and China would have to make a very difficult bargain with Japan for getting its troops out of Chinese territories. Not until the Cairo Conference of November 1943 was such a fear among KMT officials more or less alleviated. After the conference, Chiang Kai-shek cabled President Roosevelt to express his appreciation of the Allies' Germany-first strategy. Although he himself had all along urged the Allies to adopt an Asia-first strategy, Chiang now blamed "certain trouble-makers" in China for complaining about "the Allies' letting China fight Japan alone."[10]

While trying to mold public opinion in Chongqing on Japan's future, members of the RC were cautious with regard to what concrete political reforms should be carried out in postwar Japan. Privately, people like Wang Pengsheng hoped that a popular revolution would eventually develop in Japan to overthrow the existing political system and create a democracy there. But since Chiang did not provide guidelines on issues such as how the Japanese imperial institution should be treated, the RC never seriously considered what form of government Japan should adopt after the war. When some members of the RC did try to bring up the subject at the committee meetings, Wang Chonghui dismissed it as being irrelevant to the committee's central concern, which was a new world security organization. Within the committee, however, the understanding was that Wang Chonghui did not want to spend time on the subject because it was a political issue probably being considered by Chiang Kai-shek himself.[11]

Not all KMT officials were as cautious. Sun Ke (Sun Fo) was a prominent example. He was the son of Sun Yet-sen and a political figure in his own right. During the war, Sun Ke headed the prestigious yet powerless Legislative Yuan. Although having carried out some important missions

---

[9] Shao Yulin, "Ruhe jiejue Riben shijian" (How to Settle the Japanese Incident), *Da Gong Bao* (*Grand Public Daily*), 3 January 1943; Wang Pengsheng, "Xin da ke nan" (A New Answer to the Guest's Inquiry), *Da Gong Bao*, 12 June 1943.

[10] Chiang to Roosevelt, December 1943 (n.d.), ZZSC, 3(3): 287–288.

[11] Pu Xuefeng, "Wo guo dangnian duiyu zhanhou Riben tianhuang zhidu zhi lichang" (Wartime Policy of Our Government Toward the Postwar Status of the Japanese Imperial Institution), ZW, 28 (1976): 6: 51–53; *RWK*, 5(A): 342.

for Chiang to the Soviet Union and Europe before the war, Sun was not an insider within Chiang Kai-shek's power circle. Yet, Sun's family background and high official position allowed him to be outspoken without worrying too much about Chiang's own attitude. Chiang's tolerance of Sun Ke often confused foreign observers in Chongqing, who had difficulty from time to time deciding whether Sun was speaking for himself or for the government.

In July 1942, on the occasion of the fifth anniversary of the Marco Polo Bridge Incident, Sun Ke's article "Our Victory Is Imminent" became the first public statement ever made by a Chinese high official on the terms of Japanese surrender. Advocating thorough disarmament of Japan, Sun specified fifty years as the time limit for Japan's disarmament and linked it to China's own rearmament. For instance, Sun believed that it was crucial for China's postwar naval expansion to take over whatever would be left of the Japanese Navy. Sun's territorial conditions for peace included Japan's departure from all Chinese territories, including Manchuria. Korea should also regain its independence. So far as reparations were concerned, Sun wanted half of Japan's industrial establishment. Japan should transfer to China half of its merchant fleet; half of all the equipment of the Japanese iron and steel, shipbuilding, engineering, textile, and paper-making industries; and, to make the list complete, half of all the book collections in the libraries and universities of Japan. All the historical and cultural relics looted by the Japanese from China since 1895 must be returned. How should the scar in the Chinese–Japanese relationship be healed? For the moment, Sun had only a hasty measure: all printed materials in Japan containing anti-Chinese sentiment should be banned or, even better, burned. To guarantee smooth enforcement of the surrender terms for Japan, Sun concluded his plan by suggesting an Allied joint occupation of several strategic locations in Japan's home islands.[12]

In 1943, when the Allies were gradually achieving the upper hand in the Pacific, Sun Ke's edict on postwar Japan also became more radical. Calling for "just revenge," he demanded that all officers of the Japanese armed forces be tried and punished at the end of the war. These steps would necessarily be part of the "humanitarian" measures to compensate victims of Japanese aggression. But it was Sun's statement on punishment of the Japanese emperor that aroused wide attention both in China and abroad. In an article entitled "The Mikado Must Go," published in early October, Sun attacked an alleged misunderstanding in the West that held the Japanese emperor to be sacred and inviolable in the minds of Japan's common people. He contended that in the course of modern Japanese history, the emperor had been a puppet and tool enabling Japanese warlords to manipulate the

[12] Sun Ke, *Zhongguo yu Zhanhou Shijie* (China and the Postwar World) (Chongqing: n.p., 1944), 37–38.

Japanese people. A democratic system in Japan could not be established without first smashing the edifice of the feudal political structure. Nevertheless, according to Sun Ke, because a revolutionary force was absent in Japan, a political revolution for overthrowing the imperial house had to be engineered by the Allies from the outside; the Allied occupation authorities in Japan should assume the task of democratizing the Japanese political system and removing the emperor.[13]

Although Sun Ke's hard-line policy toward Japan diverged from the RC's prudent deliberation, it received support from the domain of T. V. Soong, the Waijiaobu. At a press conference held by the Waijiaobu on 13 October, when questioned about whether Sun Ke's proposals for the severe punishment of Japanese officers and for the removal of the emperor represented the official policy of the Chinese government, Wu Guozhen, the Vice Foreign Minister, tactfully replied that Sun's views were undoubtedly shared by a large number of Chinese people. He Fengshan, director of the Information Department of the Waijiaobu, was more candid than Wu when he told an American foreign service officer that at least 90 percent of informed Chinese endorsed the policy toward the Japanese emperor suggested by Sun Ke, and officials in the Waijiaobu unanimously supported Sun's stand.[14]

If these remarks were still not authoritative enough, T. V. Soong's own attitude confirmed the impression obtained by the Western Allies in 1943 that Chongqing was inclined to adopt a hard-line policy toward the Japanese emperor. Early in August, at a meeting with British Foreign Secretary Anthony Eden in London, Soong inquired into the British policy toward the House of Savoy of Italy. He admitted that the Chinese government was interested in this issue only for the sake of contemplating a postwar policy toward the Japanese emperor. According to Soong, the current view of the Chinese government was that since the Japanese emperor was used as a symbol by Japanese warlords for the purpose of carrying out their aggression, he must be removed after Japan's defeat. Eden responded that on this question he would like to turn to the Chinese government for advice. But on another occasion, when talking to two lower-ranking officials of the British Foreign Office, Soong encountered disagreement. The British did not think that the monarchies in Italy and Japan were sufficiently comparable. In Italy, as long as there was a government able to sign an armistice with the Allies, Esler Dening told Soong, the form of the Italian government was not important. But the Japanese emperor was a different matter. The removal of the throne would not have the effect of eliminating Japanese

---

[13] Sun Ke, "Chedi huimie Riben kouguo" (For the Total Destruction of the Japanese Pirate State), *Da Gong Bao*, 7 July 1943; Sun Ke, "Xiaomie Riben tianhuang" (Eliminate the Mikado), *Da Gong Bao*, 10 October 1943.

[14] Gauss to Hull, 23 October 1943, *FRUS, 1943: China*, 877–878.

militarism but could well drive the Japanese to Bolshevism. Soong was not convinced, insisting that the Japanese imperial house be abolished as a necessary prerequisite for peace and security in the world as well as in Asia. Nor could he see why the Allies should be more concerned about the danger of Bolshevism in Japan than in Italy or Germany.[15]

In both conversations, Ambassador Wellington Koo was present. Koo later recalled that he was surprised by Soong's statements on the resolution concerning the removal of the Japanese emperor. Soong had not previously mentioned the subject to Koo. In fact, before then, Koo had never heard the Chinese government's view on the subject. Koo's observation in his memoir is noteworthy: "My impression was that Soong was expressing Generalissimo's [Chiang Kai-shek's] view as well as his own, but in fact I am not sure whether the foreign minister's views at this time reflected more the American viewpoint or the Generalissimo's."[16] Koo's judgment was based on his experience in working with both Soong and Chiang, and not on evidence about this particular issue. Generally speaking, Soong's American connections rendered him prone to absorb American ideas. At the same time, it was difficult for Koo to imagine that Soong would take the risk of putting himself in contention with Chiang Kai-shek on any important policy issues. Therefore, to Ambassador Koo, although Soong might gain inspiration from his American acquaintances for his view, he must at least have a sense that his view was not contradictory to Chiang's own.

Although at the time Chiang Kai-shek's attitude toward the issue of postwar Japan was not known to the outside world, editorials of the KMT organ, *Zhongyang Ribao* (Central Daily), might offer some hints in this regard. The KMT regime was not known for its belief in a free press, and in the war years the government's censorship of the media was especially severe. During this period, Chiang Kai-shek personally checked all of the *Zhongyang Ribao*'s important editorials, and once he even ordered an editor of the paper imprisoned for his unauthorized editorship.[17] In this context, an editorial of the *Zhongyang Ribao* entitled "The Problem of Postwar Treatment of Japan," which appeared in mid-October 1943, carried

[15] "Notes of a conversation between Dr. Soong and Dr. Koo on one part and Mr. Eden and Sir Alexander Cadogan on the other," 3 August 1943, TSP, box 29; "Notes of a conversation between Dr. Soong and Dr. Koo on the one part and Messrs. Ashley Clark and Denning [sic] of the Foreign Office on the other," 4 August 1943, ibid. For more information about the view of the British Foreign Office on postwar Japan, see Christopher Thorne, *Allies of a Kind: The United States, Britain, and the War Against Japan, 1941–1945* (Oxford: Oxford University Press, 1978), 373.

[16] RWK, 5(A): 571.

[17] William L. Tung, *Revolutionary China; A Personal Account, 1926–1945* (New York: St. Martin's Press, 1973), 244; Chen Bulei, *Chen Bulei Wenji* (Writings by Chen Bulei) (Taipei: Zhongyang Wenwu Gongyingshe, 1984), 446–447; Lai Guanglin, *Zhongguo Baoye Shi*, 189.

great importance. According to the editorial, the postwar policy of the United Nations toward Japan should include (1) retention by Japan of only a minimum armed force; (2) abolition of the whole Japanese aviation capability; (3) demolition of the Japanese military industry; (4) punishment of the principal war criminals; (5) "proper solution" of the imperial and constitutional systems that were pillars of the militarist state of Japan; (6) re-education of the Japanese people with democratic ideas; (7) independence for Korea; (8) return of Formosa, the Ryukyu Islands and Manchuria to China; (9) international administration of the South Kurile Island and the Japanese Mandated Islands; (10) restoration of the Japanese-occupied territories in the Pacific to their original owners and independence for Thailand; and (11) liberation of the white Ainu people living in Hokkaido.[18]

The editorial's carefully arranged order of items (United Nations security with regard to Japan first, China's territorial claims later) and cautious wording of controversial subjects (such as the colonies in the Pacific) pointed to a meticulous editorship guided by an authoritative hand, maybe even Chiang Kai-shek's own hand. Although falling short of advocating openly the removal of the Japanese emperor, the editorial clearly incriminated the imperial house. The editorial also conveyed the old KMT suspicions of the West. In a pregnant sentence, the editorializer emphasized: "An important condition for lasting peace in East Asia will also hinge on the complete abandonment by the West of its traditional policy of sustaining Japan and repressing China." Chongqing's attitude was unmistakable: whatever policy toward postwar Japan was adopted by the Western Allies, it would also imply a policy of theirs toward China. It is noteworthy that the editorial appeared on the eve of the Cairo Conference; therefore, it was likely part of Chongqing's effort to pave the way for Chiang Kai-shek's first (and only) summit meeting with the American and British leaders.

Washington: a new Japan?

At the Casablanca Conference of January 1943, President Roosevelt proclaimed to the world that an "unconditional surrender" principle would be applied to the Axis powers. In doing so, the president was partially motivated by a concern about placating the Russians, who were disappointed by the Western Allies' reluctance to open a second front in Europe soon. No such concern seemed to exist about the Chinese. Even if Roosevelt were also thinking about China, the Chinese editorial of October 1943 indicated that KMT leaders did not take the unconditional surrender principle as a guarantee against a Western–Japanese compromise in the long run. Had officials in Chongqing known of the policy planning for postwar Japan in the U.S. State Department, they would have felt that their concern

---

[18] *Zhongyang Ribao*, 15 October 1943.

was well founded. Although never contemplating a negotiated peace in the Pacific, American planning officials tended to hold that after the war "Japan should not be reduced [to a] weak and impoverished [state] that would create a vacuum in [the] North Pacific and render Japan a prey of neighboring powers, and would also create hostile psychology within Japan."[19] Such an orientation was too pro-Japan to those KMT officials who could not see how China and Japan would be able to be strong simultaneously.

American planners agreed with the Chinese that the spider-shaped Japanese Empire in the Pacific must be dissolved after the war. Yet the Americans' reasons for doing so differed from Chongqing's. In the summer of 1942, a "tentative view" was adopted by a Political Subcommittee organized in February under the State Department's Advisory Committee on Postwar Foreign Policy. It suggested that territories acquired by Japan after the first Sino–Japanese conflict of 1894–1895 should be subject to readjustment. Thus, a long list of territories including Formosa, Korea, Manchuria, southern Sakhalin, the Japanese Mandated Islands, and some other small islands in the Pacific would be affected. The reason, for one, was that during Japan's half-century of expansion, "no comprehensive attempt at a fair territorial settlement in the Far East had been made, as had been done for Europe in 1919."[20] The peace settlement of 1919 was a model of the great powers' collective effort to redraw the political map of Europe. Thus, for the Americans, Japan was guilty for its unilateral actions. But for the Chinese, Japan's crime in 1895 and ever since was its violation of China's sovereignty and territories.

Yet, although the 1894–1895 time line could be supported by moral or legal arguments, it alone could not satisfy America's concern about postwar security in the Pacific. For instance, Japan's acquisition of the Mandated Islands in the Pacific was part of the peace agreement of 1919, but it proved to have endangered American security. Thus, a geographic criterion was also developed by State Department planners. After this war, U.S. foreign policy must not allow Japan to retain its control of the sea and air routes across the Pacific. To ensure security, Japan must be deprived of all its insular possessions south of 30° north latitude, acquired before or after the 1894–1895 war, which would reduce Japanese influence to its home islands. Chongqing would welcome such a policy, but there was also a potential for disagreement between the Americans and the Chinese. The American emphasis on security in the Pacific would likely

[19] F. S. Dunn, *Peace-Making and the Settlement with Japan* (Princeton, NJ: Princeton University Press, 1963), 19; John W. Pickersgill and David W. Foster, ed., *The Mackenzie King Record* (Toronto: University of Toronto Press, 1960–1970), 1: 431–433; T documents-366, 27 September 1943, *OJ*, 1-B-25.
[20] P document-31, 6 August 1942, *RHN*, box 54; P minute-20, 1 August 1942, *SHP*, box 350; Harley Notter, *Postwar Foreign Policy Preparation, 1939–1945* (Washington, DC: G.P.O., 1949), 82.

require that territories detached from Japan be put into "steady hands," for which a weak China might not qualify. The Chinese were certain that they wanted to regain those former Chinese territories, but planning officers in the State Department warned against any premature commitment by the U.S. government to the ultimate disposition of any territories in the Pacific that were suitable for air and naval bases.[21]

The unpredictability of China's postwar status also created uncertainty for other aspects of U.S. planning for Japan. For instance, although demilitarization of Japan was a foregone conclusion to planners in the State Department, they could not determine with accuracy the scope and characteristics of necessary policy measures. How large a police force should Japan be allowed to keep in the postwar years, which would be enough to maintain Japan's internal order but not to threaten its neighbors? Questions like this were raised in the State Department but not answered. They had to be considered in relation to the military and economic strength of other East Asian countries, especially China, at the end of the war.[22]

Even more unsettling was the question of how Japan should be treated economically after the war. Along with China's recovery of lost territories, China's receiving of substantial reparations from Japan was viewed in Chongqing as among the undisputable conditions for peace settlement with Japan. By contrast, economic policy toward Japan caused a serious debate among American officials. In the State Department, a Subcommittee on Economic Policy headed by Dean Acheson was responsible for deliberating on economic policies with regard to the Axis powers. Before the Cairo Conference, the subcommittee was sharply divided by opposing ideas about Japan. At one extreme was the concept of reducing Japan to an agricultural economy by removing all of its modern industries and foreign trade. The opposite view was that interference by the United Nations in Japan's economy should not go further than measures necessary for disarming Japan. In other words, only those industries directly connected to Japan's military capacity should be dismantled or converted to enterprises with civilian purposes. At the same time, Japan's peaceful industry and trade should be revived and the Japanese people should be allowed to have a tolerable living standard, which would be "the first prerequisite for finally ending the Japanese menace."[23]

It is well known to students of World War II that the White House once favored a "Morgenthau Plan" for "pastoralizing" Germany after the war.[24] A difference in the case of Japan is that in U.S. economic planning for

[21] P document-31, 6 August 1943, *RHN*, box 54; P document-110, 22 September 1942, *OJ*, 1-A-17.
[22] S document-18a, 2 October 1942, *RHN*, box 76; S minute-32, 19 March 1943, ibid.
[23] E document-155, 21 July 1943, *RHN*, box 64.
[24] Robert Dallek, *Franklin D. Roosevelt and American Foreign Policy, 1932–1945* (Oxford: Oxford University Press, 1979), 472–477.

Japan, hard-liners never achieved the upper hand. A reason might be that President Roosevelt, while giving encouragement to the Morgenthau Plan, never paid attention to the issue of Japan's postwar economy. From the outset of the State Department's planning for postwar East Asia, a group of specialists in Japanese affairs exercised strong influence. These officials tended to believe that any overly harsh policy toward Japan would likely be counterproductive. As expressed in a position paper of the Territorial Subcommittee, "any attempt to crush 73 million energetic, patriotic, long-suffering, aggressive, industrious and productive Japanese people not only will be abortive, but will germinate a festering sore which would contaminate and nullify any program designed to bring peace and prosperity to Asia."[25]

Another theory supportive of this view of the Japanese nation was that economically Japan would be indispensable for the postwar rehabilitation of Asia. According to the theory, there had already existed mutual compatibility between Japan and other Asian areas, with the former as the manufacturer and the latter as the consumer. This economic tie might well be used by the Allies for the purposes of postwar relief and long-term economic development in Asia. Retribution for Japan's wrongdoing in Asia, therefore, should not be achieved by demolishing the Japanese economy, but rather by compelling the sole Asian industrial power to convert itself from an exploiter to a servant of other Asian countries.[26]

Such an estimate of Japan's role in postwar Asia tended to bring America's wartime policy toward China into question. While the Roosevelt administration was promoting China as a great power to fill in a power vacuum in postwar Asia created by Japan's defeat, the State Department was planning to sustain Japan's economic strength and thus prevent a vacuum of economic power from emerging in Asia in the first place. In theory, by emphasizing China's political, not economic, role, Washington's China policy did not collide with its Japan policy. President Roosevelt never had any illusion about China's serious economic flaws. But in his China policy, Roosevelt was not impeded by China's economic weakness; he believed that China could be "in the sun even before she has the economic power."[27] In postwar Asia, the United States might well act to hold the balance wheel between a political ally (China) and an economic asset (Japan). The problem is that the Chinese themselves never believed China could be strong again without economic strength. Leaders in Chongqing were convinced that China's complete rehabilitation and the

[25] T document-392, 9 October 1943, *RHN*, box 65. The subcommittee was chaired by Isaiah Bowman and organized in February 1942. See Notter, *Postwar Foreign Policy Preparation*, 82.
[26] E document-173, 6 September 1943, *RHN*, box 65.
[27] "Record of conversation with the president and Mr. Hopkins," 16 July 1943, *TSP*, box 32.

full-scale degradation of Japan's military and economic strength were two halves of the same walnut.

The contrast between Chongqing's and Washington's policies toward Japan also extended into the realm of governmental systems. As mentioned before, although KMT leaders were reluctant to treat Japan as an international outlaw for too long after the war, they envisaged a new Chinese–Japanese relationship formed on the premise that an internal revolution would create a new Japan. To American planners, a radical revolution in Japan was hardly a favorable option. Most revealing in this respect was the State Department's consideration of postwar treatment of the Japanese imperial house. During the winter of 1942, the question was first raised in the State Department in the context of Allied psychological warfare against Japan: how would the war in the Pacific be affected if the Japanese emperor were attacked physically or through Allied propaganda?

Some in the Division of Far Eastern Affairs (FE) advised against such attacks lest they cause radical disturbances in Japan and create difficulties for Allied occupation in the postwar years. These officials also argued that democracy could not be imposed on Japan from the outside, whereas the retention and humanization of the emperor might help start a gradual course toward a progressive government in Japan.[28] Others, especially the officials at the China Desk of the FE, challenged this view. In late December, George Atcheson, a senior officer of the China Desk who would soon be assigned to the U.S. embassy in China, admitted in a memorandum that holders of the foregoing opinion were "competent students of Japan and experts on Japan." Yet, he continued, their expertise turned into a disadvantage on this particular issue: they were too much influenced by the image of Japan created by the Japanese themselves, and believed that Japan's institutions were unique and deserved special treatment, regardless of other nations' interests. Atcheson contended that the emperor cult in Japan was at the center of the aggressive and militarist forces in that country, and therefore it must not be perpetuated. Alger Hiss supported Atcheson. At the time, he was assistant to Stanley K. Hornbeck, the political adviser of the Secretary of State on Far Eastern affairs. Believing that the issue had important implications for American–Chinese relations, Hiss criticized the "Japanese officers" in the State Department for their failure to discuss in any manner "our Chinese ally's" possible attitude toward the matter. Although afterward the American government refrained from attacking the Japanese emperor physically or verbally, the issue of his postwar treatment continued to cause controversies among American planning officials.[29]

[28] Bishop to Hornbeck, 14 December 1942, *SHP*, box 237.
[29] Atcheson to Hornbeck, 28 December 1942, and Hiss to Hornbeck, 30 December 1942, *SHP*, box 237; T document-315, 25 May 1943, *RHN*, box 63; T document-381, 6 October 1943, *OJ*, l-B-28; T minute-54, 22 October 1943, *OJ*, l-C-4.

Labels like "Japan crowd" and "China crowd" tend to simplify policy disagreements among the State Department's East Asian officials, though there were indeed officials who wanted to eradicate Japan from postwar Asian politics and those who did not have much respect for China. Hornbeck belonged to the former group. Like Sun Ke and Wang Pengsheng in China, Hornbeck believed that this war should provide an opportunity for Japan to have a long-overdue revolution. Hornbeck, however, expected that such a process would mean Japan's disappearance from the international scene for a considerable period. He was not motivated by a concern about Japan's having a genuine social-political revolution. Hornbeck was simply confident that as long as a new China was on the American side, U.S. foreign policy would be able to deal with any difficult contingencies in postwar Asia.[30] Yet, in the war years, Hornbeck's influence on Far Eastern affairs in the State Department was receding. When his views on America's China policy were challenged, Hornbeck did not have much impact on the Japan policy, which was not his area of expertise. In the fall of 1943, Hornbeck was appointed to head a new inter-divisional area committee on East Asia that would coordinate the State Department's policy planning for the region. But Hornbeck did not seem interested in the job. He had designated another official as his alternate to chair the committee even before it was organized.[31]

The establishment of the area committee on East Asia indicated that in its policy planning, the U.S. government wanted to adopt a regional approach but not to base its postwar plans on individual countries. Yet, despite the implications of the Japan policy for China, American policy planners did not conscientiously try to combine their plans for Japan with America's wartime policy toward China. On the screen of the State Department's economic and political planning for postwar Japan, China usually cast only a blurred silhouette. China's relevance to most discussions on Japan in the State Department was limited to its being a receiver of some territories and reparations. Generally speaking, President Roosevelt's idea about China's acting as a policeman in postwar Asia, if not openly contradicted, was at least not substantiated by plans in the State Department. It was remarkable how quickly the inseparability of China and Japan in America's prewar Asian policy eroded in the war years. After all, one of America's principal war aims was to pull Japan out of the Asian mainland. After the Japanese knot in Asia's regional web was cut, officials in the State Department did not seem to share Roosevelt's opinion that China would be able to provide the rope to retie the area together.

[30] Memorandum of a conversation between Hornbeck and State Department officials, 28 October 1943, *RHN*, box 79; "Autobiography [of Hornbeck], 1942–1944," n.d., *SHP*, box 497.
[31] Gary May, *China Scapegoat: The Diplomatic Ordeal of John Carter Vincent* (Washington, DC: New Republic Books, 1979), 91–93; Notter, *Postwar Foreign Policy Preparation*, 178.

In mid-1943, China received some attention in the Security Technical Committee's deliberation on America's postwar military strategy in the Pacific. At one of the committee's meetings, Captain H. L. Pence, representing the Navy on the committee, made some extraordinary remarks. Viewing the war as a struggle for survival between races and civilizations, Captain Pence argued that Japan would remain America's enemy for the next hundred years unless the race was totally terminated. Therefore, the most effective solution to the problem of postwar security in the Pacific was not to allow Japan to surrender until it was extensively bombed and "there was little left of its civilization." Although this view might not have seemed radical to America's fighting men, it did not receive support from the State Department members of the committee. These officials pointed out to the captain that it was impossible to crush a nation and that the genocide idea was not feasible from a political point of view. The captain was reminded that China was an ally of the United States and that his racist version of the current war was not compatible with this reality. To this Captain Pence responded that one day China might also become an enemy of the United States. But the majority of the committee members agreed that the proper answer to the security problem in postwar East Asia should be an effective security system consisting of bases surrounding Japan and in Japan itself, but not Japan's utter destruction.[32]

Other matters to be resolved were where the projected security bases should be located and what Allied powers should be responsible for the new security system. Colonel James F. Olive of the Air Force expressed doubt that any of the Big Four would allow international bases to be installed in its own territories even for the purpose of policing Japan. The colonel questioned why "outside forces" – namely, America and Britain – had to participate in controlling Japan, suggesting that because of their geographic proximity to Japan, the Soviet Union and China were the powers most suitable for assuming the responsibility. State Department planners disagreed. They offered three reasons why the United States could not afford to be an outsider to the Pacific. First, the interests of the United States in the Far East were hardly limited to the control of Japan. America had interests in the welfare and security of areas such as the Dutch Indies and the Philippines. These matters should not be left to the Chinese and the Soviets. Second, in the long run, the responsibility for policing Japan would have to be carried out by powers that had significant naval strength, for which neither China nor the Soviet Union qualified. Last but not least, at the end of the war, China would be exhausted and would remain weak for some time, which would leave America with no other alternative but to assume a paramount military role in East Asia in the foreseeable future.[33]

[32] ST minute-16, 7 May 1943, and ST minute-17, 12 May 1943, *RHN*, box 79.
[33] ST minute-17, 12 May 1943, *RHN*, box 79.

During these discussions, China's *amour propre* was often mentioned as a condition to be satisfied in the postwar disposition of Japanese territories, especially where the territories had been related to China in the past. But due to China's weakness, Chongqing's territorial aspirations were rarely considered in light of the postwar security system in the Pacific. In other words, although willing to support certain Chinese territorial demands, American planners did not think that China's recovery of territories would contribute significantly to security in the Pacific. When President Roosevelt advocated China's role in policing Japan, State Department planners at first could not even agree on whether China's cooperation should be solicited for the purpose of Allied postwar occupation of Japan. Eventually, nevertheless, a consensus emerged from these discussions that the occupation force in Japan should not be exclusively American. A joint Allied occupation would have the advantage of distributing the material and personnel burdens among the participating powers. Other participating countries would also have to share with America the animosity of the conquered Japanese. For these reasons, China should be included in the occupation. Yet the number of Chinese occupation forces must be limited because, in the State Department's opinion, "there would be a much more salutary effect if Japan were policed by a power which it felt had been responsible for its defeat." China would not be such a power, and its prominent presence in Japan, backed by the Western Allies, would only cause Japan's resentment against the West.[34]

Clearly, the American–Chinese collaboration in war and President Roosevelt's promotion of China as one of the great powers responsible for peace did not persuade the State Department to offer China an important role in its postwar policy toward Japan. Nor did China occupy a leading position in overall East Asian planning at the State Department. This is not to say that the State Department never tried to treat China as the most important subject in its postwar planning. Soon after the United States entered the war, the Special Research Division of the State Department outlined issues that would face the United States in postwar Asia. At the time, it was believed that U.S. foreign policy had to deal with problems in four major geographical areas. In order of priorities, these were (1) China, (2) Japan, (3) dependent areas in Southeast Asia, and (4) India. The emergence of a strong, unified, independent, and prosperous China at the end of the war was regarded as the cardinal condition for eliminating big-power rivalries and aggressions and for enhancing general economic growth in the whole Asian–Pacific region.[35]

Yet, it was also understood that China presented a dual problem to

---

[34] ST minute-16, 7 May 1943, and ST minute-19, 26 May 1943, *RHN*, box 79.
[35] Memorandum by Joseph M. Jones, "Statement of Major Postwar Problems in the Pacific Area," 20 February 1942, *RLP*, box 2.

American planning. On the one hand, China should be viewed as one of the "principal voices in the determination of postwar solutions," and its cooperation ought to be solicited by the American government in all issues pertinent to worldwide postwar readjustments. On the other hand, China would be "a principal area where reconstruction may take place." China's postwar reconstruction would be different from that of any other Ally because of its own chronic problems. Before American policymakers were able to enter China as a great power into their policy equation, they had to ask questions like "how can China be unified?", "how can China be made prosperous?", and "how can China be made strong?"[36]

There were no ready answers to these questions in the war years. Consequently, although a China-centered agenda for East Asian planning was contemplated in the State Department early in the war, in practice the planning officers found it very difficult to treat China both as a great power to discharge international obligations and as a weak, internally disoriented country likely to become an international liability. The China priority in America's foreign policy planning had to remain an abstract principle or a delusion. To American planners, as an object of strategic planning, the China problem simply lacked the necessary tangible frame of reference. By contrast, the issue of a vanquished Japan was relatively easy to define. These factors, along with American officials' wartime convictions about Japan's importance to American security in the Pacific, helped shape the State Department's planning for postwar East Asia that paid more attention to the question of how to recondition a defeated Japan than that of how to promote a victorious China.

Thus, in the initial stages of their postwar planning for Japan, the Chinese and American governments shared some concepts but also had serious disagreements. Except for some extremist opinions, mainstream thought in the two capitals seemed to agree that, after the war, Japan should be rendered harmless to its neighbors but not excluded from the international life of East Asia for too long. Otherwise, Chongqing and Washington were preparing different futures for Japan. Chongqing's policy was characterized by severe economic measures against Japan and by an expectation that some drastic change in postwar Japanese politics would help bring about a new Chinese–Japanese relationship. Simply put, the Chinese wanted to reverse the historical imbalance between an isolated, weak China and a strong Japan associated with or tolerated by the Western powers. American policy planners disliked the thought of disturbances in postwar Japan in either an economic or a political sense. If they foresaw any drastic change in postwar international relations in East Asia, it was neither Japan's total elimination nor China's blossoming into a new great

[36] Memoranda by Joseph M. Jones, "What Do We Desire of China? Preliminary Considera-tion," and "China," n.d., *RHN*, box 11.

power in Asia. Rather, it was America's expansion of its influence in both Japan and China in different ways and America's bringing the two most important Asian countries into its own global system. Until the Cairo Conference of late 1943, there had been no systematic exchange of opinions between the Chinese and American governments concerning postwar Japan. This led to an awkward situation: Japan, supposedly the most important subject of both American and Chinese foreign policy planning in Asia, was far less visible in the two governments' relationship than were other issues.

3

China's lost territories

Once both the Chinese and American governments accepted the dismemberment of the Japanese Empire as a logical result of the war, the next question was how to treat Japan's imperial territorial possessions. An answer, also seemingly logical, was that those territories seized by Japan from China should be returned. Thus, China's nationalist objective of recovering lost territories and America's wartime policy of promoting China's international status could both be satisfied. By the time of World War II, China's lost territories were not limited to those seized by Japan, such as Manchuria, Taiwan, and the Ryukyu Islands. It was simply politically expedient for the Allies to focus their postwar plans on the territories in Japan's possession lest other territorial issues cause inter-Allied disunity. Yet, even in the areas just mentioned, the Chinese and the American governments did not readily agree.

Manchuria

To the Chinese government, Manchuria held a unique place in China's rehabilitation. It symbolized China's territorial disintegration in the prewar years due to the fact that, after establishing itself in Nanjing in 1928, Chiang Kai-shek's "central government" had never been able to extend its actual control to the region. During the Sino–Japanese conflict in the 1930s, although it gradually ceased reproving Western treaty powers in China in order to win international sympathy, the Chinese government never formally abandoned the objective of recovering its lost territories. Refraining from pressing other treaty powers over territorial problems, the Chinese government's persistent claim to Manchuria became the only evidence that its "revolutionary diplomacy" was still alive. Therefore, KMT officials easily regarded the status of Manchuria as a touchstone of China's internal unity and external independence. But in the decade between the Mukden

Incident and Pearl Harbor, while the Chinese government's rhetoric on recovering the Northeast kept the subject alive in the international forum, the real chance of recovery grew slimmer.

The flame of war in the Pacific at the end of 1941 sparked new hope in Chongqing. Sun Ke was among those who first articulated this hope. In a speech made in September 1942, Sun pointed out that only a thorough defeat of Japan could induce Japan to return Manchuria to China. And the goal would be attainable only after the Sino–Japanese war was integrated into the larger war in the Pacific and China and the Western powers became allies.[1] On 3 November, T. V. Soong officially clarified China's war aims at his first press conference as China's Foreign Minister. He stated that at the end of the war China would restore its sovereignty over Manchuria, Taiwan, and the Ryukyu Islands. At the same time, Korea should be granted full independence.[2]

Despite the importance of the Manchurian question to China, the Chinese government's postwar policy planning for the region was slow to begin. The subject was discussed publicly by Chinese officials and nonofficial commentators, but most commentaries were concerned with justifying China's claim over Manchuria, not with making concrete policy suggestions on how the territory should be recovered. A few months before Pearl Harbor, Wu Tiecheng, secretary-general of the Central Executive Committee of the KMT, spoke in public on the northeastern provinces' economic and strategic values.[3] In mid-1943, when the Waijiaobu prepared a "Statement on 'Manchukuo,'" the main concern was still to justify to the world that China had the right to recover the region. The points made by the statement included the following: (1) 97 percent of the Manchurian population were Chinese; (2) legally, China's sovereignty over Manchuria was indisputable; (3) the recovery by China of Manchuria was not only a matter of justice but also necessary for the existence and welfare of the Chinese nation; and (4) the return of Manchuria to China would serve as evidence of good faith on the part of the other Allied governments.[4] During the first two years of the Pacific war, Wang Chonghui's RC included Manchuria in its general agenda on the restoration of China's lost territories but undertook no concrete study of the subject.

Meanwhile, there were people in Chongqing who believed that the recovery of the Northeast would demand more than just making claims. The faculty members of the National Northeast University, who had been forced out of Manchuria and in the war years resided in Chongqing, took up the issue. By 1943, they had completed three alternative programs for

[1] *Zhongyang Ribao*, 25 September 1942.
[2] Gauss to Hull, 5 November 1942, *FRUS, 1942: China*, 174.
[3] *Zhongyang Ribao*, 18 September 1942.
[4] Memorandum by Xu Shuxi, "Statement on 'Manchukuo'," n.d. (1943?), *TSP*, box 27.

the recovery and reconstruction of the Northeast, hoping these could be useful in government planning.[5] Sun Ke also favored an early beginning of detailed planning for Manchuria. Recalling the autonomous history of Manchuria under the warlord Zhang Zuolin and then under his son Zhang Xueliang, Sun believed that the principle of centralization must be applied to the region in order to establish the real authority of the central government. A strong centripetal force in the Northeast must be fostered by reconnecting the political, ideological, economic, financial, and ethnic ties between the region and the interior of China. Especially interesting was Sun's recommendation in the economic field. He believed that socialist programs like the nationalization of heavy industries and Soviet-type agricultural collectivization would be useful for Manchuria.[6]

Sun Ke admired the Soviet model because he believed that it was congruent with his father's "Three People's Principles." As for the historical antagonism and existing discord between the Chinese and Soviet governments, Sun was willing to attribute them to misunderstandings for which neither side should be blamed.[7] Sun actually viewed Japan's destruction of old Chinese systems in Manchuria as an opportunity; it enabled the Chinese government to have a new beginning there. A new Northeast would become a model of reconstruction for the rest of China by implementing the Three People's Principles and learning from Soviet experiences.

Although not many Chinese officials in Chongqing shared Sun Ke's cordial feelings toward the northern neighbor, Sun's praise of the Soviet experience was not really heretical in wartime Chongqing. In fact, the imitation of certain Soviet practices was an official policy of the Chinese government. In December 1943, the Central Planning Board, the highest-ranking planning agency for China's domestic affairs, reviewed closely the Soviet experiences of economic development and military organization and considered how these experiences could be adapted to China.[8] Anxious as they were to prevent the restitution of Russian interests in Manchuria, KMT leaders did not exclude economic and military cooperation with the Soviet Union on a new basis. While Sun Ke's discussion of the Northeast did not elaborate on how new Chinese–Soviet cooperation would take place in the region, many in Chongqing recognized the Soviet factor in the question. In September 1943, an editorial in the *Da Gong Bao* (*Grand*

---

[5] Jin Yufu, "Jinnian jiu yi ba ganxiang" (Reflection on September 18th of This Year), *Da Gong Bao*, 18 September 1943.

[6] *Zhongyang Ribao*, 26 September 1942.

[7] Sun Ke, *Zhongguo yu Zhanhou Shijie* (China and the Postwar World) (Chongqing: n.p., 1944), 139–140; Sun Ke, *Zhong Su Guanxi* (Chinese–Soviet Relations) (Shanghai: Zhonghua Shuju, 1946), 36–37, 54–56.

[8] *GW*, 80: 58–59; "Junshi zu huitan beiwanglu" (Memoranda on the Meetings of the Military Group), 17 December 1943, and "Guofang jianshe" (National Defense Reconstruction), 21 December 1943, *HSP*, box 1.

Public Daily) on the Manchurian question admitted that China's recovery of Manchuria was pertinent to the adjustment of Chongqing–Moscow relations. The editorial argued that the recovery of the northeastern provinces would rely on both China's own military efforts and some favorable political conditions. The latter included consolidation of the Sino–Soviet friendship, solution of the problem of the Chinese Communist Party, and development of a powerful Korean independence movement.

Yet, during the first two years of the Pacific war, Soviet neutrality in the Asian conflict did not lead Chongqing to seek an understanding with the Russians over Manchuria. Instead, what worried Chinese officials in this period was the Western Allies' (especially Washington's) attitude toward postwar settlement in Manchuria. On the eve of the Pacific war, Chiang Kai-shek had personally called President Roosevelt's attention to the Chinese government's attitude toward Manchuria. In a message to the president, Chiang asserted that China would never relinquish Manchuria because its loss to China would be followed by that of Xinjiang and Tibet, and would also create great difficulty for China in the recovery of Outer Mongolia.[9] To the dismay of Chinese leaders, by the time of the Pacific war, many people in the West had already become accustomed to view Manchuria more as a region of international intrigues than as a Chinese territory.

In this regard, a conversation between President Roosevelt and Hu Shi in September 1939 was revealing. On that occasion, President Roosevelt told Hu Shi, then the Chinese ambassador to the United States, that he was contemplating a peace solution of the Chinese–Japanese dispute over Manchuria. "I have a new formula," the president announced to the ambassador. "I can settle this question of Manchuria on the same basis as the new agreement we have just signed with Britain regarding the joint interest and control over the two islands in the Pacific: Canton and Enderbury Islands. Some such arrangement can be made with regard to Manchuria for the benefit and security of both China and Japan." Not familiar with the recent American–British agreement, Ambassador Hu could not decide how to respond properly to President Roosevelt's suggestion. But later he learned some relevant facts. Canton Island, with a population of forty, was only nine miles long and 500 yards across at its widest point. Enderbury Island was even smaller: three miles long and one mile wide. Its population totaled four. In contrast, Manchuria was 413,000 square miles and had a population of 33 million. Ambassador Hu Shi was astonished by the president's analogy between Manchuria and these two tiny islands.[10]

---

[9] Wu Xiangxiang, *Di Er Ci Zhong Ri Zhanzheng Shi* (History of the Second Chinese–Japanese War) (Taipei: Zonghe Yuekanshe, 1973), 2: 775.

[10] Hu Shih (Hu Shi), "China in Stalin's Grand Strategy," *Foreign Affairs*, 24 (October 1950): 39. In 1939, Hu Shi himself was a recent convert to the noncompromising stand against

Besides, the Chinese government could not as easily make a deal over China's national territories as the American and British governments did over their imperial possessions.

When the American–Japanese conflict in the Pacific became imminent, opinions about Manchuria became chaotic even among the best-informed people in the United States. In late 1941, the U.S. Council on Foreign Relations (CFR) organized a study group to inquire into the long-term prospect of American–Japanese relations that involved people from both the official and academic circles.[11] In the group's first meeting, on 3 November 1941, Dr. Tyler Dennett, the renowned Far Eastern diplomatic historian, presented three principles for peace with Japan: (1) Japan must no longer be discriminated against in international trade in the Asian–Pacific region; (2) Japan must be granted the rights to trade peacefully in China and to enter into various engagements with China; and (3) Japan's "special position in Manchuria and her right to absorb Manchukuo into a status similar to that of Korea" should be recognized. In making these points, Dr. Dennett adopted the view that the origins of the Asian conflict lay in the unsatisfactory living conditions of the Japanese nation and its unfulfilled legitimate demands. In the following discussion, Hornbeck and others questioned the effectiveness of the Dennett formula of offering Manchuria to Japan in exchange for Japan's ceasing its expansionist policies on the Asian mainland. Yet some also suggested that the establishment of Manchuria as a truly "independent state" might be an easier solution to the Sino–Japanese dispute over the territory.[12]

Japan's attack on Pearl Harbor did not effect a consensus on Manchuria in the study group. When the group again turned its attention to the issue in early March 1942, Nicholas J. Spykman argued for a new balance of power in postwar East Asia that should give America and other Western powers a chance to exert influence on the Asian continent. In the new configuration of power, Spykman believed, the West could afford to allow Japan to remain a strong power; the Russians would be preoccupied with

Japan. Not long after the Marco Polo Bridge incident, Hu was in the United States lobbying for American aid to the Chinese government. In a speech sponsored by the New York Foreign Policy Association, he stated that if Japan withdrew from China proper, China in return was willing to recognize the Manchukuo. Afterward, it was Henry Stimson who asked Hu reprovingly: "How could you say this in the name of the thirty million people of Manchuria?" See Zhang Zhongfu, *Miwang Ji* (Perplexed Reminiscences) (Taipei: Wenhai Chubanshe, 1978), 117.

[11] Some members of the group – George H. Blakeslee (chairman), Hugh Borton, Stanley K. Hornbeck, and Grayson Kirk – would also be participants in the State Department's wartime foreign policy planning. For the relationship between the CFR and the postwar planning of the State Department, see Dan Smoot, *The Invisible Government* (Dallas: Dan Smoot Report, Inc., 1962).

[12] CFR study group reports, "First Meeting: United States Peace Terms. November 3, 1941," *PRC*, box 174.

European problems; and China was likely to achieve supremacy in Asia. Spykman took the last possibility as a major challenge to U.S. policy: "If China is restored from Manchuria to Hainan, then we shall have restored the sort of thing we are trying to destroy in Europe. A China–Manchuria–Korea combination would establish a concentration of power comparable to a Hitler victory in Europe. The resources in China plus a population of 350 million people could make that nation the greatest war potential in the Far East." To prevent such a nightmarish future, Spykman suggested that the Western Allies work to contract the Japanese Empire in the Pacific but, at the same time, retain Manchuria and Korea for Japan in order to use Japan to balance China.[13]

Nathaniel Peffer contested Spykman's fear of a powerful and aggressive China as groundless: in the foreseeable future, China would not be able to become strong enough to exert its will throughout the Far East; furthermore, the Russians might not be as passive in Asia as Spykman predicted. "In any case," Peffer argued, "a strong China will check Russia, but a weak China will mean the retention of foreign rivalries as in the past." Nor could Peffer accept the notion that the Japanese possession of Manchuria would bring stability to the Far East. Instead, it seemed more likely that Japan would continue to use Manchuria as a power base for further infiltration into North China.[14]

No one in the group doubted that Manchuria held a vital position in the power structure of East Asia. The possession of the region by whatever state would significantly enhance that state's strength and strategic position in Asian politics. Despite their disagreement on the future of Manchuria, members of the group approached the issue from the same power political premise, and no one made an argument based on China's rights and sovereignty. Even those who believed China should regain Manchuria based their contention on the consequential ground that this would facilitate a stable power relationship in postwar East Asia. In the meantime, legal or moral arguments based on Chinese sovereignty seemed impotent and ineffectual.

Furthermore, in these discussions, Manchuria was considered mainly as an issue between China and Japan, and the Russian factor was reduced to a minimum. Moscow's pledge to "respect the territorial integrity and inviolability of Manchukuo" in its 1941 neutrality pact with Tokyo might affect these American observers' opinions. Still, considering the fact that the participants in these discussions were among the best-informed and most learned students and experts on Far Eastern affairs, it comes as a surprise that not a single member of the group predicted that the Russians

---

[13] CFR study group reports, "Fourth Meeting: Concrete Issues in a Postwar Settlement with Japan. March 3, 1942," *PRC*, box 174.
[14] Ibid.

would stage a comeback in Manchuria. What makes this neglect of Soviet intentions even more curious is that at about the same time the aforementioned meetings took place, another study group of the CFR was considering the issue of military cooperation with the Soviet Union in the Pacific war, which would inevitably lead to the question of possible Soviet entry into the war in northeastern Asia.[15]

The deliberations in the CFR were important because when the State Department began to consider the postwar status of Manchuria in 1943, its contemplation of the subject fell into the same pattern. But this time, officials in the State Department substituted the Soviet Union for Japan as the principal postwar contender in Manchuria aside from China. Although the department planners had by now achieved a better forecast than had their CFR forerunners about the nature of postwar politics in Manchuria, their planning operation was seriously hindered by a lack of reliable information about Soviet intentions toward East Asian issues. The Russians were reluctant to reveal their intentions even when pressed. For instance, in mid-March 1943, Harry Hopkins queried Soviet Ambassador Maxim Litvinov about Russian demands at the peace table. Litvinov was blunt about Soviet aims toward the Baltic states, Finland, Poland, and Germany, but he was evasive on Asia.[16]

The State Department succeeded no better than the White House in taking a cue from Moscow. Consequently, for the moment, planning officials could only use induction. They speculated about Soviet aims in East Asia according to known Soviet postwar aspirations in Europe. In August, the Far Eastern Division prepared a memorandum on "U.S.S.R. Aims in the Far East." The "perhaps primary motivating factor in Soviet policy," the authors surmised, "is a natural desire to promote national security" in East Asia as well as in Europe, and the method for Moscow to achieve this goal would be "the creation of well disposed and ideologically sympathetic governments in nearby areas." But to what extent, if any, Moscow would expand its influence in the Far East depended on developments in the East Asian countries themselves more than on the intentions of the Soviet government. Accordingly, these officials predicted that following Japan's defeat, a political vacuum in the North Pacific would provide Soviet Russia with an opportunity to move in. Any serious disturbance in China and throughout the Far East at the end of the war would likewise put the Soviets in a strong position to achieve substantial influence in Asia. The areas where the Russians might seek to create "Sovietized governments,"

[15] Hanson W. Baldwin, "Russian Military Cooperation in the Pacific War," 12 January 1942, *SAI*, A-B 38. For the history of the Japanese–Soviet Neutrality Pact, see James W. Morley, ed., *The Fateful Choice: Japan's Advance into Southeast Asia, 1939–1941* (New York: Columbia University Press, 1980), 13–114.

[16] Robert E. Sherwood, *Roosevelt and Hopkins: An Intimate History* (New York: Harper, 1948), 713.

FE officials predicted, included Inner Mongolia, Manchuria, Korea, and some other areas in the western Pacific. The Soviet government might also want to restore its commercial privileges in Manchuria, such as facilities of warm-water ports and transit rights via the railway across that territory.[17]

The memorandum was one of the earliest official documents that took the Soviet Union, not Japan, as America's principal rival in East Asia in the postwar years. But at the time, American policymakers were not yet prepared to deal with the Soviet Union as a hostile force. Consequently, Washington's postwar policies toward Japan and the Soviets evolved in different directions. Briefly, the policy toward Japan was to contract Japanese influence to its original geographical limits prior to its overseas expansion, but the policy toward Russia was to draw a line confining Moscow's territorial ambitions in East Asia. The trick in the latter was to draw the line in such a way that it would not alienate the Russians but rather facilitate the continuity of the wartime Grand Alliance in the postwar years.

Interestingly, both sets of policies would require restrictions on America's wartime ally, China. Although Japan was to be contracted, American policy did not want to encourage Chongqing to go too far in making excessive demands for retribution. So far as the strategy toward the Soviet Union was concerned, Chongqing disturbed American policymakers on two counts: it was at once too weak to stand by itself in dealing with Soviet power and too militant in its attitude toward Moscow to give compromise a chance. In the State Department's opinion, after the war no other great power would be in a position to balance Soviet power in Asia. Although the American government would not endorse any Soviet initiative for taking advantage of the dire conditions in China, Washington could not afford to allow Chongqing's reckless attitude to provoke Moscow into incorrigible actions. Such a projection of the postwar situation in East Asia prompted planning officials in the State Department to support a policy for "a direct settlement of all issues outstanding" between China and the Soviet Union. The settlement, they hoped, would prevent any serious crack in the Big Four's cooperation for global peace and save the United States from becoming involved in a Sino–Soviet confrontation under the worst possible circumstances in Asia.[18]

But a settlement of the Sino–Soviet disagreements was no simple matter. In 1943, the State Department made a long list of the issues between the Chinese and the Russians, ranging from the Chinese Communists to a series of disputes over territories. The territorial controversies between China and the Soviet Union involved Outer Mongolia, Tannu Tuva, Manchuria,

---

[17] Memorandum by Hornbeck et al., "U.S.S.R. Aims in the Far East," 19 August 1943, *FRUS, 1943: China,* 317–320.

[18] PG document-28, 2 October 1943, *RHN,* box 119.

and Xinjiang, and all, in the State Department's opinion, fell into the same pattern: the Chinese government claimed sovereignty over these territories, but the Soviets either had practical control or probably intended to establish such control. Although conditions in the other territories were relatively stable, Japan's expected relinquishment of Manchuria after the war would most likely cause unpredictable developments. State Department planners thus expected Manchuria to become "the most important of all the areas in which the interests of China and Soviet Russia may come into postwar conflict."[19]

Seeing no need to duplicate the many statements made by the Chinese on China's rights and interests in Manchuria, officials in the State Department focused their attention on how Russia's legitimate interests in Manchuria should be defined. They thought it doubtful but possible that after the war Moscow would want to renew the old tsarist objectives in Manchuria. If such demands came along with Soviet entry into the Pacific war through Manchuria, a serious situation would arise. The Soviet government would likely reassert an interest in the control of the Chinese Eastern Railroad and also in a warm-water port in southern Manchuria. Under such circumstances, in the State Department's opinion, a solution to the Manchuria question would depend both on Russia's not making excessive demands and on China's willingness to satisfy "the real needs of Soviet Russia," such as "favorable traffic privileges across Manchuria and possibly port facilities in Dairen [Dalian]." American officials were trying to draw a very fine line between old tsarist rights and legitimate Soviet interests. They believed that although the former had impaired Chinese sovereignty, the latter would not. But when planners in the department tried to explain why the latter would not constitute an infringement of Chinese sovereignty, they advanced an ambiguous and feeble argument: "Transit privileges, . . . granted to the Soviet government could be supported by *precedent*."[20] No further definition of the "precedent" was attempted. Obviously, it was very difficult to find a precedent in Chinese–foreign relations that concerned Chinese territories but did not damage Chinese sovereignty; this was the case to an even greater extent in the international history of Manchuria.

The difference between the contemplation of the Manchuria question in the State Department and the aforementioned discussions by the CFR group is important. Once the State Department substituted the Soviet Union for Japan as the principal contender for a privileged position in Manchuria, the Manchurian question escalated from an old Far Eastern problem to a current issue of global importance. To American officials, the significance of Manchuria changed mainly because Russia was a Eurasian power

[19] PG document-34, 4 October 1943, *RHN*, box 119.
[20] Ibid.

and its cooperation in world affairs in the postwar years should be solicited. They presumed that Russia would continue to cooperate with the West in the postwar years only if the Western Allies appreciated its interests in different parts of the world. In the 1930s, the American government had treated the Chinese–Japanese conflict over Manchuria as mainly a regional issue and therefore adopted a detached attitude. But in the war years, when American officials reevaluated the Manchuria question against their grand design for the postwar world order, America's stake in a settlement of the problem rose significantly. The planning for Manchuria in the State Department did take into account Chinese sovereignty in the area. Yet the problem remained how to interpret Chinese sovereignty. Due to the significance of Manchuria to the postwar survival of the Grand Alliance, Washington's support of Chinese sovereignty had to be conditional. In fact, in American government plans concerning former Chinese territories, Chinese sovereignty was never interpreted as an unbending precondition.

Taiwan

If, earlier in history, the Pacific Ocean constituted an almost insurmountable barrier that separated peoples living in the two land masses on its eastern and western banks, in modern times it was transformed into a thoroughfare that enabled one of the oldest civilizations and the youngest to communicate with each other. Yet in the eighteenth and nineteenth centuries, the Chinese and the Americans entertained different feelings about the vast ocean: to the former, the water washed to the China shore a new kind of "barbarian"; to the latter, it provided opportunities for seeking a new manifest destiny beyond their own continental limits. During the Pacific war, perhaps for the first time in the history of the Pacific region, the Chinese and Americans found a common goal in removing the lobster-shaped Japanese Empire in the western Pacific that threatened to close the ocean again to free traffic. The lobster shape included Japan's home islands as the body; the two capturing pincers consisted of Korea in the north and the Ryukyu Islands and Taiwan in the south. While China was suffering from Japan's monstrous embrace, the United States was also denied access to the Asian continent.

During the Pacific war, in the official language of Chongqing, Taiwan was an "old enemy-occupied territory." The terminology was intended to give the island a status similar to that of Manchuria. Yet, before Pearl Harbor, the Chinese government had not been able to treat the two territories in the same terms. The difference between them had to do with legality. Taiwan had been ceded to Japan by China in a treaty (the Treaty of Shimonoseki of 1895), but Japan's control of Manchuria since 1931 had not resulted in China's relinquishment of its sovereignty there. In the

1930s, Chinese official statements often referred to Taiwan as a bad precedent in Sino–Japanese relations that must not be repeated in the case of Manchuria. Meanwhile, although mourning Taiwan's loss, the Chinese government did not publicly advocate the island's return to China.[21]

The beginning of the undeclared Sino–Japanese war in 1937 did induce the Chinese government to readjust quietly its stand with regard to all the historical territorial disputes between China and Japan, including Taiwan. First, in 1938, Chiang Kai-shek took the lead within KMT circles in advocating China's recovery of Taiwan. He described Japan's seizure of Taiwan and the Ryukyu Islands in the last century as the beginning of a master plan for first encircling and then subjugating China.[22] Given the ambiguous state of the war with Japan, Chiang's statement remained unpublicized before Pearl Harbor. At the same time, the KMT regime began to use its party apparatus to develop a Taiwan program. In the spring of 1940, provoked by the formal inauguration of Wang Jingwei's regime in Nanjing, Chiang Kai-shek instructed Zhu Jiahua, Chen Lifu, and some other KMT officials to study the issue of "sponsoring revolutionary movements in Japan, Taiwan and Korea . . . in order to create unrest in the enemy's rear and weaken the enemy's strength of aggression." This led to the establishment in September of an agency known as the "Preparatory Office of the KMT for a Regional Branch of Taiwan." Another development in 1940 was Chongqing's endorsement of a "Taiwanese Volunteers Corp" that had already existed for more than a year. Early in 1941, the KMT authorities further supervised the formation of a "Taiwanese Revolutionary Alliance" (TRA) in Chongqing.[23]

These early steps were contemplated mainly to enhance Chongqing's war effort. After the Pacific war began, however, measures of long-term significance followed. Along with its declaration of war on Japan at the end of 1941, the Chinese government nullified all treaties between the two countries. For Chongqing, the legal obstacle to reclaiming the territories lost to Japan was thus removed. Beginning in 1942, the Chinese government formally and publicly included the recovery of Taiwan in its war aims.[24] In 1943, Chiang Kai-shek added his name to the policy in his book

[21] *CSYZ*, 4: 150–151.
[22] *GW*, 76: 370.
[23] Zhu Jiahua to Chiang, 29 April 1940, *HDYS*, 551–554; Lü Fangshang, "Kangzhan shiqi zai dalu de Taiwan kang Ri tuanti jiqi huodong" (The Taiwanese Anti-Japanese Organizations and Activities on the Mainland during the War of Resistance [Against Japan]), *Jindai Zhongguo* (Modern China), no. 49 (October 1985), 11–23; *Taiwan Shi* (History of Taiwan), comp. Documentary Committee of Taiwan Province (Taipei: Zhongwen Tushu, 1979), 708; Zhang Bilai, "Taiwan yirongdui" (The Taiwanese volunteer corps), *Gemingshi Ziliao* (Materials on the History of Revolution), 8 (1982): 54–55, 70–71; Hu Songping, *Zhu Jiahua Nianpu* (A Chronicle of Zhu Jiahua's Life) (Taipei: Zhuanji Wenxue Chubanshe, 1969), 51.
[24] Gauss to Hull, 5 November 1942, *FRUS, 1942: China*, 174.

China's Destiny, leaving no doubt to the outside world about the serious-
ness of Chongqing's intention. In the book, Chiang delineated a "physical
configuration" of China that formed an integral defense system. Peripheral
areas of this system, including the Ryukyu Islands, Taiwan, the Pescadores,
the northeastern provinces (Manchuria), Inner and Outer Mongolia,
Xinjiang, and Tibet, "are all strategic regions for safeguarding the nation's
existence; to lop off any one of them from China is to destroy her national
defense."[25]

Along with publicizing its aspiration to regain Taiwan, during the first
two years of the Pacific war the Chinese government initiated personnel
training programs that would be put to use when Chinese administration
was reestablished in Taiwan. Surprisingly, Chongqing seemed less handicapped in taking action with regard to Taiwan than Manchuria. In December 1941, the KMT Central Training Committee opened a "training class
for the Taiwanese administrative cadre." The director of the class was
Chen Yi, former governor of Fujian. Before its termination in April 1945,
the training class undertook various programs that would eventually enroll
about a thousand trainees.[26] The aforementioned KMT's Preparatory Office for Taiwan also ran a short-term program, known to outsiders as the
"Shaoguan battlefield training class on party affairs." A noteworthy feature of the program is that its organizers and trainees were all Taiwanese
in origin. Between late 1942 and early 1943, about sixty young Taiwanese
devoted themselves to discussions and seminars on serious issues like the
postwar status of Taiwan, international intentions toward the Taiwanese
problem, and every kind of historical, cultural, and social problem that
might conceivably affect the political reintegration of Taiwan with mainland China.[27] Yet, given the background of the participants (mainly enthusiastic Taiwanese youths), the low profile of the program within the KMT
power structure (organized by a parachapter of the KMT without its own
provincial basis), and the duration of the class (only three months), these
discussions did not have a significant impact on Chongqing's policymaking
with regard to Taiwan.

In a sense, Chongqing encountered problems in its Taiwan policy similar
to those in its Korea policy. As in the case of Korean independence, the
cause of Taiwan's liberation had an organized constituency of expatriates
on the mainland. Although in the war years Taiwanese political activists
on the mainland were really of Chinese, or "Han," nationality, the long

[25] Chiang Kai-shek, *China's Destiny* (New York: Roy Publishers, 1947), 9–10.
[26] *Taiwan Shi*, 715–716.
[27] Huang Chaoqin, et al., *Guomin Geming Yundong yu Taiwan* (The Nationalist Revolutionary Movement and Taiwan) (Taipei: Zhonghua Wenhua Chuban Shiye Weiyuanhui,
1955), 51; Lü Fangshang, "Kangzhan shiqi," 20. In this study, "Taiwanese" means not
only the native people of Taiwan but principally the Han people whose ancestors had
migrated to the island from the mainland long before the war.

separation between Taiwan and China did allow them to cherish certain
aspirations of their own that were not in complete agreement with
Chongqing's policy. Therefore, the development of Chongqing's postwar
policy toward Taiwan must be understood in the context of encounters
and exchanges between the Chinese government and Taiwanese partisans.

In the war years, Taiwanese political activists on the mainland included
both veterans of anti-Japanese movements in the island and Taiwanese
youth who were squeezed out of Taiwan by the high-handed policies of
the Japanese authorities. By the end of the 1930s, more than forty Taiwanese anti-Japanese organizations existed in China. The KMT regime's influence on these groups also became increasingly evident. In the spring of
1940, an "Association of Taiwanese Revolutionary Organizations," the
forerunner of the TRA, proclaimed: "In terms of race and history, Taiwan
is inseparable from the motherland [China]. China's war of resistance and
Taiwan's revolution are actually two aspects of the same process, and they
cannot achieve rapid victory without helping each other." The association
submitted itself completely to the leadership of "our national leader Chiang
Kai-shek." In February 1941, when the TRA was formally launched as a
Chongqing-endorsed organization, it included all five important Taiwanese
groups in South China.[28]

Wong Junming, a Taiwanese leader, proved instrumental in bringing
these Taiwanese groups under the aegis of the KMT. Unlike many Taiwanese political figures on the mainland, who began their association with the
Chinese government only during the war, Wong was a KMT veteran. In
his early years, Wong had worked in Taiwan as a correspondent for Sun
Yat-sen's Revolutionary Alliance. During most of his life, Wong traveled
in Chinese provinces close to Taiwan, trying to organize a unified Taiwanese liberation movement on the mainland. In 1938 and 1940, Wong flew
twice to Chongqing, urging the KMT leadership to consider Taiwan's
reunion with China at the end of the war, as well as steps for unifying
Taiwanese anti-Japanese groups on the mainland. Wong's political career
was cut short when he was fatally poisoned, allegedly by Japanese spies,
on the eve of the Cairo Conference in 1943.[29] Wong's and other Taiwanese

[28] *Taiwan Shi*, 705–706; Xie Dongmin et al., *Guomin Geming yu Taiwan* (The Nationalist
Revolution and Taiwan) (Taipei: Zhongyang Wenwu Gongyingshe, 1980), 54–56, 59–65;
Huang Chaoqin et al., *Guomin Geming*, 18.
[29] Huang Chaoqin et al., *Guomin Geming*, 49–54; *Taiwan Guangfu Sanshi Nian* (Thirty
Years after Taiwan's Restoration), comp. News Bureau of the Provincial Government of
Taiwan (Taizhong: Taiwan Sheng Xinwenju, 1975), 26–28; Chen Sanjing, "Wong Junming
yu Taiwan dangbu chengli de yiduan jingwei" (Wong Junming and the Establishment of
the Taiwan Branch of the Party), in *Zhonghua Minguo Shiliao Yanjiu Zhongxin Shi
Zhounian Jinian Lunwenji* (Essays for the Tenth Anniversary of the Research Center of
Historical Materials on the Republic of China) (Taipei: Zhonghua Minguo Shiliao Yanjiu
Zhongxin, 1979), 555–567.

leaders' proposition for Taiwan's reunion with China and their voluntary acceptance of the KMT's leadership made the Taiwanese movement on the mainland a convenient instrument of Chongqing's policy. During the war, Wong Junming and other Taiwanese managed to establish some twenty-five secret cells of the KMT in Taiwan, but they were never able to launch a home-based Taiwanese liberation movement.[30] This may help explain why, despite their occasional discontent about Chongqing's policy toward Taiwan, Taiwanese leaders saw no alternatives other than relying on the KMT regime to realize their aspirations.

In mid-1940, frustrated by Chongqing's ambiguous attitude toward the status of Taiwan, some leading Taiwanese figures raised a series of questions with the KMT leadership. The foremost was whether the Chinese government would want Taiwan's return to China or would rather support an independent Taiwan under Chinese protection. After Chongqing definitely confirmed the former, Taiwanese partisans focused their attention on the status that Taiwan would achieve after its reunion with China.[31] Remarkably, TRA leaders did not seek any special treatment for Taiwan but believed that Taiwan must reintegrate with China on an equal footing with the other Chinese provinces. In April 1943, the second assembly of the TRA appealed to the Chinese government to establish a provincial government for Taiwan. The contention was that such a step would not only clarify the island's legal position but would also accelerate the mobilization of all Taiwanese anti-Japanese elements.[32]

Not waiting idly for Chongqing's response, the TRA in November took further actions and set up committees on postwar political, military, and cultural reconstruction in Taiwan. These were intended as preparatory bodies to be transformed into branches of a new provincial government on the island. The TRA undertook these seemingly hasty steps mainly to induce the KMT regime to clarify its attitude. Leaders of the TRA were anxious because there were signs that Chongqing might not want to restore Taiwan's original provincial status. For instance, commenting on a Taiwanese inquiry about Chongqing's long-term policy toward Taiwan, Zhu Jiahua suggested that "Taiwan used to be an appendage of the Fujian Province." Chongqing's leading newspapers, such as the *Da Gong Bao*, adopted the same line.[33] Ironically, in 1943, it was the TRA leaders who were on the defensive. Xie Nanguang, one of the TRA leaders, argued

[30] *Taiwan Shi*, 709; Chen Sanjing, "Wong Junming," 564–566.
[31] Chen Sanjing, "Wong Junming," 561–562.
[32] *Taiwan Wenti Yanlunji* (Speeches and Writings on the Taiwan Question), comp. Taiwan Geming Tongmenghui (Chongqing: Guoji Wenti Yanjiusuo, 1943), 1: 104–106; Huang Chaoqin et al., *Guomin Geming*, 35–36; Xie Dongmin et al., *Guomin Geming*, 71–72, 88 n. 65.
[33] Chen Sanjing, "Wong Junming," 562; Xie Dongmin et al., *Guomin Geming*, 66–67, 72, 87 n. 62; *Da Gong Bao*, 7 January 1943.

publicly that restoration of Taiwan's provincial status had a precedent in Chongqing's policy toward Manchuria, and that the TRA's purpose was to mobilize the Taiwanese people to struggle for a distinct goal but not to select any particular Taiwanese leader for the governor's position.[34]

Yet, Xie Nanguang's argument revealed what was really bothering the KMT leadership. Chongqing was playing for time, hoping to postpone a showdown with the Taiwanese over the question of who would control the local affairs of Taiwan in the postwar years. The Chinese government certainly had no desire to transform the TRA into a political power that could dominate Taiwanese affairs after the war. The usefulness of Taiwanese partisans to the Chinese government was confined mainly to waging wartime propaganda, collecting information, and sabotaging against the Japanese. But after the war, either in the form of a special region or a restored province, Taiwan must be tightly controlled by the central government, not the Taiwanese. Chongqing's intention to have mainland control over Taiwan in the postwar years was reflected in the backgrounds of the officials in charge of the government's training programs for Taiwan. These included Chen Yi (born in Zhejiang, governor of Fujian, 1934–42), Chen Guofu (born in Zhejiang, member of the KMT Central Supervisory Committee), Wu Tiecheng (born in Guangdong, secretary-general of the Central Executive Committee of the KMT), Zhang Lisheng (born in Chahar, commander-in-chief of the Shanxi–Chahar–Suiyuan Border Area Assault Army), Duan Xipeng (born in Jiangxi, acting chairman of the KMT Central Training Committee), and Xiong Shihui (born in Jiangxi, governor of Jiangxi, 1931–42).[35] These "big names" of the KMT indicated that the Chinese government did not treat the status of Taiwan lightly. The list did not include a single Taiwanese figure. The political future in store for Taiwan was to be a transplant of the KMT political system from the mainland to the island.

Nevertheless, in the war years, Taiwanese leaders in mainland China not only maintained that Taiwan should be granted an equal position with other Chinese provinces, but also thought that Taiwan deserved even better treatment. In 1943, Xie Dongmin, a Taiwanese leader in charge of propaganda activities for the Taiwanese branch of the KMT, wrote an article contending that Taiwan had all the favorable conditions to become a model province in pursuance of Sun Yat-sen's Three People's Principles.[36] In wartime China, behind such talk about constructing model provinces in the peripheral regions of China was disillusionment with conditions in the so-called free China. Without much leverage in dealing with the KMT

[34] *Taiwan Wenti Yanlunji,* 1: 51–53.
[35] *Taiwan Shi,* 715; Chinese Ministry of Information, *China Handbook, 1937–1943* (New York: Macmillan, 1943), s.v. "Chinese Who's Who."
[36] Lü Fangshang, "Kangzhan shiqi," 22.

authority, Taiwanese partisans contemplated using international support to enhance their cause. Yet this was a sensitive field in which the Taiwanese could not afford to overplay their hands. After the Pacific war began, Wong Junming suggested that the Chinese government should broach the issue of its sovereignty over Taiwan at international conferences for peace.[37] Wong's motive can only be speculated on. Possibly, realizing Chongqing's weakness, Wong did not believe that the Chinese government would be able to recover Taiwan unilaterally without international support. It is also possible, however, that he hoped to internationalize the Taiwan question in order to obligate the Chinese government to follow a moderate and liberal approach in postwar Taiwan.

If Wong was discreet enough to work through the Chinese government, there were others who tried to establish direct contact with the Americans. Some time before the Cairo Conference, in a report to the American Military Intelligence Service, Xie Nanguang introduced important TRA leaders on the mainland as a group different from leaders of a prewar home-rule movement in Taiwan. The latter had actually sought a compromise with Japanese rule. More significant was his request that the American government provide direct financial assistance to the TRA on the mainland. An American officer familiar with the report later remarked that Xie Nanguang was "maneuvering toward what he hoped would be a prominent role in Formosa affairs under a postwar [American] Occupation."[38] It is doubtful that in 1943 the TRA leaders expected to return to an American-occupied Taiwan after the war. But Xie's action clearly aimed at some sort of international recognition of the Taiwanese movement in its own right, not just as an adjunct to the KMT.

During the first two years of the Pacific war, foreign opinion on the Taiwanese issue did not appear favorable to Taiwan's reunion with China. An occasion that caused concern in Chongqing was the annual conference of the Institute of Pacific Relations (IPR) held in Canada in the winter of 1942. Although IPR meetings were unofficial events, governments of the member states often used them to launch trial balloons on issues concerning the Pacific region. The Chinese delegation used the conference of 1942 to reiterate its government's policy of recovering the lost territories at the end of the war. But to the annoyance of the Chinese delegates, they did not receive unanimous support. Some British representatives suggested that Taiwan should be made an international base for peace and security in the Pacific. So far as the Chinese delegates were concerned, China should recover all of its lost territories with no conditions attached, though they also indicated that the Chinese government would be willing to talk about

[37] *Taiwan Guangfu Sanshi Nian*, 26; Lü Fangshang, "Kangzhan shiqi," 20.
[38] George H. Kerr, *Formosa Betrayed* (Boston: Houghton Mifflin, 1965), 14–15.

using Chinese territories as security bases as part of a worldwide discussion of the matter.[39]

The proposal for internationalizing Taiwan also had its supporters in the United States. In August 1942, a committee of editors of *Time, Life,* and *Fortune* published a "memorandum" entitled "The United States in a New World, II: Pacific Relations." Concerning the structure of a new peace order in the Pacific region, a section of the pamphlet was devoted to "a trans-Pacific highway." The authors proposed that a U.S.–United Nations defense belt be established across the Pacific. It should begin with Hawaii in the east and end with Taiwan in the west as "the logical anchor of the line and the mighty western terminus for the air armadas of the United Nations." Admitting China's predominant interest in Taiwan, the authors were willing to allow the island to be included in the Chinese customs and currency system. "But," they argued, "to make Formosa [Taiwan] Chinese territory seems impolitic in view of the necessity for a United Nations base there." Under a United Nations government, according to the proposition, the Chinese population of the island would enjoy full autonomy and civil rights, though the foreign affairs, armed forces, and security measures of the island would be controlled by the UN authorities.[40]

The Chinese reaction came forcefully. On New Year's Day 1943, Sun Ke published an article in the KMT official organ, the *Zhongyang Ribao,* attacking the American pamphlet for ignoring China's sovereignty over Taiwan. He also contended that Taiwan under Chinese control could also make a contribution to international security in the Pacific. Editors of the *Da Gong Bao* also expressed their astonishment that Americans should place the issue of security above the principle of self-government. They asserted that China's cooperation for international security should not be expected by its allies unless Chinese sovereignty over the lost territories was unconditionally restored. TRA leaders did not remain silent either. They made it clear that the Taiwanese people had no interest in autonomy under an international authority. In a "Statement on the Issue of Postwar Taiwan" dated 30 January 1943, they criticized the *Time–Life–Fortune* memorandum for its "ignorance of historical facts and violation of the Taiwanese people's aspirations." The statement concluded: "The postwar disposition of Taiwan must restore China's full sovereignty. Taiwanese people will object to any other kind of settlement that is intended either to maintain or merely modify the current situation of Taiwan."[41]

[39] *RWK*, 5 (A): 56; "Draft Memorandum for the Delegation to the I.P.R. Conference," 7 November 1942, *WKP*, box 58; Shi Zhaoji (Alfred Sao-ke Sze) to T. V. Soong, 19 December 1942 and 22 December 1942, *TSP*, box 11.
[40] "The United States in a New World, II: Pacific Relations," an insert supplementary to *Fortune*, August 1942, 11–12.
[41] *Da Gong Bao*, 15 May 1943; Xie Dongmin et al., *Guomin Geming*, 74.

In fact, in the United States, people close to the government tended to be more sensitive to Chongqing's feelings toward Taiwan than were the authors of the *Time–Life–Fortune* memorandum. In 1942 and 1943, some studies done by the research staff of the CFR were quite aware of the complexity of the Taiwan question. Believing that, in general, a successful settlement of territorial issues in the Pacific must precede any international security arrangement there, CFR researchers admitted that Taiwan presented a dilemma in this regard. On the one hand, Taiwan was such a key spot for sea control in the western Pacific that it should not be confidently delegated to a weak and disoriented China. On the other hand, denial of Taiwan to China would damage that country's relations with the Western Allies, and "suspicion of all Occidental schemes and motives [in China] may be so great [as] to frustrate, or at least, seriously limit, postwar Chinese collaboration in security matters with the other United Nations."[42] Accordingly, the CFR suggested, under the auspices of the United Nations or not, the United States must achieve a base in Taiwan in a way that would not irritate the Chinese government.

Japan's expansion in the Asian–Pacific region before Pearl Harbor was the immediate reason for a new interest on the part of the American government in the Pacific islands. As early as 1938, the State Department asked the U.S. Navy to make an estimate of the value of certain Pacific islands as possible seaplane bases, many of which at the time were owned or claimed by Britain or France. In mid-1940, President Roosevelt also began to take a personal interest in the matter.[43] Toward the end of 1941, American officials' concern was vindicated when Japan attacked U.S. territories in the Pacific and launched military operations against Western countries from its own insular possessions in the ocean. Throughout the Pacific war, postwar disposition of the Pacific islands became an obsessive subject for the U.S. government. In the Pacific War Council, consisting of the principal countries at war with Japan, President Roosevelt returned frequently to the subject. He was convinced that after the war, islands in the Pacific must be prevented from being used again for anti-American purposes. In the president's mind, postwar territorial readjustment in the area should include the Japanese Mandated Islands and many other islands in the central and western Pacific. From time to time, he also expressed a preference for United Nations responsibility for these islands.[44]

American strategists had a simple and immediate reason to pay strong

---

[42] "Postwar Security Arrangement in the Pacific Area," 11 September 1942, *SAI*, A-B 69; "Political Problems Involved in the Selection of Bases for Use in International Policing," 3 May 1943, *SAI*, A-B 87.

[43] R. Morre to Roosevelt, 4 June 1940, *RPOF* 4351.

[44] Memorandum by John L. McCrea on the 8th meeting of the Pacific War Council, 23 May 1942, and memorandum by Wilson Brown on the 13th meeting of the Pacific War Council, 31 March 1943, *RPMF*, box 168.

attention to the issue of the postwar disposition of Taiwan. Just one day after the Japanese attack on Pearl Harbor, fifty-four Japanese bombers and thirty-six Zero fighters took off from their bases in Taiwan and attacked Clark Field in the Philippines. This attack resulted in the destruction of nearly half of General Douglas MacArthur's best aircraft and crippled American air power in the Pacific.[45] This disaster, though not as well publicized as the debacle at Pearl Harbor, made Taiwan a thorn in the flesh of American strategists. During the first two years of the Pacific war, when deliberating on the Taiwan issue, the State Department placed great emphasis on the strategic importance of the island.

In May 1943, a study by the Territorial Subcommittee echoed the aforementioned CFR studies, emphasizing that "with the exception of Singapore, no location in the Far East occupied so controlling a position [as Taiwan]." The problem was what kind of settlement would be able to make the island beneficial rather than harmful for the United States. The subcommittee outlined four alternative solutions. Continuance of Japanese sovereignty was summarily rejected. Aside from military reasons, the retention of Japanese rule would be antithetic to the self-government principle approved by the Atlantic Charter. Members of the subcommittee did not believe that after the war the populace of Taiwan could possibly want to remain within the Japanese Empire. The second alternative, the independence of Taiwan, was viewed as unlikely. There was no movement for independence in the island. Moreover, the economic interdependence between the island and Japan tended to raise a question about Taiwan's ability to achieve true independence. Noteworthy is the subcommittee's conviction that the odds were also against the internationalization of Taiwan, the third alternative. China's objection was not the only obstacle to any international solution. Another problem was that an international entanglement with the civil affairs of a predominantly Chinese population in the island might not be worthwhile or practical, even for the strategic importance of Taiwan. Therefore, the fourth choice, the restoration of Chinese sovereignty in Taiwan, became the "one logical alternative."[46]

The logical solution was by no means a perfect one, and it had pros and cons. State Department officials admitted that the historical and ethnic relationship between Taiwan and China justified restoration of Chinese sovereignty. Information on the psychological reactions of the Taiwanese to China's armed resistance against Japan in recent years indicated "an outlook which is more Chinese than Formosan." American planners also suggested that future administration of the island should be entrusted mainly to experienced personnel from the mainland because the Japanese

[45] Ronald H. Spector, *Eagle Against the Sun: The American War with Japan* (New York: Vintage, 1985), 107–108.
[46] T documents-325, 25 May 1943, *RHN*, box 63.

rule of Taiwan since 1895 had afforded few opportunities for the development of political talents among the local population. In the meantime, difficulties could be expected in the economic field. Due to its long-term economic integration with the Japanese Empire, Taiwan's economy might not be able to adapt itself to the Chinese economic system without suffering serious dislocations. Also, because of China's own low-level technological development, at the beginning the Chinese government would probably not be able to provide sufficient numbers of skilled personnel to replace the Japanese in the management of Taiwanese industry.[47]

Yet, in terms of American interests, the most awkward problem in the China–Taiwan reunion was that the Chinese government would not be "capable of making use of Formosa in execution of the international interest in security," nor would it accept any strings attached to the restoration of China's sovereignty in Taiwan. A two-step solution was therefore suggested: Chinese sovereignty over Taiwan should first be fully restored, and then the Chinese government should be persuaded to consent to "stipulated rights" of an international body to establish and maintain base facilities in the island solely for the purpose of maintaining international security.[48] Such a scheme was actually supported by President Roosevelt. Between 1942 and 1943, on different occasions, Roosevelt indicated that he was in favor of both returning Taiwan to China and having American bases on the island, which, in his words, was one of the "strong points of the world."[49]

Given their knowledge of the KMT regime's prejudice against foreign interference in its policymaking, State Department officials' confidence in Chongqing's willingness to comply with the American solution to the Taiwan question deserves exploration. It was known in Washington that Chongqing's wartime reliance on America's assistance had not extinguished KMT officials' antiforeign sentiment. After Chiang Kai-shek published *China's Destiny*, the Far Eastern Division of the State Department became so concerned with the possible negative impact of Chiang's "reactionary nationalism" on China's internal and external affairs that it suggested that the matter be brought to the attention of President Roosevelt.[50] Therefore, the State Department's plan was based less on Chongqing's good feelings toward the United States than on the U.S. government's bargaining position with regard to the postwar settlement of Taiwan.

The strongest condition that would probably help Washington prevail

[47] Ibid.

[48] Ibid.

[49] Memorandum, "Indications of Contact with President on Post-War Matters," n.d., *RHN*, box 54; memorandum by Hopkins, "Eden Conferences," 22 March 1943, *HHP*, box 329; memorandum by Wilson Brown on the 13th meeting of the Pacific War Council, 31 March 1943, *RPMF*, box 168.

[50] FE memorandum for the Secretary of State, 2 September 1943, *SHP*, box 70; note by Hornbeck, 24 June 1943, *SHP*, box 114.

over Chongqing on the Taiwan question was the military reality in the western Pacific. By 1943, it had become clear to both the Chinese and the Americans that no matter how tenaciously the Chinese government might assert its determination to recover Taiwan, it could not possibly develop and master the means of liberating Taiwan from the Japanese. In 1943, American military and civilian planners both agreed that if the island was to be liberated by military force, it would have to be done by American troops.[51] Consequently, before the Cairo Conference, the State Department developed a few tentative principles for a Taiwan policy: (1) for prosecuting the war against Japan, America had an interest in temporarily controlling the military government in Taiwan after it was captured, in which Britain's or other foreign powers' participation should be minimal lest it cause Chinese–foreign friction; (2) Taiwan should be returned to China as soon as possible; and (3) the permanent settlement of Taiwan was a matter of China's concern, "modified somewhat by the requirements of American defense."[52] According to this scenario, China would get Taiwan back sometime after the war, but not from the Japanese. American military authorities would transfer Taiwan to the Chinese government, which presumably would facilitate the desired modification of permanent Chinese sovereignty over Taiwan.

In the State Department's opinion, such a conditional restoration of Taiwan to China would not compromise Chinese external sovereignty. Yet department officials could not agree on whether American influence should be used in matters concerning China's internal sovereignty in Taiwan. In March 1943, Hornbeck wrote a memorandum to Under Secretary of State Sumner Welles, using Taiwan as an example of applying the self-government principle to particular cases:

> The bulk of the people of Formosa are of Chinese race. But, at no period in recent times have they been ruled by China or representatives of the Chinese government. Should they be turned over, lock, stock, and barrel, to China, which is to say, to the none too tender mercies of political leaders, mostly military, who live in China, and who, through the Kuomintang, rule over the Chinese in China? To what extent, and by what procedure, would this fit into the picture of "Self-determination"? I happen to believe that Formosa should be placed under the aegis of China, but I am by no means convinced that the United Nations, after they have thrown the Japanese out of Formosa, probably largely through efforts which will be American, should "restore" the Formosans to China on a basis devoid of conditions, qualifications and reservations.[53]

[51] Grace P. Hayes, *The History of the Joint Chiefs of Staff in World War II: The War against Japan* (Annapolis, MD: Naval Institute Press, 1982), 459–462; Spector, *Eagle Against the Sun*, 418.
[52] T minute-54, 22 October 1943, *OJ*, 1-C-4.
[53] Hornbeck to Welles, 5 March 1943, *SHP*, box 333.

Compared with the view of the Territorial Subcommittee, which was mainly concerned with Taiwan as a place, Hornbeck's opinion made a pointed reference to "Formosans" as a people. At the time, Hornbeck probably did not know much about the official Chinese policy regarding the postwar internal affairs of Taiwan. But his understanding of Chinese politics enabled him to predict with accuracy how the Chinese government would reestablish itself in Taiwan.

Nevertheless, as a principle, self-government was to be applied only to meet political contingencies, not to pursue ideological perfection. The development of the State Department's Taiwan policy indicated no intention to complicate the issue further. Although both Welles and Hornbeck were in a position to bring up the issue in the discussions of the Territorial Subcommittee, there is no evidence that they did so.[54] The subcommittee took the position that the residents of Taiwan were of Chinese nationality, thus rendering the issue of their right to self-government under China irrelevant. The subcommittee did not want to make a distinction between a "Chinese interest" and a "Taiwanese interest"; nor did it regard American entanglement in the civil affairs of a basically Chinese population on the island as a wise move.

It is notable that when discussing the issue of self-government in Taiwan, neither Hornbeck nor the Territorial Subcommittee attended much to factual evidence about the attitude of the Taiwanese themselves. It is doubtful that these officials had authentic knowledge about the aspirations of the Taiwanese population. There were those who believed that the State Department's policy preparation for Taiwan suffered from a lack of firsthand knowledge about the conditions in the island and the Taiwanese movement in China. Yet, given the predominant concern of the State Department about working through the Chinese government to obtain bases in Taiwan, whatever the Taiwanese wanted was not really important to American officials.[55]

---

[54] Harley Notter, *Postwar Foreign Policy Preparation, 1939–1945* (Washington, DC: G.P.O., 1949), 64, 117.

[55] George H. Kerr, *Formosa: Licensed Revolution and the Home Rule Movement* (Honolulu: University of Hawaii Press, 1974), 219, points out that Joseph W. Ballantine, chief of the FE in 1943, was the only official on the planning staff of the State Department who had once served in Taiwan. He took part in the work of the Territorial Subcommittee. In wartime, Kerr himself was involved in the issue of postwar Taiwan as a member of the military planning staff. He called State Department officials responsible for the Taiwan policy "China firsters" and he himself did not believe the Chinese government would be able to run Taiwan either for the strategic interests of the United States or for the welfare of the Taiwanese people (see Kerr, *Formosa Betrayed*, 18–22). But, as indicated in this discussion, the planners in the State Department were really America firsters who were mainly concerned with achieving the American goal in Taiwan in the least difficult way.

The Ryukyu Islands

Another insular possession of Japan, the Ryukyu Islands, did not occupy a primary position in wartime foreign policy planning in either China or the United States. Before the Cairo Conference, Chinese official thinking on the subject was at best confused. Publicly, the Chinese government included these islands in China's lost territories. But when the aforementioned *Time–Life–Fortune* memorandum suggested that these islands should also be part of the string of international bases in the Pacific, Chongqing did not protest in any manner, as it did in the case of Taiwan. The reason was that, at the time, the Chinese government itself did not have a definite policy on these islands.

After China's war with Japan began, within KMT circles Chiang Kai-shek tended to put the Ryukyu Islands and Taiwan in the same category. Once, he suggested mistakenly that the Ryukyu Islands had come under Japan's control as a result of the Sino–Japanese War of 1894–1895. Consequently, after the beginning of the Pacific war prompted the Chinese government to adopt formally the 1894–1895 war as the time line for its territorial readjustment with Japan, KMT leaders also included the Ryukyu Islands in their list of China's lost territories.[56] Historically, however, the Ryukyu Islands and Taiwan had had different relations with China, and they had been seized by Japan in different circumstances. Briefly, the Ryukyu Islands had never been a formal part of China, as Taiwan had, nor had Japan's conquest of the islands taken place during the war of 1894–1895. For more than a century and a half, before Japan made these islands into an "Okinawa Prefecture" in 1879, the rivalry between China and Japan over the suzerainty of the Ryukyu Islands, a quasi-independent kingdom, had been growing. The government of the Qing Dynasty had eventually lost its tributary patronage over the Ryukyus through an ambiguous and gradual process. Therefore, in the war years, Chongqing's claim of sovereignty over the Ryukyu Islands in reference to the war of 1894–1895 would not be able to stand careful scrutiny at international peace conferences.[57]

Some Chinese officials were cognizant of the confusion. In June 1942,

---

[56] *CSYZ*, 19: 348; *GW*, 76: 369–370; Gauss to Hull, 5 November 1942, *FRUS: China, 1942*, 174.

[57] For an American interpretation of the Chinese–Japanese conflict over the Ryukyu Islands, see John K. Fairbank, Edwin O. Reischauer, and Albert M. Craig, *East Asia: Tradition and Transformation* (Boston: Houghton Mifflin, 1973), 195, 511, 601. Michael H. Hunt, *The Making of a Special Relationship: The United States and China to 1914* (New York: Columbia University Press, 1983), 118–125, offers a detailed account of the role played by former president Ulysses S. Grant in the negotiations of 1880 between China and Japan on the Ryukyu question. For Chinese views, see Fu Qixue, *Zhongguo Waijiao Shi* (Diplomatic History of China) (Taipei: Sanmin Shuju, 1966), 104, and Song Shushi, *Liuqiu Guishu Wenti* (The Question of the Ownership of the Ryukyu Islands) (Taipei: Zhongyang Wenwu Gongyingshe, 1954).

Waijiaobu official Yang Yunzhu told John Service of the U.S. embassy that the overture on China's recovery of the Ryukyu Islands was one of those "unfortunately inevitable . . . [and] exaggerated statements by private individuals concerning [China's] war aims." The truth, according to Yang, was that the people living in these islands were not Chinese, and the islands themselves, though at one time existing within the tributary system of China, had been entirely separated from China for almost eighty years. Unimportant economically and strategically to China, the Ryukyu Islands were now in effect an integral part of Japan. Yang firmly stated that the Chinese government would not expect the return of these islands in the peace settlement.[58] Although expressing what he believed proper, Yang failed to anticipate T. V. Soong's aforementioned statement on China's war aims of November 1942 and Chiang Kai-shek's book, *China's Destiny*, both asserting that China wanted to recover the Ryukyus.

Knowledgeable officials within the Chinese government remained doubtful even after Soong and Chiang publicly committed themselves to Chinese sovereignty over the Ryukyu Islands. For instance, in May 1943, Xu Shuxi, adviser to the Foreign Minister and director of the Western Asiatic Affairs Department of the Waijiaobu, pointed out in a memorandum to Soong that, in contrast to Taiwan but similar to Korea, the Ryukyu Islands had been a semisovereign state before their annexation by Japan. China's traditional "rights" over the Ryukyus were obsolete in the twentieth century; therefore, China should not attempt to recover them. According to Xu, the only realistic course for the Chinese government was to support these islands' freedom from Japan. Yet, Xu doubted that, without its own independence movement, the formerly insular kingdom would be able to achieve self-government. Therefore, a period of international supervision and assistance was in order. Xu emphasized that no matter what type of international administration was established for the Ryukyu Islands at the end of the war, its eventual purpose must be to set these islands free from Japan. Japan must not be allowed to use them again as bases of aggression.[59] Soon, at the Cairo Conference, the Chinese government would make an effort to redefine its postwar intention toward the Ryukyu Islands. But, as is shown in Chapter 6, the effort would not be very effective in altering the public image, fostered by Soong and Chiang, of Chongqing's postwar ambition concerning the Ryukyu Islands.

Before the Cairo Conference, despite President Roosevelt's general interest in the Pacific islands, the Ryukyus seemed to escape his attention. During the first two years of the war, in the State Department the Ryukyu question was also considered only tentatively. In the summer of 1943, when contemplating the subject, the Territorial Subcommittee of the State

[58] Service to Gauss, 17 June 1942, *FRUS, 1942: China*, 732–733.
[59] Xu Shuxi to T. V. Soong, 31 May 1943, *TSP*, box 26.

Department treated it as a sequel to the Allied policy toward Taiwan. The predominant concern was that these islands' strategic location lay "athwart the approaches to the China coast and parallel to the great circle trade route." The Territorial Subcommittee did not think Chinese control of the Ryukyu Islands would be a proper solution. First, in view of the fact that the Chinese in the past had allowed these islands to pass to Japanese control "by default," Chongqing's current claim for sovereignty was at best "tenuous." Furthermore, should the Ryukyu populace really want to be freed from Japanese rule, they would not necessarily welcome a Chinese government, which would be even more alien to them than the Japanese. An alternative to Chinese control could be international administration if these islands had to be separated from Japan. But in the subcommittee's opinion, the prospective international agency should concern itself only with military matters, leaving civil administration to the Japanese. The inclination was, therefore, to allow Japanese control to continue. It was held that after Japan was disarmed and deprived of the Mandated Islands, Korea, and Taiwan in the postwar years, the Ryukyu Islands alone, even in Japanese hands, would no longer constitute a threat to the security of other nations. Of course, these islands must be thoroughly demilitarized as well. The principle of self-government, in the subcommittee's opinion, did not seem to have a very strong case here. Japanese efforts at assimilation of the islanders seemed to have been quite successful: "Through education, conscription, and [a] closely supervised system of local government, the population undoubtedly has come to consider itself an integral part of the Japanese Empire."[60]

To sum up, although all three areas were categorized by the Chinese government as China's lost territories, Manchuria, Taiwan, and the Ryukyu Islands represented different problems in postwar readjustment in East Asia. Clearly, the Chinese and American policymakers had different understandings of Chinese sovereignty. The Chinese conception was uncompromising and exclusive; the American one was flexible and accommodating to foreign interests. In Manchuria, the United States did not have a direct political stake, yet the prospect of possible postwar Chinese–Soviet controversies in the region made Manchuria a serious concern in Washington. Taiwan, due to its strategic importance, was a place that American planners believed would affect their country's security in the Pacific. In both Manchuria and Taiwan, American solutions pointed to China's accommodation of foreign interests, which was not congenial to wartime nationalism in China. The divided opinions among Chinese officials on the Ryukyu Islands typically reflected the confusion experienced by the Chinese government in trying to reestablish China's traditional influence in East Asia in a modern context. To wartime Chinese–American diplomacy,

[60] T document-343, 2 July 1943, *RHN*, box 64.

legal arguments for or against Chongqing's claim on the Ryukyu Islands eventually proved secondary. The two governments' potential disagreement was really over whether these islands should be allowed to remain under Japanese control; and China's and America's different geostrategic interests in the Pacific, not their views of the legal status of the Ryukyus, were decisive. As will be shown in the next chapter, such differences were best exposed in the Sino–American wartime diplomacy concerning Korea.

4

Korea's independence

Contiguous to three stronger neighbors – China, the Soviet Union, and Japan – Korea suffered frequently from its geopolitical location. Historically, its neighbors just could not leave Korea alone and alternately used the peninsular country as a buffer state, a defensive barrier, or a stepping stone against one another. World War II became another historic juncture for Korea. Although the Korean people had always wanted to be masters of their own fate, their country again became a target of the intrigues among the big powers. Japan's doomed military future in the Pacific war would disqualify it from participation in the new round of international contests over Korea. For the better part of the war, the Soviet Union's nonbelligerent status in the Asian conflict tended to obscure its intentions toward Korea. Meanwhile, in China, the KMT government maintained intense interest in postwar settlement in the country, and in the United States, policymakers were awakening to the importance of the Korea question. Inevitably, Korea became an important item in the two allies' postwar planning and in their wartime diplomacy.

Chongqing's intentions

Korea occupied a unique position in the wartime foreign policy of the Chinese government. In a sense, the Chinese support of Korean independence was a trademark of wartime Chinese nationalism. During World War II, the resurgence of Chinese nationalism could be detected not only in the temporary internal cohesion of Chinese politics and a new drive in China toward regaining full independence, but also, more significantly, in the publicized intention of the Chinese government to support other Asian peoples' struggle to liberate themselves from colonialism. Korea was an area for which the Chinese government developed detailed policy measures.

In this matter, for the first time since the collapse of the traditional Chinese Empire, Chongqing attempted to act as a great power.

Yet, the dual identity of wartime China as both an emerging Asian country and one of the Big Four complicated Chongqing's foreign policy task. Leaders in Chongqing were certainly pleased by the wartime American policy of treating China as one of the big powers, but more often than not, they felt that the Chinese government could serve itself better by acting as a spokesman on behalf of Asian nationalism. Chongqing tried to play such a role soon after the Pacific war began. On 7 January 1942, Chiang Kai-shek dispatched a telegram to President Roosevelt, urging the president to impress on the British and Dutch governments the need to act in accordance with the spirit of the Atlantic Charter in their own colonial affairs. The liberalization of these governments' colonial policies, Chiang reasoned, would win the Asian peoples over to the Allied war effort. In the following several months, Chiang actively interfered in the troublesome affairs of India, attempting ineffectively to persuade British and Indian leaders to make mutual concessions for the sake of the common cause against Japan.[1] As mentioned earlier, in the same period, the RC proposed to use a "Pacific Charter" to amend the Atlantic Charter in order to establish a universal anticolonial principle.

The Western Allies were suspicious of the motives behind Chongqing's anticolonial rhetoric. In June 1942, in a message to the Secretary of State, American Ambassador Clarence Gauss commented that some Chinese leaders' statements on postwar freedom for dependent areas in Asia reflected "[a] Chinese tendency to consider [that] China should be the leader of Asiatic peoples." About a month later, Lauchlin Currie, President Roosevelt's personal envoy to Chongqing, conveyed a similar concern to Chiang Kai-shek. He told Chiang that some people in the United States were reluctant to support President Roosevelt's policy of aid to China due to their fear of a militarist and antiwhite China. It was advisable, in Currie's opinion, for the Chinese government to improve China's internal democracy and especially to avoid using antiforeign expressions and phrases like "China as the leader of Asia" in its public statements. Chiang had no intention of upsetting the Americans over this matter, and afterward he cautioned Chinese officials against stating that China was the leader of Asia.[2]

If Western observers feared that China would succeed Japan in establishing an anti-Western Asian sphere, in wartime they could find little evidence that the Chinese government had either the strength or the will

[1] Chiang to Roosevelt, 7 January 1942, ZZSC, 3(1): 154–155. For Chiang's role in wartime Indian affairs and the British reaction, see Aron Shai, *Britain and China, 1941–1947* (London: Macmillan, 1984), 58–61; and John Sbrega, *Anglo–American Relations and Colonialism in East Asia, 1941–1945* (New York: Garland, 1983), 68–69, 72–73.

[2] Gauss to Hull, 17 June 1942, *FRUS: China, 1942*, 732; minutes of conversation between Chiang and Currie, 4 August 1942, ZZSC, 3(1): 698–703; CSYZ, 19: 347.

to step into Japan's shoes. Indeed, in December 1942, when talking to Wellington Koo, then Chinese ambassador to London, Chiang Kai-shek professed that "China herself had no intention to dictate or dominate in Asia. Her policy of favoring the liberation of weak and small peoples was a fundamental one, but there was no intention on her part to take any active steps to realize it, [though] these countries would themselves look to China as a natural leader and her civilization as a great heritage for Asia." On a different occasion, Chiang commented that no one would accept China's leadership if China lacked sufficient strength, and that although morally and spiritually deserving the status of a great power, China was currently ill-qualified in terms of material strength and progress.[3]

These are rare exposés of Chiang's thought. His discourse on China's "natural" superiority among Asian countries indicated that in his heart Chiang was very much a traditionalist. He could not think of China's proper position in Asia without mentally traveling back to the old glorious days of the Confucian Empire of China. But Chiang was also a down-to-earth realist who did not fantasize that spiritual right would be able to overcome material might. Then how could a weak country like China hope to recover its presumed proper position in Asia? Should this goal be postponed until China obtained the necessary material strength? Chiang saw another alternative–support from friendly Western powers, especially the United States. Diplomacy therefore became the most important instrument for China to improve its international image and enhance its international status. Chiang imparted this idea emphatically to officers in the Chinese foreign service, whom he called China's "spiritual soldiers."[4] He was quite honest with Ambassador Koo when he admitted that the Chinese government had no intention of taking any active steps to liberate other submerged Asian nations. The anticolonial oratory of Chongqing, therefore, was neither sustained by a strong foreign policy, as in the case of Japan's expansion in the Pacific, nor derived from a blind antiforeign antagonism, as in the case of the Boxer Rebellion of 1900. Instead, it was a calculated tactic originating in a weak position. In the war years, Chongqing's moderate anticolonialism was designed not to alienate the Western powers but to strengthen its own bargaining position with them; not to add burdens to the Chinese government for the sake of improving Asian colonial peoples' conditions but to reestablish its spiritual appeal among them.

Yet, in the long run, KMT leaders did not want to limit their goals in foreign policy to reestablishing China's traditional cultural superiority in Asia. Recovery of lost territories, abrogation of unequal treaties, and achievement of Asian peoples' respect for China were merely fundamental preconditions

[3] RWK, 5(A): 249; CSYZ, 19: 347.
[4] CSYZ, 19: 162–168.

for China to play a new role in modern international politics. When these conditions were fulfilled, additional steps would have to be implemented for China to function as a great power in the modern sense.

In the war years, these additional objectives were rarely divulged to the other Allies, though at times there were occasional disclosures. For instance, in May 1942, Wang Chonghui told an American official that due to its deep concern about the dire conditions of overseas Chinese living in Indochina, Burma, Thailand, Malaya, the Dutch East Indies, and the Philippines, the Chinese government hoped to establish some sort of Chinese control over these areas after the war. This was not a casual remark made by Wang on impulse. Two years later, when the Waijiaobu conducted a comprehensive review of China's postwar foreign policy, further thought would be devoted to Indochina and other areas in the southern Pacific. It was suggested that after the war China should use military force to control upper Vietnam and Laos in order to achieve the effect of "whipping on Vietnam, reining the Mid-South Peninsula [*Zhongnan Bandao*, a Chinese name for the peninsula consisting of Indochina, Burma, Thailand, and Malaya], and watching closely Thailand and Burma." Politically, however, the Chinese government should still foster pro-Chinese feelings among the Vietnamese, "restore the spirit in the past of mutual assistance and mutual trust between China and Vietnam," and help Vietnam to achieve self-government.[5]

In Chongqing's policy aimed at restoring China's influence among its neighboring states, Korea and the countries of Southeast Asia belonged in the same category. Both were subject to KMT leaders' penchant for *cunwang jijue jiruo fuqing*. But in the war years, for Korea alone, the Chinese government developed not only general principles but also concrete plans. Korea became a focus of Chongqing's wartime diplomatic effort for good reasons. At first, Japan's conquest of Korea being a major cause of Sino–Japanese antagonism, postwar settlement in Korea would directly affect China's physical security in Northeast Asia. Then, in the war years, there was an active Korean independence movement in China whose association with the KMT could be traced back to the prewar years. Furthermore, because Korea was a colony in the Axis domain, Chongqing's support for its independence would not bear directly on the issue of Western colonialism in Asia and therefore would not greatly disturb Chinese–Western cooperation in the war.

The Chinese government's contemplation of postwar settlement in Korea started right after the Sino–Japanese war began. In the spring of 1938,

---

[5] U.S. Senate Committee on the Judiciary, *Morgenthau Diary: China* (Washington, DC: G.P.O., 1965), 887 (hereafter cited as *Morgenthau Diary*); Waijiaobu memorandum, "Taipingyang shang zhiminti wenti yu yiban anquan wenti" (Colonial Problems in the Pacific and General Security Problems), 7 June 1944, *VHP*, box 3.

Chiang Kai-shek told some KMT party functionaries that Dr. Sun Yat-sen had bequeathed to the party a revolutionary strategy calling for "strengthening China through restoration [*huifu*] of Korea and Taiwan." Chiang interpreted this policy as a countermeasure against Japan's continental expansion. He summarized the rationale of the policy as follows:

> Korea used to be a vassal state of China and Taiwan a Chinese territory. Geographically speaking, both are lifelines on which China's very existence and safety hinge. If China seeks to establish a substantial national defense and secure a lasting peace in East Asia, it must not allow imperialist Japan to control Korea and Taiwan. The meaning of the Premier's [Sun's] policy is that only by helping our compatriots [*tongbao*] in Korea and Taiwan to regain their independence [*duli*] and freedom, can the Republic of China strengthen its own defense and lay the foundation of peace in East Asia.[6]

Chiang's purpose of detaching Korea from Japan was clear, but his use of *tongbao* and *duli* for both Taiwan and Korea obscured his ideas about exactly how postwar settlement in these countries should be implemented. Unmistakable were his stress on the connection between Korea and China's national defense and his notion that China must exert strong influence in any postwar settlement with regard to Korea.

After the Pacific war began, Chongqing publicized its support for Korea's independence. Yet, given Chiang Kai-shek's estimate of China's limited ability to influence even regional affairs in Asia, Chongqing never believed that its postwar policy toward Korea should be a unilateral undertaking. In the war years, Chongqing worked at two different levels to implement its program for Korea. Within China, to foster long-term Chinese influence in Korea, the KMT regime sponsored Korean expatriates, mainly those affiliated with a "Korean Provisional Government" (KPG) in Chongqing. On the international scene, the Chinese government consulted with the Western Allies, principally the United States, to obtain their consent for Korean independence and their endorsement of the KPG as the legitimate authority in postwar Korea.

The wartime relationship between the Chinese government and Korean nationalists had its roots in an earlier period. After the anti-Japanese March First Movement of 1919 was suppressed by the Japanese in Korea, Korean revolutionaries in exile came to China and established the KPG in Shanghai. The political situation in China at the time was not at all congenial to Korean partisans. When the KPG began to consider its political program at the beginning of 1920, which gave China a prominent position in the KPG's foreign policy, it realized that an effective central government was absent in China. In the following years, the KPG not only made

[6] *GW*, 76: 370.

contact with the two "central governments" in Beijing (Peking) and Guangzhou (Canton), but also had to deal with the various provincial and local authorities and the seemingly countless *dujun* (military governors). In October 1921, the KPG sent an emissary to Sun Yat-sen's government in Guangzhou, requesting recognition and financial aid. In responding to this request, Sun consented to the first demand "in principle" but declined the second on the ground of his own government's financial difficulties. Sun told the Koreans that so far as material aid was concerned, his government could not do anything before its northward expedition achieved complete victory, meaning the reunification of China.[7] Sun Yat-sen died four years later and never had the chance to honor his promise to the Koreans.

In the 1920s, when presiding over the Whampoa Military Academy, Chiang Kai-shek had some Korean cadets under his authority. But his personal interest in Korean partisans' activities in China began only after Manchuria was taken by Japan. In the early 1930s, some sensational assassinations by Korean patriots of Japanese high officials caught Chiang's attention. Early in 1933, Chiang Kai-shek received Kim Ku (known to the Chinese by the name of Jin Jiu or Bai Fan), a prominent figure of the KPG and organizer of those assassinations. According to Kim Ku's memoir, at the beginning of their conversation, Chiang said that Sun Yat-sen's Three People's Principles would be a good program for all Asian peoples. Kim agreed and then stated that if the Chinese government gave the KPG substantial financial aid, it would be able to start uprisings in Japan, Korea, and Manchuria within two years. The next day, Chen Guofu, who was then head of the organizational department of the KMT and instrumental in bringing about the Chiang–Kim meeting, told Kim that Chiang Kai-shek hoped that the Korean nationalists would shift their attention from terrorist activities to making long-term preparations for a war of liberation. For this purpose, Chiang was willing to help the KPG train military cadets. A training program was soon initiated in Luoyang. But due to Japan's protest, the program continued only for a year.[8]

The meager beginning of KMT–KPG cooperation was followed by troubles and mutual misgivings. First, there was the problem of Chinese financial aid to the Koreans. During the 1930s, according to Kim Ku, the Chinese authorities' response to Korean nationalists' appeal for financial aid was

---

[7] Chong-sik Lee, *The Politics of Korean Nationalism* (Berkeley: University of California Press, 1963), 129; Fan Tingjie, "Hanguo geming zai Zhongguo" (Korean Revolution in China), ZW, 27 (1975): 1: 36–41, 27 (1975): 4: 84–87, and 28 (1976): 2: 86–91.

[8] Jin Jiu (Kim Ku), *Bai Fan Yizhi* (Autobiography of Bai Fan) (Taipei: Youshi Shudian, 1969), 187–189; Hu Chunhui, "Chen Guofu yu Hanguo duli yundong" (Chen Guofu and the Korean Independence Movement), in *Zhong Han Guanxishi Guoji Taolunhui Lunwenji* (Essays from an International Symposium on the History of Chinese–Korean Relations), comp. Institute of Korean Studies of the Republic of China (Taipei: Zhonghua Minguo Hanguo Yanjiu Xuehui, 1983), 273–281.

"very cold."[9] Overseas Koreans, mainly those living in the United States and Mexico, constituted the main source of financial assistance and provided about $3,000 a month to the KPG based in China. This austere self-reliance could no longer continue when the Pacific war began and severely reduced the funds from Koreans on the other side of the Pacific. At about this time, the Chinese government began to increase gradually its allowance to the Koreans. By the time of the Cairo Conference, the original figure of $6,000 (Chinese) a month would have been increased to $200,000. This money kept Korean activists and their families from starvation and allowed the KPG to operate as a political organization. But Korean leaders were far from satisfied. In the summer of 1942, Kim Ku tried to persuade the Chinese government to grant his "government" a loan of $500,000 (American). H. H. Kung, the Chinese Minister of Finance, demurred by suggesting that the Koreans turn directly to Washington for American dollars.[10]

The fragmentary condition of the Korean independence movement was another problem that seriously hindered Chongqing's ability to carry out a consistent Korean policy. In 1938, Zhu Jiahua, successor to Chen Guofu as head of the KMT organizational department and director of the Central Bureau of Investigation and Statistics (CBIS), began to take charge of the Korean affair. Zhu and his aides found themselves dealing with not one but seven Korean parties that were separated into two "fronts." From 1938 to 1941, the number of Korean parties was reduced due to reorganization, but the division would continue throughout the war. The two principal contending parties were the Korean Independence Party (KIP) under Kim Ku and the Korean National Revolutionary Party (KNRP) under Kim Won-bong (known to the Chinese as Chen Guobin or Jin Roshan). At the beginning, Chongqing's policy was to aid the two Kims in order to bring all Korean factions into a unified movement. Ineffectual in this effort, the Chinese government beginning in 1941 increasingly favored Kim Ku's organization.[11]

Koreans' inability to unify themselves was puzzling to Zhu and his associates. Kim Ku insisted that the problem was manufactured by the "reds," his name for the KNRP. The accusation was fiercely denied by Kim Won-bong and his supporters. Probably for the purpose of professing its ideological innocence, the KNRP organized the translation of Sun

[9] Jin Jiu, *Bai Fan Yizhi*, 201. Hu Chunhui in "Chen Guofu" argues differently, suggesting that after 1932 Kim Ku and his followers began to receive "major," "regular and reliable" financial aid from the Chinese government. The disagreement between the two should not obscure the importance of overseas Koreans' contributions to the KPG before Pearl Harbor.

[10] Zhu Jiahua to Chiang, 10 December 1941, *HDYS*, 436–438; Kim Ku to Zhu, 24 June 1942, ibid., 453–454; Zhu to H. H. Kung, 27 June 1942, ibid., 456–457; Kung to Zhu, 8 July 1942, ibid., 462; He Yingqin to Zhu, 24 July 1942, ibid., 492.

[11] Shao Zheng to Zhu, 4 November 1938, *HDYS*, 3; minutes of conversation between Chinese officials and Korean partisans, 2 April 1940, ibid., 76–81.

Yat-sen's lectures on the Three People's Principles into the Korean language and then reported the feat to Chongqing.[12] Chinese officials were also suspicious of Kim Ku's assertion. In October 1939, in a report to Zhu Jiahua, Wang Rongsheng of the CBIS attributed Koreans' disunity to several factors. These included the Korean nationality's lack of a cooperative spirit by nature, absence in the Korean movement of leaders of high caliber and a guiding ideology, and the mutual suspicions entertained by the Korean parties. While admitting the existence of some left-wing factions among the Koreans, Wang did not consider them serious obstacles to unity.[13] In the summer of 1941, however, Chongqing's impartial attitude began to change. The immediate reason was that certain members of the KNRP and its military organization, the Korean Volunteers Corps, went to the CCP region in northwestern China. Officials of the CBIS still did not regard the KNRP as a radical organization. They attributed the exodus to opportunism among KNRP members who were confused by some of the year's international events, such as the Soviet–Japanese neutrality pact and the Soviet–German war. Nevertheless, from this point on, Zhu and his associates began to take the view that among the existing Korean factions in Chongqing, Kim Ku's group was the most promising and deserved special attention from the Chinese government.[14]

The rivalry among the Korean parties also spread to the Chinese government. The issue was the status of a "Korean Restoration Army" (KRA) under the Korean Provisional Government. Kim Ku's party had actual control over both. Zhu Jiahua's agencies were disposed to offer effective support to the KRA and recognize the KPG diplomatically at the proper time. But their opinions were not decisive in these matters. The first Korean military organization in China was the Volunteer Corps affiliated with the KNRP, which had been established in October 1938 and ever since had been controlled in practice by the Chinese National Military Council.[15] In September 1939, without Chongqing's approval, the KIP established its own military group, the KRA. During the next two years, although Chiang granted the KRA the right to exist, Kim Ku wanted it to be different from the Volunteers Corps, which had no independent position. Hoping to use the KRA as the core of a national army under the KPG,

[12] Kim Ku to Xu Enzeng, 26 January 1940, *HDYS*, 65–68; Zhu to Kang Ze, 3 June 1940, ibid., 83; Kang Ze to Zhu, 9 June 1940, ibid., 84–85; the secretariat of the Standing Committee of the KMT Central Committee to Zhu, 13 October 1940, ibid., 105–106.

[13] Wang Rongsheng to Zhu, 5 October 1939, *HDYS*, 15–28.

[14] Xu Enzeng to Zhu, 1 November 1941, *HDYS*, 107–121.

[15] Chongqing's allowance to the Volunteers Corps reached $16,000 (Chinese) a month before Pearl Harbor. Xu Enzeng to Zhu, 1 November 1941, *HDYS*, 107–121; Fan Tingjie, "Hanguo geming"; Hu Chunhui, *Hanguo Duli Yundong zai Zhongguo* (Korean Independence Movement in China) (Taipei: Zhonghua Minguo Shiliao Yanjiu Zhongxin, 1976), 47–48, 153–154.

Kim Ku argued with Chinese authorities that although the KRA would follow Chinese instructions in military affairs, it should also maintain complete autonomy as far as its administration was concerned. Actually, KPG leaders hoped that Chongqing would recognize the KRA as an ally's army. They wanted the KRA to expand as rapidly as possible, which, they hoped, would significantly enhance the prestige of the KPG. In the long run, the KRA was expected to assist "China's general counteroffensive" and to participate in a "gigantic rebellion and tangled warfare" against Japan in many Japanese-occupied areas.[16]

In 1940 and 1941 the KRA became a controversial issue within the Chinese government. The direct sponsor of the Volunteers Corps, the political department of the National Military Council under General He Yingqin, was opposed to the KRA's claim as a national army. He and his department refused to grant the KRA more freedom of action than the Volunteers Corps. This was why, in the spring of 1941, after Chiang gave his personal approval for the establishment of the KRA, the National Military Council issued a puzzling order to Chinese military commanders in the northwestern provinces that prohibited the KRA's activities.[17]

The Koreans saw the attitude adopted by the Military Council as chauvinistic. They complained to Zhu Jiahua that in respect to the KRA, the Chinese government ought to treat Korea as a "sovereign unit," not a "province of China." Zhu Jiahua then blamed He Yingqin's office for the inconsistency of Chongqing's policy toward the KRA. In his correspondence with Chiang Kai-shek and He Yingqin, Zhu contended that the Chinese government should not conduct its Korean policy with too many regulations but should adopt a broad view. It was to be generous and benevolent toward weak and small nations and to "let those alien peoples who admire and yearn for China know to whom they ought to pay their gratitude." Zhu questioned why Chongqing could not treat Kim Ku and his KRA the same way as the British government treated Charles de Gaulle and his "freedom fighters."[18]

The dispute over policy was temporarily settled in July 1941, when Chiang Kai-shek decided to approve the KRA for the second time. But this time, Chiang instructed He Yingqin and Zhu Jiahua to work out a formal policy toward the KRA. He Yingqin's political department was given the

[16] Xu Enzeng to Zhu, 1 November 1941, *HDYS*, 114–115; minutes of conversation between Chinese officials and Korean partisans, 23 May 1940, ibid., 217–225; Zhu to He Yingqin and enclosures, 3 July 1940, ibid., 236–242.
[17] Kim Ku to Zhu, 28 April 1941, *HDYS*, 259–264; Jin Xuekui and Wang Juncheng to Zhu, 1941 (after May), ibid., 291–298; memorandum by Jin Xuekui on the KRA, 1941 (after May), ibid., 299–305; memorandum on the status of the KRA in terms of international laws, n.d., ibid., 420–424.
[18] Memorandum by Jin Xuekui on the KRA, 1941 (after May), *HDYS*, 299–305; Zhu to Chiang and enclosures, 3 July 1941, ibid., 314–325; Zhu to He Yingqin, 3 July 1941, ibid., 329–331.

task.[19] To the dismay of Kim Ku and others in the KPG, the resultant policy merely put the KRA under the Chinese government's rigid and humiliating regulations. In November, the National Military Council informed Li Qingtian (Korean name unknown), commander of the KRA, that from now on the position and activities of the KRA would be regulated by a "nine-point code." The code included conditions under which the KRA would be allowed to operate, recruit troops, hire Chinese personnel, establish headquarters, and issue orders.[20]

In addition to these "technical" limitations, the KPG leaders had to accept certain political rules diminishing the image of the KPG as an independence movement. Under these rules, the KPG was deprived of any power to control its own military force. According to the code, in wartime the KRA would be subject to the direct control of the Chinese National Military Council and would maintain only a "nominal relationship" with the KPG. Before either of the two following conditions would happen, the KRA "ought only to accept orders from the supreme commander of the Chinese military forces but not from any other authorities." These conditions were the end of the Sino–Japanese war and the advance of the KPG into Korea. If the KPG reached Korean territories before the conclusion of the Sino–Japanese war, the KRA's position would be reconsidered, although the KRA "should still principally accept the orders of this [Chinese National Military] Council and cooperate with China's war effort." But if by the end of the war the KPG was still unable to march into Korea, the future deployment of the KRA would be decided solely by the Chinese government.[21] Notably, Allied diplomatic recognition of the KPG was not mentioned as a condition that would change the KRA's subordination to the Chinese government.

In the final analysis, the difficulty caused by the KRA reflected Chongqing's uncertainty about the legal status of the KPG itself. In May 1940, at a meeting with Chinese officials, Kim Ku admitted that "no matter how important military affairs may be, they are only part of the issue, and [we] wish to establish a permanent comprehensive relationship [with the Chinese government]." At the time, Kim did not want to appear too ambitious and only urged Chongqing to recognize the KIP as the "orthodox and central force" of the Korean independence movement. Kim was pragmatic enough to leave the legal status of the KPG to the future. For the moment, he was content to work through an interparty relationship between the KIP and the KMT to gain whatever assistance Chongqing was willing to offer.[22]

[19] Chiang to Zhu, 18 July 1941, *HDYS*, 332.
[20] General Office of the National Military Council to Li Qingtian, 13 November 1941, *HDYS*, 335–336.
[21] Ibid.
[22] Minutes of conversation between Chinese officials and Korean partisans, 23 May 1940, *HDYS*, 217–225.

Yet, this restrained policy did not last. In the summer of 1941, two developments incited the Koreans to seek better treatment in Chongqing. One took place on the international scene: Hitler's military conquests in Europe made London an international capital for more than half a dozen exile governments. Chongqing, acting in line with the Western Allies, continued to maintain full diplomatic relations with these governments.[23] This policy seemed to KPG leaders a useful precedent for requesting Chongqing to grant their own government the same treatment. The second development was the migration of some of Kim Won-bong's followers to areas in northern China controlled by Yan'an. Kim Ku and his associates seized this opportunity to destroy the reputation of their most powerful competitor for Chongqing's support, claiming that only their party represented the "genuine nationalist" force of Korea. Consequently, in the summer of 1941, the KPG made an oral request to the Chinese Ministry of Foreign Affairs for formal diplomatic recognition. Then, in January 1942, after Pearl Harbor drastically changed the context of the struggle in Asia, the KPG made recognition a principal item in its relations with Chongqing. In a five-page letter to the Chinese government, Kim Ku urged the KMT leadership to act, as one of the Big Four, to honor Sun Yat-sen's unfulfilled promise of recognizing the KPG. In addition to citing the precedents of the European exile governments in London and reasserting that political disunity among Korean revolutionaries had ceased to be a problem, Kim tried to arouse Chongqing's concern about Moscow's intentions in Korea. He warned that unless the Chinese government took a decisive step now to grant the KPG diplomatic recognition, it might in the future find a red Korean government emerging in Soviet Siberia.[24]

Opinions on the matter varied among Chinese officials, though they shared a concern about the Soviet factor. Advising Zhu Jiahua on the issue, Wang Rongsheng favored a waiting period due to the allegedly poor quality of the KPG leadership. But Xu Enzeng, deputy chief of the CBIS, recommended early recognition. He emphasized the international aspect of the issue, arguing that after Pearl Harbor, a recognition policy became imperative due to two factors. One was the KPG's recent overtures to the American government for recognition, and the other was the existence of "thirty to forty thousands" of Korean troops in the Soviet Army. Believing that Chongqing should maintain its position as the principal sponsor of the Korean cause, Xu was more troubled by the prospect that Moscow might create a Korean soviet government when it decided to enter the war with Japan. Although inclined to favor early recognition, Zhu knew that

---

[23] Jin Wensi (Wunsz King), *Waijiao Gongzuo de Huiyi* (Reminiscences on Diplomatic Missions) (Taipei: Zhuanji Wenxue Chubanshe, 1968), 90–102.
[24] Xu Enzeng to Zhu, 1 November 1940, *HDYS*, 116; memorandum by Kim Ku on recognition of the KPG, 30 January 1942, ibid., 565–569.

a decision had to be delayed. Commenting on a memorandum by Xu dated 11 December 1941, Zhu reasoned: "This matter [recognition of the KPG] has been processed several times but cannot be materialized for the moment. Should the United States be willing to recognize [the KPG], we then would certainly be able to implement [a recognition policy]."[25] After the Pacific war began, many in Chongqing no longer felt it proper for the Chinese government to make decisions concerning Korea without consulting the other Allied governments. A comprehensive review by the KMT of its Korea policy was therefore in order.

On 20 August 1942, a senior advisory committee was organized by the Standing Council of the KMT Central Committee to review the government's Korea policy. Closely supervised by Chiang Kai-shek himself, the committee completed its job before the end of the year.[26] The committee started with a "Guiding Plan for Helping and Using the Korean Revolutionary Forces in China," which was originally drafted by the National Military Council. The document held Korea's "complete independence" as a fundamental objective of Chongqing's policy, stipulated close Chinese supervision over Koreans' military and political activities in China, and supported Kim Ku's KPG as the designated government of a unified Korean independence movement. Furthermore, an important policy objective was to foster pro-Chinese feelings among Korean nationalists in order to prevent them from falling under the influence of other foreign powers. The plan did not state which foreign powers were meant. But during the discussions of the committee, it was clearly understood that the Chinese government needed to be vigilant in regard to Moscow's intentions.[27]

Chiang Kai-shek was not satisfied with the plan. He wanted a clearly defined central authority responsible for Korean affairs, which the plan failed to offer. Chiang also felt that the plan was too rigid in endorsing only one Korean group, the KPG. He wanted his government to have a more flexible policy that would be able to meet different contingencies. To be prepared for unpredictable developments within the Korean movement, the Chinese government must not close its door to other anti-Japanese Korean groups. At the same time, Chiang approved the notion that the KPG be treated as China's principal protégé. Thus, the KPG would continue to receive the lion's share of Chongqing's financial assistance and would also gain diplomatic recognition in due course.

In late December, a revised "Guiding Plan for Helping the Korean Restoration Movement" was finally adopted with Chiang's approval. The

[25] Xu Enzeng to Zhu, 1 November 1940, *HDYS*, 107–121; Xu Enzeng to Zhu, 11 December 1941, ibid., 562–564.

[26] Members of the committee included some big names in the KMT, such as Chen Guofu, Zhu Jiahua, He Yingqin, Dai Chuanxian, Wang Chonghui, Wang Shijie, and Wu Tiecheng. *HDYS*, 570, 574–576.

[27] Hu Songping, *Zhu Jiahua Nianpu*, 53; Hu Chunhui, *Hanguo*, 97, 101–104.

new version established the Three People's Principles as the ideological basis of Chongqing's Korea policy and explicitly stipulated that Chongqing would take the lead among the Allies in granting recognition to the KPG. The timing for the action would be decided by Chiang Kai-shek himself. A division of labor between the KMT party organization and the National Military Council was adopted, and they would separately be responsible for financing Koreans' political and military activities in China. In return, the Koreans were obliged to collect intelligence information for the Chinese government, to conduct psychological warfare within enemy troops, and to expand their contact with Korean people both within Korea and abroad. The KPG had to agree to submit its military force, the KRA, to the direct control of the Chinese National Military Council.[28]

Thus, there were a few distinct elements in Chongqing's Korean enterprise that would not change much before the end of the war. First was the continual intramural competition over the Korea policy. Before the guiding plan was adopted, Zhu Jiahua was designated as the principal official in charge of Korean affairs, but He Yingqin's office tended to contradict Zhu's position on some important issues. Despite Chiang's intention to have a single authority for carrying out the Korean policy, the plan only clarified the different responsibilities of Zhu and He. At the end of 1942, Chiang had to take further action and handpicked Zhu, He, and Wu Tiecheng to form a triumvirate to oversee Chongqing's relations with the KPG. The measure, however, only created a new forum for the quarrel between Zhu and He.[29]

The division between Chiang's two principal aides in Korean affairs reflected a second, pretentious feature in Chongqing's policy. Officials in Chongqing could not help but see a mirror image of the KMT government in the KPG: it was a government claiming legitimacy and orthodoxy for the whole nation but in practice representing only a faction. A factional force would be useless to Chongqing's postwar purposes in Korea, but after the 1941 exodus of the KNRP, the KPG was regarded by many KMT officials as the only supportable force. In a report to Chiang, Zhu Jiahua argued that whereas Kim Won-bong's KNRP was following an "internationalist line," the KPG represented the only true Korean nationalist force. Evidence presented by Zhu and his colleagues against the KNRP included its programs for "land revolution," "reduction of working hours," "freedom of speech and assembly," and "coalition among anti-aggression states."[30]

During the Pacific war, in practice Chongqing abandoned serious efforts

---

[28] Hu Chunhui, *Hanguo*, 105–107. For the text of the plan, see Appendix 1.
[29] Ibid., 108; Zhu to Chiang, 5 March 1943, *HDYS*, 577–586.
[30] Zhu to Chiang, 12 September 1942, *HDYS*, 407–410; Zhu to Chiang, 5 March 1943, ibid., 577–586.

to promote unity among the Koreans. In August 1943, to settle the continual policy dispute between Zhu and He, Chiang Kai-shek decided that in the future, Chinese policy would no longer force the Koreans to reach a "reluctant unity" but would "choose the best to support." There was merely a vain hope that this clearly KPG-centered policy would discourage competitions from other Korean factions and therefore facilitate the elimination of internal disunity in the Korean movement.[31] Although the KPG was identified as the best of the Korean factions, Chinese officials were not blind to the fact that it was still a factional organization. Despite Chongqing's diplomacy with the Allies in peddling the KPG as the legitimate representative of the Korean people, in its own relations with the KPG the KMT regime never seriously treated the KPG as a national government.

The contradiction between Chongqing's presentation and its actual treatment of the KPG movement indicated another feature: the restrictiveness of Chongqing's sponsorship of the Korean independence movement. The issue of the KRA clearly reflected the diminishing effect of Chongqing's policy toward the KPG. Bound by the nine-point code and other regulations, the KRA became an auxiliary of the Chinese military machinery, not a metal fist of the Korean independence movement. The chief of staff of the KRA was a Chinese general named Yin Chengfu, who was appointed by Chiang Kai-shek. All important positions in the KRA, except that of commander-in-chief, were held by Chinese officers, with Koreans serving as their deputies. The Chinese government was never enthusiastic about the idea of helping the Koreans develop an effective military force. Chongqing approved the organization of the KRA principally as a political ploy to appease the KPG leaders. Before the end of 1944, membership of the KRA had never exceeded 600. Chongqing had no intention of using the KRA for combat purposes either. The Chinese National Military Council did not begin to consider training programs for the KRA until May 1945.[32]

The KMT–KPG military relationship became evidence to Kim Ku's critics of the KPG's fawning on foreign (Chinese) influence. Early in 1943, KPG leaders made an appeal to Chongqing to revise its policy toward the KRA. The Chinese refused to comply on the ground that before receiving international recognition, the KPG could not execute command over the KRA properly. The command of the KRA would not be transferred to the KPG until mid-1945. Deprived of actual control over the KRA and the chance to engage the Japanese in real combat, the KPG remained an echelon of idle talk throughout the war. It is not surprising that in the postwar years, with little exaggeration, Kim Ku would mock his own wartime sojourn in China with these words: "My life in Chongqing consisted in taking shelter [from Japanese air raids] with the members of the Provisional

---

[31] Zhu to Chiang, 5 March 1943, *HDYS*, 577–586.
[32] Hu Chunhui, *Hanguo*, 165–167, 169–171, 182–183.

Government and eating and sleeping once in a while."[33] The restrictive character of Chongqing's policy did lead the Koreans to consider moving the KPG from Chongqing to Washington. The agony for the KPG leaders was that, conscious of the limits of Chinese patronage, they could not find any other government among the Allies willing to develop a *de facto* relationship with the KPG and to offer some assistance.[34]

Chongqing's support of the KRA was also inadequate due to the overall lack of military planning for Korea. The "guiding plan" of 1942 contemplated neither China's military role in liberating Korea nor the possibility of expanding the KRA to such a size that it would be able to drive into Korea. Devoid of any military planning, Chongqing's long-term objectives in Korea would depend completely on how successful the KMT leaders would be in persuading the other Allied powers to endorse the KPG. This approach was in concert with Chongqing's general orientation toward Asian colonies. Chinese troops would not be used to drive the Japanese out of Korea, but Chiang's "spiritual soldiers," the diplomats, would work to induce the Allies to accept the Chinese conception of Korean affairs.

But the spiritual or diplomatic battle was no easy undertaking. The fact that the 1942 plan included the principle of China's first recognition of the KPG but not a timetable reflected a dilemma for Chongqing. The dilemma, as depicted by a Chinese official, was that "premature recognition might cause displeasure on the part of Great Britain and therefore also affect America's attitude, but a delay of recognition would encourage a Soviet conspiracy regarding the Korean problem." In 1942 and 1943, the issue of recognition was seriously discussed on a few occasions within the Chinese government, but Chongqing could not find a way out of its predicament. Loathing the conservative British policy toward colonialism and fearing Soviet intentions in East Asia, the KMT leadership could see only Washington as the potential cosponsor of its Korean program.[35]

Washington's concerns

Although the KPG could not avoid relying on Chongqing's sponsorship, the Americans refused to be manipulated by the Chinese in Korean affairs. It is enlightening to make a comparison between the Chinese–Korean–

---

[33] Ibid., 184–185, 193; Lee, *Politics of Korean Nationalism*, 223–225, 230.

[34] Gauss to Hull, 9 December 1942, *FRUS, 1942*, 1: 880–881.

[35] Hu Chunhui, *Hanguo*, 306; Zhu to Soong, 25 September 1942, *HDYS*, 571–573. For the British and Soviet attitudes toward the Korean question, see Christopher Thorne, *Allies of a Kind: The United States, Britain, and the War Against Japan, 1941–1945* (Oxford: Oxford University Press, 1978), 160–161; Michael C. Sandusky, *America's Parallel* (Alexandria, VA: Old Dominion, 1983), 97–98; and James I. Matray, *The Reluctant Crusade: American Foreign Policy in Korea, 1941–1950* (Honolulu: University of Hawaii Press, 1985), 18–19.

United States triangular relationship in the late nineteenth century and the one during World War II. In 1882, Li Hongzhang, a prominent figure in the Qing government's foreign affairs, was instrumental in bringing about the first treaty between Korea and the United States. During the Pacific war, therefore, for the second time in history, the Chinese government tried to act as a broker between the Koreans and the Americans. On both occasions, Chinese policies were conditioned by China's weakness and motivated by the notion of maneuvering the United States into Northeast Asian politics in order to promote Chinese interests. But there are also remarkable differences between the two occasions. In the early 1880s, the influence of the Manchu court in Korea was still strong, and the Americans needed Chinese help to get into the Korean trade as much as the Chinese needed the American presence in that area to check other powers.[36]

By the time of the Pacific war, the two countries' positions in East Asia had changed beyond recognition. China had lost its redeemer's position in Asia long before. In the war years, the KMT government in Chongqing did not have any tangible means to influence Korean affairs. The practical value of its protégé, the KPG, was in serious question. In approaching the U.S. government in regard to Korea, therefore, Chongqing acted less as a broker for the KPG's legitimacy than as a supplicant for China's own lost patronage over Korea. By contrast, the United States was no longer a peripheral state in Asian politics. The war had made it the strongest military influence in the Asian–Pacific region. This new position prompted American policymakers to contemplate positively a U.S. role in the postwar settlement for Asia. American interests in Korea could no longer be defined only by trade.

Although repeatedly prodded by Chongqing and Korean partisans in the United States, Washington was slow to develop a policy for Korea. In the war years, the two best-known Korean figures in the United States based their credentials on connections with the two principal factions of the Korean independence movement in Chongqing. Syngman Rhee, a veteran of the Korean independence movement, acted as chairman of the Korean Commission, a self-designated mission for the KPG in the United States that was never recognized as such by the U.S. government. Rhee's principal purposes were to achieve Washington's recognition of and assistance to the KPG. He was supported by a Korean–American Council that included both Korean and American members and was presided over by James H. R. Cromwell, former American ambassador to Canada. Another

---

[36] Michael H. Hunt, *The Making of a Special Relationship: The United States and China to 1914* (New York: Columbia University Press, 1983), 126–132; Hilary Conroy, *The Japanese Seizure of Korea, 1868–1919* (Philadelphia: University of Pennsylvania Press, 1960), 184–185; Robert R. Simmons, *The Strained Alliance: Peking, Pyongyang, Moscow and the Politics of the Korean Civil War* (New York: Free Press, 1975), 8.

Korean figure, Kilsoo K. Haan, head of the Sino–Korean Peoples' League, claimed to represent Kim Won-bong's KNRP. Although not appealing for formal recognition by Washington, Haan was nevertheless a powerful rival of Rhee in the task of gaining favorable treatment from Washington. Haan's political capital was an alleged espionage network in some Pacific countries, including Japan. Haan was also helped by his American friends in getting Washington's attention.[37]

These two men, along with their American friends' lobbying activities, were effective enough to persuade the State Department to consider how to deal with the situation. In February 1942, in a memorandum to Under Secretary of State Sumner Welles, Assistant Secretary Adolph A. Berle expressed his concern about the buildup of a "very considerable sentiment in the United States in respect to Korean independence," fearing that continual passivity on the part of the U.S. government might invite public criticism. Berle himself believed that an anti-Japanese rebellion in Korea was only a matter of time and thought that it would contribute to the Allied war effort in the Pacific. What the Koreans needed most were recognition and encouragement. To Berle, the American government's refusal to meet these demands amounted to "almost criminal negligence to overlook the weapons we have." Berle's charge caused a rebuttal from Stanley K. Hornbeck and the Far Eastern Division. In an informal communication to Welles, Hornbeck and the FE attributed the Berle memorandum to ignorance and lack of sound judgment about both the nature of the Koreans' activities in the United States and the current policy of the department. According to Hornbeck, the Korean independence movement was not as potent as Berle maintained, nor was the departmental policy one of indifference to the fate of the Korean people.[38]

At the same time, the FE expressed its opinion through a memorandum entitled "Some Aspects of the Question of Korean Independence," prepared by William R. Langdon, who had served as a foreign service officer for many years in Japan and Manchuria before the war. The importance of the Langdon memorandum is threefold. First, it was paternalism at

[37] Syngman Rhee to Stanley K. Hornbeck, 29 November 1941, *SHP*, box 268; memorandum of conversation between John W. Staggers and Hornbeck, 27 March 1942, ibid.; Edward C. Cater and Robert W. Barnett to Kilsoo K. Haan, 24 and 30 November 1942, *PRC*, box 62; Kilsoo K. Haan and Dakin K. Chung to Harry E. Yarnell, 1 December 1942, ibid.; Senator Guy M. Gillette to Yarnell, 2 December 1942, ibid.; Kilsoo K. Haan to Robert Barnett, 24 December 1942, ibid.; Dakin K. Chung to Edward C. Carter, 28 December 1942, ibid.; four letters between James H. R. Cromwell and Cordell Hull, 5 May 1942, 20 May 1942, 3 June 1942, and 23 June 1942, ibid.; T document-319, 26 May 1943, *RHN*, box 63. For detailed accounts of the exchanges between the Koreans and their American supporters and the State Department, see Matray, *Reluctant Crusade*, 8–12, and Sandusky, *America's Parallel*, 65–92.
[38] Berle to Welles, 17 February 1942, and the FE memorandum to Welles, 20 February 1942, *SHP*, box 268.

work. According to Langdon's analysis, due to the Japanese rule for thirty-seven years, the Korean people "[were] emasculated politically" and therefore were not in a position to manage a state on their own. Consequently, after the war, "for a generation at least Korea would have to be protected, guided, and aided to modern statehood by the great powers." Second, as far as the existing Korean independence movement was concerned, the document established a quality standard: to qualify for American support, Korean nationalists outside Korea must achieve internal unity and demonstrate that they were the true representatives of the Korean people at home. Such a standard would not only militate against U.S. recognition of "any shadow organization of Koreans" as a provisional government for Korea, but would also oppose the development of a *de facto* relationship between Washington and any Korean group during the war. In fact, the document even argued against public support by the U.S. government of Korean independence.[39]

Third, disposed against any premature and unilateral action on the part of the United States, the document emphasized the necessity of consultation among the leading Allies. China and the Soviet Union were suggested as two powers that had particular interests in Korea. However, while mentioning the possibility of creating an international commission charged with the responsibility of helping Korea, the document failed to clarify the U.S. stake and role in such a commission. The Langdon memorandum did not comment directly on the Chinese policy toward Korea, but the proposed orientation implied disapproval. At the end of the document especially, Langdon warned American military authorities against attaching too much importance to the "Korean volunteers" under the auspices of the Chinese government. He remarked contemptuously: "Koreans in China have been largely rascals and running dogs of the Japanese Army," and hence were untrustworthy. This sweeping verdict set the State Department's evaluation of the KPG far apart from Chongqing's. At the same time, the only positive remarks from the FE were directed to a small group of Korean guerrilla fighters known to be active in Manchuria.[40]

The seemingly determined stand of the State Department on not dealing with the Korean groups either in Washington or in Chongqing should not obscure the fact that in 1942 Korea was still a new issue to American policymakers. The connotation of Korean independence to American interests was by no means clear to the informed minds in Washington. In March, a study group of the CFR tried but failed to define the Korean question in postwar settlement. The participants' opinions were so divergent that they had to shelve the subject.[41] Similar discussions also took

---

[39] Memorandum by William R. Langdon, 20 February 1942, *SHP*, box 268.
[40] Ibid.; Hornbeck to Hull, 13 August 1942, *SHP*, box 269.
[41] Blakeslee to Hornbeck, 3 April 1942, *SHP*, box 29.

place in the State Department. In the summer of 1942, when reviewing postwar security measures against Japan, the Security Subcommittee decided that for security reasons Korea should not remain under Japanese control at the conclusion of the war, but the committee had difficulty anticipating what would become of Korea when it was detached from Japanese control. The Political Subcommittee experienced similar confusion. The record of one of its meetings reads: "No consensus was arrived at concerning the disposition of Korea. . . . The possibilities that Korea might be independent, a member of a possible Chinese federation, or under some form of trusteeship were discussed."[42]

Nevertheless, from the beginning, American officials were conscious of the importance of the issue to the power relationship in East Asia in the postwar years. The subject of Korean independence was not discussed for its own sake but as one of the possible avenues for reaching a new political stability in Northeast Asia. Hornbeck once remarked: "The question [of] what to do for and with and about Korea will be, when the peace settlement is made, a perplexing question; and it will be a question which should be decided in the light of conditions which then exist and disposals [of] which are being made for far larger questions." The uncertainty about the "far larger questions" or relations among the leading Allies at the end of the war convinced Hornbeck that "a pledge [by the U.S. government] that Korea shall be made an independent state might become a source of most embarrassing involvement."[43] Thus, it was anxiety about international intrigues in postwar Northeast Asia that helped shape many American officials' thoughts about Korea. After Japan's defeat, the Soviet Union and China would be the two countries likely to be engaged in competition for control in Korea. While anticipating such a prospect with certainty, State Department officials in 1942 were not yet ready to prescribe a policy to be pursued by the U.S. government. Although a trusteeship formula and America's participation in a regional solution of the Korean problem were considered in the State Department, the international approach remained tentative until President Roosevelt committed himself to the idea in 1943.[44]

Between 1938 and 1941, Korean leaders in Chongqing and in the United States made efforts to appeal directly to President Roosevelt for support. For instance, when Lauchlin Currie went to Chongqing in the spring of 1941, Kim Ku asked him to bring a personal letter to the president. But Roosevelt usually turned these overtures over to the State Department for

---

[42] S minutes-10, 12 August 1942, and S documents-18a, 2 October 1942, *RHN*, box 76; P document-31, 6 August 1942, *RHN*, box 54.

[43] Hornbeck to Welles, 11 April 1942, *SHP*, box 269.

[44] Memorandum of conversation between Staggers and Hornbeck, 27 March 1942, *SHP*, box 268; Sandusky, *America's Parallel*, 74–75; P document 118, 21 October 1942, *RHN*, box 54.

response.[45] In early 1942, Roosevelt began to show some personal interest in Korea. In a note he sent to Mrs. Snow (Helen Foster Snow, or Nym Wales) in February, Roosevelt expressed his gratitude for some books he had received from her, saying: "I have learned a great deal from them, especially about Korea." But throughout the year, the president continued to encourage the State Department to take the necessary action regarding Korea without giving any specific instructions. In April 1942, Chiang Kai-shek and T. V. Soong began to work separately in Chongqing and in Washington to enlist the U.S. government as a cosponsor of the KPG. Suspicious of the self-serving character of the Rhee group and concerned about the uncertain Soviet factor, Secretary Hull recommended to the president that Chongqing's premature recognition of the KPG be discouraged. Typically, Roosevelt limited his remark on the recommendation to "very good." In the same month, at a meeting of the Pacific War Council, a memo from Soong concerning support of the KPG was brought to the participants' attention. Roosevelt merely read it to those present, along with a written comment on the memo by Sumner Welles, which proposed postponing any commitment to the KPG or to Korean independence.[46]

Early in 1943, however, due to the Chinese government's persistent pressure on Washington to clarify its policy toward Korea, President Roosevelt began to consider the issue seriously. At the end of 1942, in a communication with the president, Chiang Kai-shek insisted that the Russians be excluded from any postwar settlement in Korea. To this the president explicitly expressed his objection.[47] On 22 February 1943, still fresh from his correspondence with Chiang Kai-shek, Roosevelt conferred with Hull, Welles, and some senior members of the research staff of the State Department, expressing in generalities his opinion on peace settlement for the world. For East Asia, the president said that Taiwan and Manchuria should be returned to China, and a trusteeship should be arranged for Korea. He also indicated that Indochina should not be returned to France. For some time, Roosevelt had been flirting with the idea of resetting colonial territories in Asia with trusteeship, but this was the first time that he unequivocally applied the idea to Korea. In March, President

[45] Chief of Protocol of the State Department to M. H. McIntyre, 28 July 1938, RPOF 3342; Roosevelt to Hull, 11 April 1941, and Currie to Roosevelt, 9 April 1941, RPOF 1143.

[46] Hull to Roosevelt, 29 April 1942, RPSF, box 27; Hull to James Cromwell, 20 May 1942, PRC, box 62; Roosevelt to Hull, 8 December 1942, RPOF 1143; memorandum by J. L. McCrea on the third meeting of the Pacific War Council, 19 April 1942, RPMF, box 168; Roosevelt to Welles, 8 April 1942, FRUS, 1942, 1: 867–869; Hull to Gauss, 1 May 1942, ibid., 1: 873–875. Secretary Hull's principal consideration was the uncertain Soviet factor, but in their communication with Chiang, President Roosevelt and Secretary Hull advised that the Chinese government might wisely wait for the clarification of the Indian issue and the military situation in the Pacific before taking any action about Korea.

[47] Draft of letter from Lattimore to Chiang (18 December 1942), FRUS, 1942: China, 185–187.

Roosevelt brought up similar ideas to British Foreign Secretary Anthony Eden, who was visiting in Washington. According to Secretary Hull's record of a meeting held on 27 March, President Roosevelt categorically stated to the British that although a trusteeship should be set up for Indochina, Korea should be placed under an *international* trusteeship, "with China, the United States and one or two other countries participating." Eden expressed his support. Soon the Chinese government also learned about the president's idea through its representative at the Pacific War Council.[48]

During World War II, when the ideology of decolonization was in its heyday in Washington, trusteeship was considered a device that would allow the former colonial powers to have a part in a peaceful and gradual burial of their own empires. Considering the interests of some wartime allies, especially Great Britain, Washington was prepared to endorse trusteeships of different forms that would allow former owners of colonies to play a role.[49] But President Roosevelt's suggestion of an international trusteeship for Korea distinguished this area from the old European colonies. From Washington's point of view, a special arrangement for Korea was necessary. For after the Japanese Empire was destroyed and when the prospect of immediate Korean independence was viewed as impractical, this peninsula would become a "public land" devoid of either a sovereign government or a suzerain owner. A special arrangement would be needed to prevent international intrigues. The planning staff of the State Department agreed with Roosevelt. In the State Department, the Korea issue boiled down to which of the victorious powers in the United Nations should exercise control over Korea until it was ready for independence. Since China and the Soviet Union were the two most interested powers, and since each would object to the other's predominant position in Korea, the only feasible and safe course would be some machinery for international control.[50]

Interestingly, officials in the State Department interpreted Chongqing's intentions in Korea in terms rather similar to those they themselves employed to define U.S. policy toward China. When Chongqing continued to perform poorly in the war, American officials kept changing their opinions on whether China in postwar Asia would be able to function as a principal stabilizing power. Nevertheless, a constant theme in the State Department's

---

[48] Memorandum, "Indications of Contact with President on Post-War Matters," n.d., *RHN*, box 54; memorandum by Secretary of State Hull on the president's meeting with Eden, 27 March 1943, *RHN*, box 19; memorandum by Wilson Brown on the thirtieth meeting of the Pacific War Council, 31 March 1943, *RPMF*, box 168; Wm. Roger Louis, *Imperialism at Bay: The United States and the Decolonization of the British Empire, 1941–1945* (New York: Oxford University Press, 1978), 156–157.

[49] P documents-118, 21 October 1942, *RHN*, box 54; Robert E. Sherwood, *Roosevelt and Hopkins: An Intimate History* (New York: Harper, 1948), 718.

[50] ST minutes-18, 19 May 1943, *RHN*, box 79.

wartime papers on China was that America's interests in Asia would require the emergence of a "unified, friendly, prosperous, strong and progressively democratic" China. Among these adjectives, only "democratic" was not used by American planners when they described Chongqing's objectives in Korea. Chinese aspirations in that peninsula were viewed as nonexpansionary and basically defensive. It was suggested that for historical, ideological, and security reasons, China would want Korea to be detached from the Japanese Empire and to become an independent and friendly neighbor. China wanted Korea to be strong so that in the future it would not serve again as a stepping stone for foreign invasions of China.[51] It was also suggested that traditionally, China's foreign policy had been motivated by "a question of closeness of interest" but not "geographic proximity." In other words, in the postwar years, the Chinese government would follow this tradition and seek opportunities to develop its own peripheral regions, such as Xinjiang, Mongolia, and Manchuria, but not to expand into Korea. In addition, there was the question of China's capability. China was not capable of unilateral control over Korea, and the Chinese leaders would not seek such control.[52]

When using American terms to define Chongqing's intentions with regard to Korea, State Department officials overlooked the possibility that China's weakness and lack of security might be the very reasons for Chongqing to seek influence in geographically proximate regions like Korea. Surprisingly, the wartime relationship between the KMT and the KPG never underwent careful analysis in the State Department. This was not due to lack of information. Policy planners in the State Department knew of the Chinese control of the KRA under the nine-point code. They were also aware of Chongqing's jealousy of other foreign powers' interference in the course of Korean independence. In fact, Ambassador Gauss had warned in late 1942 that the wartime KMT–KRA relationship would have a long-term effect on postwar Chinese–Korean relations. But planning officials in Washington did not seem impressed with the information. The State Department did not expect any difficulty from Chongqing in regard to its own postwar plans for Korea. In fact, on the eve of the Cairo Conference, the planning staff of the State Department believed that an international trusteeship over Korea "would be in harmony with the statement of the Chinese Government that 'Korea must be free and independent.'"[53]

[51] PG documents-34, 4 October 1943, *RHN*, box 119; SR document, "China," n.d., *RHN*, box 11; memorandum by the Division of Chinese Affairs of the Department of State, "Outline of Long-range Objectives and Policies of the United States with Respect to China," 12 January 1945, *TSGR*, box 1.
[52] T minutes-51, 25 June 1943, *OJ*, 1-C-1; ST minutes-18, 19 May 1943, *RHN*, box 79.
[53] T documents-319, 26 May 1943, *RHN*, box 63; PG documents-32, 2 October 1943, *RHN*, box 119; Hong-kyu Park, "From Pearl Harbor to Cairo: America's Korean Diplomacy, 1941–1943," *Diplomatic History*, 13 (Summer 1989): 355–356.

Although they seemed comfortable with Chongqing's Korea policy, State Department planning officers entertained acute concern about Soviet intentions toward Korea. In 1943, despite the neutrality of the Soviet Union in the Pacific war, American planners firmly regarded Moscow as a contender for the control of Korea. It was believed that whether or not the Soviet Union eventually entered the Pacific war, it would certainly want to move into the political vacuum in northern China and Korea after the defeat of Japan. According to State Department planners, Moscow's Korean policy was designed "to apply the Soviet conception of proper treatment of colonial peoples, to strengthen enormously the economic resources of the Soviet Far East, to acquire ice-free ports, and to occupy a dominating strategic position in relation both to China and to Japan." They predicted: "A Soviet occupation of Korea would create an entirely new strategic situation in the Far East, and its repercussions with China and Japan might be far-reaching." Exclusive Soviet influence in Korea would sever China's connection with the outside world in Northeast Asia and thus would not only "seriously undermine Chinese confidence in the postwar settlement, but would provoke China to undertake similarly unilateral actions there and elsewhere."[54]

The State Department's anticipation of Moscow's intentions in Korea agreed in substance with that of KMT officials. This rendered the difference between the two sides' solutions even more remarkable. Unlike the Chinese, the Americans maintained a conciliatory approach to the Soviet factor. At the time, the State Department's consideration of the postwar status of Korea had a clear reference point: Korea must be prevented from becoming a source of trouble after Japan's defeat. Like Manchuria, Korea was categorized as one of the controversial territories between China and the Soviet Union. American officials hoped that these two powers would be able to reach agreements on these territories in order to avert a conflict in postwar Asia. Since, according to the State Department's judgment, between the Chinese and the Russians the latter was the expansionary party in regard to Korea, a solution to the Korean question had to contain elements that could at once satisfy Moscow's legitimate interests and curb its unreasonable demands. An international trusteeship seemed able to achieve such an effect.

On the eve of the Cairo Conference, the State Department's planning for Korea made some progress as far as Korea's eventual status was concerned. Recognizing the inconsistency between the self-government principle of the Atlantic Charter and Washington's silence in regard to the issue of Korean independence, planning officers now recommended that the American government adopt a more positive attitude. This would mean America's "formal recognition of the right of Korea to be free and independent at the

[54] PG documents-28, 2 October 1943, *RHN*, box 119.

close of the war, and of actual Korean independence after an interim period of limited self-government under supervision or trusteeship." Thus, the U.S. government would be able to set straight its own record on the self-government principle without becoming entangled with any Korean groups; in the meantime, the door would be left open for an international trusteeship in postwar Korea.[55]

In addition, America's future responsibility in that country was further clarified. Since a single-power trusteeship (by either China or the Soviet Union) or a Sino–Soviet condominium in Korea would be neither practical nor desirable, the United States could not avoid joining with the other two powers in the postwar international supervision of Korea. But a "three's company" arrangement might place the United States in the middle of a cross-fire between the Chinese and the Russians over Korea, and it might also cause ill will from other influential countries excluded from the trusteeship administration. Consequently, in the State Department's opinion, only a multinational authority would be able to supervise a steady and peaceful transformation of Korea from a Japanese colony to an independent state. Besides the aforementioned three powers, Britain, Canada, or the Netherlands might be considered as candidates in such an operation.[56]

In 1943, expecting all possible complications in such an international operation, the political strategists of the State Department were concerned that at the end of the war the U.S. government would lack the means to back its policy in Korea. Conventional wisdom held that the power physically in control of a territory at the war's end would exert decisive influence on postwar development there. Planning officers in the State Department could not see how the U.S. military strategy as it stood in the Pacific would be able to establish America's controlling position in Korea at the end of the war. Most likely, Korea would be the last Japanese-occupied territory to be liberated by the United Nations, and American armed forces might be too distant from the peninsula to make any decisive contribution to its reconquest. The Soviet Union, and less likely China, would be in a much better position than the United States to reconquer and occupy Korea in the conclusive stage of the Pacific war. Thus, U.S. policy toward Korea contained a discrepancy between its political goal and its military strategy that resembled a similar discrepancy in Chongqing's policy. Similarly, State Department planners came up with a remedy in diplomacy. They viewed the positive support of other Allies, especially the Soviet Union, of the trusteeship formula as a crucial condition for its success.[57]

In sum, from the point of view of American foreign policy planners, in

---

[55] T documents-319, 26 May 1943, *RHN*, box 63.
[56] Ibid.; PG documents-34, 2 October 1943, *RHN*, box 119; T minutes-51, 25 June 1943, *OJ*, 1-C-1.
[57] T minutes-51, 25 June 1943, *OJ*, 1-C-1.

postwar Korea immediate independence would be impractical, Chinese domination improbable, Soviet control undesirable, and Chinese–Soviet rivalry unacceptable. Although the feasibility of the international trusteeship formula remained questionable due mainly to America's military incompetence in Northeast Asia, it seemed the only way to preempt trouble in postwar Korea and thereby to keep intact the postwar cooperation among the Big Four in Asia, as well as in global affairs. Just before the Cairo Conference, the State Department adopted the formula as a "preferred solution" to the Korean question.[58]

By the time of the Cairo Conference, both the American and Chinese governments had made considerable efforts to develop their postwar policies in Korea. In 1943, it was hard to tell which one would have a better chance of succeeding at the end of the war. Chongqing's policy suffered from the fact that the Chinese government, being weak and factional itself, was sponsoring a similarly questionable "Korean Provisional Government." Consequently, KMT leaders had to look for help in Washington. Across the Pacific, the American government merely developed an untested idea. Calling for international supervision in Korea, the American solution ignored completely the aspirations of the Korean people and relied completely on unpredictable power politics. In the winter of 1943, when the Chinese and American leaders meet at Cairo, they discovered that there was much to be patched up between them with regard to Korea and other postwar issues in East Asia.

[58] PG documents-32, 2 October 1943 and PG documents-33, 2 October 1943, *RHN*, box 119.

5

The road to Cairo

Conspicuously, during the first two years of the Pacific war, despite their professed desire to establish a long-term partnership in postwar East Asia, Chongqing and Washington held only sporadic discussions of the matter. There was no consistent, regular working arrangement between American and Chinese planning staffs for the purpose of exchanging opinions on postwar issues. Consultations about postwar issues did take place between Chongqing and Washington, but these depended on the impulse and improvisation of the top leaders on both sides. In a sense, the consultations during the first two years of the Pacific war paved the way to the only wartime summit between the Chinese and American governments in Cairo in late 1943. Yet, it also proved a trying road to travel for Roosevelt and Chiang Kai-shek to reach the pinnacle of their wartime relationship. The different intentions of the two sides on issues like postwar territorial settlement in Asia and control of Japan really reflected a most troubling problem in their search for a long-term partnership. Namely, the two governments could not identify the same potential enemy in the Asian–Pacific region that would disturb peace in the postwar years. Chiang Kai-shek held firmly that in the postwar years the Soviet Union would be the most serious threat to China's security. Therefore, he wanted to steer Chinese–American cooperation in the direction of containing the Russians. By contrast, Roosevelt based his postwar foreign policy on continuous cooperation among the Big Four and held Moscow's good will as essential to such a regime. Thus, when the American–Chinese alliance for fighting Japan brought President Roosevelt and Chiang Kai-shek to their summit meeting in Cairo, the prospect of the two governments' collaboration for reorganizing peace in Asia turned dim because of their disagreement on the Soviet Union.

Early signs of disagreement

In the summer of 1942, Lauchlin Currie visited China for the second time as Roosevelt's personal emissary. Aside from investigating China's economic situation, Currie had the tasks of ironing out misunderstandings between Chongqing and its Western Allies and of exploring with Chiang conditions for long-term Sino–American cooperation. In a directive drafted by Currie himself for his mission, President Roosevelt authorized Currie to "give assurance [to the Chinese leaders] that China will be fully consulted on all matters touching the postwar settlement and adjustments."[1] Accordingly, Currie conversed with Chiang Kai-shek on postwar problems in East Asia.

On 3 August, in Chiang's villa in Huangshan (the Yellow Mountains), the two engaged in their most important conversation on the subject. On this occasion, Currie told Chiang that President Roosevelt was reluctant to make any premature pledges concerning postwar territorial settlement, though generally the American government favored an international trusteeship as a substitute for the mandate system created by the peace conference after World War I. He conveyed an opinion existing "in some quarters in Washington that Manchuria should be made a buffer state between Japan and Russia after the war." Currie also urged Chiang to improve Chongqing's relations with London. As for the direction of China's development, Currie posed these questions to Chiang: Would China in the postwar years become a peaceful and democratic country or a militant and chauvinistic power? Would the current leadership in China be able to maintain stability in postwar China? Currie attributed these concerns to important American leaders, including President Roosevelt himself.[2]

Although agreeable on the other issues, Chiang Kai-shek displayed vexation on three subjects. First, he fervently opposed the notion of making Manchuria a buffer state and attributed it to "propaganda conducted by Japan, the communists and Soviet Russia." Chiang asserted that China had made sacrifices in its armed struggle against Japan "solely for the recovery of Manchuria," and that "if the Soviet design should succeed, there would be no peace in the Pacific." Second, regarding the American concern about the ability and methods of his government in handling domestic problems, Chiang insisted that he would "take actions [in domestic politics] which on the surface seem undesirable" as long as the war with Japan continued. Third, as for the relations between Chongqing and

---

[1] Currie to Roosevelt, 9 July 1942, and memorandum by Currie, "Tentative Draft of Instructions to Lauchlin Currie for Mission to China," July 1942, *LCP*, box 5; John P. Davies, Jr., *Dragon by the Tail: American, British, Japanese, and Russian Encounters with China and One Another* (New York: W. W. Norton, 1974), 250–254.

[2] Minutes of Currie's interviews with Chiang, 3 August, 4 August, and 5 August 1942, *LCP*, box 4.

the other Allied governments, Chiang promised that China would make an effort to improve its relationship with Britain and the Soviet Union. But, he stated, "we do not wish to follow any leadership other than that of America." Later, Chiang clarified what he meant by China's following America's leadership: China would not join any international agreement to which America was not a party. Chiang also showed his disapproval of the close ties between the United States and Britain: "We do not wish to see American leadership directed by a second country."[3]

On returning to Washington, Currie submitted to the president a lengthy report. He pointed out that Chiang's attitude toward Britain and the Soviet Union was especially alarming. Currie told the president that according to Chiang, America must dissociate itself from Britain in Asian affairs, or else anti-British sentiment in China would turn into an antiwhite movement. Chiang's apprehension about Soviet intentions toward Manchuria, and about the connection between Yan'an and Moscow, was profound. He would be willing to cooperate with the Russians in postwar settlement in East Asia only if this were necessary to forestall any Soviet unilateral action to harm China's security. Currie faithfully told the president how Chiang felt about the Manchurian question. Yet he left out Chiang's adamant statement on his unchangeable domestic policy. What the president read in the report was a reassuring sentence about Chiang's determination "to push along the Chinese economic and social revolution toward democratic goals."[4]

The next person sent by Roosevelt to Chongqing was Wendell Willkie, the Republican presidential contender in 1940. Willkie arrived in Chongqing in early October 1942. His behavior in China impressed Ambassador Gauss as "more that of a visiting prominent American politician than of a distinguished American acting as a 'special representative of the President.'" The American embassy in Chongqing did not expect Willkie's flaunting performance to have much positive effect on wartime Chinese–American relations.[5] But the Chinese government took Willkie seriously. T. V. Soong made a judgment in Washington that Willkie might either be the next American President or be seated at the peace conference at the war's end. This impressed Chiang Kai-shek. He also liked Willkie's attitude toward certain issues. In his meetings with Chiang, Willkie not only asserted his "profound understanding" of the American people's "very pro-Chinese" psychology, but also shared Chiang's criticism of President Roosevelt's dealings with the imperialistic British. Chiang was thus encouraged to

[3] Ibid.
[4] Currie to Roosevelt, "Report on Visit to China," 24 August 1942, LCP, box 4.
[5] Gauss to Hull, 8 October 1942, FRUS, 1942: China, 161–165; Michael Schaller, The U.S. Crusade in China, 1938–1945 (New York: Columbia University Press, 1979), 118–119; Davies, Dragon by the Tail, 254–255; Gary May, China Scapegoat: The Diplomatic Ordeal of John Carter Vincent (Washington, DC: New Republic Books, 1979), 84–86.

express his thoughts bluntly and also come to a personal understanding with the American Republican.[6]

During these conversations, Chiang stressed four points. The first was that the United States should guarantee Indian independence within three years after the conclusion of the war. Chiang believed that racial relations would be among the most important issues in postwar settlement. Yet, according to him, the indecisiveness of the U.S. government regarding the situation of India was tarnishing its liberal and democratic image. Chiang reasoned that an American commitment to a timetable for Indian independence could at once avert further inter-Allied disagreements and add just cause to the United Nations' war aims.

Chiang's second point was that China and America should establish a close postwar partnership in order to block Soviet expansion. At the end of the war, in his opinion,

> [the] central issue in the Pacific will be whether or not China can successfully prevent the Soviet aggression. In other words, the issue boils down to whether or not China can achieve America's assistance and become a Far Eastern barrier protecting democratic countries. . . . A strong China will be able to assume the responsibility for preventing the communists from becoming rampant in the Pacific. Before the war, China used to be a buffer between Japan and Russia. After the war China will be a buffer between America and the Soviet Union. But China can accomplish little without American assistance.

After disclosing his fundamental view on postwar Pacific politics, Chiang tried to convince Willkie that the Pacific in the postwar years should be a sphere dominated by America and China. Both the British and the Russians were hypocritical in their statements favoring the liberation of weak nations. Therefore, any Big Four consultation on the problems in the Pacific would accomplish nothing.

Chiang's next two points were concrete proposals. He called for joint Sino–American use of bases in Port Arthur, Dalian (Dairen), and Taiwan to maintain security in the western Pacific. He also proposed to establish a Sino–American "sisterhood" relationship, implying some sort of peacetime alliance. Chiang wanted Willkie to convey all these ideas to President Roosevelt except the last. Knowing that the Roosevelt administration was willing to participate in joint actions with other countries but did not favor an alliance, Chiang preferred, for the time being, to treat the sisterhood idea as an understanding between Willkie and himself.[7]

[6] Minutes of conversations between Chiang and Willkie, 4 October, 5 October, and 7 October 1942, *ZZSC*, 3(1): 753–778; Gauss to Hull, 8 October 1942, *FRUS, 1942: China*, 163.

[7] Minutes of conversations between Chiang and Willkie, 4 October, 5 October, and 7 October 1942, *ZZSC*, 3(1): 753–778.

President Roosevelt's intention in sending Willkie to Chongqing was not very clear. The latter's internationalist persona obviously did not effect any change in Chiang's anti-Soviet tendency and narrow focus on a bilateral approach. Although smooth during his encounter with Chiang, Willkie was not convinced by the Chinese. Soon after he returned to the United States, Willkie published a book entitled *One World*. As if he had never learned about Chiang's foreign policy orientation, Willkie praised the Soviets and Chiang's China in the same terms. As for his mission for the president, Willkie now put it aside as a political liability that might cause criticism in his own party. He did not even make a report to Roosevelt about the mission.[8]

Nevertheless, President Roosevelt's personal diplomacy worked well at least in one sense. Chiang was thrilled and encouraged by these talks, and he wanted to continue his dialogue with American leaders to foster long-term cooperation between the two governments. Before the end of the year, Chiang summoned Owen Lattimore and outlined a program for postwar settlement in East Asia. Chiang was anxious to transmit the program to President Roosevelt as a basis for further formal discussion between the two governments. According to what had been recorded by Lattimore, Chiang wanted Taiwan to be returned to China, "but with America having the privilege of having a naval and air base there." Korea should become "semi-independent under American and Chinese tutelage which, of course, means Chinese." Russian influence must be excluded from Korea. In Manchuria, joint Chinese–American naval and air bases should be established for the purpose of "protection against Japan." As for Indochina, Chiang opposed its return to France and supported its independence. But before Vietnam could achieve self-government, China would act as a "big brother." "That would work out all right," Chiang told Lattimore, "because Indo-China was far distant from Russia." Thus, Chiang implied that his need for the presence of American influence in East Asia was proportional to the proximity of Soviet Russia and his fear of Soviet power. Later, Lattimore obliged Chiang and delivered his proposals to Roosevelt through Lauchlin Currie.[9]

President Roosevelt's response, also via Lattimore, reached Chongqing in late December. Advocating the trusteeship formula for former colonies in Southeast Asia, Roosevelt evaded Chiang's specific suggestion for a joint Chinese–American enterprise in postwar Indochina. Showing interest in Chiang's offer regarding joint American–Chinese bases in Manchuria and

---

[8] Roosevelt to Chiang, 26 October 1942, ibid., 779; Robert A. Divine, *Second Chance: The Triumph of Internationalism in America during World War II* (New York: Atheneum, 1967), 103–105; Cordell Hull, *Memoirs of Cordell Hull* (New York: Macmillan, 1948), 2: 1182–1183.

[9] Memorandum by Lattimore, "Chinese Postwar Aims," 4 December 1942, *LCP*, box 5.

Taiwan, Roosevelt nevertheless did not commit himself at this time. He explicitly refuted Chiang's two other principal points. One was for a Chinese–American coalition against the Soviet Union in Northeast Asia; the other was for an early formal understanding between Chongqing and Washington on general postwar settlement in East Asia. Chiang was told in effect that the Big Four would have to act in concert to prevent any aggression in the postwar world. Therefore, it "would be undesirable to attempt to exclude Soviet Russia from such problems as the independence of Korea." Probably to avoid a direct contradiction of Chiang by the president himself, most of the communication was carried in Lattimore's words. Yet Roosevelt did take personal responsibility for dissuading Chiang from the idea of a formal, detailed American–Chinese discussion of postwar problems at the moment, suggesting that because these problems could be discussed "through regular channels" in due time, Chiang and the president should not commit themselves to any ideas in advance.[10] Having received Roosevelt's personal envoys, Chiang must have been taken aback by the president's new preference for "regular channels."

Chiang's envoys

In early 1943, at a meeting of the Pacific War Council, President Roosevelt declared: "There is at least 95 percent agreement among all of the United Nations on almost all subjects having to do with the war and postwar period."[11] Given the troubled American–Chinese military relationship during the war and the emerging disagreements between the two governments on postwar issues, Roosevelt's depiction distorted the reality across the Pacific. With the war with Japan continuing, Chiang had already begun to anticipate that the Soviet Union, hitherto neutral in the Asian conflict, would emerge as the cardinal threat to China in the postwar years. He sought to counter such a danger by creating an exclusive Sino–American partnership. This intention underlay nearly all of Chongqing's proposals to the American government with regard to postwar territorial readjustments and security arrangements in the Asian–Pacific region. To enlist American support in his dealings with the Russians, and to a lesser degree with the British, Chiang was willing to attach China's diplomacy to America's global enterprise and to provide the United States with base facilities in Chinese territories yet to be recovered, such as Taiwan and Manchuria. American officials had their own doubts about Moscow's postwar intentions,

[10] Draft of letter from Lattimore to Chiang (18 December 1942), *FRUS, 1942: China*, 185–187.
[11] Memorandum by Wilson Brown on the thirtieth meeting of the Pacific War Council, 31 March 1943, *RPMF*, box 168.

and they also wanted to integrate China into America's foreign policy undertaking. But at the time, the Roosevelt administration had no intention of allowing Chiang's rampant anti-Sovietism in East Asia to ruin its search for a global security system based on continual cooperation among the four leading Allied powers.

Aside from its propaganda value, President Roosevelt's remark to the Pacific War Council might also have reflected optimism about his ability to bring the other Allies along with him. He did not see any insurmountable difficulties with Chongqing. After reading Currie's report on his trip to Chongqing, Roosevelt commented on the relationship between his government and Chongqing: "There are many bridges to be gapped but none of the gaps are wide enough to keep them from being bridged." In Roosevelt's opinion, the key to improving American–Chinese cooperation was to find the "right people" on both sides to handle that relationship.[12] At the time, Lauchlin Currie thought that he was qualified for the job and tried to persuade the president to send him to China as ambassador. But even Currie did not believe that the right people were all that was needed to put American–Chinese relations on the right track. In November 1942 he wrote to Roosevelt:

> If he [Chiang Kai-shek] hopes to make an ally of America against the U.S.S.R. in the Far East, to bring about a forcible liquidation of the Chinese communists, and to secure financial and economic help from America regardless of the trend toward or away from democratic processes in China, I would be an awkward representative [of the U.S. government] to deal with and he would prefer a man who did not care so much for the maintenance of the conditions of peace and democracy in the postwar world.[13]

Although he shared Currie's misgivings about the KMT leaders' intransigence on the Soviet factor, Roosevelt did not give up the hope of converting them to his ideas. But he needed more time to temper the Chinese. That is why, at the end of 1942, after his surrogate diplomacy during the year had exposed the differences between the two sides, Roosevelt decided to postpone further consultations with Chongqing on postwar issues.

President Roosevelt was unable to shelve issues for long. In the summer of 1943, he became supportive of the idea of having a summit with Chiang Kai-shek. The resultant Cairo Conference in November 1943 would commit the American, British, and Chinese governments to important decisions on peace settlement in East Asia. It is quite possible that the summit with the Chinese was a by-product of the president's contemplation of his first summit with the Soviet leader, Joseph Stalin. He might have been mindful of possible discussions with Stalin of issues concerning China, and

---

[12] Roosevelt to Currie, 12 September 1942, *RPOF* 3719.
[13] Currie to Roosevelt, 11 November 1942, *RPSF*, box 132.

he also might not have wanted to create an impression in Chongqing that China was the only leading Allied power forgotten by Washington.[14] All these reasons granted, the Chiang–Roosevelt summit would probably not have happened without Chiang's dogged efforts, through his personal emissaries, to convince Roosevelt to hold such a meeting.

In 1943, Chiang Kai-shek sent his wife, Song Meiling, and his brother-in-law T. V. Soong, to Washington to maintain the momentum of the personal diplomacy started by Roosevelt. In the war years, for officials of the Waijiaobu in Chongqing, T. V. Soong was an absentee boss, but for officers of the Chinese Embassy in Washington, Soong's long sojourn in the United States made the role of the Chinese ambassador embarrassingly insignificant. A prominent political and financial figure in Chongqing politics, Soong also demanded that American leaders take him into their confidence. Once he told Harry Hopkins that ever since finishing school in the United States and returning to China, he had committed himself to the mission of bringing about "close and lasting political and ideological associations between our two countries." Yet in China, opinions varied about his ability and courage to think and act independently from Chiang Kai-shek.[15]

From March to September, Soong met with President Roosevelt and his aides several times. Generally, these meetings were characterized by American leaders' promise of supporting China as a great power in Asia and Soong's request for cashing in the promise now in the form of financial and military aid to Chongqing. But postwar issues were also discussed occasionally. In March, after British Foreign Secretary Anthony Eden visited Washington, Soong became interested in finding out what the president and Eden had discussed with regard to postwar issues in East Asia. Soong's inquiry gave rise to American officials' sympathetic statements concerning Chongqing's war aims. They agreed that after the war, Manchuria, Taiwan, and the Ryukyu Islands should be returned to China. Yet the Americans also insisted that Russian interests should not be ignored. Sumner Welles told Soong that in Manchuria China's sovereignty was not in question, but the Chinese government should recognize the Soviet Union's "legitimate commercial interest" there. President Roosevelt said that the Chinese should approach the Russians directly to settle "the question of railways and other pending questions in Manchuria." Soong protested that the Chinese Eastern Railway (CER) was a closed issue because the

---

[14] Keith Sainsbury, *The Turning Points: Roosevelt, Stalin, Churchill, and Chiang-Kai-Shek [sic], 1943: The Moscow, Cairo, and Teheran Conferences* (New York: Oxford University Press, 1985), 126–127.

[15] Hu Songping, *Hu Shizhi*, 1640, 1688, 1706, 1777; Hornbeck, "Note on Conversation with the President on Aug. 30, 1943," TSP, box 32; Soong to Hopkins, 4 April 1942, HHP, box 220.

Russians had transferred it to the Japanese several years before. The president apologized for his ignorance on this matter and said: "This clears the way for the settlement." Yet, when talking to Secretary Hull, Soong was advised again that although the Russian–Japanese deal over the railway now seemed "fortunate" for China, the Chinese government still needed to settle the problem of Outer Mongolia with the Soviets.[16]

In these March conversations, Korea was also mentioned. American leaders repeatedly disclosed to Soong their confidence in the formula of international trusteeship. Conscious of the distance between Chongqing's and Washington's policies toward Korea, Soong only listened. Yet, on another occasion a few months later, Stanley Hornbeck, suspicious of Chinese intentions, raised a question about the Chinese "popular concept, from [the] point of view geographically, historically and politically, regarding Korea." Soong replied:

> [The] Chinese in no sense think of Korea as a part, or a lost part, of an existing or a once having existed Chinese empire. Nor . . . do they so think of Indo-China. . . . [The] prevalent Chinese opinion runs . . . to the idea that Korea should be put under an international trusteeship. Indo-China also, . . . the disposal of which would best be made in terms of a trusteeship.

This improvised response was the first and also the only support for the trusteeship solution in Korea expressed by a high-ranking Chinese official. The statement was certainly reassuring to American officials, but its real significance is no more than Soong's echo of his American hosts' chorus.[17]

Song Meiling seemed able to function more effectively than her older brother in presenting Chiang's views to American leaders. In early spring 1943, after living incognito for a few months in New York while receiving medical treatment, Song Meiling started her well-publicized speaking tour in the United States. Secretly, she also carried out Chiang's instructions and engaged in conversations with Roosevelt, trying to bridge the distance between the president's and her husband's thoughts with regard to American–Chinese cooperation during and after the war. Chiang Kai-shek especially instructed his wife to discuss thoroughly with Roosevelt issues pertaining to postwar settlement in East Asia. He was anxious to have some "conclusions" from these discussions. In February, Song Meiling told Harry Hopkins that the time had come for President Roosevelt to take the lead in getting the Big Four together to talk about postwar issues, promising that China would line up with the United States at the peace table. In June,

---

[16] Memorandum of conversation between Soong and Hull, 31 March 1943, *TSP*, box 30; memorandum of conversation between Soong and Roosevelt, 31 March 1943, ibid., box 32; Soong to Chiang, 2 April 1943, *ZZSC*, 3(1): 159–161.

[17] *RWK*, 5(A): 449–450, and 5(B): 370; memorandum of conversation between Soong and Welles, 29 March 1943, *FRUS, 1943: China*, 845–846; memorandum of conversation between Soong and Hornbeck, 28 September 1943, ibid., 133–137.

she reiterated to the president a desire on Chiang Kai-shek's part to establish an American–Chinese military cooperation in the western Pacific in the postwar years. Either charmed by Mrs. Chiang or just acting as a good host, Roosevelt appeared more positive than before to the Chinese proposal that America and China jointly use naval and air bases in Dalian, Port Arthur, and Taiwan in the postwar years. At the same time, the president maintained his stand that the future of Korea should be delegated to an international trusteeship including America, China, and the Soviet Union. There is no evidence that Song Meiling took any explicit stand on the issue.[18]

Like her brother, as a result of observing American politics at close range, Song Meiling was more familiar than her husband with Washington's determination to accommodate the Soviet Union in its postwar plans, though she was as disappointed as Chiang by the attitude of American leaders. At one point, Hopkins told Song Meiling in unmistakable language about Washington's attitude toward the Soviets, saying that despite their broad demands in Eastern Europe, Africa, and the Far East, President Roosevelt would be unlikely to resort to military force against the Soviets even if they occupied their neighbors' territories. Reporting this conversation to Chiang, Song Meiling observed: "[I]n the postwar years, America, Britain and Russia will immerse themselves in their own interests and they will have no scruples regarding China." She also warned Chiang against having any illusion that China would be able to get foreign aid after the war.[19] Yet, findings like this one did not lead to the reorientation of Chongqing's foreign policy. Chiang Kai-shek held to the idea of a bilateral partnership with America as tenaciously as Roosevelt wanted to accommodate the Russians.

An important omission in the pre-Cairo consultations between Chongqing and Washington was how to deal with their current enemy, Japan, after the war. The issue did emerge in the Pacific War Council in mid-1942. At a meeting of the council, T. V. Soong expressed his disapproval of the U.S. decision not to bomb the Japanese imperial palace in Tokyo, saying: "I think it's about time to remove the sacred halo with which the Japanese have almost surrounded their emperor; in other words, blow up Heaven!" President Roosevelt let the issue pass by equivocating that "without getting into postwar problems," the council might "adopt the slogan of 'Japan for the Japanese.'" Postwar Japan was hardly a subject of the surrogate

---

[18] Sterling Seagrave, *The Soong Dynasty* (New York: Harper & Row, 1985), 380–391; Chiang to Song Meiling, 18 June 1943, ZZSC, 3(1): 853–854; memorandum of conversation between Song Meiling and Hopkins, 27 February 1943, HHP, box 331; Song Meiling to Chiang, 25 June 1943, ZZSC, 3(1): 855.

[19] Song Meiling to Chiang, 24 December 1942, 2 January 1943, and January (n.d.), ZZSC, 3(1): 784–787.

diplomacy between Roosevelt and Chiang in 1942 and 1943, though in 1943 T. V. Soong did try to determine the British attitude toward the issue.[20]

An explanation for this omission is that from the early stages of their foreign policy planning for East Asia, American officials tended to regard policies toward postwar Japan as an American responsibility, not one for inter-Allied discussion.[21] And ever since Pearl Harbor, paradoxically, KMT leaders had viewed the Soviet Union, not Japan, as their most dangerous potential enemy. That was why, during her visit in the United States, Song Meiling aimed at two different targets during her public speaking tour and her secret diplomacy. When speaking to the American public, she followed Chiang Kai-shek's advice and attacked *Japan* as a long-term adversary for the American–Chinese partnership to deal with in the Pacific after the war. Yet, in her private conversations with American leaders, Song Meiling focused on the presumed *Soviet* threat in the postwar years and made extra efforts to convince the Americans of Chongqing's point of view.[22]

The Soongs' performance in Washington did not eliminate the two sides' disagreement on the Soviet Union, but they succeeded in reviving the idea of a Chiang–Roosevelt discussion on postwar issues. In the late spring and summer of 1943, Roosevelt began to warm up to the idea of having a meeting with Chiang. In early June, he asked T. V. Soong to convey a proposal to Chiang that a Big Four summit be held soon. Chiang disliked the idea on the grounds that he could not properly sit at the same meeting with Stalin, whose country was still at peace with Japan. He preferred a bilateral discussion with the president. In July, having wound up his conversations with Song Meiling, President Roosevelt became completely committed to the idea of meeting Chiang personally. Soon, through General Joseph Stilwell, he informed Chiang of his satisfaction with the discussions with Mrs. Chiang and emphasized that it was very important for them to meet in the fall at a location between Chongqing and Washington. After a few more exchanges in the following months, Roosevelt granted Chiang his wish that they and the British should hold a conference in Cairo in late November before the president met with Stalin.[23]

At one point, Hopkins expressed his opinion that the Chiangs were

[20] Memorandum by John McCrea on the eighth meeting of the Pacific War Council, 23 May 1943, *RPMF*, box 168; Soong to Chiang, 2 April 1943, *ZZSC*, 3(1): 159–161.
[21] ST minutes-16, 7 May 1943, and ST minutes-17, 12 May 1943, *RHN*, box 79.
[22] Four messages from Chiang to Song Meiling, 12 and 13 February 1943, *ZZSC*, 3(1): 790–793.
[23] Soong to Chiang, 2 April 1943, *ZZSC*, 3(1): 161; Chiang to Soong, 7 June 1943, *ZZSC*, 3(3): 491; four messages from Roosevelt to Chiang, 4 July, 28 October, 1 November, and 12 November 1943, ibid., 491–492, 494–497; minutes of conversation between Soong and Roosevelt and Hopkins, 16 July 1943, *TSP* box 32; memorandum of conversation between Soong and Hopkins, 15 September 1943, ibid., box 29.

"supreme artists in diplomatic propaganda in sucking folks in and deceiving them."[24] President Roosevelt could not be deceived by the Chinese easily. But after talking to the smooth Soongs, he might feel more optimistic than before about persuading Chiang Kai-shek to accept his ideas. After two years of cooperation in war, Chongqing and Washington already had many knots between them that needed to be untied. While the Americans remained dissatisfied with Chongqing's performance in the war, KMT leaders in Chongqing constantly complained about the unequal treatment of the Chinese government by the Western Allies in matters concerning lend-lease aid and inter-Allied consultation on common strategy. In 1943, the American, British, and Chinese governments became deadlocked in their exchanges concerning an offensive strategy in Burma. The friction between Chiang Kai-shek and General Stilwell also cast a shadow on the existing Chinese–American military collaboration. The conversations between the Soongs and American leaders in 1943 touched on all these difficulties and also seemed to have a soothing effect. There was also the issue of the KMT–CCP confrontation in China. In a conversation toward the end of August, T. V. Soong promised Roosevelt that after the war the Chinese government would have a non-Communist "but strongly socialist" policy. The president was pleased. He told Soong: "I do hope, . . . there will not be war against the 8th People's Army [sic]. There are good germs of sound socialism and democracy in those boys. You must not squander these values."[25]

Roosevelt certainly had his own reasons to meet with Chiang in 1943. In the short run, by meeting with Chiang in person, Roosevelt hoped to allay the tensions in Sino–American wartime cooperation and to pave the way for his meeting with Stalin. His long-term objective was also clear. Once Roosevelt observed to Soong: "Chiang may die . . . and still there will be China. Split she may into North and South, and still it will be China. Split into Communist and Kuomintang, China will still be China. China, . . . with her 425 millions is bound to become the strong power in the Far East and she will be the necessary adjunct to the success of our great enterprise."[26] The significance of this statement is twofold. The president acknowledged that by the time of World War II, China had reached a turning point both in its internal revolution and its foreign relations, and Western powers had to come to terms with the new China. Meanwhile, China was important to Roosevelt only because it was a "necessary adjunct" to the enterprise of the Western Allies. Therefore, the coming summit with

[24] John M. Blum, ed., *The Price of Vision: The Diary of Henry A. Wallace, 1942–1946* (Boston: Houghton Mifflin, 1973), 148.
[25] Memorandum of conversation between Soong and Roosevelt, 30 August 1943, *TSP*, box 32.
[26] Ibid.

Chiang would be an important step toward incorporating China into America's global enterprise in the postwar years.

Preparation for the summit

Symbolically, the Cairo Conference would end the old era of Chinese–Western estrangement and open a new one of equity and reciprocity in Chinese–foreign relations. Yet, as will be shown in the next chapter, the historical revision of the Chinese–Western relationship was incomplete. Although Chiang and Roosevelt were anxious to meet, they would not be able to overcome the psychological barrier between East and West that had existed for hundreds of years. The British were not even trying. At Cairo, they were reluctant participants so far as discussions with the Chinese were concerned. British Prime Minister Winston Churchill was eager to hold with Roosevelt the SEXTANT, his code name for the Cairo Conference. Having won Anglo–American unity of purpose, he would then be ready to confer with the Russians. But Churchill had no interest whatsoever in holding a discussion with Chiang Kai-shek. Churchill merely went along with the president's idea of meeting with the Chinese. He only thinly concealed his contempt for the Chinese. In a communication to Roosevelt, Churchill assured the president that the British authorities in the Middle East would prepare satisfactory accommodations for the three powers' delegations; then he added insolently that for Chiang Kai-shek, to whom he referred as "Celestes," he had gotten "an option on Tutankhamen's tomb."[27]

The Cairo Conference was built on ambiguous diplomacy from its preparatory stages. Between June and November, despite their commitment to a summit, the American and Chinese governments failed to work out a common agenda. To a large extent, this was due to Chiang Kai-shek's mistake. In mid-September, Harry Hopkins told T. V. Soong that the forthcoming conference between Roosevelt and Chiang ought to result in an agreement confirming the two governments' "specific commitments" to each other in the future. Therefore, Hopkins emphasized, it was imperative for the two sides to prepare a common agenda in advance. But Chiang Kai-shek disliked the idea. Earlier, when Soong had made a similar suggestion to Chiang on his own initiative, Chiang retorted that a preconference agenda would be superfluous because he and the president might well discuss topics of common interest face to face. After Soong informed Hopkins of Chiang's objection, the Americans did not press the issue

[27] Warren F. Kimball, ed., *Churchill and Roosevelt: The Complete Correspondence* (Princeton, NJ: Princeton University Press, 1984), 2: 562, 566, 576, 585, 577–578. Tutankhamen was an Egyptian pharaoh who began his reign about 1358 B.C.

further.[28] No matter what Chiang's true intention might have been, the consequence was that when preparing separately for the conference, Chongqing and Washington had general ideas about each other's attitudes toward postwar issues but did not know their counterpart's exact intentions about the conference.

Chiang's conference preparation was carried out by the National Military Council and the Supreme Council of National Defense. T. V. Soong's Waijiaobu was excluded from the process. This amounted to a disgrace for Soong and a disappointment to Washington, especially after Hopkins explicitly expressed his wish that Soong accompany Chiang to the summit. On the eve of the Cairo Conference, T. V. Soong was suddenly dropped from the front line of Chinese diplomacy. In President Roosevelt's words, Soong fell "out of the good graces of the Generalissimo [Chiang]."[29] This development tended to render the outcome of the forthcoming summit even more unpredictable.

Contemplating his first meeting with the Western Allies, Chiang established certain specific objectives. He wanted to end the conference with a communiqué including the following items: (1) the application of the Atlantic Charter to the whole world; (2) an "unconditional victory" over Japan; (3) China's recovery of Manchuria and Taiwan; (4) Korean independence plus the redefinition of the status of Asian countries such as Indochina, Thailand, Burma, and Malaya; (5) a new international peace organization, (6) a combined chiefs of staff for military operations in the Pacific, and (7) American financial aid to China during the war, along with Sino–American economic cooperation in the postwar years. Chiang also needed an understanding with the American government to arrange for the two countries' postwar strategic cooperation. In his view, China's continental location required that its national defense focus on the Asian mainland. On the high seas, China had neither the ability nor the intention to compete with America and Britain. Therefore, in Chiang's view, a sound security system in the Asian–Pacific region should include China's responsibility for the continent and America's responsibility for the ocean. Responsibility for air defense in the region should be divided in the same manner. Chiang showed special concern about the situation of northwestern China in his defense system. At the time, the CCP had its stronghold in the region and Soviet influence was ominous in Xinjiang. So far as postwar control over Japan was concerned, Chiang preferred to defer responsibility completely to the United States. Curiously, in his instructions to his planning staff, Chiang

---

[28] Memorandum of conversation between Soong and Hopkins, 15 September 1943, *TSP*, box 29; Chiang to Soong, 21 July 1943, *ZZSC*, 3(3): 492–493.

[29] Memoranda of conversations between Soong and Hopkins, 5 and 15 September 1943, *TSP*, box 29; Joseph W. Esherick, ed., *Lost Chance in China: The World War II Despatches of John W. Service* (New York: Random House, 1974), 79; Roosevelt to Summerlin, 30 December 1943, *RPPF* 2907.

did not discuss the status of Manchuria in China's defense system. This might have reflected Chiang's uncertainty about whether he would be able to rely on America's cooperation in curbing Soviet ambitions in the area.[30]

Following Chiang's instructions, the National Military Council and the Supreme Council of National Defense separately prepared several programs to cover the Chinese government's attitudes toward general principles in world peace settlement, postwar treatment of Japan, and American–Chinese bilateral cooperation. For general peace, the Chinese government supported the modish ideas of the time, such as self-determination of nations and a new world organization for peace. To manifest China's Asian identity, the principle of racial equality was also included. Chongqing's postwar policy toward Japan focused on retribution: China would recover lost territories and receive reparations from Japan. In Asia and the Pacific, Japan must withdraw from all territories seized since September 1931; return to China Manchuria, Taiwan, the Pescadores, and the Ryukyu Islands; and restore Korea's independence. The Chinese programs especially emphasized that China's sovereignty in Manchuria must also include Dalian, Port Arthur, and the railways in the area. For the Ryukyu Islands, depending on circumstances, Chongqing could afford to be flexible to the extent of accepting international control. Chongqing intended to demand that Japan pay reparations for the Chinese people's and government's losses since the Mukden Incident. Part of the reparations could be paid in kind by transferring to China Japan's merchant fleet, aircraft, weapons, and other war materials. So far as the postwar control of Japan was concerned, the Chinese programs only proposed some general measures. It was suggested that the Allied forces occupy Japan for a number of years and that an inter-Allied supervision committee be placed in charge. Disarmament, trial of war criminals, and dissolution of jingoist organizations should also be carried out in postwar Japan. What was missing from these programs was a definition of China's role in postwar Japan.[31]

So far as China's relations with the other Allied powers were concerned, these programs only paid lip service to the unity among the Big Four. Meanwhile, Chongqing would call on the other big powers to take unlikely actions. For instance, the Chinese programs proposed a four-power declaration on Indian independence, which could not possibly be accepted by London. On the other hand, Chongqing did not intend to use the conference to discuss with the British such thorny issues as Hong Kong and Tibet. The Chinese programs also called for the Big Four's immediate

---

[30] Zhang Qiyun, *Zhonghua Minguo Shigang* (A Historical Outline of the Republic of China) (Taipei: Zhonghua Wenhua Chuban Shiye Weiyuanhui, 1956), 7: 130, 152.

[31] Program for the Cairo Conference prepared by the Counsellors Office of the National Military Council for Chiang, November 1943 (n.d.), ZZSC, 3(3): 498–501; three programs for the Cairo Conference prepared by the secretariat of the Supreme Council of National Defense for Chiang, November 1943 (n.d.), ibid., 503–506.

recognition of Korean independence and their commitment to guarantee that independence after the war. In this regard, the Chinese government really sought the other three Allies' endorsement for its protégé, the KPG.

KMT leaders viewed the Cairo Conference more as an opportunity for China to strengthen its relationship with the United States than to contribute to the harmony among the Big Four. They expected Washington's commitment to continuing American military aid to their government in the postwar years, which would enable the KMT government to possess powerful land, air, and naval forces trained and equipped by the United States. The Chinese programs also made American assistance a vital condition for China's postwar economic rehabilitation and industrialization. At Cairo, American leaders would be asked to agree to help China stabilize its currency, rebuild its industrial and transportation systems, develop new vital heavy industries, and train various technical personnel. The KMT expected not only American capital in large volume but also American "war surplus," including merchant ships, trains, automobiles, airplanes, and machines. Chinese policymakers believed that an "American surplus for the China market" formula would make the Cairo arrangement beneficial to the United States as well. This formula simply repeated what Chiang had already told Currie and Willkie. The assumption was that after the war, although China would need American capital and technology for industrialization, the American economy would also need China's enormous market and untapped resources to avert its own difficulties in the process of postwar demobilization.[32]

Not all the topics listed in these programs were to be discussed at Cairo. Unwilling to be limited to a preconference common agenda with the U.S. government, Chiang would find it necessary to make some last-minute revisions in the Chinese programs on his arrival in Cairo. Therefore, these programs reflect the distance between Chongqing's expectations and the reality of the Cairo Conference. Chinese officials expected that the conference would be comprehensive and definite so far as the postwar settlement in East Asia was concerned. They had very high hopes of achieving some concrete results in terms of postwar American–Chinese military and economic cooperation. They also expected China to emerge from the conference a champion of racial equality in world affairs. Briefly, the KMT regime treated the coming meeting at Cairo as a quasi-peace conference for East Asia, something that it was not to be.

Whatever else would characterize the Chinese programs, the actual policy of the Chinese government at the Cairo Conference depended on Chiang Kai-shek's own performance. Before Cairo, however, Chiang was in an anguished mood. Conscious of his weakness, Chiang was troubled about

---

[32] Minutes of conversation between Chiang and Currie, 15 February 1941, ZZSC, 3(1): 558–561; minutes of conversation between Chiang and Willkie, 5 October 1942, ibid., 760–775.

how to present himself in his first meeting with the leaders of the two most powerful Western countries, which not long before had been among China's imperialist foes and whose recent friendship with China remained frail. A few days before the conference, Chiang entered into his diary these sentences:

> I will talk with Roosevelt and Churchill in accordance with a spirit of demanding nothing and offering nothing. I am going to exchange opinions frankly with them on military, political and economic affairs, not being troubled by any anxiety about gains and losses. . . .
>
> My orientation for the coming meeting with Roosevelt and Churchill ought to be one of seeking no fame and wealth but self-sufficiency. Not expecting benevolence from the others, I can avoid inviting humiliation. I'll also avoid taking the initiative on the issues like disposal of Japan and Japan's compensation for China's losses, and wait for the Americans and the British to make the first move. Then, Britain and America will be able to appreciate and respect our selfless stance in this world war.[33]

Clearly, on the eve of Cairo, Chiang was more troubled by the question of how to impress the Western leaders with his fair motives than how to achieve the objectives listed in his programs. It is interesting to note that before Cairo, President Roosevelt expressed his concern to T. V. Soong about the language barrier between himself and Chiang. He wished Chiang Kai-shek to master at least 800 English words. But at Cairo, where Chiang tried to surround himself with a wall of alleged oriental virtues, Roosevelt would not be able to penetrate the Chinese leader even with the help of the fluent English-speaking Song Meiling.[34]

Despite the State Department's work in foreign policy planning for East Asia, such efforts were bypassed by President Roosevelt in his preparation for the Cairo Conference. Roosevelt's own preparation was anything but systematic. In 1943, the U.S. secretaries of State, War, and the Navy unanimously agreed that they had a common difficulty in maintaining communication with their chief relative to international matters. In the words of Secretary of War Henry Stimson, people who "used the back door of the White House" more freely than himself occupied most of the president's time.[35] In the fall of 1943, Sumner Welles was one of the few persons with whom Roosevelt tested his ideas about the coming summits at Cairo and Teheran. At the time, however, Welles had already resigned from his under-secretary position in the State Department. Welles later recalled that on that occasion the president mentioned to him all the principles that would appear in the Cairo Communiqué governing the postwar settlement of East Asia. But what impressed him most was Roosevelt's desire to achieve a "meeting of minds" with Stalin. Although,

[33] *CZM*, 8: 108–109.
[34] Memorandum of conversation between Soong and Roosevelt, 30 August 1943, *TSP*, box 32.
[35] Entry of 4 May 1943, *HSD*, 43 (reel 8): 12–13.

in Welles's opinion, Chiang Kai-shek was the only one among Chongqing's leading figures unknown to the Americans, Roosevelt did not seem to anticipate difficulties from him.[36] In his postwar memoirs, Secretary of State Hull complained that he received information on the Cairo and Teheran conferences only after these events from sources other than the president. Yet before leaving for Cairo, the president talked at least once with Hull about the forthcoming conferences. That discussion took place in early November, soon after Hull returned from the inter-Allied conference of foreign ministers in Moscow. From Hull's recollection, what can be learned about their conversation is that the president talked more than he listened.[37]

At least Harry Hopkins once contemplated using the State Department's personnel in planning for the Cairo Conference. In September, when talking to T. V. Soong about an American–Chinese common agenda for the conference, Hopkins solicited Soong's opinion on who in the State Department was "the proper person to be the American spokesman in preparing these topics for discussion [at Cairo]." To Hopkins's surprise, Soong mentioned Dean Acheson. During the war, Acheson served as Assistant Secretary of State for Economic Affairs and had no special knowledge of Chinese affairs. So far as Acheson's views of Far Eastern affairs were concerned, in the State Department he was known for his hard-line orientation toward Japan before and after Pearl Harbor. Acheson was also not among those officials who advocated the use of American aid as leverage for applying pressure on Chongqing to carry out reforms. These might have been the qualities in Acheson that Soong appreciated, but they were not what Hopkins wanted. Hopkins rejected Soong's notion, saying: "The trouble is that he [Acheson] does not understand much about China." At this point, Soong made it clear that the Chinese government would not want Joseph Ballantine, one of Secretary Hull's three "ranking Far Eastern experts," to handle the issue because he was "essentially an expert on Japan." The other two "ranking experts" were Stanley Hornbeck and Maxwell Hamilton. Soong did not mention their names, probably because he knew that although their attitudes toward Chongqing were more favorable than those of many other Far Eastern officials in the State Department, their influence was in decline.[38] It is not clear whether Hopkins reported his conversation with Soong to Roosevelt. If he did, it would

[36] Sumner Welles, *Where Are We Heading?* (New York: Harper, 1946), 28–30; Welles, *The Time for Decision* (New York: Harper, 1944), 283.

[37] Hull, *Memoirs*, 2: 1110, 1313. Kimball comments in *Churchill and Roosevelt*, 2: 572, that Roosevelt deliberately used his meeting with Hull to delay his own departure for Cairo in order to avoid meeting with Churchill prior to the formal Cairo talks.

[38] Memorandum of conversation between Soong and Hopkins, 15 September 1943, *TSP*, box 29; David S. McLellan, *Dean Acheson: The State Department Years* (New York: Dodd, Mead, 1976), 44–46, 52; Paul A. Varg, *The Closing of the Door: Sino–American Relations, 1936–1946* (East Lansing: Michigan State University Press, 1973), 96–97; Hull, *Memoirs*, 1: 894–895; May, *China Scapegoat*, 91–93.

certainly not have encouraged the president to delegate the preparatory tasks for the Cairo Conference to the State Department. Hopkins never found his "proper person" in the State Department. Before leaving for Cairo, President Roosevelt asked the State Department only for some memoranda on the formula of trusteeship and on postwar aviation policies to read.[39]

Heading toward his 1943 summit meetings, President Roosevelt tried to sort out his agenda only when his party was halfway to Cairo. Between November 15 and 19, aboard the presidential warship U.S.S. *Iowa*, Roosevelt instructed the military advisers of the Joint Chiefs of Staff to prepare the conference agenda for him. The result was three lists of questions for the president to discuss separately with the Chinese, the British, and the Russians. Roosevelt's military advisers did not venture beyond their areas of responsibility and, inevitably, these lists gave high priority to military issues. In fact, only the list for Roosevelt's meeting with Chiang Kai-shek included questions of postwar significance. These were (1) the possibility of Chinese participation in the occupation of Japan and China's recovery of territories seized by Japan; (2) arrangements for American–Chinese cooperation on mutual security; (3) military bases in the Pacific to be made available to both parties for mutual assistance; (4) the extent of American military commitment for peace in the Orient; (5) continuing American military aid to China in the postwar period; and (6) a mechanism for military consultation between America and China in the event of future aggression in the Orient. The Joint Chiefs of Staff planners proposed that these postwar problems be discussed only if they were brought up by the Chinese.[40]

Aboard the *Iowa*, Roosevelt and his aides (Hopkins, Admiral William D. Leahy, Admiral Ernest J. King, General George C. Marshall, General Henry H. Arnold, and Rear Admiral Wilson Brown) only briefly discussed postwar issues in the Asian–Pacific region. Although his military advisers thought it wise to avoid postwar issues at Cairo, Roosevelt knew that a discussion of them with Chiang would be inevitable. He predicted that China's claims in Manchuria and Outer Mongolia would be troublesome topics in his meeting with Chiang. Without giving further elaboration, however, Roosevelt expressed confidence that the Chinese–Soviet territorial disagreements could be resolved "on the basis of free zones." Perhaps

[39] Stettinius to Roosevelt, 9 November 1943, *FRUS: The Conferences at Cairo and Teheran, 1943*, 167–171 (hereafter cited as *FRUS: Cairo and Teheran*); memorandum of conversation between Roosevelt and officials of the State and War departments, 11 November 1943, ibid., 177–179.

[40] Minutes of meeting between Roosevelt and members of the Joint Chiefs of Staff, aboard the U.S.S. *Iowa*, 15 November 1943, *FRUS: Cairo and Teheran*, 194–199; paper prepared by the Joint Chiefs planners on President Roosevelt's agenda at Cairo and Teheran, aboard the U.S.S. *Iowa*, n.d., ibid., 245–246.

misled by his conversations with the Soongs, the president also reported that Chiang Kai-shek "desires" an American–Chinese–Soviet trusteeship for Korea. His other presumption was that "the Chinese will undoubtedly want to take part in the occupation of Japan." Roosevelt also expressed his conviction that the Mandated Islands in the Pacific should be removed from Japanese control and placed under the authority of the United Nations, with American occupation of the military bases there. The Chinese, the president informed those present, also wanted Formosa and the Bonins (the latter were mistaken for the Pescadores). At this point, Hopkins commented that, if requested, the Chinese would be willing to allow the United States to use bases in Formosa. President Roosevelt agreed but pointed out that Chiang would agree to grant such right to America only on a temporary basis.[41] Apparently, Roosevelt thought that he knew Chongqing's intentions well and expected no surprises at Cairo.

[41] Discussion aboard U.S.S. *Iowa* of proposed agenda for President Roosevelt's conferences with Chiang, Churchill, and Stalin, n.d., *FRUS: Cairo and Teheran*, 257–259.

6

A divisive summit

In late 1943, there were both favorable and unfavorable developments in the American–Chinese relationship that might affect the atmosphere of their first summit conference. Favorable developments included the Western Allies' agreement to abrogate their old treaties with China earlier in the year and China's inclusion among the signatories of the Moscow Declaration that clarified the leading Allies' general war aims and their intention to cooperate after the war. Both events symbolically lifted China from its traditionally dire diplomatic situation to an equal status with the leading Allied powers. Otherwise, Chongqing continued to perform poorly in the war. The relationship between Chiang Kai-shek and his American chief of staff, General Joseph Stilwell, also became more and more irritating to both governments. These developments formed the background for the summit between Roosevelt and Chiang Kai-shek and made events at Cairo and afterward, in one historian's opinion, "counterpoints of military and political decision-making of [the] highest order."[1]

Although students of World War II have long been aware that the conference did not improve the Chinese–American military relationship, they have rarely questioned the political achievements of the summit. The conferees' agreement on postwar settlement in East Asia, which would lead to China's recovery of lost territories from Japan and the removal of the Japanese Empire in the Pacific, seemed to reduce their frustrations over the alliance for war. As summarized deftly by one historian, when the British, American, and Chinese military authorities at Cairo still debated

[1] Cordell Hull, *Memoirs of Cordell Hull* (New York: Macmillan, 1948), 2: 1256–1258, 1306–1307; Michael Schaller, *The U.S. Crusade in China, 1938–1945* (New York: Columbia University Press, 1979), 104–105, 109–110, 125–145; Wm. Roger Louis, *Imperialism at Bay: The United States and the Decolonization of the British Empire, 1941–1945* (New York: Oxford University Press, 1978), 274–275.

the priority of the Asian theater in the global war, Roosevelt and Chiang redrew the political map of the Far East.[2] But the American–Chinese agreements at Cairo with regard to postwar disposition of the Japanese Empire were far from definite. Furthermore, the undercurrent of the Chiang–Roosevelt disagreement with regard to the Soviet Union also prevented the two leaders from launching an effective and solid American–Chinese partnership in international affairs.

A thorough analysis of the political aspect of the Cairo Conference is still hindered by lack of documentation. The key political discussion between Roosevelt and Chiang took place on the evening of 23 November 1943. Also present were Harry Hopkins and Song Meiling. This meeting was followed by a number of brief political sessions of a supplementary nature.[3] In keeping with Roosevelt's wishes, American participants in these meetings did not keep any records. Two months before his summit trip to Cairo and Teheran, President Roosevelt directed the State Department to refrain from publishing the records of the Big Four meetings at Paris in *1919*. He opposed publication of these records for fear that readers would be likely to "draw untrue conclusions and parallels between 1919 and 1943." He told Secretary Hull that the minutes of those meetings should never have been recorded in the first place because "four people cannot be conversationally frank with each other if somebody is taking down notes for future publication."[4] Strangely, in all the summit meetings that he held with the other Allied leaders afterward, Roosevelt thoroughly objected to record keeping only when he conferred with Chiang Kai-shek at Cairo. Consequently, the only available American impression of the Roosevelt–Chiang meetings appears in a book by Elliott Roosevelt, the president's son, published in 1946, based on Roosevelt's alleged recollections of his meetings with Chiang.

In 1956, the KMT government in Taiwan provided the State Department with a "summary record" of the Roosevelt–Chiang conversation on 23 November 1943. The basis of this record remains obscure. The Chiangs were the only Chinese participants at the meeting, and Chiang's wife served as the interpreter. Therefore, any Chinese record must have been based either on notes taken by Song Meiling during the session or on the Chiangs' later recollections of the meeting. The authenticity of both Elliott Roosevelt's account and the Chinese summary record has been questioned by historians, but these have also been the principal sources of information on

[2] Louis, *Imperialism at Bay*, 280.
[3] Log of the Cairo Conference presented by Wang Chonghui to Chiang, n.d., *ZZSC*, 3(3): 508–525; editorial notes on Roosevelt–Chiang meetings, 25 and 26 November, Roosevelt–Chiang–Churchill meeting, 26 November, and Hopkins–Chiang meeting, 26 November 1943, *FRUS: Cairo and Teheran*, 349–350, 366–367.
[4] Roosevelt to Hull, 16 September 1943, *RPSF*, box 74.

which the existing literature is based.[5] In 1981, the KMT government in Taipei published a document collection, *Zhonghua Minguo Zhongyao Shiliao Chubian: Dui Ri Kangzhan Shiqi* (Preliminary Compilation of Important Historical Records of the Republic of China: The Period of the War of Resistance Against Japan), which makes available additional documents concerning the Roosevelt–Chiang summit. Other documents pertaining to the conference have also emerged from American archives. Supported by these documents, a reassessment of the political aspect of the Cairo Conference can now be attempted.

A common agenda

Without a common agenda for their summit, both the Americans and the Chinese at Cairo were sure to be surprised. No sooner had the Chinese made their initial contact with Western leaders than Chiang Kai-shek decided to make some important changes in his original plans. On the afternoon of 22 November, Harry Hopkins paid a visit to the Chinese delegation and made arrangements for the Roosevelt–Chiang meeting the next evening. What Hopkins told the Chinese cannot be documented. But judging from the behavior of the Chinese afterward, it is reasonable to speculate that on the basis of the brief discussion between Roosevelt and his aides aboard the U.S.S. *Iowa*, Hopkins may have informed the Chinese of what the president expected to discuss with Chiang. In view of his concern about having a Sino–American common agenda for the conference, it is plausible that Hopkins made a last-ditch effort to reduce the uncertainty about the first American–Chinese summit.[6] At that point, Chiang Kai-shek and his staff must have realized the gap between their own extensive program and the Americans' highly selective agenda. Consequently, Wang Chonghui and Guo Binjia, a counsellor from the Waijiaobu, were put to work to abbreviate and restructure the original Chinese program.

The two accomplished their task in haste, and the next morning they presented to Chiang four memoranda. These covered separately Chongqing's attitude toward a postwar international peace organization, worldwide

---

[5] Elliott Roosevelt's account of the Roosevelt–Chiang meetings is in his book *As He Saw It* (New York: Duell, Sloan & Pearce, 1946), 158–159, 164–166, 204. The Chinese "summary record" is published in *FRUS: Cairo and Teheran*, 322–325. Louis, *Imperialism at Bay*, 18–21 and Keith Sainsbury, *The Turning Points: Roosevelt, Stalin, Churchill, and Chiang Kai-Shek [sic], 1943: The Moscow, Cairo, and Teheran Conferences* (New York: Oxford University Press, 1985), 188–191, raise questions about the reliability of Elliott's account of the president's statements at Cairo, though they also acknowledge that it may be accurate in certain aspects. The latter work also suggests that the Chinese record may have been doctored.

[6] Log of the Cairo Conference, n.d., ZZSC, 3(3): 514.

security arrangements, conditions affecting Germany's surrender, and peace settlements in East Asia. Among the general principles for world peace organization and international security, racial equality was deleted lest it cause difficulties for the summit. The subject of Germany was added not because the Chinese government had any particular policy to discuss with the Western Allies, but because Chongqing, now one of the Big Four, wanted to be notified of any Allied decision with regard to Germany that might later become a precedent for the peace settlement in Asia. Although the memorandum on East Asia was basically a condensed version of the original programs, an important addition was made with respect to inter-Allied administrative arrangements for "liberated territories." It indicated the Chinese leaders' expectation that certain Chinese territories to be recovered from Japan might possibly be liberated by Allied forces other than the Chinese. Intended for Chiang Kai-shek's use in his discussion with President Roosevelt, all four documents were translated into English.[7]

Yet even these compact programs proved too much for Chiang to handle. On the morning of 23 November, during their first formal session on military affairs, Chiang and Churchill disagreed sharply over the projected Burma campaign while Roosevelt remained aloof, not taking sides. Disheartened by this experience, Chiang became more anxious than ever to obtain some positive results in the political arena. For this he needed a more focused agenda.[8] Shortly before his meeting with Roosevelt that evening, Chiang told his staff assistants that unlike the Soviet–Western relationship, long-term cooperation between China and the Anglo–American powers would not pose serious problems. There was therefore no need for the three governments to devote precious time at Cairo to general principles. Instead, he wanted to use the opportunity to reach a "definite understanding" with the American and British leaders over just two issues. First, he would continue to work for readjustment of the Allied military strategy against Japan, which meant raising the levels of British and American action in the war against Japan. Second, he would try to obtain a conclusive agreement with the Western Allies over postwar punishment for Japan and the eventual disposition of its empire. All other issues, Chiang decided, could either be dealt with tentatively during the conference or included in some aide-mémoires to the Western Allies for future consideration. Consequently, in his meeting with Roosevelt that evening, Chiang did not use the four memoranda. They were to be handed to Harry Hopkins by Wang Chonghui the next day as Chiang's informal opinions.

[7] Memoranda by the Chinese government, 24 November 1943, *FRUS: Cairo and Teheran*, 387–389; "Zhengzhi wenti huishang jingguo" (Course of the Consultations on Political Issues), appendix (1) to the log of the Cairo Conference, n.d., ZZSC, 3(3): 525–527.
[8] "Junshi wenti huishang jingguo" (Course of the Consultations on Military Matters), appendix (2) to the log of the Cairo Conference, n.d., ZZSC, 3(3): 535–538; minutes of the plenary meeting on 23 November 1943, *FRUS: Cairo and Teheran*, 311–315.

Later, the Chinese would solicit President Roosevelt's comments on these documents without avail.[9]

This is not to say that Chiang went to his first meeting with President Roosevelt lacking an agenda. After making the decision to shelve the four memoranda, Chiang instructed his aides to prepare a new agenda to meet his desire for "selecting topics from the original [four] memoranda according to their relative importance." Hence a fifth memorandum was drafted. This time, the drafting officers closely consulted Hopkins's information about American leaders' discussion aboard the *Iowa*. The fact that the fifth memorandum was also translated into English indicates that, like the previous four documents, it was prepared not merely as a guide to Chiang but also as a proposal to be presented to President Roosevelt.[10] The striking resemblance between the items listed and the language used in the published Chinese "summary record" of the Roosevelt–Chiang meeting and the "fifth memorandum" leaves no doubt that the two leaders in their discussion used the latter as a common agenda.

The Roosevelt–Chiang meeting on the evening of 23 November lasted three hours. A Chinese log of the Cairo Conference published by Taipei in 1981 asserts that only oral exchanges occurred at this meeting, and Chiang Kai-shek did not provide the Americans with any written proposal.[11] Yet the existence of the fifth memorandum suggests differently. Although the memorandum can confirm the Chinese summary record with regard to what subjects were discussed between Chiang and Roosevelt, the resemblance between the wording of the two documents tends to cast serious doubts on the conventional impression of the meeting based on the summary record.[12] A point-by-point comparison of the two documents is illuminating.

---

[9] "Zhengzhi wenti huishang jingguo," ZZSC, 3(3): 527–529; memoranda by the Chinese government, 24 November 1943, *FRUS: Cairo and Teheran*, 387–389.

[10] "Zhengzhi wenti huishang jingguo," ZZSC, 3(3): 527. In the late 1940s, while working on his book, *Roosevelt and Hopkins: An Intimate History*, Robert Sherwood encountered the fifth memorandum in the Harry Hopkins papers. He listed the document in his catalog for the Hopkins papers as a "memorandum setting forth Chinese desires." But obviously, Sherwood did not ponder the importance of the document, and, of course, he could not compare the document with the Chinese summary record which would not be published until 1961. See item 18, Sherwood Catalog, Book III: Teheran (A), p. 3, *HHP*, box 297.

[11] "Zhengzhi wenti huishang jingguo," ZZSC, 3(3): 527.

[12] Notably, the ZZSC does not include a Chinese version of the summary record; nor does it hint at the existence of such a record, even though to date it is the most authoritative and complete publication of Chinese official documents on the period. Liang Jingtong, a scholar who had access to unpublished official documents of the KMT government in Taiwan, mentioned in his *Kailuo Huiyi* (The Cairo Conference) (Taipei: Taiwan Shangwu Yinshuguan, 1978), 87, that Dong Xianguang (Hollington Tung) kept a ten-point record of the Chiang–Roosevelt meeting. At Cairo, Dong was handling the press for the Chinese delegation and also served as Chiang's interpreter for daily matters. It is therefore possible that having returned from their meeting with the president, the Chiangs asked Dong to

Disposition of Japan

The first item in the fifth memorandum concerned "Chinese participation on [an] equal footing in all deliberations, decisions and machinery
of the Four Powers Group acting as such." According to the summary
record, President Roosevelt suggested and Chiang concurred that "China
should take her place as one of the Big Four and participate on [an]
equal footing in the machinery of the Big Four Group and in all its decisions." Therefore, what according to the summary record represented a
Roosevelt initiative was actually a simple endorsement by the president
of the idea already in the fifth memorandum.[13] In principle, this was a
subject on which the two leaders were able to reach agreement readily,
though in practice the two governments had different definitions of what
"equal footing" meant for China's wartime relations with the other three
Allies.

The second item in the memorandum concerned armistice terms with
Japan and included three issues: "(1) deposition of [the] Japanese Imperial
House, (2) Chinese participation in [the] occupation of Japan, [and] (3)
part compensation [to China] by transfer of Japanese industrial plants,
shipping, rolling stock, etc." As alleged in the summary record, Chiang
and Roosevelt discussed the same three issues in the same sequence. The
impression created by the record is that the president took the initiative in
asking Chiang's view on whether the Japanese emperor should be removed
after the war. Yet, considering Roosevelt's cautious attitude toward the
subject during the deliberations of the Pacific War Council, as treated in
the previous chapter, here he might have, in reality, merely raised a question about the wisdom of deposing the Japanese emperor by the Allies, as
prescribed by Chiang's fifth memorandum. According to the record, Chiang
responded to the president's question with a moderate hands-off policy
toward the issue of the form of Japanese government. Having decided to
include the deposition policy in the memorandum in the first place, however, what Chiang actually said was more radical.

This judgment can be supported by Chiang's New Year's message of 1
January 1944, in which he recalled his discussion with Roosevelt in these
words:

prepare a memorandum based on their still fresh memory. Dong's own recollections of the
Cairo Conference in his *Dong Xianguang Zizhuan* (Autobiography of Dong Xianguang)
(Taipei: Xinsheng Baoshe, 1973), 192–195, remain silent on the episode. Surprisingly,
although he extensively used the then unpublished archival materials on the Cairo Conference in Taiwan, in his work Liang did not use the alleged Dong record but instead cited
the content of the summary record as if it were of American origin.

[13] Unless otherwise indicated, the comparison between the two documents is based on the
Chinese summary record as published in *FRUS: Cairo and Teheran*, 323–325, and an
undated memorandum of Chinese origin, the fifth memorandum in this discussion, located
in Hopkins papers, box 331: Book 8: Teheran (A) En Route: First Cairo Meeting.

It is my opinion that all the Japanese militarists must be wiped out and the Japanese political system must be purged of every vestige of aggressive elements. As to what form of government Japan should adopt, that question can better be left to the awakened and repentant Japanese people to decide for themselves. . . . If the Japanese people should rise in a revolution to punish their war mongers and to overthrow their militarist government, we should respect their spontaneous will and allow them to choose their own form of government.[14]

This was the first authoritative public statement on Japan's political future ever made by the Chinese government. Clearly, the intended emphasis of the statement was to incite a political revolution in Japan *during* the war, not simply to promise the Japanese that *after* the war they would have the freedom to choose their own form of government. Such a stand was more flexible on the question of the imperial house of Japan than the deposition policy in the fifth memorandum at Cairo. Chiang's change of attitude may have been caused only by whatever opinion President Roosevelt voiced at that meeting. In essence, however, Chiang's statement did not depart from Chongqing's wartime policy toward Japan, which included the goal of fomenting turmoil in Japan in order to expedite Japan's defeat. Wang Pengsheng, one of Chiang's top advisers on Japanese affairs, had been in charge of certain special operations for this purpose for some time.[15]

Another conceivable inspiration for Chiang's stand on the issue of Japan's postwar government came, interestingly, from an American source. A month before the Cairo Conference, Ambassador Wellington Koo dispatched to Chiang a report of a recent conversation between himself and Stanley Hornbeck. On that occasion, Koo told Hornbeck that the British might favor retaining the Japanese emperor after the war lest his removal cause chaos in Japan. Hornbeck remarked: "The issue of the Japanese Emperor's removal or retention should be left to the Japanese themselves to decide. But if the Japanese people will rise and want to overthrow the emperor, the Allied powers need not to support the [Japanese] Imperial House." On the British concern for preventing anarchy in postwar Japan, Hornbeck continued: "In the future Japan will survive in isolation in its own home islands, and its stability or anarchy will have no important effect to the world."[16]

[14] Chinese Ministry of Information, *The Collected Wartime Messages of Generalissimo Chiang Kai-shek, 1937–1945* (New York: John Day, 1946), 779.

[15] Zhu Jiahua to Chiang, 29 April 1940, *HDYS*, 551–552. In one of the earlier four memoranda, Chongqing's stand on the issue was less explicit but just as clear as in the fifth memorandum: postwar treatment of Japan should be decided according to the same principles used with regard to Italy that had been established by the Moscow Conference of Allied Foreign Ministers in October 1943. These principles included complete destruction of fascism in Italy and the Italian people's right to establish new governmental and other institutions based on democratic principles. See the memoranda by the Chinese government, 24 November 1943, *FRUS: Cairo and Teheran*, 389; Hull, *Memoirs*, 2: 1284.

[16] Koo to Chiang and Soong, 15 November 1943, *WKP*, box 57.

The resemblance between Chiang's statement and Hornbeck's comment is easily recognizable. Yet there was also an important difference between the two. Ready to disregard Japan as an important force in international politics, Hornbeck supported unconditional freedom for the Japanese to choose their government *after* the war, and he could not care less about the chaotic situation in Japan that might result from the emperor's removal. But Chiang was actively seeking a revolution in Japan *now* to end China's predicament. In his thinking, the Japanese had to earn the right to choose their own form of government by launching such a revolution.[17]

The next item in both the fifth memorandum and the summary record was China's role in a postwar military occupation of Japan. According to the record, President Roosevelt suggested that China play "the leading role in the postwar military occupation of Japan." In this regard, the president was not only contradicting the opinion of the State Department but was also inconsistent with himself. In mid-1942, speaking to Soviet Foreign Minister Vyacheslav Molotov, the president had advocated the idea that in the postwar years the Big Four, including China, should perform the duty of policing the world. Yet he also stated: "[I]t was [sic] not clear whether they [the Chinese] could [sic] set up a strong central government adequate to act as a policeman for Japan. Only events can determine that." In March 1943, when peddling his China policy to British Foreign Secretary Anthony Eden, Roosevelt came back to the subject, saying that "China might become a very useful power in the Far East to help police Japan." Eden expressed his doubts exactly as Roosevelt had expressed his own to Molotov.[18] China's supplementary role in America's postwar control of Japan was one thing; its "leading role" was quite another. Therefore, by making the suggestion at Cairo, the president might have intended to bolster Chiang's morale by embellishing China's role, or perhaps he was simply launching a trial balloon to encourage Chiang to disclose his intention about China's role in postwar Japan.

Never before had Chiang seriously considered his government's military responsibilities overseas. Occupation of Japan was included in Chiang's original programs for Cairo, but only the fifth memorandum explicitly

[17] In the postwar years, in a different international environment, commentators in Taiwan adopted the interpretation that at Cairo Chiang Kai-shek favored preserving the Japanese imperial institution and was instrumental in persuading the American government to adopt the same orientation. See Zhang Qun, *Wo yu Riben Qishi Nian* (I and Japan for Seventy Years) (Taipei: Zhong Ri Guanxi Yanjiuhui, 1980), 17; Pu Xuefeng, "Wo guo dangnian duiyu zhanhou Riben tianhuang zhidu zhi lichang" (Wartime Policy of Our Government Toward the Postwar Status of the Japanese Imperial Institution), *ZW*, 28 (1976): 6: 51–53; Liang, *Kailuo Huiyi*, 111–112.
[18] Memorandum on the conversation between Roosevelt and Molotov on 29 May 1942, *HHP*, box 311; memorandum on the meetings between Roosevelt and Eden, 22 March 1943, ibid., box 329.

indicated China's participation. This may have been added to the memorandum by Chiang's aides at Cairo in order to keep abreast of American intentions as conveyed by Hopkins on 22 November. But Chiang was not prepared for Roosevelt's promotion of China in such a manner. After the meeting, Chiang mused in his diary with suspicion: "His [Roosevelt's] insistence on China's leading role [in the occupation of Japan] must have been based on some profound calculation. I was not able to express my support or objection right away."[19]

Yet Chiang was not rendered speechless by Roosevelt's surprising proposal, and he immediately turned the situation to his own advantage. He responded that China was not "equipped" to shoulder such "considerable responsibility," but pledged nevertheless that his government was willing to follow American leadership in performing the task. Thus, it was made clear to Roosevelt that if the president expected China to assume international duties in the postwar Pacific, he ought to speed up U.S. aid to Chongqing forthwith. By so declaring, Chiang Kai-shek was not improvising. KMT officials had always thought that the president's idea of "four policemen" afforded them a bargaining chip when urging the U.S. government to increase its aid to China. In the summer of 1943, Roosevelt had already heard T. V. Soong complaining: "You are assigning police functions to us. But policemen must be armed."[20] Thus, Chongqing's stand at Cairo on China's participation in the projected postwar occupation of Japan was partly intended to serve its own wartime needs. The subject provided Chiang with an avenue for urging the U.S. government to arm the "Chinese policeman." So far as the occupation was concerned, Chiang made no commitment but told the president that the final decision "could await further development of the actual situation."

The last issue of the memorandum relative to Japan had to do with Japanese reparations in kind. Chongqing had always had a serious concern about this matter. Whereas Chinese officials considered substantial Japanese reparations in kind an important condition for their country's postwar reconstruction, President Roosevelt's attitude toward the issue remained ambiguous. Before the Cairo Conference, Roosevelt had remarked to T. V. Soong that Japan had taken twenty-five years (from 1880 to 1905) to become a great power, and although China was much bigger than Japan, the Chinese people were also "much cleverer than the Japanese, who are just imitators." Yet the president also admitted that something should be done to accelerate China's progress in becoming a great power.[21]

---

[19] CZM, 8: 116.
[20] "Note on Conversation with the President on Aug. 30, 1943 from noon to 12:45 pm," TSP, box 32.
[21] "Record of Conversation with the President and Mr. Hopkins, July 16, 1943," TSP, box 32.

Despite the comparison, unlike officials in Chongqing, Roosevelt did not suggest that Japan should be deprived of its industrial achievements for the purpose of strengthening China. At the time, Far Eastern officials in the State Department were sharply divided over America's postwar economic policy toward Japan. Whereas one group advocated complete dissolution of Japan's industrial base, another saw such a drastic measure as unnecessarily punitive and counterproductive for stability in the Pacific.[22] Although he chose not to guide the State Department on this issue, President Roosevelt was nevertheless aware that it was one of those postwar complexities with which he did not want to get involved, at least for the time being.

Chinese records are not clear about what agreement Roosevelt and Chiang may have reached concerning the future of Japanese industry. As the summary record shows, after Chiang basically reiterated what was in the fifth memorandum – "Much of *Japan's* industrial machinery and equipment, war and merchant ships, rolling stock, etc., could be transferred to China" (emphasis added) – the president expressed agreement. But the Chinese log of the Cairo Conference, published only in 1981, reads: "With regard to the proposition that after the war the Chinese government take over all Japanese public or private properties *in China*, President Roosevelt expressed his full endorsement" (emphasis added). Nothing is mentioned in this document about industries and equipments in Japan.[23] Without further evidence, it is difficult to decide which version of the Chinese documents is more reliable: if the president was anxious to placate Chiang at Cairo, he might have been generous enough to give his oral endorsement to the fifth memorandum; but if the president was consistent with his usual cautious attitude toward postwar problems, he would likely have made only a limited commitment to the disposal of Japanese properties in China.

Chiang was conscious that difficulties might arise over reparations after the war. Before talking to Roosevelt, he had supported the idea that at the end of the war, captured Japanese equipment, including aircraft and warships, should be placed at the disposal of a tripartite authority consisting of American, British, and Chinese representatives. After his meeting with Roosevelt, however, Chiang had second thoughts. He instructed Wang Chonghui to suggest to Hopkins that the president might want to consider whether an American–Chinese body would be preferable to a tripartite authority for handling Japanese equipment and weapons. The American side did not express any opinion at the time as far as the record shows.[24]

[22] E document-155, 21 July 1943, *RHN*, box 64; E document-173, 6 September 1943, and T document-392, 9 October 1943, ibid., box 65.
[23] "Zhengzhi wenti huishang jingguo," *ZZSC*, 3(3): 528.
[24] Ibid., 529.

Due to its ambiguous nature, the Chiang–Roosevelt understanding on Japanese reparations would not help much when the two governments were faced with the issue again after the war.

China's lost territories

After dealing with the issue of Japan, Roosevelt and Chiang turned to China's territorial aspirations, as shown in the fifth memorandum. The two leaders' agreement on China's recovery of Manchuria, Taiwan, and the Pescadores was consistent with their governments' stated policies. Yet, the inclusion of the Liaodong Peninsula in the memorandum reflected a special concern of the Chinese government. Chiang was anxious to pinpoint the issue because, legally, the Japanese had not seized the Liaodong Leased Territory directly from China, but rather from Russia through the Treaty of Portsmouth of 1905.[25] The Liaodong Peninsula, therefore, was a region in Manchuria where the Russians could easily make a claim after Japan's defeat. Before the Cairo Conference, knowing that the American government was willing to support Russia in regaining its so-called legitimate interests in Manchuria in exchange for its postwar cooperation, KMT leaders had striven without much success to dissuade Washington from that notion.

The gap between the two sides' views on the issue was not bridged at Cairo, despite the fact that, according to the summary record, Roosevelt concurred with the Chinese stand. The real issue here was not China's sovereignty in Manchuria or in any part of the territory, but how to define that sovereignty. Aboard the *Iowa*, the president had spoken of a "free zone" formula for solving a likely Chinese–Soviet dispute in Manchuria after the war. Although the formula is not mentioned in the Chinese records, it is very likely that at their meeting of 23 November, President Roosevelt tried out the formula with Chiang. For, three days later, in a conversation between Chiang and Hopkins, the Chinese leader conceded that Dalian (Dairen), one of the two important ports in the Liaodong Peninsula, might be treated as a free port after its return to China. At the same time, hoping that the Russians themselves would not press the issue, he exhorted Hopkins that the Americans must not leak the discussion of Dalian at Cairo to the Russians in their forthcoming meeting at Teheran. Chiang's request would not be heeded. At Teheran, President Roosevelt would actively seek to accommodate Russian interests in the Far East. At one of his meetings with Stalin, Roosevelt encouraged the Russian desire

[25] Shumpei Okamoto, *The Japanese Oligarchy and the Russo–Japanese War* (New York: Columbia University Press, 1970), 150–166. That treaty had come into being with the help of an American president named Theodore Roosevelt, the fifth cousin of Franklin D. Roosevelt.

to have a warm-water port in the Far East, suggesting that Dalian might be a possible choice and that the Chinese would like the idea of making it a free port under international guarantee.[26]

With regard to the status of the Ryukyu Islands, the summary record conveys the wrong impression that President Roosevelt was the one who brought up the subject and was anxious to offer it to China. In concert with Chiang's original plans for the Cairo Conference, the fifth memorandum clearly indicated Chongqing's intention to regain the Ryukyu Islands along with other lost territories. Instead of being generous, Roosevelt's attitude toward the subject must have put Chiang on the defensive, for, as the record indicates, Chiang appeared flexible and indicated his willingness to participate in a joint American–Chinese administration of the Ryukyus on behalf of the postwar international peace organization. This position constituted a retreat from both the memorandum and Chiang's own earlier claim regarding the Ryukyus that had been made public in his book *China's Destiny*. But, it should be recalled, the retreat was a contingency anticipated in Chiang's original plans. After the meeting with Roosevelt, Chiang explained his stand in his diary, saying that he had proposed to the president a joint American–Chinese control of those islands to end the Americans' anxiety (about China's expansionism?). Later, within KMT circles, Chiang also admitted that the Ryukyus had been part of Japan for so long that it would be better to institute joint American–Chinese control for security purposes rather than to restore China's unilateral influence there.[27]

Unfortunately for Chiang, his gesture of self-denial over the Ryukyu Islands at that meeting was somehow obscured by the back-and-forth translation between the two languages. The task was performed with difficulty by Song Meiling, who, in the opinion of Churchill's doctor in Cairo, "was always tired" that day because of lost sleep over her nettle rash. Whatever the reason might be, Chiang's proposal did not get across to the president. After his meeting with Chiang, Roosevelt remembered only what he learned from the fifth memorandum and continued to believe that the Chinese government was anxious to obtain the Ryukyu Islands.[28]

Following the Ryukyus in the memorandum came the question of Hong Kong. In its preconference documents, the Chinese government revealed its

[26] Discussion aboard U.S.S. *Iowa* of the proposed agenda for the president's conferences with Chiang, Churchill, and Stalin, n.d., *FRUS: Cairo and Teheran*, 257; note on Hopkins–Chiang conversation, 26 November 1943, ibid., 366–367; Bohlen minutes on Roosevelt–Stalin–Churchill luncheon meeting, 30 November 1943, ibid., 567.
[27] CZM, 8: 116; Zhang Qiyun, *Zhonghua Minguo Shigang* (A Historical Outline of the Republic of China) (Taipei: Zhonghua Wenhua Chuban Shiye Weiyuanhui, 1956), 7: 143.
[28] Lord Charles Moran, *Churchill: Taken from the Diaries of Lord Moran* (Boston: Houghton Mifflin, 1966), 139; minutes of a meeting of the Pacific War Council, 12 January 1944, *FRUS: Cairo and Teheran*, 869.

doubt that the coming summit with the Western Allies would be able to reach any decision concerning Hong Kong. Yet, obviously, Chiang saw no harm in including the subject in the memorandum for his, in Churchill's grumbling words, "closeted" talk with Roosevelt. Wartime improvement in Chinese–British relations did not include a breakthrough in the two governments' continual disagreement over Hong Kong. Although focusing its diplomatic effort on gaining the Western Allies' support for China's recovery of territories occupied by Japan, Chongqing had not ceased to argue that Hong Kong was also a lost territory to be returned. When the British government agreed to abrogate its old treaties with China in late 1942, Chiang Kai-shek almost refused to accept the gesture unless British "goodwill" also included Hong Kong's return to China. The Chinese stand had its sympathizers and opponents in both London and Washington, and President Roosevelt's own attitude was regarded by Chongqing as sympathetic.[29]

Roosevelt's attitude toward Hong Kong was directed by both the conviction that British imperialism was obsolete and by the fear that unless a solution could be found, the issue would become an obstacle to his scheme for Big Four cooperation. As with Manchuria, Roosevelt sought a fair solution for Hong Kong in terms of readjusting the interests of America's two wartime allies. He had made his intention clear even before the Cairo Conference. At the end of March 1943, T. V. Soong asked the president at one point whether he had discussed Hong Kong with British Foreign Secretary Anthony Eden. Roosevelt replied: "I wanted [sic] the proposed settlement to be a magnanimous gesture by both Great Britain and China, and I want it to be kept secret from everybody, and without anyone knowing it two simultaneous declarations to be made in due time, the one about handing over [Hong Kong back to China] and the other about [making Hong Kong] the free port." Neither Hopkins's nor Hull's records on the Roosevelt–Eden conversations in March indicate that they discussed Hong Kong. Yet, after listening to the president, Soong reported to Chiang that he saw no further need to discuss the thorny issue with the British himself.[30]

[29] Winston Churchill, *The Second World War* (Boston: Houghton Mifflin, 1950–51), 5: 328–329; *RWK*, 5(A): 27, 30–33. For different arguments within the British government on a postwar policy toward Hong Kong, see Louis, *Imperialism at Bay*, 188–192. U.S. Secretary of State Hull was reluctant to press the British for Hong Kong's return to China, arguing that "Hong Kong had been British longer than Texas had belonged to the United States," and certainly no one in the United States "would welcome a move to return Texas back to Mexico." See Hull, *Memoirs*, 2: 1599.

[30] "Memorandum on Dr. Soong's Conversation with the President, March 31st, 1943," *TSP*, box 32; note on Soong–Eden conversation on 26 July 1943, ibid., box 29; Soong to Chiang, 28 July 1943, ibid., box 15; memoranda by Hopkins on Eden's visit, 17, 22, and 27 March 1943, *HHP*, box 329; memorandum by Hull on Roosevelt–Eden meeting, 27 March 1943, *RHN*, box 19.

Fully aware of the difficulty of negotiating with the British for Hong Kong's recovery, Chiang appreciated the wisdom of Soong's approach and expected to use the Americans to overcome the bullheaded British. Before he came to Cairo, Chiang had decided to avoid any discussion of bilateral problems with Churchill, and that issues like Hong Kong and Tibet should be discussed only if the president were willing to mediate the Chinese–British relationship. When Chiang Kai-shek and Churchill met on 22 November, both expressed their hope for long-term British–Chinese co-operation but both were evasive about concrete issues.[31]

In contrast, Hong Kong was discussed in the Chiang–Roosevelt conversation on the following day. In light of the fifth memorandum, the summary record is again misleading in suggesting that Roosevelt raised the subject first. Chiang's request that the president discuss the matter with the British, however, was made with sincerity. In this regard, Elliott Roosevelt's account is useful. The president's son quoted his father as saying to him: "You see, he [Chiang] wants very badly to get our support against the British moving into Hong Kong and Shanghai and Canton with the same old extraterritorial rights they enjoyed before the war." Allegedly, Roosevelt wanted Chiang to form a "unity government" with the Chinese Communists as a condition for American support of China's regaining of Hong Kong.[32] According to Ambassador Koo's postwar memoirs, Wang Chonghui told him that at Cairo, President Roosevelt did urge Churchill to give Hong Kong back to China. That Roosevelt discussed Hong Kong with Churchill at Cairo is also supported by John P. Davies's recollection. The question is how the issue was discussed. As an assistant to General Joseph Stilwell, Davies joined the general in a conversation with President Roosevelt a few days after the Cairo Conference. The president recalled an earlier discussion with Churchill in which Churchill revealed his intransigence over British imperial possessions. "Therefore," Davies recalled, "in the case of Hong Kong, Roosevelt would agree to the British flag being raised, but then as a generous gesture, the British should the next day declare it to be an open port." Thus, although consistent in supporting his free-port idea, the president seemingly promised both the Chinese and the British that their own flags would fly over the territory.[33]

---

[31] Zhang Qiyun, *Zhonghua Minguo Shigang*, 7: 31–32; log of the Cairo Conference, n.d., ZZSC, 3(3): 513–514. According to Chinese records, the only Chinese–British political discussion took place between Wang Chonghui and Anthony Eden and Alexander Cadogan on 26 November. They only outlined their respective stands on the issue of Tibet and exchanged opinions on British aid to Chongqing. See ibid., 534–535.

[32] E. Roosevelt, *As He Saw It*, 164.

[33] *RWK*, 5(A): 27; John P. Davies, Jr., *Dragon by the Tail: American, British, Japanese, and Russian Encounters with China and One Another* (New York: W. W. Norton, 1972), 280. There is no evidence that at Cairo Roosevelt mentioned the free-port idea to Chiang in relation to Hong Kong. Later, President Roosevelt claimed that in his communication with

A military alliance?

The next category in the memorandum reveals Chiang Kai-shek's desire at Cairo to solicit a long-term military alliance with the United States. Chongqing's preconference documents, while emphasizing wartime and postwar cooperation between China and the United States, did not mention a bilateral military alliance with America at all. KMT officials' knowledge of President Roosevelt's negative attitude toward such an undertaking was the reason for suppressing the fundamental objective of Chongqing's wartime foreign policy. But suddenly, at his meeting with Roosevelt, Chiang Kai-shek put aside all his previous prudence and presented the president with a proposal that amounted to no less than a full-scale military alliance between the two governments. According to the memorandum, postwar Chinese–American military cooperation should include (1) mutual assistance against aggression; (2) American military presence at Pacific bases to prevent aggression; (3) U.S. aid to China for equipment of Chinese land and air forces; (4) arrangements on bases for mutual security; and (5) mutual consultation with regard to decisions pertinent to the Pacific region and the Asian mainland.

How should Chiang's improvised diplomatic offensive be explained? Without further documentation, a scenario can nevertheless be imagined. Aboard the U.S.S. *Iowa*, in their tentative agenda for Roosevelt's meeting with the Chinese, planners of the Joint Chiefs of Staff raised five questions with regard to postwar arrangements with China for mutual security in the Orient. Chiang's fifth memorandum provided exact answers to all five questions. This cannot have been a coincidence. The Chinese must have taken advantage of Hopkins's information about the *Iowa* agenda and decided to seize the opportunity to reveal their intentions. Because the memorandum was merely a response to the Americans' own questions, Chiang could avoid appearing imprudent. Skillfully transforming these questions into positive policy objectives, the fifth memorandum was aimed at creating an American–Chinese military bloc in the Asian–Pacific region mainly sustained, at least for a considerable period after the war, by America's military strength and large-scale aid to China. In 1943, when postwar settlement in East Asia was just beginning to show its complexity,

Chiang Kai-shek, he obtained the Chinese leader's promise to make Hong Kong a port "open to the entire world on equal terms." But in 1944, when the Waijiaobu contemplated steps to regain Hong Kong, a free port was not one of the options. These steps were (a) direct negotiation between the Chinese and British governments for a special agreement on Hong Kong's return to China; (b) Chinese purchase of British public properties in Hong Kong after its return; (c) the Chinese government's guarantee of British economic interests in China; and (d) the Chinese government's promise to use the returned territory as a base for Chinese–British cooperation and to assist British defense needs in certain areas. Louis, *Imperialism at Bay*, 438; Waijiaobu memorandum, "Wancheng wo guo lingtu zhi wanzheng" (Implement Our Country's Territorial Integration), 7 June 1944, *VHP*, box 3.

such an arrangement would have been especially reassuring to the Chinese government, which was not only concerned about China's postwar security vis-à-vis Japan, but was even more worried about the Soviet threat.

Is it plausible to believe that at Cairo, President Roosevelt became willing to be drawn into the Chinese scheme? According to the summary record, not only did Roosevelt support all the arrangements just mentioned for postwar U.S.–Chinese military cooperation, but allegedly it was the president who offered some of these arrangements to Chiang. In light of the fifth memorandum, the record obviously misinforms historians. The mutual consultation promise was especially incriminating to President Roosevelt because, in early 1945, he would make a secret deal with Stalin over East Asian problems at Yalta without even notifying the Chinese government. Although the Yalta diplomacy remains an action on Roosevelt's part that violated his Chinese ally's rights, the fifth memorandum at Cairo at least proves that at Yalta the president did not intentionally overthrow his earlier promise to the Chinese government. For at Cairo, all the so-called Roosevelt proposals for U.S. military and diplomatic obligations to China were derived from Chinese ideas; at most, Roosevelt was guilty of being unwilling to disappoint the anxious Chiangs by directly repudiating their excessive desires.

Colonial issues

So far as colonial problems were concerned, the fifth memorandum included Korea, Indochina, and "other dependent areas" for the Chiang–Roosevelt discussion. To make Sino–American cooperation complete in this regard, the memorandum also proposed Chinese participation in any international administration of Pacific territories to which America would be a party. Yet, Chiang was not ready to accept the formula for multinational administration in China's close neighboring areas. As the summary record shows, on the issue of Indochina, Chiang limited his promise to cooperate with the United States in helping that territory achieve independence. This can be compared with Elliott Roosevelt's account that at the meeting his father used the opportunity to enlist Chiang's support of his trusteeship idea for Indochina. But Korea proved to be the most difficult issue that continued to separate the two governments. As mentioned in the previous chapter, aboard the *Iowa* Roosevelt had expected Chiang to support a trusteeship for Korea. After his meeting with Chiang at Cairo, the president would also discuss with Stalin a "40-year tutelage" for Korea at Teheran.[34]

At this point, a question arises: since the trusteeship formula served

---

[34] E. Roosevelt, *As He Saw It*, 165; minutes of a meeting of the Pacific War Council, 12 January 1944, *FRUS: Cairo and Teheran*, 869.

Roosevelt as a proper solution for Korea throughout his summit experience in 1943, why was it never mentioned in any record pertaining to the Roosevelt–Chiang discussion of Korea? The Chinese summary record is vague about what was agreed between Roosevelt and Chiang. Allegedly, after Roosevelt advanced his view that the two governments should reach a mutual understanding on the future of Korea, Indochina, and other dependent areas, "Chiang stressed on [sic] the necessity of granting independence to Korea." The Chinese log of the conference published in the 1980s suggests a complete meeting of minds between the two, though the so-called agreement never addressed America's trusteeship formula. The Chinese log summarizes the discussion in these words:

> [The two leaders agreed that] Korea should be granted its independence after Japan's defeat. . . . As for the method of helping Korea achieve freedom and independence, the two sides had an understanding that China and the United States should cooperate in assisting the Koreans.[35]

The quotation is more specific than the summary record on two important points. One is the time at which Korea should regain independence: "after Japan's defeat," neither earlier nor later. The other is a bilateral U.S.–Chinese partnership to assist the Koreans. These two points accurately represented the Chinese government's policy toward Korea up to the time of the conference. Yet, they certainly contradicted President Roosevelt's trusteeship solution which would delay the timing for Korean independence and call for multinational cooperation.

The real exchange between Roosevelt and Chiang over Korea may never be reconstructed, but it must have had a much less pleasant aura than that conveyed by the Chinese records. After the meeting with Chiang on 23 November, Roosevelt must have been annoyed by his previous misconception of Chongqing's attitude toward Korea. The next day, at a meeting of the Combined Chiefs of Staff, he revealed to the participants that "there was no doubt that China had wide aspirations which included the reoccupation of Manchuria and Korea." After the conference, a story about the Roosevelt–Chiang contention over the issue of Korea also began to circulate among State Department officials. Allegedly, during his conversation with Chiang, President Roosevelt rebutted Chiang's intentions, whatever they may have been, toward Korea: "You may have Manchuria. You may have the Pescadores and you may have Formosa, but you may not have Korea, which is to be detached from Japan and is to be given its independence after a period of international supervision." It cannot be verified whether the president really said these words to Chiang, but so far as Korea was concerned, the words are consistent with what he had said to his aides aboard the *Iowa*. The crux of the Chiang–Roosevelt disagreement on Korea was the Soviet role in the matter. After his meeting with the president, Chiang Kai-shek entered these words in his diary: "I cautioned him [President Roosevelt] that judgement about Russia must be based on facts and its action in the future, and I also explicitly told him that I really dare not trust the Russians."[36]

Despite the disagreement between Roosevelt and Chiang, the Cairo Conference marked notable progress in the Allied policy toward Korea. In the final communiqué of the conference, the three participating governments committed themselves to the ultimate goal of Korean independence. In this regard, Chiang claimed a diplomatic victory and believed that he was successful at Cairo in winning President Roosevelt over to China's policy for Korean independence.[37] Yet insofar as policy planning for Korea proceeded in Chongqing and Washington, the ultimate goal was less important than the means of achieving it. In this regard, Chiang had to accept his failure, which was reflected in a qualifying phrase in the communiqué for Korean independence: "*in due course* Korea shall become free and independent" (emphasis added).

At Cairo, the British were invited to express their opinions on postwar issues in East Asia only at the stage when the final communiqué was discussed. The British tried but failed to make fundamental changes to a draft communiqué already accepted by the Americans and the Chinese. "In due course" was a contribution by Churchill and exemplified the British prime minister's ability to use terse language to convey complicated political concepts. In substance, however, the difference between the Churchillian "in due course" and the original American phrases, "at the earliest possible moment after the downfall of Japan" or "at the proper moment after the downfall of Japan," was trivial.[38] The change made no great difference to the American policy. Both the American and British choices of words provided for an interim period between Japan's defeat and Korean independence. Having failed to prevail over Roosevelt with his plan for Korea, Chiang showed no interest in how the decision on Korea was worded in the final document. Listening to Wang Chonghui reading from the Chinese versions of the original American draft and the final draft of the communiqué, Chiang did not even notice the difference between the two documents' wording about Korea.[39]

---

[36] Minutes of the meeting of the Combined Chiefs of Staff with Roosevelt and Churchill, 24 November 1943, *FRUS: Cairo and Teheran*, 334; D (CDA) minutes-2, 8 February 1945, *RHN*, box 134; *CZM*, 8: 117.

[37] *CZM*, 8: 116.

[38] American draft of the Communiqué, *FRUS: Cairo and Teheran*, 401–404; final text of the Communiqué, ibid., 449; Louis, *Imperialism at Bay*, 281–282.

[39] "Zhengzhi wenti huishang jingguo," *ZZSC*, 3(3): 528–533. The Chinese version of the American draft translated "at the proper moment" into *yu shidang shiqi*, and that of the final draft translated "in due course" into *zai xiangdang shiqi*. There is no significant difference between the two.

The last item in the fifth memorandum was U.S. financial aid for China's postwar economic reconstruction. According to the summary record, Roosevelt promised sympathetic consideration of this issue. More urgent was China's current economic situation, and Chiang did not let the opportunity pass without asking the president in person for more aid. Allegedly, either on 23 November or on later occasions, the two discussed topics like currency stabilization in China, a U.S. loan to Chongqing, and a Sino–American economic commission. The two governments' cooperation in the economic field was really an ongoing subject, and their consultation in this respect would continue after Cairo.[40]

The shadow of Moscow

The summary record also included two other issues that were not listed in the memorandum. One was the status of Outer Mongolia, along with a related territory named Tannu Tuva. Another was China's participation in the U.S.–British Combined Chiefs of Staff. In different ways, each indicated an aspect of the Cairo Conference not known to most contemporaries. Despite the fact that the Cairo Conference would be known in history as a landmark in the development of the Allied policy toward Japan, what also loomed large in the Chiang–Roosevelt political discussion was the issue of the Soviet Union. In 1943, President Roosevelt devoted his diplomatic efforts to forming a Big Four coalition in which the United States would hold the balance wheel. Before the Cairo Conference, the president told his son Elliott: "The United States will have to lead and use our good offices always to conciliate, help to solve the differences which will arise between the others, between Russia and England, in Europe; between the British Empire and China and between China and Russia, in the Far East."[41] Yet Chiang and other KMT leaders around him seriously doubted that the difference between their government and the Soviet Union could be reconciled, even though they were anxious to enlist American support in their dealings with Moscow.

In their meeting on 23 November and during other unrecorded conversations at Cairo, Chiang and Roosevelt did not avoid the Soviet presence. According to the summary record, Chiang indicated his intention to negotiate directly with the Russians to restore China's control of Outer Mongolia and Tannu Tuva. Roosevelt's response was not recorded, but later Hopkins recalled as a laughable matter Chiang's intention to regain Outer Mongolia. Chiang and Roosevelt also discussed other issues pertinent to

---

[40] Editorial note on Roosevelt–Churchill–Chiang meeting, 26 November 1943, *FRUS: Cairo and Teheran*, 366–367.
[41] E. Roosevelt, *As He Saw It*, 129–130.

Russia, such as Xinjiang, the Soviet participation in the war against Japan, and the Communist problem in China and in the world.[42] Because the president would soon join Stalin at Teheran, it seemed natural that at Cairo these topics would be brought up between Chiang and Roosevelt. But, more important, both Chiang and Roosevelt realized that the Soviet Union would be a force to be reckoned with in Asian affairs at the end of the war. Soviet neutrality in the Asian conflict at the time created special difficulties for the Chinese and American governments in predicting how peace would supersede war in Asia. Although they had a common concern about the uncertain Soviet factor, the Chinese and the Americans remained unable to agree on a common strategy for dealing with the Russians. To Chiang, the best solution was a Chinese–Western entente for containing Soviet power, which, it was hoped, would prevent the Russians from reaping profits in Asia by entering the war against Japan in the final stage. For this very reason, at Cairo he pressed Roosevelt to form a bilateral American–Chinese command or a trilateral command including the British in the Asian war. But aware of Roosevelt's disposition toward Big Four cooperation, Chiang could not put the reason on the table when talking to the president. For Roosevelt's part, he treated Chiang's proposal as one more instance of Chongqing's ongoing demand for equal treatment by the Western Allies and referred the issue to his military advisers.[43]

Roosevelt himself preferred a circuitous approach when dealing with the Chongqing–Moscow impasse. As mentioned earlier, in conversations with Chiang, the president assumed that American support of China on the issue of Hong Kong and Chongqing's liberalization of its policy toward the Chinese Communists could be combined in a deal, which, aside from its expected benefits for the Chinese–British relationship and for China's domestic situation, would indirectly ease the tension between Chongqing and Moscow. But Chiang preferred a different arrangement for involving the president in his strategy to deal with the Russians. Chiang agreed to form a coalition with the CCP only if he had American assurance that the Soviet Union would agree to respect Chinese sovereignty in Manchuria.[44] Chiang, of course, was aware that what he discussed with Roosevelt at Cairo would likely be carried by the Americans to Teheran. Therefore, he asked Roosevelt to act as a broker with Moscow on behalf of Chongqing. Chiang would soon regret this request because Roosevelt proved willing to play the role only in his own way. At Teheran, Roosevelt would indeed obtain Stalin's oral support for the general idea of the Cairo communiqué including the restoration of China's sovereignty in Manchuria. Against Chiang's wishes, however, the president also used port privileges

[42] Davies, *Dragon by the Tail*, 278; Zhang Qiyun, *Zhonghua Minguo Shigang*, 7: 134–135.
[43] Chiang to Soong, 11 September 1943, ZZSC, 3(3): 263–264.
[44] E. Roosevelt, *As He Saw It*, 164.

in Dalian to entice Stalin, hoping to gain the Soviet leader's cooperation in East Asia.[45]

When the Cairo Communiqué was published, Chiang was not thrilled. He wrote in his diary: "Public opinions at home and abroad unanimously praised [the Cairo Conference] as an unprecedented victory in the diplomatic history of China, but I only feel worried and apprehensive at heart." As for his principal goal in foreign policy, close bilateral cooperation with the United States, Chiang had only achieved vague promises from President Roosevelt at Cairo. He sensed that, given Roosevelt's attitude toward the Soviet Union, these promises meant very little.[46] If President Roosevelt's Cairo diplomacy was intended to enhance Chinese morale in the war against Japan, its effect on Chiang Kai-shek himself was minimal. President Roosevelt was also frustrated by the experience. In his postconference communication with H. H. Kung, Roosevelt called his meeting with Chiang a "true success" and said: "It is the beginning of many such conferences. I hope." At the same time, Roosevelt confessed privately that he simply failed to understand Chiang Kai-shek.[47] Throughout the rest of the war, Roosevelt would never attempt to meet with Chiang again.

At Cairo the language barrier was a problem, but the differences between the two sides' policies also proved substantial. The final document of the conference included only those items on which no serious disagreement occurred between Roosevelt and Chiang; the other items discussed were simply shelved. In view of the Western Allies' commitment to a thorough defeat of Japan and their support of China's recovery of its lost territories from Japan after the war, the Cairo Conference could be interpreted in China as a success. Yet the decisions made at Cairo only skimmed the surface of the complicated Chinese–American relationship at the time.

At Cairo, in regard to Chongqing's postwar aspirations, President Roosevelt acted more cautiously than conventional wisdom tends to suggest. Convinced that after the war lasting peace would have to rely on successful cooperation among the four leading Allies, the president maintained his international approach with regard to issues like settlements in Manchuria and Korea. Conscious of a strong anti-Soviet bias behind Chiang's proposal for a postwar Chinese–American military alliance, Roosevelt responded with rhetoric but did not make a definite commitment. So far as the seemingly single important issue of postwar Japan was concerned, the president did not make any commitment to China that might in the future hinder America's own policymaking concerning Japan.

---

[45] Bohlen minutes of Roosevelt–Churchill–Stalin luncheon meeting, 30 November 1943, *FRUS: Cairo and Teheran*, 566–567.

[46] *CZM*, 8: 117, 119.

[47] Roosevelt to H. H. Kung, 26 November 1943, *RPPF* 1178; Edgar Snow, *Random Notes on Red China, 1936–1945* (Cambridge, MA: Harvard University Press, 1974), 127.

For his part, Chiang Kai-shek was certainly not a passive recipient of Roosevelt's generosity. In his meeting with Western leaders, Chiang functioned as both head of a Chinese government and leader of the KMT. This dual capacity reflected Chiang's fragile position as a weak leader of a weak state. He planned, improvised, and strove to get the most out of his negotiations with American leaders. Since Chiang's predetermined policy was to rely on American support to achieve all his important objectives in postwar foreign and domestic policies, at Cairo he was able to make some arguments but was in no position to bargain. Yet, neither was he converted by Roosevelt's approach to postwar issues. In this last sense, the Cairo Conference was a failure for both Roosevelt and Chiang. The two leaders were so concerned with evading commitment to each other's postwar programs that, except for a communiqué valuable for propaganda, they failed to lay a solid foundation for long-term American–Chinese cooperation.

Nevertheless, for foreign policy planners in China and America, the Cairo Conference indeed constituted a landmark. It was so not only because their leaders formalized certain previously tentative policies in the Cairo Communiqué, but also because the discussions at Cairo created new confusions. Now foreign policy planners in the two capitals had the task of interpreting the "decisions" of Cairo and also of seeking clarification of those "understandings" not included in the final document. The full meaning of Cairo was yet to unfold.

7

Yan'an and postwar East Asia

Despite the many cosmetic features of the Cairo Conference, the summit represented a radical departure in the history of Chinese foreign relations. The conference signified China's emergence as an equal among the great powers in the United Nations coalition. Even more important, the Cairo Conference led to a new international definition of the Chinese state by restoring its lost territories. Most astonishing was that these events occurred at a time when China was represented at Cairo by only a single faction in Chinese politics. At the time, the effective authority of the KMT government was limited to the southwestern corner of China. Before continuing this narrative of Sino–American diplomacy with regard to postwar arrangements in East Asia, therefore, it is necessary to examine the views of the CCP, the chief rival of the KMT for power and the party that then controlled extensive territories and population in northern China.

For the purpose of official foreign policymaking, the KMT's monopoly of power was absolute. Other political parties in China, including the CCP, lacked the means to exert direct influence in international affairs. Therefore, Yan'an's views on international affairs became known to the outside world only gradually. Observers of CCP policies had to seek information from reports by a small number of foreign journalists who had opportunities to visit the Communist areas, from the CCP's own propaganda organs, and from occasional contacts between Western diplomats and CCP officials in Chongqing. In 1944, when a U.S. Army Observer Group, dubbed the "Dixie Mission," arrived in Yan'an, the American government for the first time learned the CCP's views through direct contacts. Yet throughout the war, Washington's China policy was based on the assumption that the KMT regime would continue to retain political power in China after the war; American policymakers paid attention to Yan'an's views about postwar issues in East Asia only occasionally.

Nevertheless, an inquiry into Yan'an's wartime intentions regarding peace settlement in East Asia is worthwhile for two reasons. First, they anticipated the CCP's foreign policy in the postwar years. Second, they constituted an important point of reference for comparison with Chongqing's wartime foreign policy. The question posed here is whether in the war years there was a "Chinese perspective" on international affairs that transcended the KMT–CCP contention for power at the time and might in the long run provide a new point of departure for Chinese foreign policy during the postwar era.[1]

CCP–KMT competition in foreign affairs

If World War II was a vital period for China's resurgence in international politics, it was also a most important time in the Chinese Communists' struggle for national leadership. The two processes did not overlap completely. Without question, the vigor of the CCP in its social reforms and warfare against the Japanese aggressor helped win Allied sympathy for China's cause. Since it was not part of the KMT government, however, the CCP was not in a position to participate in Chinese diplomacy during the war aimed at reestablishing China's international status. To discern the secret of the CCP's eventual success in China's power struggle, many scholars have sensibly focused their attention on the CCP's domestic programs. Studies of the CCP's wartime encounter with international politics are limited in number, and they tend to agree on the futility of Yan'an's effort to persuade foreign powers, chiefly the United States and the Soviet Union, to act on its behalf.[2] Indeed, in competition with the KMT, the CCP did

[1] Opinions vary among scholars of Chinese history and culture as to whether there is a continual "Chinese perspective" on world order from traditional to contemporary China. Two opposing views are expressed in Mark Mancall, "The Persistence of Tradition in Chinese Foreign Policy," *Annals of the American Academy of Political and Social Science*, 349 (September 1963): 14–26, and Benjamin Schwartz, "The Chinese Perception of World Order, Past and Present" in John K. Fairbank, ed., *The Chinese World Order: Traditional China's Foreign Relations* (Cambridge, MA: Harvard University Press, 1968), 276–288. The "Chinese perspective" in the following discussion is a relatively narrow and simple conception in the sense that it should have been acceptable to different political groups in China, especially to both the KMT and the CCP.

[2] Chalmers A. Johnson, *Peasant Nationalism and Communist Power: The Emergence of Revolutionary China, 1937–1945* (Stanford, CA: Stanford University Press, 1962); Mark Selden, *The Yan'an Way in Revolutionary China* (Cambridge, MA: Harvard University Press, 1971); and Lyman P. Van Slyke, *Enemies and Friends: The United Front in Chinese Communist History* (Stanford, CA: Stanford University Press, 1967), are noteworthy classic studies of the CCP's domestic programs. For the CCP foreign policy in the war years, see John W. Garver, *Chinese–Soviet Relations, 1937–1945: The Diplomacy of Chinese Nationalism* (New York: Oxford University Press, 1988), chaps. 4 and 8; John Reardon-Anderson, *Yenan and the Great Power: The Origins of Chinese Communist Foreign Policy, 1944–1946* (New York: Columbia University Press, 1980); and Kenneth E. Shewmaker, *Americans and Chinese Communists, 1927–1945: A Persuading Encounter* (Ithaca, NY: Cornell

not occupy as favorable a position on the diplomatic front as it often did on the domestic front.

Whereas the KMT exercised control over the formal state machinery, the CCP relied mainly on its contacts with peasant groups. These positions served the two parties differently in the domestic political struggle and in the theater of diplomacy. In the former, the issue of "heaven's mandate" was to be determined by the Chinese population, but in the latter, the issue of "legitimacy" depended on attitudes prevailing in the international community. The history of modern China has repeatedly shown that the disposition of the Chinese population and the preference of foreign governments have not always been consonant. Although to the Chinese peasants the CCP had much to offer, to the Allied governments Yan'an was never a legitimate or proper political organization for official diplomacy. Throughout the war, the Chinese Communist leadership was conscious of its difficult relationship with the Allied powers, desiring only to be treated as one of the principal anti-Japanese forces in China deserving of Allied assistance. No significant foreign assistance ever reached Yan'an from either the Western Allies or the Soviet Union. Bound by its obligations under the wartime KMT–CCP united front, Yan'an in the war years did not claim to be a sovereign government despite the fact that it functioned like one in the Border Regions.[3] In this regard, the CCP's leadership was so cautious that in the middle of the war CCP officials actually announced to their American contacts that any foreign assistance to China's war effort must be conveyed through the so-called central government in Chongqing and that aid to the Border Regions should not be provided in a manner that might alienate Chongqing.[4]

This cautious attitude began to change only in the last year of the Pacific war. In the summer of 1944, Mao Zedong complained to a member of the U.S. Army Observer Group in Yan'an that Washington's policy of

University Press, 1971). A recent work by a Chinese scholar, Niu Jun's *Cong Yan'an Zouxiang Shijie – Zhongguo Gongchandang Duiwai Guanxi de Qiyuan* (Approach the World from Yan'an: The Origins of the Foreign Relations of the Chinese Communist Party) (Fuchou: Fujian Renmin Chubanshe, 1992), is based on the CCP's internal documents and discusses the party's foreign policies from 1936 to 1949.

[3] The areas and population of the Border Regions expanded drastically during the war. In 1937, the CCP controlled only one Border Region, which included part of three northwestern provinces (Shaanxi, Gansu, and Ningxia) and a population of about 2 million. By the end of the Pacific war, however, there were nineteen Border Regions that extended into twenty-one provinces in northern and southern China and governed a population of 95.5 million. Chen Lian, *Kangri Genjudi Fazhan Shilüe* (History of the Development of the Anti-Japanese Bases) (Beijing: Jiefangjun Chubanshe, 1987), 4–5.

[4] U.S. Senate Committee on the Judiciary, *Morgenthau Diary: China* (Washington, DC: G.P.O., 1965) (hereafter cited as Morgenthall Diary), 872–874; U.S. Senate, Committee on the Judiciary, *The Amerasia Papers: A Clue to the Catastrophe of China* (Washington, DC: G.P.O., 1970), 697 (hereafter cited as *Amerasia Papers*).

providing one-sided aid to Chongqing could only have an unfo~~r~~
effect on Chinese politics. In January 1945, Yan'an took even bold~~e~~
tion by sending a message to President Roosevelt offering to send a s~~e~~
mission to Washington. What the Communist leaders included in th~~e~~
agenda cannot be documented, though a meeting as such would have ha~~e~~
great symbolic meaning. It is noteworthy, however, that even in this dramatic appeal, the CCP leaders exercised restraint: they wanted to meet with
President Roosevelt as "leaders of a primary Chinese party," not as representatives of a government. These overtures indicated the beginning of
what was defined by an internal directive of the CCP as "semi-independent
diplomacy" of the party.[5]

Throughout the war, as "leaders of a primary Chinese party," Mao and
his associates acknowledged the KMT regime as a "formal holder of power."
But at the same time, they claimed that the CCP provided vital "practical
leadership" to the Chinese people in the war of resistance against Japan.[6]
Although such juxtaposition between "formal" and "practical" did not
occur in China's wartime foreign relations, the CCP competed rhetorically
with the KMT for the right to speak about China's aspirations on the
international scene. In contrast to the KMT–CCP divergence in domestic
politics, the two parties tended to converge on the significance of China's
war against Japan for China's international status. For instance, leaders in
both Chongqing and Yan'an agreed that the current military struggle in
East Asia would lead to a general readjustment of China's foreign relations. For, in view of Japan's aggression, the other "imperialist powers" in

---

[5] Joseph W. Esherick, ed., *Lost Chance in China: The World War II Despatches of John W. Service* (New York: Random House, 1974), 300–302; Michael Schaller, *The U.S. Crusade in China, 1938–1945* (New York: Columbia University Press, 1979), 204–206; Niu Jun, *Cong Yan'an Zouxiang Shijie*, 25 nn. 3, 111, 172; "Zhongyang guanyu waijiao gongzou zhishi" (Directive of the Central Committee [of the CCP] on Diplomacy), 18 August 1944, *Zhonggong Zhongyang Wenjian Xuanji* (Selected Documents of the Central Committee of the Chinese Communist Party), comp. Zhongyang Dang'anguan (Central Archives) (Beijing: Zhongyang Dangxiao Chubanshe, 1992), 14: 314–315 (hereafter cited as *Zhongyang Wenjian*). The decision to propose to the Americans a CCP mission to the United States must have been made by Mao and Zhou under some unusual circumstances. According to Hu Qiaomu's (Mao's political secretary during the Yan'an period) recollections, he and all others around Mao at the time were not aware of such a decision, and no evidence regarding the episode has surfaced from the CCP archives. See Hu Qiaomu, *Hu Qiaomu Huiyi Mao Zedong* (Hu Qiaomu Remembers Mao Zedong) (Beijing: Renmin Chubanshe, 1994), 89. For interpretations of the proposed trip by CCP leaders to Washington, see Barbara W. Tuchman, "If Mao Had Come to Washington: An Essay in Alternatives," *Foreign Affairs*, October 1972, 44–64, and Steven M. Goldstein, "Chinese Communist Policy Toward the United States: Opportunities and Constraints, 1944–1950," in Dorothy Borg and Waldo Heinrichs, ed., *Uncertain Years: Chinese–American Relations, 1947–1950* (New York: Columbia University Press,1980), 235–278.

[6] Edgar Snow, *Random Notes on Red China, 1936–1945* (Cambridge, MA: Harvard University Press, 1974), 21–22.

. would be compelled to change their old policies toward China.
y also agreed that a new system of international relations must emerge
postwar East Asia, one in which China and other Asian peoples would
njoy a stronger position than before when dealing with the Western powers.

Another conviction shared by the Communists and the Nationalists was
China's role as a model for other Asiatic peoples. Both made the predic-
tion that after the war, the new China, with its successful revolution,
would serve as the spiritual inspiration to other colonial peoples in Asia.
Although, for practical or ideological reasons, the KMT and the CCP
identified the United States and the Soviet Union, respectively, as an organizing influence in the postwar world, both believed in principle that China
had to stand on its own. At the onset of the war of resistance against
Japan, Mao made a categorical remark to the American journalist Edgar
Snow: "We are certainly not fighting for an emancipated China in order
to turn the country over to Moscow!" Despite the internationalist character of Communist ideology, the CCP was critical of the KMT government's passive military policy toward Japan, citing Chongqing's overreliance
on foreign aid and its lack of "national self-esteem." Not surprisingly, in
1944, after talking to CCP officials in the Border Regions, Gunther Stein,
a British journalist, concluded that there was no disagreement between the
principles articulated by the CCP and the KMT in their foreign policies,
and that the CCP leaders' criticism of the KMT's foreign policy was mainly
against its lack of a democratic basis at home and inconsistencies between
its principles and its diplomatic practice.[7]

There was a good reason for the KMT–CCP consensus on principles
guiding Chinese foreign policy. Expressed in different terms according to
changing circumstances, these principles generally reflected the desire of
the Chinese nation to change the unfortunate external conditions that
had developed during the preceding century. Any political party contending for national leadership in China could not disregard these aspirations.[8]
During World War II, therefore, when Chinese diplomacy had opportunities to change China's status in world politics, the CCP adopted the role

[7] Edgar Snow, *Red Star Over China* (New York: Random House, 1968), 103, 444–445;
Nym Wales, *My Yenan Notebooks* (Madison, CT: Helen F. Snow, 1961), 134, 145; Zhou
Enlai, "Lun muqian zhanju" (On the Current Military Situation), *Jiefang Ribao* (Liberation
Daily), 14 June 1941; Gunther Stein, *The Challenge of Red China* (New York: McGraw-
Hill, 1945), 447.

[8] Using different connotations of "nationalism," scholars of modern China date the beginning of Chinese nationalism differently, but there seems to be no disagreement on a significant departure made by modern Chinese nationalism at the beginning of the twentieth
century. See Mary C. Wright, ed., *China in Revolution: The First Phase, 1900–1913* (New
Haven, CT: Yale University Press, 1968), 3; Fairbank, *Chinese World Order*, 284–285,
Jonathan C. Spence, *The Search for Modern China* (New York: W. W. Norton, 1990),
230–231; and Hu Sheng et al., *The 1911 Revolution: A Retrospective After 70 Years*
(Beijing: New World Press, 1983), 128–130.

of constructive critic. While Chongqing conducted China's wartime foreign relations, Yan'an's occasional suggestions intimated that the CCP
might handle these affairs in a more effective manner. This contention over
who should speak for the Chinese nation was reflected in the CCP's commentary on important events in China's wartime foreign relations.

One of these events was the American and British governments' agreements with Chongqing to abrogate their old unequal treaties with China.
With regard to the issue of "treaty revision," Japan's aggression in China
had persuaded the CCP to adopt a stand similar to that of the KMT in
softening its attitude toward the other treaty powers in China. In May
1937, Luo Fu (Zhang Wentian), a prominent member of the CCP's political bureau, published an article advocating China's alliance with all friendly
countries for the purpose of opposing the Axis powers. In his opinion, the
unequal treaties between China and the West should not become a hin-
drance to such an alliance, for a solution of the issue could be found
through "peaceful negotiations and discussions."[9]

When the unequal treaties between China and the United States and
Britain were ultimately abrogated in early 1943, the *Jiefang Ribao* (Liberation Daily), an official newspaper of the CCP, responded favorably. According to its editorial, the new treaties agreed on by the Western Allies
differed fundamentally from the hypocritical "new treaty" concluded earlier between Tokyo and its puppet, Wang Jingwei's regime in Nanjing.
Their conclusion was "a great development concerning our nation, an
indication of closer cooperation among the United Nations, and a cornerstone for a permanent world peace to come." But to what extent should
the diplomacy of the KMT regime be credited for this achievement? The
Jiefang Ribao conveyed the view of the CCP Central Committee that the
old treaties' abrogation was a logical result of the general wartime internal
and external conditions of China and was especially the product of wartime cooperation between the KMT and the CCP. The Central Committee
emphasized that the KMT and the CCP should continue their cooperation
in order to achieve victory in the war and transform the new treaties from
"a mere scrap of paper" into substantial results. In an interview with the
Jiefang Ribao, Gao Gang, head of the Northwestern Bureau of the CCP
Central Committee, stated that before the unequal treaties were formally
abrogated, China's population in the Border Regions had long been freed
from these treaties, implying that the CCP was really in the vanguard of
the struggle to revoke them.[10]

Although generally viewing China's wartime participation in inter-
Allied diplomacy as evidence of the improvement in China's international

[9] Luo Fu, "Women dui minzu tongyi gangling de yijian" (Our Opinion on a Platform for
National Unity), *Jiefang* (Liberation), 8 May 1937.
[10] *Jiefang Ribao*, 12, 13, 14, and 29 January 1943 and 4 February 1943.

status, Yan'an did not attribute the achievement to the KMT government. Instead, CCP leaders preferred to regard the inter-Allied diplomacy as an effective instrument for disciplining the KMT regime, which was at best an uneasy collaborator with the Allied cause. According to the *Jiefang Ribao*, the inter-Allied conferences at Moscow and Cairo in 1943 were significant to China not only because they had the collective effect of elevating China to the position of a great power, but also because the other Allied governments endeavored on these occasions to forestall a "surrender conspiracy" between the Japanese and the "defeatist elements" in the KMT. The CCP leadership emphasized the Cairo decision concerning Japan's total defeat and unconditional surrender as being highly significant. After these conferences, the *Jiefang Ribao* told its readers, the Chinese people should not indulge themselves in self-congratulation but should act to see that Chongqing honored its obligation under the Moscow Four-Power Declaration and the Cairo Communiqué, namely, to prosecute the war against Japan to a final decisive victory. While supporting the territorial decisions made at Cairo, the Communist organ attached much importance to the three participating governments' renunciation of all expansionist ambitions. For, in its judgment, this provision would thwart those imperialists within the KMT government who were promoting "China's cultural superiority." This can be taken as a conscious renunciation by the CCP of a premise in the traditional Chinese view of the world order. If the CCP leadership also believed in China's role as a model for other Asian peoples, it would have to emphasize the revolutionary spirit, not the traditional cultural values, of China.[11]

Despite their censure of certain KMT officials' imperialist tendencies, CCP leaders did not appear to believe that imperialism would become a feature of China's relations with its neighbors. Zhou Enlai once ventured the opinion that the fear of Chinese imperialism in postwar Asia among some people in America and Britain was caused by the wartime crises in their own countries. Such anxiety would disappear after these countries achieved victory in the war. So far as China was concerned, Zhou contended, the nation did not have the economic and military strength to pursue an imperialist future.[12]

Because the war with Japan provided the chief incentive, the military objectives of Chongqing's diplomacy naturally could not escape criticism from the CCP. As mentioned earlier, before the United States entered the war, Yan'an castigated Chongqing for its lack of confidence in the Chinese people's own ability to resist Japanese aggression and for its passive military strategy based on speculations concerning the likelihood of an American–Japanese conflict. After the American–Japanese war in the Pacific began,

[11] *Jiefang Ribao*, 21 July, 6 November, and 10 December 1943.
[12] *Morgenthau Diary*, 877–878.

the CCP leadership continued to stress self-reliance as the fundamental principle in China's war effort. At the same time, it professed complete support for the European priority of the Allied military strategy. Chongqing's attempt to persuade the Western Allies to accept an Asia-first strategy was attacked by the Chinese Communists as selfish and irresponsible. According to Yan'an, such an attempt was both harmful to the Allied war effort and dangerous to China's political future. Chongqing's attempt to persuade the Western Allies to accept an Asia-first strategy was the reason for its lackluster military effort and for its repressive policies against the Chinese people. Although it wished to shift the burden and responsibility for defeating Japan to the other Allies, the KMT leadership was first and foremost concerned with retaining its own military strength to maintain dominion in China. In other words, the Communists thought it absurd for Chongqing to use the Allied military concentration in Europe to absolve itself of responsibility for vigorously prosecuting the war in China's own theater. The precondition for a more active role of China in the Allied war effort, in Yan'an's view, was that the KMT regime must agree to carry out meaningful social and political reforms in China.[13]

Yan'an and the lost territories

During the war, the CCP leadership popularized its war and peace aims by codifying "ten anti-Japanese principles" for the Eighth Route Army. These principles were designed for the peasant-soldiers to comprehend. Prominently placed at the beginning of the document was a call for recapturing territories seized by Japan.[14] In the CCP leaders' statements governing postwar objectives, China's recovery of the lost territories was usually juxtaposed with other Asian peoples' regaining their independence. China's postwar security, along with territorial dispositions, was also discussed in relation to the interests of China's allies. But if the CCP leadership ever considered the meaning of China's territorial recovery in its plans for gaining power in China, the connection was never explicitly revealed in the CCP literature during the war.

In view of its strategic and economic importance and physical proximity to the CCP bases in northern and northwestern China, Manchuria was a region most likely to attract the CCP strategists' attention. As early as 1936, in a conversation with Edgar Snow, Mao Zedong observed: "It is the immediate task of China to regain all our lost territories, not merely to defend our sovereignty south of the Great Wall. This means that Manchuria must be regained." Despite such rhetoric, the Communists themselves in 1936 had neither the intention nor the ability to implement the

---

[13] *Jiefang Ribao*, 17 June 1941, 2 July 1943, and 8 June 1944.
[14] Evans F. Carlson, *Twin Stars of China* (New York: Dodd, Mead, 1940), 251–252.

"immediate task." At that time, the boldest military strategy that leaders in Yan'an could contemplate aimed at penetrating into Suiyuan and Mongolia, enlarging the CCP's military influence in Ningxia and Gansu, and establishing communications between the Border Regions and Xinjiang. In other words, the CCP first wanted to consolidate its current position in northwestern China and to improve its lines of communication with Moscow.[15]

The truth was that in Manchuria the CCP experienced difficulties in its military operations even when conducting a "people's war." During the four years before Japan attacked Pearl Harbor, the Japanese authorities in Manchuria succeeded in reducing guerrilla activities in the area to an insignificant level. In mid-1937, Zhu De, commander-in-chief of the Eighth Route Army, was optimistic about the future of guerrilla warfare in the northeastern provinces, expecting the "systematic" growth of small-group military actions against the Japanese forces there. Actually, within the year, the development of the anti-Japanese guerrilla forces in Manchuria reached its climax. Then the Communist-led Northeastern Anti-Japanese Allied Army had eleven "army units," with troops never numbering more than 30,000. In the next three years, these units suffered serious losses and were reorganized into three "route armies." Throughout the winter of 1940, the three route armies successively retreated into the Russian territory, eventually becoming the Training Brigade of the Northeastern Anti-Japanese Allied Army, known to the Soviet authorities as the Eighty-Eighth Infantry Brigade of the Soviet Far Eastern Front Army. Thus, before the Pacific war even began, any respectable force of the CCP had ceased to exist in Manchuria. During the Pacific war, Yan'an's contact with the remaining guerrilla forces in Manchuria had to be maintained through Moscow. Yan'an's reliance on channels in Moscow to conduct its partisan activities in Manchuria served constantly as an annoying reminder of its dependent position.[16] Under these circumstances, although determined to "fight [the Japanese] back to the Yalu River," the CCP did not possess any means for achieving that goal.

Like the KMT officials in Chongqing, the CCP leaders were keenly aware that Manchuria would be beyond the reach of any Chinese forces for a period of time. International complications in postwar Manchuria

---

[15] Snow, *Random Notes*, 62–63; idem, *Red Star*, 110; Niu Jun, *Cong Yan'an Zouxiang Shijie*, 25.

[16] T. A. Bisson, *Yenan in June 1937: Talks with the Communist Leaders* (Berkeley: Center of Chinese Studies, University of California at Berkeley, 1973), 40; Jin Yuzhong and Chang Haoli, "Dongbei kangri lianjun zuzhi xulie" (The Organization of the Northeastern Anti-Japanese Allied Army), *Zhonggong Dangshi Ziliao* (Materials on the History of the Chinese Communist Party), 18 (1986): 226–258; Chang Cheng et al., *Xiandai Dongbei Shi* (Modern history of the Northeast) (Harbin: Heilongjiang Renmin Chubanshe, 1986), 295, 338–339, 367–369, 383–384, 391; Garver, *Chinese–Soviet Relations*, 262.

were therefore expected. In 1942, Zhou Enlai revealed his thoughts to an American interviewer. Zhou predicted that in the event of a Soviet–Japanese war, Manchuria would likely fall under the occupation of Soviet forces. Probably the Russians would prefer a Chinese government there, but, according to Zhou, "unless the Chinese [KMT] Government drives the Japanese out of China, no victory can be won in the Far East. The Central Government cannot drive the Japanese out of China without [first] adopting democratic methods." Accordingly, Manchuria should be liberated by a KMT–CCP coalition rather than be reconquered and possibly restored to China by Soviet forces.[17]

It is noteworthy that although both anticipated Soviet interference in Manchuria, during most of the war neither the KMT nor the CCP expected the territory to become the first hot spot in their postwar rivalry for power. In the summer of 1942, Mao Zedong did envisage a scenario looking beyond Japan's defeat, when the "whole Eighth Route Army and the New Fourth Army must be concentrated in the three northeastern provinces." But such military maneuvers would not serve to initiate an armed struggle against the KMT. At that time, the CCP forces in the southern provinces of China were deemed a thorn in the flesh by Chongqing, which became the cause of much friction between the two sides. The best-known event was the New Fourth Army incident. In January 1941, when the Communist New Fourth Army to the south of the Yangtze River was moving north, it was ambushed by Chiang Kai-shek's troops and its principal commanding officers were captured. Therefore, aside from viewing Manchuria as a new base for the CCP, Mao expected that CCP forces would move to the northeast at the end of the war in order to ease tensions between Yan'an and Chongqing and to create "conditions of a continual KMT–CCP cooperation" in the postwar years.[18]

During the last year of China's war against Japan, the CCP policy toward Manchuria typically reflected the uncertainty of the KMT–CCP relationship. In the summer of 1944, 100,000 KMT troops in Henan collapsed under Japan's *Ichigo* offensive (Operation No. 1). The debacle shocked the CCP Central Committee into making the decision that the Communists, not the impotent KMT, must now assume the responsibility for expelling Japanese troops from urban areas in eastern China. Therefore, the party had to escalate its efforts in the cities. While directing its

---

[17] *Morgenthau Diary*, 879. Peter Vladimirov's *The Vladimirov Diaries: Yenan, China: 1942–1945* (Garden City, NY: Doubleday, 1975), 38, 230, 371, 394, 440, 464–465, 495–496, 498, 501, presents some alleged views of CCP leaders on Manchuria and its position in the Yan'an–Moscow relationship. The reliability of these "diaries" has been questioned by scholars. What emerges from this source is not an accurate and consistent depiction of the CCP policy toward Manchuria but the fact that this issue was a trouble spot in the Yan'an–Moscow relationship.

[18] Niu Jun, *Cong Yan'an Zouxiang Shijie*, 123–124.

regional bureaus to strengthen their work in the cities, the Central Committee realized that Manchuria was an uncharted land in terms of the party's activities. Consequently, the Central Committee commanded its organizations in Hebei, Jehol, and Shandong each to establish a "working committee on Manchuria." In its directives the Central Committee pointed out: "The development of [the party's] work in Manchuria not only will affect enormously the future conditions in China, but also is an urgent task demanding immediate attention."[19] From the spring of 1945, when Yan'an's relations with both Chongqing and the United States were deteriorating and the Soviet entry into the Pacific war seemed imminent, CCP leaders began to consider turning Manchuria into one of their most important bases in a new round of power struggles against the KMT regime. Meanwhile, Yan'an continued to make preparations for a renewed civil war in southern China, where the KMT's nerve center could be attacked directly. A new strategy calling for military advances in the north but defense in the south would not be adopted by the CCP until a month after Japan's surrender.[20]

Taiwan was another lost territory often mentioned in CCP leaders' wartime statements. Yan'an's orientation toward Taiwan, like that of the KMT regime, also went through several readjustments. Conferring with CCP leaders in 1936, Edgar Snow learned about Mao Zedong's attitude toward Korea and Taiwan:

> We do not . . . include Korea [in China's lost territories], formerly a Chinese colony, but when we have re-established the independence of the lost territories of China, and if the Koreans wish to break away from the chains of Japanese imperialism, we will extend them our enthusiastic help in their struggle for independence. *The same thing applies for Taiwan.* (Emphasis added)[21]

[19] "Zhongyang guanyu chengshi gongzou de zhishi" (The Central Committee's Directive on the Work in the Cities), 5 June 1944, *Zhongyang Wenjian*, 14: 243–252; "Zhongyang guanyu kaizhan Manzhou gongzou gei Jin Cha Ji fenju de zhishi" (The Central Committee's Directive to the Jin Cha Ji Bureau on the Development of [the Party's] Work in Manchuria), 4 September 1944, ibid., 321.

[20] Niu Jun, *Cong Yan'an Zouxiang Shijie*, 178–179; "Zhongyang guanyu huanan zhanlue fangzhen he gongzou bushu gei Guangdong qu dangwei de zhishi" (The Central Committee's Directive to the Party Committee of the Guangdong District on the Military Strategy and the Work Plans in Southern China), 16 June 1945, *Zhongyang Wenjian*, 15: 145–147; "Zhongyang guanyu huazhong wojun de zhanlüe bushu gei huazhong ju de zhishi" (The Central Committee's Directive to the Central China Bureau on the Military Strategy in Central China), 12 August 1945, ibid., 234–235; "Zhongyang guanyu queding xiang bei tuijin xiang nan fangyu de zhanlüe fangzhen zhi Zhonggong fu Yu tanpan daibiaoduan dian" (The Central Committee to the Communist Delegation of Negotiation to Yu [Chongqing] on the Decision Concerning the Strategy of Advancement in the North and Defense in the South), 17 September 1945, ibid., 278–280.

[21] Snow, *Red Star*, 110.

Mao's attitude toward Taiwan, as reflected here, is subject to different interpretations. In 1936, the issue did not seem important enough to warrant Snow's special attention. But thirty-two years later, in preparing a new edition of his *Red Star Over China*, Snow noticed intricacies surrounding the issue and thought it necessary to explain Mao's stand. Snow did not think it conceivable that in 1936 Mao had really meant Taiwan's independence. This view is supported by researchers in the People's Republic of China but challenged by others.[22]

Other evidence indicates that Mao's statement was not a careless, isolated remark. It represented a consistent policy of the CCP that did not change until early 1942. For instance, the fifth item of the aforementioned Eighth Route Army's ten anti-Japanese principles stipulated that the Chinese anti-Japanese forces should "join the Japanese, Korean and Formosan peasants in an anti-Fascist movement," categorizing the Chinese and the Taiwanese as two separate units in an Asia-wide international united front. In the spring of 1937, writing about the CCP's political strategy in the war against Japan, Luo Fu expressed the same idea: in their struggle for national independence, the Chinese people should join forces with "the suppressed people in Japan and the suppressed nations such as Korea and Taiwan." As late as June 1941, the *Jiefang Ribao* treated the anti-Japanese struggle of the Taiwanese people as a "national independence movement," which was "one of the troops in the anti-imperialist movement of the Oriental suppressed peoples and part of the world force that loves peace and opposes imperialist war." All these voices treated the Taiwanese movement as an independent force on the international scene rather than an integral part of China's struggle.[23]

It would be an exaggeration to argue either that the CCP leadership in this period was committed to a policy of supporting an independent Taiwan, or that, although CCP leaders talked in terms of Taiwanese independence, what they really meant was Taiwan's reunion with China. Both arguments tend to simplify the historical record. CCP leaders always contemplated their revolution in China in terms of a phased struggle. It is therefore plausible that they applied the same principle in addressing China's external affairs. CCP leaders viewed the war against Japan as both a military process for national defense and a process of revolution.

[22] Ibid., 421. A view from the People's Republic of China can be found in Zhang Bilai, "Taiwan yiyongdui," *Geming Shi Ziliao*, 8 (1982): 46–90. Two different interpretations are Frank S. T. Hsiao and Lawrence R. Sullivan, "The Chinese Communist Party and the Status of Taiwan, 1928–1943," *Pacific Affairs*, 52 (Fall 1979): 446–467, and Lu Xiuyi, *Ri Ju Shidai Taiwan Gongchandang Shi, 1928–1932* (A History of the Taiwanese Communist Party in the Period of the Japanese Occupation, 1928–1932) (Taipei: Qianwei Chubanshe, 1989), 161.

[23] Carlson, *Twin Stars of China*, 251–252; *Jiefang*, 8 May 1937; *Jiefang Ribao*, 17 June 1941.

Accordingly, they saw the recovery of China's lost territories as both a foreign policy issue and a revolutionary act. Elements to be considered included not only the progress of China's revolution and the international conditions for China's diplomacy, but also the aspirations of the populations in those territories who had been alienated from China for a considerable time.

In the CCP's statements and writings of the war years, Yan'an's strategy for recovering China's lost territories concentrated on three components. The first was for China to achieve complete independence, political unity, and democratization of its internal politics. These were necessary preconditions for China to discharge its responsibility for and obligations to the diverse nationalities along China's peripheries. The second was that these nationalities, through their participation in the international anti-imperialist struggle, must break away from foreign control and regain their right to make decisions governing their own political future. The third was a process of federation making, in which China would be the leader but would be joined voluntarily by the peripheral peoples on an equal footing. Depending on the circumstances, the order of the first two stages might vary and the attainment of the third might occur at different times for different territories. In the war years, such a strategy, at least in theory, held the advantage of providing the CCP with tremendous flexibility in dealing with China's external affairs. In practice, Yan'an had to focus its attention on the life-and-death struggle with both Japan and Chongqing in China.

Mao Zedong himself best delineated this strategy on territorial subjects when he talked to Snow in 1936. Among Japan's principal overseas possessions, Manchuria had been alienated from China for less than five years. Manchuria's identification with China was indisputable. Therefore Mao, like other leaders, definitely categorized the region as a lost territory to be recovered by China. For Taiwan and Korea, the formidable task was to achieve their liberation from Japan, and the two peoples' struggle for freedom would certainly weaken Japan and assist China's resistance. A people's republic had already come into existence in Outer Mongolia, and this state would automatically join a Chinese federation once the Chinese people won their own revolution. Inner Mongolia and Tibet would also go through the same process from autonomy to membership in the Chinese federation. Mao did not claim original authorship for this program but attributed it to Sun Yat-sen. In 1936 and in the years to come, however, Mao did not think that the current KMT leadership could sponsor a proper program for a democratic Chinese republic unless it returned to Sun's principles.[24]

Mao's attitude toward the status of Outer Mongolia might well have been

---

[24] Snow, *Red Star*, 110.

regarded as a precedent for Taiwan. Although he endorsed the current Mongolian independence from the KMT China, Mao contended that Mongolia would want to rejoin a new, democratic China. In light of the phased revolutionary strategy, therefore, Yan'an's support of Taiwanese independence in the late 1930s and early 1940s reflected a policy of expediting the immediate anti-Japanese struggle, but not for a permanent settlement of Taiwan's status. Throughout the war, the Chinese Communists would continue to hold this independence-autonomy-federation formula as a proper policy for the peoples living in alienated territories of China.[25]

Another matter that affected the CCP's approach to the issue of Taiwan was the stand taken by the Comintern, which treated the island as a colony of Japan but not a lost territory of China. Accordingly, the Taiwanese Communist Party (TCP, founded in 1928) affiliated organizationally with the Japanese Communist Party. In concert with the Comintern's policy of national liberation for colonial peoples, the TCP's goals included the establishment of a "Taiwanese Republic." There was a brief period of cooperation between the CCP and the TCP after the latter was crushed by the Japanese authorities in Taiwan in 1932. But when the Sino–Japanese war began, the CCP no longer conducted its Taiwan policy via the TCP. Nevertheless, the established objectives of the Taiwanese left-wing movement, which bore a Comintern trademark, continued to affect the CCP's own policy.[26]

During the war of resistance against Japan, the CCP endeavored to cultivate contacts with non-Communist Taiwanese groups on the mainland. Its most important achievement in this regard was to gain influence over the Taiwanese Independent and Revolutionary Party (TIRP). In 1938, Li Youbang, a Taiwanese graduate of the Whampoa Academy, organized the TIRP in Zhejiang with assistance from the CCP. In fact, Li's deputy was a secret CCP member. Later, the TIRP was instrumental in encouraging Taiwanese groups on the mainland to consolidate to form the Taiwanese Revolutionary Alliance (TRA).[27] Yan'an hoped to use the TIRP to influence other Taiwanese. In April 1939, Zhou Enlai personally instructed secret CCP members in the TIRP to make full use of its connections with

---

[25] Guan Feng, "Menggu minzu yu kangri zhanzheng" (The Mongolian Nationality and the Anti-Japanese War), *Jiefang*, 29 February 1940; Stein, *Challenge of Red China*, 442; *Amerasia Papers*, 696.

[26] Lu Xiuyi, *Taiwan Gongchandang*, 147–160; Wu Guo'an, "Lun Taiwan tongbao canjia zuguo kangri zhanzheng de huodong jiqi yiyi" (On the Taiwanese Compatriots' Activities of Participating in Our Nation's Anti-Japanese War), *Jindaishi Yanjiu* (Study of Modern History), no. 29 (Fall 1986), 227; Hsiao and Sullivan, "Chinese Communist Party and the Status of Taiwan," 455–456.

[27] Zhang Bilai, "Taiwan yiyongdui," 46–48, 63–67, 70; Wu Guo'an, "Taiwan tongbao," 224; Xie Dongmin et al., *Guomin Geming*, 61–68.

the KMT but cautioned against exposing its relationship with the CCP. Li Youbang's Whampoa background proved crucial. For instance, with the help of his Whampoa classmate, Kang Ze, a senior member of the Political Committee of the KMT Military Council, Li won the KMT military authorities' support for organizing a "Taiwanese Volunteer Corps."[28]

In the late 1930s, the TIRP's program was unique among Taiwanese organizations but closely resembled Yan'an's own. Li Youbang once explained why his party's name included both "independent" and "revolutionary." "Why independent?" Li asked. "Because Taiwan was in the hands of the Japanese imperialists, the Taiwanese revolution must at first achieve independence and then, after that, return to the motherland [China]. Why revolutionary? Because China was still an old state ruled by feudal warlords, only a revolution could create a new China." In addition to its two-phase program for Taiwan, the TIRP stood alone among the Taiwanese groups on the mainland in not accepting the KMT regime's leadership. Instead, it proposed to establish a "body of political alliance" between the Taiwanese movement and Chongqing. This policy of conditional cooperation with the KMT authorities was obviously influenced by the CCP's united-front strategy.[29]

Eventually, it was the united-front strategy that prompted Yan'an to shift the focus of its policy from Taiwan's independence to reunification with China. In March 1940, when Taiwanese partisans formed a unified organization in Chongqing, they adopted the TIRP formula for independence from Japan first and reunification with China later. Yet, the next year, the reorganized Taiwanese Revolutionary Alliance adopted a new platform that formally accepted KMT leadership as a vital condition for Taiwan's liberation. The Taiwanese made this move in order to arouse Chongqing's interest in their movement. From then on, Taiwanese partisans strove to achieve Chongqing's recognition of Taiwan's proper position in China. They first demanded that Taiwan be regarded as an old lost territory of China, and then that the island be restored to its position as a province of China. Consequently, in early 1942, when the Taiwanese revolutionaries capitalized on the beginning of the Pacific war and used the

[28] Zhang Bilai, "Taiwan yiyongdui," 47, 52–55, 60–62, 70–71. Although the Chongqing government had suspicions about the political connection of the TIRP, there is no evidence that in the war years they knew of the TIRP–CCP cooperation. After the Japanese surrender, Li Youbang went to Taiwan but maintained contacts with the CCP underground on the island. Eventually he was arrested and died in prison. The year of his death is unknown to this writer.

[29] Zhang Bilai, "Taiwan yiyongdui," 48–52, 71–76; Li Yunhan, "Kangzhan qijian Taiwan geming tongmenghui de zuzhi yu huodong" (The Organization and Activities of the Taiwanese Revolutionary Alliance during the War of Resistance), in Wang Shounan et al., ed., *Zhongguo Jindai Xiandai Shi Lunwenji, Di Ershijiu Bian* (Essays on the Modern and Contemporary History of China, Volume 29) (Taipei: Taiwan Shangwu Yinshuguan, 1986), 714.

occasion to press Chongqing for more concrete and positive support, the CCP joined in the chorus.[30]

In the spring, the CCP's two organs, the *Jiefang Ribao* in Yan'an and the *Xinhua Ribao* (New China Daily) in Chongqing, began to report various Taiwanese partisans' activities aimed at achieving Chongqing's active support for Taiwan's reunification with China. The latter even instituted a special column on the "Taiwanese Restoration [*guangfu*] Movement." Thereafter, the term "restoration movement" replaced "independence movement" in the CCP rhetoric on Taiwan, and the island's reunification with China became Yan'an's official policy.[31]

At the outset, the CCP's support was well received by the TRA. In April 1942, the TRA held its second assembly, which urged the KMT government to organize a Taiwanese provincial government and to accelerate its preparatory work for recovering the island. On that occasion, the *Xinhua Ribao* published an editorial criticizing the government for being "always too slow" in responding to the Taiwanese cry for help. Meanwhile, the editorial emphasized that "the destiny of Taiwan will finally have to be decided by the Taiwanese people themselves." Later, the TRA reprinted the editorial and published it along with the manifesto of its own second assembly.[32]

During the Pacific war, Yan'an's ability to exert direct influence over the Taiwanese movement gradually eroded. At first, in the wake of the New Fourth Army Incident, Yan'an had to readjust its infrastructure in southern China. This led to a change in the CCP personnel that weakened the CCP's influence on the TIRP. Then Li Youbang's position within the TRA also visibly declined before the end of the war. During the first two years of the Pacific war, Li was one of the three members of the TRA's presidium. Some time in 1944, according to a TRA report to the KMT's Organization Department, Li was removed from that position and relegated to a powerless supervisory committee. At the same time, he continued to participate in the work of a committee on postwar military affairs in Taiwan. When the war ended and the TRA was making preparations to return to Taiwan, Li's name disappeared completely from its leading group.[33]

[30] Xie Dongmin et al., *Guomin Geming*, 57–65; Wu Guo'an, "Taiwan yiyongdui," 226–228.

[31] *Jiefang Ribao*, 23 March 1942; *Xinhua Ribao* (New China Daily), 25 March, 5 April, 6 April 1942, 17 April and 17 June 1943; *Amerasia Papers*, 696; Esherick, *Lost Chance in China*, 252–255. Hsiao and Sullivan, in their "Chinese Communist Party and the Status of Taiwan," suggest that the CCP did not begin to support Taiwan's reunion until the issue was decided at the Cairo Conference of 1943. They made this mistake probably because their discussion relies mainly on materials in the Japanese language but not on Chinese materials, including these two CCP newspapers.

[32] *Taiwan Wenti Yanlun Ji*, 92–106.

[33] Zhang Bilai, "Taiwan yiyongdui," 84, 89–90; Xie Dongmin, *Guomin Geming*, 64, 67, 77, 80; Li Yunhan, "Kangzhan qijian," 715, 724 n. 6.

Yan'an and Korean independence

In its policy toward Korea, Yan'an experienced less uncertainty than in the case of Taiwan. After Mao Zedong first professed his support for Korea's independence in his conversation with Edgar Snow in 1936, the CCP continued to uphold this policy. Their slogan, "Fight back to the Yalu River," indicated that CCP leaders did not regard Korea as a lost territory of China. Information is not available about the CCP's attitude toward, or even its knowledge of, the Chongqing–Washington disagreement over postwar trusteeship in Korea. After the Cairo Conference, the *Jiefang Ribao* praised the Cairo Communiqué for its renunciation of territorial ambitions by any participating government, suggesting that the announcement would frustrate those in China who believed in "China's cultural superiority" and in China's own imperialism. In an interview with the U.S. Army Observer Group in 1944, Buo Gu, a member of the CCP Political Bureau in charge of party propaganda, explicitly condemned Chongqing's policy toward Korean expatriates as "typical Kuomintang imperialism." He emphasized that Yan'an's policy was to help Korea achieve "full freedom."[34] Obviously, Chongqing's wartime sponsorship of the Korean Provisional Government (KPG) was interpreted in Yan'an as a means for control and manipulation. Yet, in view of the CCP's idea about national liberation for colonial peoples and its consistent belief that in Korea, as well as in China, Japan, and Taiwan, the people must fight for freedom through their own revolution, it is plausible that Yan'an shared Chongqing's misgivings about any trusteeship solution for Korea.

Without further documentation, it is impossible to know which parts of the KMT program for Korea were favored and which were opposed by the CCP leadership. Only the CCP's own support of a Korean group in the Border Regions can be compared with the KMT policy. Like leaders in Chongqing, CCP leaders did not limit their postwar concern to China's lost territories. The importance of Korea for China's anti-Japanese war and China's postwar security was as plain to Yan'an as it was to Chongqing. Whereas the KMT used the Three People's Principles to formulate its Korea policy, the CCP employed the concept of an international revolutionary united front in defining China's relationship with Korea. The two Chinese parties also supported different political wings of the Korean independence movement. In terms of geographical proximity, Manchuria was the most convenient place for the CCP and Korean revolutionaries to cooperate in a common struggle against Japan. In 1930, Korean Communists in Manchuria actually dissolved their own organization to join with the CCP. Yet, in terms of political conditions, Manchuria was a terribly

[34] *Jiefang*, 8 May 1937; *Jiefang Ribao*, 10 December 1943; *Amerasia Papers*, 696; report by John Service, 23 September 1944, *FRUS, 1944: China*, 587.

repressive place for anti-Japanese groups. Before the Pacific war began, most CCP guerrilla fighters with Korean Communists in their ranks had to withdraw across the Russian border.[35]

Wartime CCP–Korean cooperation developed mainly in northern China, starting in 1940. In one important aspect, Yan'an's relationship with Korean partisans was different from its involvement with the Taiwanese. Yan'an favored unity among the various Taiwanese groups and avoided exposing any direct connection between itself and the Taiwanese expatriates. By contrast, wartime collaboration between the CCP and a Korean group in northern China reflected factional strife within the Korean movement in China. Students of Korean nationalism and Communism have debated whether or not the CCP intentionally incited divisiveness in the ranks of the Korean partisans. Yet, like KMT leaders in Chongqing, the CCP leaders had to live with the divisive condition of the Korean movement.

Until now, the only source confirming the theory of a conspiracy by Yan'an is Sima Lu's published recollections. In the war years, Sima Lu was a secret CCP member serving as Kim Won-bong's private secretary in Chongqing. Sima alleged that in the early 1940s Zhou Enlai and his associates in Chongqing instructed him to arrange for the migration of certain members of the Korean Volunteer Corps (KVC) to northern China. This account cannot be verified.[36] In the meantime, there is evidence indicating that the northward migration of these Koreans was undertaken on their own initiative. A report of the KMT's Central Bureau of Investigation and Statistics, dated 29 October 1941, analyzed the development in these words:

> The components of the Korean National Revolutionary Party are always mixed. Since the beginning of the second European war and the conclusion of the Japanese–Russian [neutrality] pact, the unstable elements of the party have believed that the situation of the Sino–Japanese war will change soon and they have gone one after another to Shaanbei to collude with the CCP. They try to obtain favor from Yan'an through a regimental commander of the Eighth Route Army's artillery troops named Wu Ting, who is a Korean and has an influential position within the CCP.

The report complained that by "throwing themselves into the CCP's arms," these Koreans were ungrateful for the KMT regime's assistance to them

---

[35] *Jiefang Ribao*, 17 June 1941; Dae-sook Suh, *Documents of Korean Communism, 1918–1948* (Princeton, NJ: Princeton University Press, 1970), 372–376, 385–397. It should be noted that the dissolution of the Manchurian Bureau of the Korean Communist Party in 1936 was carried out in accordance with a regulation of the Comintern, which required foreign Communists to join the Communist organizations of their current residential countries.

[36] For two interpretations of the issue, see Chong-sik Lee, "Korean Communists and Yenan," *The China Quarterly*, no. 9 (January–March 1962), 182–192, and Dae-sook Suh, *The Korean Communist Movement, 1918–1948* (Princeton, NJ: Princeton University Press, 1967), 220–230. Sima is the last name in Sima Lu.

and acted "extremely foolishly."[37] In the war years, KMT officials operated under the conviction that the CCP would use any opportunity to weaken the government's position and prestige. Therefore, it is noteworthy that the report did not indicate even a suspicion of any contact between the Koreans and the CCP representatives in Chongqing.[38]

It is true that after World War II, Yan'an's Korean connection fostered in the war years would prove an asset for the CCP's military struggle with the KMT in Manchuria. But in 1941, the CCP leadership had no good reason to weaken Kim Won-bong's KVC by drawing his followers to northern China. The Koreans coming from the KMT areas would add extra burdens to Yan'an's already meager resources. More important, in Chongqing, the Kim Won-bong faction was the most likely ally to the CCP's united front policy. In fact, before moving to Chongqing in 1941, the KVC had already cooperated closely with Li Youbang's TIRP. An immediate beneficiary of the KVC's split was the right-wing KPG under Kim Ku. Previously, Kim Ku had tried without much success to convince Chongqing that Communist elements were responsible for the disunity within the Korean movement. After the most radical Koreans migrated to northern China, the Kim Won-bong faction was weakened and discredited in the eyes of the KMT authorities. This development influenced Chongqing's decision to use the Kim Ku group as the pivot for its Korean policy.[39]

The Koreans who proceeded to the CCP region in 1941 numbered about 100. Their arrival led to organizational readjustment for Koreans who were already there. In August 1942, in Tonggu, Shaanxi, a North China Korean Independence League (NCKIL) was established. Soon the headquarters of the NCKIL moved to Yan'an.[40] Yan'an's influence on the NCKIL and its forerunners in northern China was easily recognizable.

[37] Xu Enzeng to Zhu Jiahua, 29 October 1941, and enclosures, *HDYS*, 118–119. Wu Ting (also known as Mu Rong or Mu Chong) probably joined the CCP in the late 1920s or early 1930s. He was a participant in the Long March. During World War II, he commanded a Korean military unit in northern China.

[38] Suh, *Korean Communist Movement*, 221; Lee, "Korean Communists and Yenan," 184–185. As related in the Lee article, the alleged CCP conspiracy to lure the Koreans to North China was developed at a dinner meeting between Sima Lu and Zhou Enlai in Zhou's mansion in Chongqing and several other meetings between Sima and Zhou's delegates. Given the fact that both the KVC and the CCP delegation in Chongqing were watched closely by the KMT authorities, it seems unlikely that all of these meetings escaped the government's attention.

[39] Zhang Bilai, "Taiwan yiyongdui," 55–56, 84–89; Zhu Jiahua to Chiang Kai-shek, 26 January 1940, *HDYS*, 63–64; Zhu to Kang Ze, 3 June 1940, ibid., 83; Kang to Zhu, 9 June 1940, ibid., 84–86; Xu Enzeng to Zhu, 1 November 1941, ibid., 107–122.

[40] Tang Pingzhu, "Yi Chaoxian zhanyou" (Korean Comrades-in-Arms Remembered), in *Xinghuo Liaoyuan; Xuanbian Zhi Qi* (A Single Spark Can Start a Prairie Fire, Volume 7 of an abridged edition) (Beijing: Zhanshi Chubanshe, 1982), 193–194; Suh, *Korean Communist Movement*, 225–229.

Subscribing to the CCP's united-front policy, the NCKIL during the remainder of the war made an effort to attract additional Koreans into its
ranks. Yet it scrupulously targeted its propaganda at Koreans in northern
China and other Japanese-occupied territories. The NCKIL never recognized the KPG in Chongqing as the central body of the Korean national
movement. Nor did it make such a claim on its own behalf. The NCKIL
always called itself a "local organ" of the Korean revolutionary movement, which paralleled Yan'an's claim that it was not functioning as a
government but rather as a principal anti-Japanese force in China.[41]

Throughout the war, the NCKIL expanded. In the spring of 1945, some
Korean leaders in Yan'an talked to members of the U.S. Army Observers
Group. They told the Americans that at the time the NCKIL had about
100 cadres, fewer than 20 of whom were Communist Party members. The
majority of these cadres came from Chongqing, and there were also about
thirty who came from Manchuria and Korea. The NCKIL claimed more
than 1,000 members in the CCP region alone, as well as a significant
number of secret members acting behind the Japanese lines. Compared
with the Koreans in Chongqing, the Yan'an Koreans were a much younger
and more vigorous group (the majority were bachelors between twenty
and thirty-five). They were especially proud of their well-trained military
units. With these advantages, the NCKIL claimed to be the strongest Korean
fighting force in China. Meanwhile, these leaders remarked with obvious
contempt that the KPG was "split within and has no mass support . . .
represents only the reactionary Korean landlords and has no idea what the
common people of Korea think or feel. . . . In twenty-four years of existence, it has done virtually nothing." Nevertheless, the Americans were
informed that the KPG would not be excluded from the Korean people's
common struggle for independence.[42]

One aspect of the CCP–Korean cooperation was the training provided
for Korean military and political cadres through crash programs or direct
participation in the operations of the Eighth Route Army. The military
force under the NCKIL was named the Korean Volunteer Army (KVA). A
few hundred strong, the "army" consisted of units of different sizes that
rarely operated together in the same area. Politically, the KVA was under
the leadership of the NCKIL. Militarily, it had to follow the direction of
the Eighth Route Army Headquarters, though there were also small units
that operated independently. A noticeable difference between the KVA and
its Chongqing counterpart, the Korean Restoration Army, was that the
former actually participated in the war against Japan. In May 1942, for

---

[41] Suh, *Documents of Korean Communism*, 412–425.
[42] "Current Information from the Korean Independence League," 22 March 1945, and
"Reports from Korean Revolutionary Political & Military School, Yenan," 2 May 1945,
RDCA, box 8.

instance, during a battle against Japanese forces in the Taihang Moun-tains, a unit of about 100 KVA troops proved decisive in rescuing the Political Department of the Eighth Route Army's Headquarters from the enemy's siege.[43]

If there was any undertaking in the Yan'an–Korean cooperation that involved the CCP's long-term designs on Korea, it was the Korean Revo-lutionary Military and Political School. Established in the winter of 1942 in the Taihang Mountain area, the school moved to Yan'an in April 1944. Leaders of the NCKIL were ambitious to organize a force of 10,000 troops in the final stage of the war. This contingent was intended to act in concert with the Allied forces in operations to liberate Manchuria and Korea. The training school was expected to produce an adequate number of military cadets and political functionaries for the future army. By mid-1945, about 250 Korean youths had received training in the school. At the end of the war, these cadets would become the core of a stronger KVA that num-bered some 2,500 troops and was ready to march into Korea.[44]

Yan'an and postwar Japan

Mao Zedong once remarked that in the postwar era, China's role would be "tremendous in maintaining peace in the world and decisive in preserv-ing peace in the East."[45] In the war years, Yan'an developed relations with revolutionaries of other Asian areas for both winning the war and promoting revolutions in postwar Asia. Among these relations, the best publicized was the cooperation between the CCP and the Japanese Communist Party (JCP). China's war with Japan induced Chinese political parties to seek contact with Japanese antigovernment elements. While KMT officials in Chongqing indulged in idle talk about conspiring with Japanese dissidents to incite political unrest in Japan, Yan'an was forming a working relationship with Japanese radicals. The CCP leadership prized this partnership and treated Japan as one of its most important policy concerns. This can best be under-stood by noting the salient position occupied by the topic of Japan at the CCP's seventh congress in April 1945. On that occasion, after Mao delivered his report "On the Coalition Government" and Zhu De talked about the military situation, Nosaka Sanzo, leader of the JCP, served as the promi-nent third speaker to address the congress on the issue of postwar Japan.[46]

[43] Ibid.; Tang Pingzhu, "Yi Chaoxian zhanyou," 194–196.

[44] "Reports from Korean Revolutionary Political & Military School, Yenan," 2 May 1945, RDCA, box 8; Suh, *Documents of Korean Communism*, 422; Robert R. Simmons, *The Strained Alliance: Peking, Pyongyang, Moscow and the Politics of the Korean Civil War* (New York: Free Press, 1975), 23.

[45] *Mao Zedong Ji* (Works of Mao Zedong) (Tokyo: Hokubosha, 1970–1971), 8: 190.

[46] Nosaka Sanzo, *Yeban Cansan Xuanji: Zhanshi Bian* (Selected Works of Nosaka Sanzo: Wartime Writings) (Beijing: Renmin Chubanshe, 1963), 204, 349.

During the war, Yan'an had its own "Japan hands." CCP members who had studied in Japan were instrumental in a very active "Yan'an Society for Returned Students from Japan" and a "Research Office of the Japanese Problem" under the Central Committee of the CCP.[47] But until Nosaka Sanzo came to Yan'an in 1940, Yan'an's views on Japanese affairs were confined to a Leninist macroanalysis of Japanese imperialism. Japan was categorized as a "military feudal imperialist" country, with the cult of the emperor as the most prominent symbol of feudalism. This "feudal imperialism," according to CCP theoreticians, was bound to perish in the war. As early as 1937, Mao Zedong asserted to a few American journalists that "it is impossible to reason that after Japanese imperialism is driven out of China, it can still retain its position in Japan." During the first half of the Pacific war, Mao was optimistic that a revolution in Japan was not only possible but also imminent. He predicted that a revolution would start in Japan once the Japanese Army suffered a few severe military setbacks.[48]

Before the end of the war, these sketches about the future of Japan were replaced by a more sophisticated view. In September 1944, Buo Gu, chief of CCP propaganda, outlined a refined party line on Japan to John Service. At the end of the war, Buo Gu indicated, Japan must be deprived of all its colonies, Japan's monopoly capitalism must be liquidated, and Japanese armed forces must be reduced to a small number and reorganized according to democratic principles. In the meantime, Allied peace terms for Japan should not be unnecessarily severe. This meant that no heavy indemnity should be inflicted by the Allies, the imperial family should be left in place, and the Japanese themselves, through the democratic process, should be allowed to determine whether the monarchy should continue. Bo Gu also suggested that the socioeconomic system in postwar Japan should be one of "democratic capitalism," not Communism. Democratization of Japan should be implemented principally through education (by following the CCP example of reeducating Japanese war prisoners) but not by force. Japan should be given the opportunity for peaceful commercial development, as well as access to markets and raw materials. And, lastly, Japanese business would be welcome to contribute to China's industrialization program.[49]

On the question of reparations, Yan'an's position was more moderate than Chongqing's. But it was Yan'an's attitude toward the Japanese emperor that drew special attention from American officials in China. According to a report from the Office of Strategic Service, CCP leaders believed that, given the deeply rooted veneration of the emperor among the Japanese masses, the emphasis for social and political reforms in postwar

---

[47] *Jiefang Ribao*, 16 December 1941.
[48] Wales, *My Yenan Notebooks*, 134; Snow, *Red Star*, 109; *Jiefang Ribao*, 25 June 1943; *Amerasia Papers*, 696.
[49] Report by Service, 23 September 1944, *FRUS, 1944: China*, 585–587.

Japan should first be placed on ridding the country of militarist organizations and the *zaibatsu* (great business combines). After these were destroyed, the imperial institution would lose its pillars of support and the Japanese people might then be persuaded to remove the monarchy. At the same time, the CCP leadership was firmly opposed to any suggestion that after the war the emperor should be used by the Allies for any purpose. The phased revolutionary strategy was again useful. But eventually, Yan'an shared Chongqing's negative attitude toward Japan's imperial institution.[50]

Apparently, Yan'an's refined view of Japan was achieved with the help of Nosaka Sanzo. Before his arrival in Yan'an in the spring of 1940, Nosaka had spent nine years in the Soviet Union, working for the Comintern under the name Okano Susumu. When World War II began in Europe, Nosaka decided that it was time for him to return to Japan. In March 1940, he arrived in Yan'an with Zhou Enlai, who had been in Moscow for a few months in order to receive medical treatment. CCP leaders persuaded Nosaka not to continue his almost certainly suicidal journey to Japan but to stay in Yan'an in order to help the CCP improve its work regarding Japan.[51] From 1940 to 1943, Nosaka's presence in China was a well-kept secret even in the Communist region. Using a Chinese name, Lin Zhe, he directed the work of the Research Office of the Japanese Problem and also wrote editorials concerning Japan for the *Jiefang Ribao*. After the war, Nosaka's contribution to the CCP's comprehension of Japanese affairs in the war years would be acknowledged publicly by the CCP leadership.[52]

Nosaka's activities in Yan'an helped the CCP in three ways. First, his work with the Research Office in Yan'an brought Yan'an's intelligence information about Japan up to date. Nosaka painstakingly collected newspapers and other publications from Japan. Eventually, he managed to obtain more than forty different publications on a regular basis, all of

---

[50] "Chinese Views of the Japanese Emperor," 24 August 1945, *OSSR*, reel 2.
[51] Zhonggong Zhongyang Wenxian Yanjiushi (Documentary Research Office of the Central Committee of the Chinese Communist Party), *Zhou Enlai Nianpu, 1898–1949* (The Chronicle of Zhou Enlai's Life, 1898–1949) (Beijing: Zhongyang Wenxian Chubanshe, 1989), 453; Nosaka Sanzo, *Wangming Shiliu Nian* (Sixteen Years in Exile) (Hong Kong: Wenjian Chubanshe, 1949), 10–11, 39–40; idem, *Yeban Cansan Xuanji*, 198–204.
[52] Nosaka, *Yeban Cansan Xuanji*, 202–205, 208–210, 403–406, 410. Nosaka's own reminiscences do not provide a satisfactory explanation for the secrecy of his staying in Yan'an. Two possible explanations can be considered. One is that because his original destination was Japan, and this was not definitely abandoned for some time, Nosaka's open activities in China would have aroused the suspicion of the Japanese government and thus would have frustrated any future attempts on his part to sneak into Japan. Another explanation is that Nosaka went to Yan'an as a functionary of the Comintern but not as a representative of the Japanese Communist Party, and his anonymity would avoid unnecessary complications between Yan'an and the Comintern. Perhaps that is why Nosaka publicly emerged in Yan'an only after the dissolution of the Comintern in May 1943.

which were smuggled into the Communist area by connections in northern Chinese cities then under Japan's occupation. After one year's effort, Yan'an's intelligence analysis of Japan became less speculative because of its newly reliable sources. A concrete result of this development was the publication by the Eighth Route Army's political department of *Diguo Ziliao* ("Information on the Enemy State"), which circulated among senior CCP officials.[53]

The second area in which Nosaka assisted Yan'an was in the Eighth Route Army's psychological warfare against Japanese troops. This work was mainly carried out by the Anti-War League for the Japanese in China and its successor, the Japanese People's Emancipation League (JPEL). Interestingly, the first Japanese Anti-War League was established in Chongqing in the spring of 1939 but then was dissolved by the KMT government in the summer of 1941.[54] To the Eighth Route Army's own propaganda directed toward the enemy, the league's antiwar activities constituted a valuable supplement. While the Eighth Route Army focused on propagating its lenient policy toward war prisoners, the League's literature in the Japanese language was able to reach the common Japanese soldiers by exploiting their discontent about the harsh conditions of the war and their treatment by superior officers. The purpose of the League was to convert these daily frustrations into antiwar consciousness. Nosaka insisted that the League's propaganda be based on detailed, accurate information about the conditions and morale of the Japanese Army. This was not difficult to achieve because most members of the League were Japanese soldiers captured by the CCP forces or deserters from the Japanese Army.

Usually, before being admitted to the League, captured Japanese soldiers received indoctrination or "reeduction" in Yan'an's Japanese Workers' and Peasants' School. Nosaka was the president of the school and Japanese-speaking cadres of the Eighth Route Army staffed the faculty, which in the later years of the war was joined by graduates from the school itself. Yet the most important function of the school was to accommodate captured Japanese soldiers for a period of time and then send them back to the Japanese Army. During the war, the CCP forces captured a few thousand

[53] Nosaka, *Wangming Shiliu Nian*, 41–42; idem, *Yeban Cansan Xuanji*, 205; Stein, *Challenge of Red China*, 413–414.

[54] Li Yongpu, "Riben beifu shibing zai Zhongguo Guomindang tongzhiqu de fanzhan huodong" (The Anti-War Activities of the Captured Japanese Soldiers in Chinese Territories under the Kuomintang), in *Zhong Ri Guanxi Shi Lun Ji* (Historical Essays on Chinese–Japanese Relations), comp. Dongbei Diqu Zhong Ri Guanxishi Yanjiusuo (Research Institute of the Northeastern Region on the History of Sino–Japanese Relations) (Changchun: Jilin Renmin Chubanshe, 1984), 2: 309–317; Guo Muoruo, *Hong Bo Qu: Kangri Zhanzheng Huiyilu* (Melody of Mighty Torrent: Reminiscences on the War of Resistance Against Japan) (Hong Kong: Yixin Shudian, 1972), 45–47; John K. Emmerson, *The Japanese Thread: A Life in the U.S. Foreign Service* (New York: Holt, Rinehart & Winston, 1978), 180.

Japanese soldiers, most of whom eventually returned to the Japanese Army after receiving reeducation either in Yan'an or at other CCP bases.[55]

Nosaka's last, most far-reaching service to Yan'an was to enable CCP leaders to see the emergence of a long-term united front between the Chinese and the Japanese revolutionaries. During the Sino–Japanese war, the CCP leadership always believed that a worldwide antifascist front and a national anti-Japanese front in China must be supplemented by an anti-war front among the Japanese people.[56] The former two came into existence successively as a result of political developments in China and the anti-Axis wars in Europe and the Pacific. But only after Nosaka arrived in Yan'an in 1940 was the CCP leadership able to find an effective bridge to reach the Japanese people. When conditions allowed Nosaka to emerge under his true identity in May 1943, Yan'an arranged a spectacular welcome ceremony for him. The *Jiefang Ribao* published a special report on the whole event. Pretending that Nosaka had just arrived in Yan'an, the report conveyed genuine enthusiasm on the part of the CCP leadership. The party organ predicted that "fascism will be crushed under the joint strength of the Chinese and the Japanese peoples, and China and Japan will thereafter be reborn as two independent, free, and happy new states."[57]

A few months later, in January 1944, the Anti-War League was reorganized into the Japanese People's Emancipation League (JPEL). Thus, the cooperation between Yan'an and the Japanese revolutionaries was elevated from a wartime undertaking to a long-term collaboration. As reported in the *Jiefang Ribao*, Mao Zedong, Zhu De, Nosaka Sanzo (under the name Okano Susumu), and other CCP leaders participated in the inaugural assembly of the JPEL as members of the honored presidium. Zhu De spoke on behalf of the CCP leadership. He called the foundation of the JPEL the starting point of a new Chinese–Japanese relationship, predicting that when the JPEL's struggle resulted in the establishment of a "people's government" in Japan, China and Japan would then become "genuinely cordial and reciprocal friends."[58]

In the wake of the event, John Service talked to Nosaka. He found a "striking" resemblance between the platform of the JPEL outlined by Nosaka and Yan'an's stand regarding postwar Japan. Service correctly surmised that this was the result of close contact between the Japanese and the CCP leaders.[59] The relationship between Nosaka and the CCP leadership was mutually influential. Nosaka was frank about his intellectual debt to Mao Zedong's theory of a "new democratic revolution" in China.

---

[55] *Jiefang Ribao*, 20 February 1944; Stein, *Challenge of Red China*, 409–410.
[56] Li Xin, "Lun kangri zhanzheng" (On the War of Resistance Against Japan), *Lishi Yanjiu* (Study of History), no. 179 (February 1986), 166–179.
[57] Nosaka, *Yeban Cansan Xuanji*, 209–210.
[58] Ibid., 249–251; *Jiefang Ribao*, 18 January 1944.
[59] *Amerasia Papers*, 847.

Using Mao's model, he envisaged the revolution in postwar Japan as a phased development. In the primary stage, the JPEL must strive to achieve a hearing among Japanese soldiers in China and the people at home. Therefore, the JPEL program had to be moderate and tolerant of certain popular misconceptions in Japan and in the Japanese Army. At that time, the JPEL should not even support publicly the relinquishment of Taiwan and Korea by Japan because many Japanese still held these colonies to be under the emperor's divine imprimatur. The CCP's consistent demand for recovering all Chinese territories from Japan was therefore purposely omitted from the JPEL platform. So far as Japan's internal reforms were concerned, according to Nosaka, severe measures against the emperor and the zaibatsu should be delayed and the immediate task of reform in Japan should be to destroy the political influence of the headquarters of the Japanese Army and other militarist institutions.[60]

The CCP leadership agreed completely with this policy. The *Jiefang Ribao* carried the JPEL platform in full. Unable to comprehend the phased revolutionary strategy behind the platform, the *Da Gong Bao* in Chongqing criticized the program for its moderation toward the Japanese emperor and the zaibatsu, its ambiguous attitude toward Japan's disarmament, and its silence about Japan's colonies. Later, Nosaka had to explain to the Chongqing newspaper why the JPEL needed to hold a view on postwar Japan less radical than the editors of the *Da Gong Bao* expected. Nosaka's activities in Yan'an also attracted attention from U.S. officials in China. In the fall of 1944, two Japanese-speaking officers were added to the U.S. Army Observer Group in Yan'an in order to investigate the Japanese there. In the process, naturally, the Americans also learned about the CCP leaders' attitude toward postwar Japan.[61]

When Mao and Nosaka were contemplating a "new democratic revolution" for China and a phased transformation for Japan, they could not possibly have known exactly how these formulas would be implemented in their countries during the postwar years. They also could not predict at the time which program would have a better chance of succeeding in its own country. In April 1945, when Mao Zedong and Nosaka Sanzo delivered their reports to the seventh congress of the Chinese Communist Party, both entertained the same cautious optimism about the revolutionary

---

[60] *Jiefang Ribao*, 7 July 1943 and 18 January 1944; Stein, *Challenge of Red China*, 409–410, 413–421.

[61] *Jiefang Ribao*, 20 February 1944; *Da Gong Bao*, 23 March 1944; Nosaka, *Yeban Cansan Xuanji*, 310–316. Emmerson, *Japanese Thread*, 181, 190–203, contains an interesting account of his experience with the Japanese in Yan'an. The success of the CCP's and Nosaka's policy on Japanese POWs confirmed Emmerson's own belief that the U.S. government had to begin to pay close attention to the psychological preparation of the Japanese people for the Allied occupation. But he doubted that his suggestions would be received favorably by the U.S. government.

movements in their own countries. But Mao saw more difficulties in China than Nosaka did in Japan. In his report "On the Coalition Government," Mao warned that the defeat of Japan would not automatically ensure the success of the Chinese revolution. The CCP and the Chinese people would have to make a determined effort to overcome the KMT's reactionary policies in order to prevent the new danger of civil war.[62] In contrast, Nosaka did not see any significant political force in Japan that would be able to compete with the Japanese Communist Party after Japan's defeat. In his report "Construct a Democratic Japan," Nosaka contended that the militarist rule in Japan had created an explosive revolutionary situation for the Japanese Communist Party to exploit. He predicted that once the Allies launched their last offensive against Japan, the JCP would expand rapidly and play a decisive role to end the war by attacking the militarists from inside Japan.[63]

About four months after Mao and Nosaka made their predictions, the war came to a sudden conclusion. Although Mao Zedong immediately went to Chongqing to negotiate with Chiang Kai-shek, China was no closer than before to achieving a coalition government. In January 1946, Nosaka Sanzo returned to Japan. Before he left Yan'an, Nosaka and Mao talked through the night. Mao was angry about the organization of the first postwar cabinet in Japan, saying that this cabinet was essentially not different from the militarist government that had existed during the war. Mao also said that China's modernization would need the assistance of Japan's technology and industry, and Japan would need to depend on China's resources. But such a "coprosperous" relationship could be established only after Japan achieved democratization. Nosaka was to return to his country and work for the dream that he and Mao shared. However, no matter how confident Nosaka might be in the Japanese Communists' ability to start a revolution in Japan, postwar Japan would follow a course of development controlled by the Allied occupation forces. It is symbolic that, when departing from Yan'an, Nosaka had to travel on an American airplane.[64]

[62] *Mao Zedong Ji*, 8: 214–215.
[63] Nosaka, *Yeban Cansan Xuanji*, 349–389.
[64] Nosaka, *Wangming Shiliu Nian*, 60, 67–69.

8

Diplomacy without action

Symbolically, the summit at Cairo formalized Chongqing's partnership with the Western Allies in prosecuting the war and in planning for peace. Practically, however, the Cairo Conference did not result in the definite American–Chinese alliance sought by the KMT leadership. At Cairo, exposure of the difficulties in Chongqing's relations with the Allies did not result in the alteration of Chiang Kai-shek's attitude toward cooperation with the United States. Actually, the experience only made him more anxious than ever to maintain the momentum of the wartime Chinese–American partnership. Nevertheless, the anticlimax of the Chongqing–Washington military cooperation in war came in 1944. In that summer, amid the KMT regime's military disaster inflicted by Japan's new offensive, the U.S. government pressed Chiang Kai-shek to delegate the command of the Chinese Army to General Joseph Stilwell. Chiang's stubborn resistance to the pressure eventually resulted in Stilwell's departure from the China theater. The Stilwell affair showed Chiang's intractable character whenever he sensed a threat to his power. Yet, strangely, Chiang's defense of his sovereign status in the command crisis unfolded along with Chongqing's retreat on the diplomatic front as far as postwar East Asia was concerned. When President Roosevelt saw no other choice but to recall General Stilwell from China, the State Department realized that in international affairs Chongqing was becoming more manageable than before.

American alliance in question

The effect of the Cairo Conference on Chongqing's foreign policy planning was similar to that of American entry into the war on its military strategy: once Washington decided to take a stand, leaders in Chongqing became disposed to defer to the U.S. government even on issues that involved China's concerns more than those of America. After Cairo, Chinese officials seemed to believe that since the American government had committed itself to peace settlement in East Asia, the provisions of the Cairo Communiqué would automatically ensue. "It is only a matter of time" became a popular phrase in Chinese planning papers during the post-Cairo period.[1] The Cairo Conference affected China's postwar policy preparation in yet another sense. Now officials in Chongqing fell under a spell characterized by China's obligation to the Western Allies (mainly the United States), as embodied in the Cairo understandings. During the last two years of the war, Chongqing took almost no diplomatic initiative with reference to the postwar issues of East Asia. Officials in Chongqing became concerned that if Washington and London detected any sign of unilateral action by China, they would likely break the "Cairo understanding." Having argued ineffectively with the Americans at Cairo, Chiang in the next two years preferred a passive posture for Chongqing's diplomacy. He did not want to rock the already perilous boat of the Chongqing–Washington partnership.

During the remainder of the war, the paralyzing effect of Chiang Kai-shek's Cairo experience recurred in Chongqing's diplomacy. For instance, during the inter-Allied conferences at Dumbarton Oaks in October 1944 and then at San Francisco in April 1945, Chiang Kai-shek sent his delegates over with strict instructions limiting any diplomatic initiative on China's part. On both occasions, Chongqing's foreign policy planning staff painstakingly prepared position papers on the postwar treatment of Japan and on territorial issues in East Asia. Twice, however, Chiang Kai-shek's instructions prohibited the Chinese delegations from bringing up these subjects to their American and British counterparts. Instead, the Chinese delegates were instructed to wait for the Allies to introduce these subjects into the discussion and then decide how to respond. Chiang preferred Chinese diplomacy to act like a clam with its valves open: it made no noise and did not pinch unless first touched. Consequently, because the other governments at the conferences were mainly interested in discussing a future world peace organization rather than Japan or other East Asian problems, Chongqing's taciturn diplomacy did not even stir up any dust.[2]

Within Chongqing's official circles, there were dissenting opinions on China's stranded alliance with the United States. The Cairo Conference did

[1] Waijiaobu memorandum, "Tingzhan hou chuli Riben zhu fang'an" (Various Plans for Postwar Treatment of Japan), 7 June 1944, VHP, box 3.
[2] T. V. Soong to Wei Daoming, 29 July 1944, WKP, box 70; Chiang Kai-shek to Soong, 3 April 1945, ibid., box 81; Waijiaobu memorandum, "Lianheguo huiyi wo guo yingdang zhunbei zhi gexiang wenti" (The Problems That Should Be Considered by Our Government for the United Nations Conference), n.d., VHP, box 8; Waijiaobu memorandum, "Ni ju Jiujinshan huiyi huiwai ying yu Mei Ying Su shangtan zhi gexiang fang'an qingshi you" (Report for Approval on the Programs That Should Be Discussed with America, Britain and the Soviet Union Outside the San Francisco Conference), n.d. (March 1945), WKP, box 81.

cause some Chinese officials to question the direction of China's foreign policy. Soon after the Cairo Conference, for instance, Xu Shuxi, director of the Waijiaobu's western Asiatic affairs department, told T. V. Soong that despite the Cairo decisions on China's recovery of Manchuria and Taiwan, certain prominent persons in the United States believed that China was not yet qualified to assume responsibility for these territories. Fearing that after Cairo a complacent attitude might grow in Chongqing, Xu stressed the urgent need for the Chinese government to make more concrete and vigorous preparations for recovering these territories.[3]

Within the Chinese government, there were always officials who were concerned that Chongqing's foreign policy was too narrowly focused on developing relations with the United States. They favored a more broadly defined and assertive foreign policy. Wellington Koo was one such spokesman. Throughout the war, Ambassador Koo tried to persuade the top leadership in Chongqing to enlarge the basis of Chinese foreign policy from one of bilateral cooperation with the United States to at least a trilateral partnership including Great Britain. Koo's deepest apprehension was that unless there was more than one option for China's foreign alignment, China could find itself forced to return to its traditional isolation at the end of the war. He tended to regard the lofty international status of wartime China and its cooperation with America as very fragile. Although he shared Chiang Kai-shek's suspicion of Roosevelt's prescription for a harmonious postwar world, Koo had no confidence in a bilateral Sino–American collaboration. For one thing, it was difficult to imagine that, given the Anglo–American kinship, America would support the Chinese in any serious dispute that might arise between China and Britain. For another, since the tradition of American foreign policy went against entering into an alliance in peacetime, the wartime American–Chinese partnership promoted by Roosevelt might not extend into the postwar years. Koo once reminded Chiang that American policy "often suffered from lack of continuity because of the quadrennial presidential elections." Therefore, in his opinion, a cordial relationship between China and Britain was needed to assure China a reliable partner in the West. Although Ambassador Koo achieved support from some high officials in Chongqing, he was unable to persuade T. V. Soong and Chiang Kai-shek.[4]

T. V. Soong could not appreciate the alleged value of an Anglo–Chinese alliance. He strongly questioned whether Washington, looking on China as its protégé, would welcome a Sino–British rapprochement. Koo also failed

[3] Xu Shuxi to Soong, 22 December 1943, *TSP*, box 30.
[4] *RWK*, 5(A): 171–172, 196–198, 214–215, 220, 360–361, 5(E): 752. Among those who reacted favorably to Koo's idea were Sun Ke and generals Bai Chongxi, Zhang Qun, He Yingqin, and Hu Zongnan. The last three were in Chiang's confidence, and Koo took Hu as the most likely successor to Chiang.

to persuade Chiang Kai-shek even by appealing to the latter's pronounced anti-Communist feelings. Koo emphasized that the British had a high regard for Chiang as a resolute anti-Communist leader and sought cooperation with China as a check on the Soviet Union. But Chiang did not think China could gain sufficient advantage from negotiations with the "shrewd and cunning" British. Nor did he want to provoke the Russians by forging an anti-Communist bloc with the British while the war was still in progress.[5]

The Russian factor proved a powerful reason for Chongqing to pursue a close connection with America. But not all high officials in Chongqing wanted a confrontational relationship with the Russians, and some supported a positive approach to solve the Chinese–Soviet dilemma. Sun Ke, for instance, called for Chongqing's Russia policy to return to Sun Yat-sen's policy for a "revolutionary alliance" between the KMT and Moscow.[6] Although not going as far as Sun Ke, other officials nevertheless favored a balanced foreign policy that would cultivate friendly relations with all three leading Allies. Wu Tiecheng, secretary-general of the KMT Central Committee, advised Chiang Kai-shek that China should look for economic assistance from America, but for political wisdom and military matters China should turn to Britain and the Soviet Union respectively. Xu Shuxi also told T. V. Soong that although a close relationship with the United States should be maintained, in the long run China must remain on friendly terms with Russia and Britain as well. "Our salvation in the future," Xu argued, "lies in the good will of all, not, as in the past, in a delicate balance of power."[7]

These opinions reflected the weariness among Chinese officials and diplomats with the old international politics of balance of power, in which China had often been a dispensable pawn to all sides. But these officials' "balanced Chinese diplomacy" did not coincide with President Roosevelt's formula of Big Four cooperation. Instead, their opinions reflected a distrust of both Washington's version of a new international order and of its China policy. They did not expect any drastic transformation of prewar world affairs either in terms of general cooperation among the big powers or in terms of a reliable Chinese–American alliance. What they longed for was an independent position for China in postwar international politics, not one tied to any side in a new round of great-power rivalry. As suggested by Ambassador Koo, after the war China would need at least ten or twenty peaceful years to complete its reconstruction and modernization.[8] Yet, although these officials were audacious enough to speak out, their opinions were not strong enough to revitalize Chongqing's diplomacy.

[5] *RWK*, 5(A): 171–173, 197–198, 5(B): 367–373.
[6] Sun Ke, *Zhong Su Guanxi* (Sino–Soviet Relations) (Shanghai: Zhonghua Shuju, 1946), 3–7, 22, 36–38, 49–51.
[7] *RWK*, 5(E): 766; memoranda by Xu Shuxi, 22 December 1943, 16 June and 25 September 1944, *TSP*, box 30.
[8] *RWK*, 5(E): 752.

Chiang Kai-shek's foreign policy was hopelessly anchored in an ambiguous partnership with the United States. Under these circumstances, Chongqing's foreign policy planners, more often than not, functioned as mere armchair strategists.

Japan again

Although the Cairo Conference showed the world unity among the leading United Nations with regard to the postwar treatment of Japan, it was a far cry from concluding Allied policymaking in this regard. The unconditional surrender principle as applied to Japan added little to the Allied surrender terms planned for Japan and revealed nothing about how Japan would be treated after surrender. By depriving Japan of its overseas territories, the Cairo decisions only solved half of the problem. The other half, the disposition of these territories after their detachment from Japan, involved additional international complications.

To Chongqing's political strategists, the Cairo pledge of the total defeat of Japan validated their conviction that Asian territories should be restored to their situation before the Sino–Japanese War of 1894–1895. A completely vanquished Japan had no right to keep any of its imperial possessions. In the meantime, the Cairo decisions also encouraged those within the Chinese government who advocated severe postwar treatment for Japan. They did not believe that leniency would be able to change the warlike characteristics of the Japanese nation. Before its military, economic, and ideological systems were completely reoriented toward peace and democracy, Japan did not deserve to enjoy equality with other countries.[9]

Although these ultimate objectives were generally accepted by officials in Chongqing, views differed on how they could best be achieved. A more difficult question was what role China should play in reforming Japan. The KMT leaders' indecision on these matters affected the Chinese government's preparation for the inter-Allied conference for a world peace organization at Dumbarton Oaks, Washington, D.C., in the fall of 1944. Hoping to carry the unfinished business of the Cairo Conference to Dumbarton Oaks, Chongqing's foreign policy planners drafted a series of documents tantamount to a comprehensive peace plan for East Asia. The Supreme Council of National Defense prepared a document listing the "Terms for Japan to Accept and Observe When It Surrenders Unconditionally." A striking feature of the document was its lack of creativity and initiative in articulating China's definition of the "unconditional surrender" policy.

[9] Memorandum, "Jiejue Zhong Ri wenti zhi jiben yuanze cao'an" (Draft Plan on the Basic Principles for Solving the Problems between China and Japan), n.d. (1942), General Record Number (GRN) 43 (Supreme Council of National Defense): file 287, DELD; Xu Mo to Waijiaobu, 19 March 1944, and enclosure, "Zhanhou tiaozheng Zhong Ri guanxi zhi fang'an" (Plan for the Postwar Readjustment of the Sino–Japanese Relations), GRN 18 (2) (Waijiaobu): file 162, DELD.

Except for a few items showing Chongqing's concern about regulating Japanese troops' behavior on their surrender in regard to Chinese personnel, properties, and territories under Japanese control, the better part of the document was based on two precedents. One was the "Allied Terms of Armistice with Germany" dated 11 November 1918, and the other was the "Instrument of Surrender for Italy" dated 29 September 1943. Neither was intended to induce unconditional surrender.[10] The KMT leaders' ambivalence about Allied interference in Japan's government after the war was also reflected in the document's confusing clauses. Although favoring a period of military occupation of Japan by United Nations forces, the document indicated that in this period a Japanese government should continue to function in order to assist and protect the UN personnel who were in Japan to carry out their occupation duties. Typically, the document was silent about China's participation in the occupation.[11]

In fact, during the last two years of the war, the Chinese government failed to come up with any definite policy with regard to the reform of Japan's governmental system. Chiang Kai-shek's disclosure of his own stand on the matter at the Cairo Conference, which appeared in his New Year's Message of 1944, seemed to support a qualified noninterference policy.[12] But afterward Chiang's statement was subject to different interpretations. Editorials of the *Da Gong Bao* and *Zhongyang Ribao* continued to favor severe measures for eliminating the "divine state" ideology and the imperial institution in Japan. They were especially vociferous about the appeasement attitude toward Japan thought to be current in the West, warning against any concessions by the Allies to Japan to buy a "premature and cheap" peace.[13]

The Waijiaobu was split on the subject. Some believed that Chiang's statement did not preclude a policy for abolition of the imperial institution in Japan, and that such a policy was justifiable in the same manner as terminating Nazism in Germany. Others were more cautious. One group

[10] "Zhengzhi wenti huishang jingguo," appendix (1) to the log of the Cairo Conference, n.d., ZZSC, 3(3): 535; John W. Wheeler-Bennett and Anthony Nicholls, *The Semblance of Peace; the Political Settlement after the Second World War* (New York: W. W. Norton, 1974), 69. During the Cairo Conference, the Chinese delegation obtained the full texts of the surrender instruments for Italy from the British, and then these documents were transmitted to the Waijiaobu. According to Robert Murphy, *Diplomat Among Warriors* (Garden City, NY: Doubleday, 1964), 240, so far as the document for the Italian surrender was concerned, President Roosevelt had wanted it to be "as close as possible to unconditional surrender," but the Italian surrender turned out to be a "conditional unconditional surrender."
[11] Memorandum by the Supreme Council of National Defense, "Riben wutiaojian touxiang shi suo ying jieshou zunban zhi tiaokuan cao'an" (Draft Program on the Terms for Japan to Accept and Observe When It Surrenders Unconditionally), n.d. (July 1944), VHP, box 8.
[12] Chinese Ministry of Information, *The Collected Wartime Messages of Generalissimo Chiang Kai-shek, 1937–1945* (New York: John Day, 1946), 776–781 (hereafter cited as *Messages of Chiang Kai-shek*).
[13] *Zhongyang Ribao*, 16 August 1944; *Da Gong Bao*, 31 May 1945.

preferred eliminating the imperial system through educational, not "surgical," measures. Another argued that the best policy was to ignore the monarchy and let it "wither away of its own accord." T. V. Soong also did not interpret Chiang's statement as a definite policy regarding the Japanese emperor. Speaking to reporters in San Francisco in May 1945, Soong commented that China's policy toward the Japanese emperor would still have to be decided before the future status of the emperor could be placed at the disposal of the United Nations.[14]

Indulging in rhetoric but unable to devise a concrete policy for China to influence Japan's postwar political process, KMT officials awakened to the reality that their aspiration of "restoring China's spiritual leadership in East Asia for millenniums" through patronizing Japan was unattainable.[15] They still believed that due to the cultural and physical proximity of China and Japan, the Chinese were in a better position than the Westerners to pass judgment on Japanese affairs. Yet they were also realistic enough to admit that in international politics, better judgments did not necessarily make them workable. So far as Japan's postwar government was concerned, a Chinese judgment, no matter how sound it was, might still need to defer to an American view, even though the latter might be misconceived. Such an attitude was best reflected in Xu Shuxi's opinion concerning the issue of the Japanese emperor. On the one hand, Xu criticized Washington's Japan experts, like Joseph Grew, for being indoctrinated by the Japanese propaganda on the indispensability of the emperor. On the other hand, he recognized the difficulty of changing the minds of these "well-informed [but] misguided men" and recommended a flexible Chinese policy toward the ruling house in Japan. When the war was approaching its end, the demand for the emperor's removal remained so high in Chongqing that a resolution on the matter was adopted by the People's Political Council. But Chiang Kai-shek, supported by the Waijiaobu, decided to follow the American policy in this regard out of deference to the relationship between his government and the United States.[16]

---

[14] Memorandum of the Supreme Council of National Defense, "Zhanhou guoji heping jigou ji qita youguan wenti" (Postwar World Peace Organization and Other Related Issues), n.d. (July 1944), VHP, box 7; Waijiaobu memorandum, "Tingzhan hou chuli Riben zhu fang'an"; T-document 567, 25 January 1945, RHN, box 69; *Zhongyang Ribao*, 3 May 1945.

[15] Memorandum (Supreme Council of National Defense), "Jiejue Zhong Ri wenti jiben yuanze cao'an."

[16] Memorandum of the Supreme Council of National Defense, "Zhanhou guoji heping jigou ji qita youguan wenti"; Xu Shuxi to Soong, 26 January and 14 July 1944, TSP, box 30; *Zhongyang Ribao*, 18 July 1945; resolution of the KMT Central Committee on receiving Japan's surrender, 11 August 1945, ZZSC, 7(4): 9; Shen Yanding, "Dui Ri wangshi zhuiji" (Reminiscences about Japan), ZW, 26 (1975): 1: 60–62. For the role and failure of the PPC to act as a democratic assembly, see Ch'ien Tuan-sheng (Qian Duansheng), *The Government and Politics of China, 1912–1949* (Stanford, CA: Stanford University Press, 1950), 278–295.

Acquiescing in the American view on the treatment of the imperial institution, Chongqing could not avoid also embracing Washington's decision on the disposition of Emperor Hirohito himself. Since October 1943, the Chinese government had participated in the organizational work for a United Nations War Crimes Commission. During inter-Allied discussions, the Chinese government took no particular stand except to demand that Japan be held accountable for its war crimes and atrocities committed in China since 18 September 1931. Although some governments questioned the validity of the date for the war crime issue in Asia, Chongqing began its investigation of Japan's war crimes in China in the spring of 1944. In July 1945, the Chinese government gave its first list of some 100 Japanese military officers to the Far Eastern and Pacific Subcommission of the United Nations War Crimes Commission. But Chongqing could not decide on its list of the major Japanese war criminals until two months after the war ended.[17] The delay caused some concern in the American government, especially after the People's Political Council in Chongqing adopted a resolution calling for the trial of the Japanese emperor as a war criminal. The State Department instructed Ambassador Patrick Hurley to do his best to prevent the Chinese government from raising the "unfortunate" question of the Japanese emperor with the Subcommission. In October, when Chongqing finally delivered its list, Hirohito's name was not on it.[18]

Aside from desire to maintain a smooth relationship with the United States over Japan, the KMT leadership had a hidden agenda in encouraging America's overwhelming responsibility for postwar control of Japan. That was to focus Chongqing's military strength in China to avoid Japan's animosity toward foreign occupation and to be prepared for a renewed military struggle with the CCP. After Cairo, high-ranking Chinese officials and Chongqing's newspapers voiced unanimous support for Allied occupation of Japan in the postwar period. But at the same time, even those hard-liners who wanted severe punitive treatment for a defeated Japan did not believe that China could afford to partake in the occupation. What the Chinese government really wanted, as T. V. Soong once told Ambassador Gauss, was China's presence in the Allied authority for controlling Japan, but not necessarily Chinese troops' participation in the occupation.[19] Without illusions about its formidable postwar problems at home, the KMT

[17] *Da Gong Bao*, 1 March 1944; *ZRWJ*, 7: 432, 444; Winant to Byrnes, 6 February 1945, *FRUS, 1945*, 6: 900; Hurley to Byrnes, 28 July 1945, ibid., 6: 901; Robertson to Byrnes, 20 October 1945, ibid., 6: 948.

[18] *Zhongyang Ribao*, 18 July 1945; Grew to Hurley, 7 August 1945, *FRUS, 1945*, 6: 905–906; Byrnes to Hurley, 8 August 1945, ibid., 907.

[19] See H. H. Kung's and Liang Hancao's statements in *Zhongyang Ribao*, 1 and 24 August 1944, and Gu Chunfan, "Ruhe chuli Riben" (How to Dispose of Japan), *Da Gong Bao*, 11 January 1945; Gauss to Hull, 25 July 1944, *FRUS, 1944: China*, 1165–1166.

authorities in 1944 adopted a plan for postwar demobilization, which set two tasks for government troops to carry out within China. One was to pacify in the "liberated areas" the "vestigial and dormant forces of the enemy and its puppets." The other was to prevent the growth of any "reactionary" influence, which obviously meant the CCP.[20]

But General Albert C. Wedemeyer, commander of American forces in China and also Chiang's chief of staff, believed that the Chinese Army had other duties as well. Two weeks before Japan's surrender, he submitted to Chiang a memorandum suggesting that at the end of the war, the Chinese government should be prepared to implement these measures: (1) deployment of troops against the Communists; (2) preventive action against local warlords; (3) dispatch of troops to participate in the Allied occupation of Japan; and (4) economic and political preparations for the liberated territories. General Wedemeyer's confidence in Chongqing's ability to carry out these tasks was based on the assumption that at the end of the war Yan'an would not receive substantial assistance from Moscow, whereas the Western Allies would continue to aid the KMT massively. In a report to General George Marshall, Wedemeyer admitted that a large portion of Chongqing's troops would have to be used to reestablish its authority in the liberated areas in China. Yet he also believed that the KMT regime would be able to provide "approximately ten divisions and one composite air group" to join the Allied occupation forces in Japan. If civil war ensued in postwar China, Chinese participation in the occupation would have to be reduced to a force of one or two divisions. Still, Wedemeyer suggested to General Marshall, no matter what happened in postwar China, that country's share in the occupational duties in Japan must be "mandatory." For China's participation would reduce America's burden, help the Chinese government learn how to discharge overseas responsibilities, enhance China's prestige, and destroy the myth among the Oriental peoples that Japan was invincible.[21] Wedemeyer's points might have been convincing to Washington, but the general was bound to fail to induce Chiang to take action.

Chongqing's military weakness was not the only reason for the KMT leaders' reluctance to become involved in the Allied occupation of Japan. The fact is that in contemplating China's postwar strategic posture in East Asia, officials in Chongqing hardly allowed their thoughts to extend to the Pacific Ocean. From Sun Yat-sen's discussion of China's national standing to Chongqing's wartime foreign policy planning, the focus was on the

[20] "Fuyuan jihua gangyao" (Outline of the Demobilization Plan), 31 July 1944, ZZSC, 7(4): 355–356.
[21] Minutes of Chiang–Wedemeyer conversation, 31 July 1945, ZZSC, 3(3): 322; Albert C. Wedemeyer, *Wedemeyer Reports!* (New York: Henry Holt, 1958), 333–334; Wedemeyer to Marshall, 10 July 1945, RCT, box 1539.

mainland of East Asia and its periphery. During the war years, the Chinese government showed much interest in participating in the postwar settlement of Korea. Although involvement in Korea could be interpreted as an "overseas" policy, Korea was a very different case from Japan. First, the Korean Peninsula is an extension of the Asian mainland. Second, Chongqing had a precedent in involvement in Korean affairs that had been established by the Qing government in the late nineteenth century.[22] Furthermore, Chongqing was headquarters for the Korean Provisional Government, and KMT leaders regarded the KPG as an instrument of its policy in postwar Korea. But in the case of Japan, there were too many uncertainties with which Chongqing was not prepared to deal.

Despite the radical rhetoric toward Japan articulated by certain government officials and private figures in Chongqing, the Chinese government never really intended or expected to eliminate Japan from international politics in postwar East Asia. Reconciliation between China and Japan would have to occur sooner or later, but China's participation in the Western Allies' occupation of Japan would cast a shadow on that process. Some of Chiang Kai-shek's close aides constantly opposed any Allied interference in the postwar developments in Japan. For instance, General Zhang Qun believed that noninterference in postwar Japan was a principle agreed on by Chiang and Roosevelt at Cairo.[23] Such a moderate attitude seemed puzzling to some Western observers in Chongqing. At one point, General Wedemeyer made a comment to General Marshall on the Chinese government's "apathetic view" toward Japan and its lack of a "deep concern" about "retribution." He attributed this attitude to an assumption in Chongqing that necessary steps concerning Japan would be automatically taken by the Allies.[24] General Wedemeyer was only partially correct. He failed to discern Chongqing's determination that after the war, it would bury the hatchet with Japan as soon as possible in order to shift attention to other urgent problems.

Toward the end of the war, KMT leaders had no doubt that the greatest postwar problem for them would be the combination of the Soviet threat along the northern border and the CCP agitation at home. The wartime partnership with America did not fundamentally change many KMT officials' perspective on Asian politics. They continued to view Russia and Japan as the two most important powers for China's destiny. In 1943 Chiang Kai-shek himself asked Ambassador Koo to comment on a postwar scenario with "China on one side and Japan and Soviet Russia on the

[22] Hilary Conroy, *The Japanese Seizure of Korea, 1868–1910: A Study of Realism and Idealism in International Relations* (Philadelphia: University of Pennsylvania Press, 1960), 184. Between 1885 and 1893, Yuan Shikai supervised Korean affairs for the Manchu court and called himself "His Imperial Chinese Majesty's Resident in Korea."
[23] Stevens to Gauss, 5 January 1944, *FRUS: Cairo and Teheran*, 864.
[24] Wedemeyer to Marshall, 10 July 1945, *RCT*, box 1539.

other." The question indicated Chiang's own uncertainty about a lasting Sino–American partnership. What Koo offered Chiang was a suggestion for cultivating a more stable relationship with the Western Allies in order to prevent such a danger. An alternative, however, was mentioned in the Waijiaobu: after the war, Japan might well be converted from an enemy to an ally of China and serve as a supplement to the Sino–American partnership.[25]

Before the war ended, Chongqing actually began to take some preliminary steps in this direction. Early in February 1945, Chiang Kai-shek sent an oral message to General Okamura Neiji, commander of the Japanese Army in China:

> China of course cannot separate itself from the United States, but in my view the most important issue in East Asia is the cooperation between China and Japan. . . . I am ready to speak on Japan's behalf [at the peace table], and I am the only one who can save Japan. But it is a thousand pities that the Japanese have hitherto misunderstood my good intention. . . . I wish that we two nations would not do excessive things to each other.[26]

General Okamura's reaction to this message is not known. But Chiang Kai-shek's call for a rapid reconciliation between China and Japan would be restated in public right after Japan's surrender.[27]

Yet, the KMT officials' conciliatory spirit toward Japan was limited to political matters. Although anxious to turn Japan politically from its Sinophobe orientation, Chongqing rejected resolutely an equal economic relationship with Japan, at least for the first few decades after the war. Chongqing's economic policy toward Japan was not conceived as part of a general plan for reforming the international economic order in Asia. In fact, KMT officials tended to view the postwar Chinese–Japanese economic relationship as an exception to any new international economic system that would likely emerge after the war in accordance with the prevailing principles of economic cooperation and interdependence. Given China's industrial weakness, they believed, its cooperation with Japan would only damage itself.[28] Consequently, the Chinese government contemplated its reparation policy for the sole purpose of expediting China's own postwar rehabilitation. On the one hand, KMT officials echoed an opinion in

---

[25] Shao Yulin et al., *Wang Pengsheng Xiansheng Jinian Ji* (Mr. Wang Pengsheng Memorialized) (Taipei: Wenhai Chubanshe, n.d.), 48; *RWK*, 5(B): 373–374; Xu Shuxi to Soong, 24 January 1944, *TSP*, box 30.

[26] Wu Xiangxiang, *Di Er Ci Zhong Ri Zhanzheng Shi* (The Second Sino–Japanese War) (Taipei: Zonghe Yuekanshe, 1982), 2: 1120.

[27] *Messages of Chiang Kai-shek*, 850–852.

[28] Memorandum, "Zhanhou chuli dui Ri jingji guanxi fang'an" (Plan for the Postwar Readjustment of the Chinese–Japanese Economic Relationship), n.d., GRN 761 (National Military Council): file 219, DELD.

the West calling for forbearance in this matter. On the other hand, they stressed China's "unique situation" that required substantial reparations from Japan.[29]

The very idea that China's reconstruction should be tied to Japanese reparations was subject to criticism in China. Qian Duansheng (Ch'ien Tuan-sheng), a prominent scholar of international politics who occasionally advised the government on foreign affairs, wrote after Cairo that "it is mere cowardice to destroy Japan's industry and commercial organism in order to clear the way for our progress."[30] Yet, in 1944, the Chinese government received some encouragement from the Americans. In September, Donald Nelson visited Chongqing as President Roosevelt's special envoy. The purpose of Nelson's mission was to explore forms of American–Chinese economic cooperation in the postwar years. The trip represented Roosevelt's personal diplomacy with China at its low ebb, and no concrete results were produced. But in his conversations with T. V. Soong and Chiang Kai-shek, Nelson asserted that President Roosevelt and the American people wanted to have Japan "licked" permanently, and that the stability of East Asia would rely on China's replacement of Japan as an "industrial and commercial power." He also suggested that after the war, China should take over Japan's economic positions in Southeast Asia and the Near East.[31] These words were music to Chiang's and Soong's ears.

Before the end of the war, four elements were well established in Chongqing's reparations policy. First, 18 September 1931, the date of the Mukden Incident, should be used as the starting point for calculating China's losses. Second, the amount of reparations to be received by the Allies in the Pacific war should be proportional to the damage they suffered respectively in the war. This formula was borrowed from the Soviet stand on German reparations, though the Soviet government also wanted the reparations to be proportional to each Allied power's contribution to the defeat of Germany. The third point was the long-standing demand for reparations in kind. And finally, Chongqing wanted to host an inter-Allied reparations commission for the Far East.[32]

---

[29] Memorandum of the Supreme Council of National Defense, "Zhanhou guoji heping jigou ji qita youguan wenti."

[30] Ch'ien Tuan-sheng, "How to Deal with Japan After Victory," *China at War* (a monthly published by the Chinese News Service, an agency of the Chinese government, in New York), 11 (June 1944): 14–16.

[31] "Highlights of the Conversation between Mr. Donald Nelson and General Patrick Hurley, and Dr. T. V. Soong on the Morning of September 7, 1944 at Dr. Soong's Residence," *TSP*, box 26; Wu Guozhen to Chiang, 27 September 1944, with enclosures on the Chiang–Nelson conversations on 19 September 1945, *ZZSC*, 3(1): 184–195.

[32] Waijiaobu memorandum, "Ni ju Jiujinshan huiyi huiwai ying yu Mei Ying Su shangtan zhi gexiang fang'an qingshi you."

Yet, Chongqing's resolve to make reparations claims was undermined by its own ineffective work in collecting the necessary supporting data. An investigation into the damage caused by the war began in China long before Pearl Harbor. In 1939 and 1940, the Executive Yuan issued special regulations to coordinate investigations at the local level. When the Pacific war began, the Waijiaobu also instructed its representatives in European countries to collect information about the nature and scope of these countries' reparations policies and their methods of calculating losses at the end of World War I. In 1943 an "Investigation Commission on the Losses in the War of Resistance" was appointed within the Executive Yuan to oversee the whole operation.[33] Despite these efforts, by the time of the Japanese surrender, the Chinese government had produced nothing definite and concrete that could be used for serious international consultation.

The forbidding conditions of the war could only partially explain Chongqing's fruitless effort. Ambassador Koo detected another reason for Chongqing's meager reparations policy. Both before and after the Cairo Conference, worried about the disparity between the government's reparations claims and the lack of supporting data collected by the government, Koo repeatedly called the attention of the Chongqing authorities to the problem. Then he learned that the government had organized the reparations commission only to absorb "many clamoring politicians whom the government had to satisfy with some kind of post."[34]

After Japan surrendered, Chiang began to worry about the serious deficiency in preparing China's reparations claims. Twice, in August and September, he set dates for the Executive Yuan to conclude its investigation of China's war losses. Eventually, the reparations commission produced a set of data based not on facts but on "statistics mainly derived from estimates." The sluggish preparation, however, did not prevent Chongqing from making reparations demands after Japan's surrender, including reduction of Japan's heavy industries to their pre-1914 level and the transfer of parts of Japanese industries, heavy and light alike, to China as reparations in kind. In contrast to its muddled account of China's war damages, the Chinese government had a clear idea about how many plants and how much equipment it wanted from Japan. The only problem for

---

[33] Soong to Jin Wensi, Wellington Koo, and Qian Tai, 4 November 1943, *WKP*, box 54; Committee on Japanese Reparations of the Chinese Mission in Japan, comp., *Zai Ri Banli Peichang Guihuan Gongzuo Zongshu* (Summary of the Work by the Mission for Reparations in Japan) (Tokyo: no publisher, 1949), 11–12 (hereafter cited as *Zongshu*); Chi Jingde, *Zhongguo Dui Ri Kangzhan Sunshi Diaocha Shishu* (A Narrative History of the Chinese Investigation of the Losses during the War Against Japan) (Taipei: Guoshiguan, 1987), 68–107.

[34] Chi Jingde, *Kangzhan Sunshi*, 68–107; *Zongshu*, 11–12; C. F. Remer, "Papers on United States Economic Relations with China," 8 August 1945, *RDCA*, box 5; *RWK*, 5(A): 772, 5(E): 883.

Chongqing was to base these claims on solid data and justify them with the other Allies.[35]

More uncertainty about lost territories

Although keeping silent about Japan's postwar treatment, the Cairo Communiqué was deceptively simple and clear with regard to Japan's imperial territories. As a document demonstrating Allied solidarity to the world, the communiqué could not possibly convey to its readers the complexities behind its territorial decisions. Although the conferees at Cairo did not agree completely on territorial readjustments in postwar Asia, they were also unable to predict the political and military conditions in Asia and the Pacific at the end of the war that would be decisive for territorial settlements. The conferees at Cairo were not blind to the inadequacy of their work. The absence of the Russians at Cairo immediately pointed to uncertainty. Since the Allies were already speculating about Soviet participation in the Asian war at the time, territories like Manchuria and Korea in northeastern Asia were bound to become, once more, focal points of international intrigue. Territories in the south, such as Taiwan, the Ryukyu Islands, and the Japanese Mandated Islands, seemed immune from Soviet influence for the time being, but the Cairo decisions were by no means conclusive for these areas either.

So far as Taiwan was concerned, the Cairo Communiqué seemed an unequivocal document that favored China's sovereignty. At least most officials in Chongqing believed so. Before Cairo, policy planners in the Waijiaobu had been anxious to find a formula for obtaining international endorsement of China's sovereignty over Taiwan. Now that problem was resolved by the Cairo decision.[36] Chinese officials knew that international support carried a price: Taiwan's postwar function as an international security base. Some in the Waijiaobu were simply resigned to the inevitable: if American forces were expected to play the leading role in reconquering Taiwan, how could the Chinese government refuse to grant Washington's demand for a base there?[37] But this was a price Chiang Kai-shek was

---

[35] Chi Jingde, *Kangzhan Sunshi*, 187–208; *Zongshu*, 27–29. When the Chinese government participated in the work of the postwar Far Eastern Commission, it was still struggling with chaotic figures. There were three or four sets of "official figures" on China's losses, ranging from $3.5 billion to $5.8 billion (U.S. dollar value as of 1937). Some figures used 18 September 1931 and others used 7 July 1937 as the starting date for the calculation. See *RWK*, 5(E), 883; *ZRWJ*, 7: 106–107, 291–301; *ZZSC*, 7(4): 612–613, 700–702, 1065, 1068; Chi Jingde, *Kangzhan Sunshi*, 208–216, 276.

[36] Waijiaobu memorandum, "Zhuxi duiyu waijiao fangmian zhishi" (Chairman's [Chiang's] Instructions on Diplomacy), n.d., *VHP*, box 3.

[37] Memorandum by Yang Yunzhu, "Gaoli, Riben, weiren tongzhidi ji wo guo shidi wenti" (Korea, Japan, the Mandated Islands and the Problem of China's Lost Territories), n.d., *WKP*, box 79.

prepared to pay, for he preferred to view Taiwan as a link to establish postwar Sino–American military cooperation within the western Pacific.

During the early months of 1944, Chiang ordered the secretariat of the Executive Yuan to study the Taiwan issue. Officials there contemplated Taiwan's significance for Chinese–American cooperation in the postwar years. Their conclusion was that many local products in Taiwan, such as sugar, salt, and camphor, were not really needed by the Western Allies, but the United States might be keenly interested in Taiwan's navigation enterprises. These therefore could serve as the basis of a Sino–American partnership on the island. They also proposed that in consulting with the Allies, Chongqing insist on Chinese control of the initial military government in Taiwan. But on this matter, Chiang preferred to wait for the development of the war in the Pacific.[38] Consequently, in April 1944, when Chiang authorized the organization of an "Investigation Commission on Taiwan" under the Central Planning Board (CPB), Chongqing's policy planning for Taiwan began with a focus on Chinese civil administration.[39] The commission drafted its plans with the assumption that at a certain point during or after the war, Taiwan would be "automatically" transferred to China by the Allied forces. By March 1945, the commission presented to Chiang an "Outline of the Plan for Taking Over Taiwan."[40]

The document reflected a pragmatic attitude toward the existing Japanese systems in Taiwan and a determination to establish the KMT's tight control over the island. At the outset, the document stated that "after taking over [Taiwan], all measures [by the Chinese authorities] will be taken in accordance with the Founding Father's [Sun Yat-sen's] bequeathed teachings and the *zongcai*'s [director-general, or Chiang Kai-shek's] instructions, and for the purpose of seeking welfare for the Taiwanese people and eliminating the influence of the enemy." This did not mean that an institutional revolution should be started in Taiwan. Although, according to the document, the Three People's Principles must replace Japan's ideological influence in Taiwan's governmental and educational institutions, the economic, financial, and judicial systems established by the Japanese

[38] Zhang Lisheng to Chiang, 15 March 1944, and Chiang to Zhang, 2 June 1944, GRN 2(2) (Executive Yuan): file 1087, *TG*, 1: 1–2.

[39] "Juwu huiyi beiwanglu" (Memoranda on Meetings of the [Central Planning] Board), 26 February, 27 March, 10 April, and 17 April 1944, *HSP*, box 1; "Hai sang ji" ("The Changing World"; this is Xiong Shihui's memoir), 5: 6, ibid., box 2; Lin Xiongxing and Huang Wangzheng, comp., *Taiwan Sheng Tongzhi*, (10): *Guangfu Zhi* (Annals of the Taiwan Province, (10): The History of Restoration) (Taipei: Taiwan Sheng Lishi Wenxian Weiyuanhui, 1976), 11 (hereafter cited as *Guangfu Zhi*). The CPB was established in July 1940; its mission was to make plans for national economic and political reconstruction. See *GW*, 80(2): 58–59.

[40] "Taiwan diaocha weiyuanhui gongzuo dashiji" (The Chronology of the Work Undertaken by the Investigation Commission on Taiwan), April 1944 to April 1945, GRN 171(2) (Central Planning Board): file 100, *TG*, 1: 4–11; *Guangfu Zhi*, 11–16.

colonial authority would continue for a considerable period. For instance, most taxes levied by Japan in Taiwan would continue to be collected by the succeeding Chinese authorities. Sun Yat-sen's land program calling for *pingjun diquan* (equal distribution of land ownership) was included in the outline, but it would not be implemented before a transitional period of preparation. The current land tenure in the island, as long as the land was not owned by a citizen of the enemy state, would be maintained. Also, the outline did not propose to integrate Taiwan's monetary system into that of the mainland. Instead, the Central Bank of China would issue a special legal tender in Taiwan that would circulate together with the old currency for a period. Likewise, except for the reprehensible political regulations, most of the Japanese civil and criminal laws would remain valid while laws of the Republic of China were introduced into the island.[41]

The outline also reflected a guarded attitude of the KMT regime toward the population of Taiwan. As a plan for civil administration, the document prominently included a military clause: "For the purpose of eliminating the remaining forces of the enemy state, Taiwan should be divided into regions to be occupied by a proper number of troops." Since planners of the Chongqing regime were expecting an American occupation force in Taiwan to carry out the duties of a military government, the stated purpose for the Chinese troops was open to question. While defining Taiwan's new position as a province of China, the outline nevertheless treated the population of Taiwan as a unique case, one that needed to "strengthen national consciousness [of China] and to purge servile mentality [toward Japan]." One article stated that after Chinese authority was restored, all popular organizations in Taiwan should immediately suspend their activities and wait for further decisions by the new authority. Guided by such an attitude, the outline did not provide for a positive role by the local people in Taiwan's reconstruction. Devoid of any clause encouraging talented Taiwanese to participate in the postwar administration of Taiwan, the document only suggested "temporary use" of Taiwanese personnel who had served under the Japanese colonial authorities.[42]

Chen Yi, head of the commission on Taiwan, was fully aware that a

---

[41] "Taiwan jieguan jihua gangyao" (Outline of the Plan for Taking Over Taiwan), 14 March 1944, GRN 5(2) (Ministry of Education): file 592, *TG*, 1: 49–57; *Guangfu Zhi*, 12–16. Shao Yulin, *Shengli Qian Hou* (Before and After Victory) (Taipei: Zhuanji Wenxue Chubanshe, 1984), 109, 117–118, 122–123, suggests that the decision to retain the old currency on the island issued by the Bank of Taiwan was made after the war ended in order to save the Taiwanese economy from experiencing the galloping inflation of postwar China. Yet the outline published by the Second Archives of China in Nanking in 1989 indicates that the policy was decided in early 1945. In 1959, when *Guangfu Zhi* published the contents of the outline in Taiwan, its compilers carefully omitted the article in question (part 6, art. 1) from the text.

[42] "Taiwan jieguan jihua gangyao," 14 March 1944, GRN 5(2) (Ministry of Education): file 592, *TG*, 1: 49–57; *Guangfu Zhi*, 12–16.

postwar Chinese administration in Taiwan would suffer greatly for want of specialized personnel in various fields. At the same time, the commission showed no interest in fully using the human resources of the Taiwanese Revolutionary Alliance to solve the problem.[43] In September 1944, when a guide for training administrative personnel for Taiwan was adopted by the CPB, it included an item on enlisting Taiwanese as trainees. But since it also required every trainee to have a higher education and a remarkable record of serving the KMT government, the screening process of these training programs tended to shut out many Taiwanese youths.[44] In February 1945, the TRA suggested to the Chinese government that its members be armed for the purpose of carrying out armed propaganda in Taiwan and assisting the landing of the Allied forces. Shortly before Japan surrendered, the TRA further organized a "Working Committee for Assisting the Recovery of Taiwan" to provide advice to the central government. These initiatives failed to impress the KMT leadership.[45]

This is not to say that the TRA was completely ignored by the KMT authority. During its preparation of the outline, the commission did include individual members of the TRA in its policy deliberations. But the process only accentuated the difference between the two sides. On three important issues KMT planners and TRA leaders stood apart. One was concerned with how to integrate Taiwan into the political and economic life of China. Using the Three People's Principles as a standard, both sides recognized the unique situation of Taiwan in comparison with other Chinese provinces. But whereas KMT planners tended to emphasize the political backwardness of the island as a result of long-term colonization, TRA leaders pointed out that in terms of economic development and governmental organization, Taiwan could become the most advanced province in China. Therefore, when the two sides talked about Taiwan as a "special province," they meant very different policies for the island. Another issue separating the two sides was how to evaluate the human resources in Taiwan. The commission wanted personnel from the mainland to govern the island, but TRA leaders urged Chongqing to adopt a policy of "drawing on local human resources," one that the Japanese had used to great effect.[46]

[43] Chen Yi to Chen Lifu, 15 May 1944, GRN 171(2) (Central Planning Board): file 103(1), TG, 1: 60–61.
[44] "Dongbei ji Taiwan dang zheng ganbu xunlian banfa cao'an" (Draft Plan on Methods to Train Party and Administrative Cadres for the Northeast and Taiwan), September 1944 (n.d.), GRN 171(2) (Central Planning Board): file 102, TG, 1: 34–36.
[45] Xie Dongmin et al., *Guomin Geming yu Taiwan* (Nationalist Revolution and Taiwan) (Taipei: Zhongyang Wenwu Gongyingshe, 1980), 79–80.
[46] Minutes of the meetings of the Investigation Commission on Taiwan, 13 and 21 July 1944, GRN 171(2) (Central Planning Board): file 99, TG, 1: 11–27; minutes of the meeting of the subcommittee on the Taiwanese administrative division, 27 February 1945, GRN 171(2) (Central Planning Board): file 141, TG, 1: 41–44.

Finally, TRA leaders expressed concern about the KMT government's "absolute optimism" that China could rely on America's support for regaining Taiwan. At one point, Ke Taishan, one of the founders of the TRA, reminded Chen Yi and other members of the commission that although the Americans were also making preparations for conquering Taiwan, they rarely consulted the Chinese government. He was worried about America's intentions toward Taiwan:

> It [the United States] recognizes other powers' rights and suzerainty [in the Pacific], but it also professes its intention to control every island in the Pacific, ... this naturally causes our concern about the relations between Taiwan and the United States: (1) strategically, America may land before other powers in Taiwan and then establish its defense system in Taiwan, which after the war can be turned into a manufactory industry to control Taiwan's economy; (2) the United States may also avenge Pearl Harbor and destroy all industries [in Taiwan]; (3) before the war Taiwan's electricity plants borrowed six hundred thousand dollars from America, and now America may want to clear this account with Taiwan.

To prevent any extreme actions on the part of the Americans, Ke urged Chongqing to train a large number of troops that would join American forces landing in Taiwan and also to come to some understanding with American military authorities concerning occupation policies.[47] The TRA leaders' concerns made no significant impact on Chen Yi's commission. When the outline was completed, it remained a typical KMT product.

When the war ended abruptly in mid-August 1945, Chongqing was caught by surprise. A "Governor-General's Office in Taiwan Province" was hastily established on 20 August, and nine days later Chen Yi was appointed "Administer General of the Taiwan Provincial Government." Because in the war years the Chinese government had never seriously considered a military plan for conquering Taiwan, a "Headquarters of the Commander-in-Chief of the Police Force in Taiwan Province" was established, also under Chen Yi, to make plans for military occupation of the island.[48] Chen Yi's dual capacity conferred on him tremendous power. But when Chen Yi established his administration at Taiwan in October, he discovered that the thousand mainlanders who came with him were far from adequate to manage the island. Hence, despite the objection in the outline to using Japanese personnel for the new Chinese administration in Taiwan, Chen Yi's regime was compelled to retain some 7,670 Japanese employees in their former positions. In contrast, only 5,568 Taiwanese employees remained in their positions. What made this situation even

---

[47] Minutes of the meeting of the Investigation Commission on Taiwan, 21 July 1944, GRN 171(2) (Central Planning Board): file 99, TG, 1: 24–26.

[48] George H. Kerr, *Formosa: Licensed Revolution and the Home Rule Movement, 1895–1945* (Honolulu: University of Hawaii Press, 1974), 233; *Guangfu Zhi*, 17–18.

more awkward was that Chen Yi and most of his Chinese subordinates spoke neither the Japanese language nor the local dialect. Nonetheless, only a few leaders of the wartime Taiwanese movement in Chongqing were offered positions in the postwar Taiwanese government.[49] In this manner, a new page in Taiwanese history was turned.

Chongqing's post-Cairo planning for the Ryukyu Islands was similarly influenced by events following Chiang Kai-shek's alliance-making effort at Cairo. Unaware of Chiang's desistance of China's claims over the islands at Cairo, planners of the Waijiaobu assumed that since these islands probably would not survive as an independent entity in the postwar years, Chinese control would be the preferred solution. In the meantime, expecting disagreement with the Allies, Waijiaobu strategists also recommended that the Ryukyu issue should be used as a bargaining chip by China when negotiating with the Western Allies. In the event of American and British objections to China's control, the Chinese government should be amenable and accept either of the following alternatives for the Ryukyu Islands: (1) international control or joint American–Chinese control or (2) a demilitarized zone. The rationale behind the first choice was that these islands would probably be occupied by American forces, which would leave China no choice but to support the American formula. The second option was included because Chongqing remained uncertain about whether the American government might favor Japan's retention of the Ryukyu Islands. In that situation, demilitarization of those islands seemed China's best hope. When negotiating with the Allies, these officials recommended, the Chinese delegation should mount some resistance at first but then ought to settle with a policy acceptable to the Western Allies. Supposedly, concessions over the Ryukyu Islands could make China a humble example for the other governments coveting their own dependent areas.[50] Until the end of the war, however, Chongqing did not give itself a chance to serve as role model for the Western Allies. Instead, Chongqing's wartime deliberation on the Ryukyu question ended with Chiang Kai-shek's endorsement of the Potsdam Proclamation. That document included the Ryukyu Islands among a group of "minor islands" whose status would be determined by the United Nations at a later time.[51]

Chongqing's "liberal" attitude toward the disposition of Pacific islands

[49] Shao Yulin, *Shengli Qian Hou,* 110, 120; Lin Hengdao, *Taiwan Shi* (Taipei: Zhongwen Tushu, 1979), 721, 725, 726, 728; Kerr, *Formosa: Licensed Revolution,* 233 note, 233–234.

[50] Chiang to Soong, 3 April 1945, WKP, box 81; memorandum by the Supreme Council of National Defense, "Riben wutiaojian touxiang shi suo ying jieshou zunban zhi tiaokuan cao'an"; memorandum by Yang Yunzhu, "Gaoli, Riben, weiren tongzhidi ji wo guo shidi wenti."

[51] The Potsdam Proclamation is printed in *FRUS: The Conference of Berlin, 1945,* 2: 1474–1476 (hereafter cited as *FRUS: Berlin*).

was also reflected in its policy toward the Japanese Mandated Islands, though the KMT leaders' real concern was again to show respect for America's leadership. Originally, the Waijiaobu's rationale was that in the past the mandate system had created new colonies but under a different name, and that after this war any interim administration for dependent areas, including the Japanese Mandates, should be internationalized in order to prevent a single power from repeating the old imperial practice.[52] Yet, after Cairo, the Chinese government decided that should the trusteeship question be raised for discussion and the American government indicate a willingness to take over the Japanese Mandated Islands, the principle of international administration could be waived in that instance. Chongqing also saw Washington's interest in these islands as an opportunity to encourage the United States to assume greater responsibility for the security of the whole Pacific region.[53]

During the Dumbarton Oaks Conference, President Roosevelt complained to Ambassador Koo, who headed the Chinese delegation, that the issue of the postwar treatment of the Japanese Mandated Islands was racking his brain.[54] The favorable Chinese attitude might help ease the president's headache. When the issue of the Japanese Mandated Islands was wrapped into a bigger controversy on the so-called strategic trust problem at the San Francisco Conference, the Chinese delegation duly gave its support to the American policy of putting these islands under U.S. control as "strategic trust territories."[55]

Korea and "in due course"

Obviously, the Cairo summit helped the KMT leaders awaken to the reality that the Chinese government was not in a position to alter Washington's policies with regard to postwar East Asia. This new awareness resulted in a modification by the KMT of its foreign policy objectives that eventually had the effect of reducing friction between Chongqing and Washington

---

[52] Memorandum of the Supreme Council of National Defense, "Zhanhou guoji heping jigou ji qita youguan wenti."

[53] Soong to Wei Tao-ming, 29 July 1944, WKP, box 70; Waijiaobu memorandum, "Tingzhan hou chuli Riben zhu fang'an."

[54] "Canjia guoji heping anquan jigou huiyi daibiaotuan baogaoshu" (Report by the Chinese Delegation to the Conference on an International Organization for Peace and Security), n.d., WKP, box 76; Koo to Chiang, 4 October 1944, ibid., box 57. Wm. Roger Louis, *Imperialism at Bay: The United States and the Decolonization of the British Empire, 1941–1945* (New York: Oxford University Press, 1978), 383–384, and 384 n. 11, suggests that according to the British record, at a certain stage of the conference the Chinese delegation proposed to establish an International Territorial Trusteeship Commission for administering trust territories.

[55] "Notes of a Conversation with Mr. Benjamin Gerig," 21 May 1945, WKP, box 77. For the "strategic trust" controversy, see Louis, *Imperialism at Bay*, 512–531.

over postwar issues. Yet, to Chongqing's Korean protégés, such a development was ominous. After the official text of the Cairo Declaration was issued in December 1943, the Koreans canceled a celebration ceremony scheduled earlier. Interestingly, they construed the "in due course" clause on Korea in the Cairo document not as an Anglo–American policy but as a Chinese scheme. Koreans in Chongqing feared that the clause might eventually put Korea under China's mandate, and therefore they pressed the Chinese government for an explanation.[56] Chinese diplomats in Western capitals were also faced with inquiries along the same line. When questioned by Western reporters about China's Korea policy, Ambassador Koo neither denied nor confirmed the assumption that China intended to recover its traditional suzerainty over Korea. He emphasized that China's so-called suzerainty had been very different from the prevailing understanding of that term in the West. It had been more cultural and spiritual than political. Koo used a metaphor of oriental brotherhood to depict the traditional Chinese–Korean relationship, suggesting that China's position as the elder brother would naturally decide its duty after this war to help Korea achieve independence.[57] Obviously, Koo also assumed that the "in due course" clause reflected Chongqing's policy. In view of the Anglo–American origin of that clause and Chongqing's dislike of it, it is ironic that this cryptic phrase should compel the Chinese government to come forward and explain its meaning to Korea.

The Chiang–Roosevelt polemic over Korea at Cairo effected some superficial readjustment of Chongqing's stand, but this only magnified the hesitant character of the KMT policy toward Korea. The occasion for Chongqing to adapt its Korean policy to the Cairo Communiqué was provided by the Koreans themselves. In the summer of 1944, during American Vice-President Henry Wallace's visit to China, the KPG intensified its effort to gain Allied recognition. Kim Ku sent a letter to Chiang Kai-shek demanding that Chongqing escalate its efforts in aiding the KPG. An appeal for recognition was also circulated by the KPG among Allied diplomats in Chongqing. KMT officials had to consider how the situation might affect their intention that China would be the first country to grant diplomatic recognition to the KPG. In early July, Chiang Kai-shek ordered his top aides on Korean affairs, including Zhu Jiahua, Wu Tiecheng, He Yingqin and T. V. Soong, to study the possibility of granting either de jure or de facto recognition to the KPG.[58]

Yet the policy recommendation made by Zhu's group had to disappoint

[56] Gauss to Hull, 7 December 1943, *FRUS, 1943*, 3: 1096.
[57] *Zhongyang Ribao*, 5 December 1943.
[58] Shao Yulin, *Shi Han Huiyilu*, 38; Waijiaobu memorandum, "Zhuxi dui waijiao fangmian zhishi"; Gauss to Hull, 3 June 1944, *FRUS, 1944*, V, 1294; Hu Chunhui, *Hanguo Duli Yundong zai Zhongguo* (Korean Independence Movement in China) (Taipei: Zhonghua Minguo Shiliao Yanjiu Zhongxin, 1976), 307.

both Chiang and the Koreans. In these officials' opinion, two developments in the past few months called for Chongqing's readjustment of its Korean policy. The first was the convening of a "parliamentary" assembly of Korean expatriates in Chongqing during April 1944. This brought about a temporary reconciliation between Kim Ku's and Kim Won-bong's factions and therefore strengthened the KPG case for diplomatic recognition. The second was the international support for Korean independence, as reflected by the Cairo Communiqué, which put further pressure on Chongqing to act on its promise to recognize the KPG's legitimacy. Zhu and others admitted that these developments required the Chinese government to upgrade its relationship with Korean expatriates in order to "strengthen its [the KPG's] confidence in us and enhance our opportunity to control and use it [the KPG]." They feared that unless the momentary unity of the Korean factions under the KPG was encouraged and strengthened, Korean expatriates in Chongqing would become disappointed and discard the KPG or even try to organize a second exile government somewhere else.[59]

But even these considerations did not warrant formal recognition of the KPG at the moment. An argument made by the Waijiaobu, obviously conveyed to Zhu's group by T. V. Soong, was used to convince Chiang. After Cairo, in the opinion of the Waijiaobu, the Chinese government should act in concert with the Western Allies in the matter of recognition; in particular, any "concrete decision [about Korea made by Chongqing] should be immediately communicated to the United States in order to keep close contact." At the time, the Western Allies were reluctant to grant recognition to the KPG because of doubts about its representativeness and their concern about Moscow's reaction. Under such circumstances, Zhu's group suggested to Chiang, the Chinese government should also postpone a de jure recognition of the KPG until a more auspicious time. An alternative for maintaining Chongqing's position as principal patron of the Korean cause was to double the monthly allowance granted to the KPG (from 500,000 to 1,000,000 yuan). It was also recommended that the Military Council relax its control over the Korean Restoration Army. The latter point was made because, by that time, the KPG's acceptance of the Chinese Military Council's nine-point code had already become a major embarrassment for the KPG in front of its critics.[60] Disposed to act more positively, Chiang nevertheless accepted these arguments. In mid-September, to placate the disappointed Koreans, Chiang instructed the Waijiaobu that the Korean Restoration Army should now be placed under the direction of the KPG and that, in the future, the KPG should receive "favorite treatment" as a de facto government.[61]

[59] Wu Tiecheng to Zhu Jiahua, 31 July 1944, and enclosures, *HDYS*, 614–630.
[60] Ibid.
[61] Hu Chunhui, *Hanguo*, 308.

Therefore, after Cairo, the Chinese government in practice abandoned its original policy of being the first to recognize the KPG. Practically speaking, Chongqing's diplomatic support of the KPG reached a dead end. For the remainder of the war, the Chinese government continued to support the Korean nationalists in the international arena, but the effort was intended more to humor the Koreans than to persuade the other Allies to accept China's particular stand. On the eve of the San Francisco Conference, Chongqing agreed to provide traveling expenses for KPG members to attend. But then the Koreans were left adrift when they failed to receive American visas. In San Francisco, outside the conference, certain members of the Chinese delegation encouraged Korean expatriates in the United States to propagate their objection to the trusteeship formula for Korea. But inside the conference, the Chinese delegation refrained from taking any initiative on the Korean question.[62]

The drift of Chongqing's Korean policy, along with the Western attitude, did not lead to any relaxation of its guard against the Soviet Union. On the contrary, because of the existence of a large number of Korean nationals in Siberia in 1944 and 1945, Chongqing grew increasingly fearful that Moscow might at some time create a "Korean Lublin Government" and then extend its influence to the Korean Peninsula.[63] This anxiety was further intensified when the Western and Soviet leaders reached their understanding on the issue of the Polish government at Yalta. To Chongqing, it was an ominous precedent for Korea. A small number of officials in Chongqing began to suggest that direct discussions of Korea between the Chinese and Soviet governments be initiated. Yet this line did not receive a favorable hearing from top KMT leaders, who preferred to pursue a common front with the Western Allies for curbing the Russians. Nevertheless, due to Washington's attitude, KMT leaders felt obliged to modify their earlier rigid anti-Soviet stand regarding Korea. Now, grudgingly, they agreed to give the Soviets an insignificant role in Korea, provided that China could forge an entente over Korea with the United States and Britain in advance.[64]

---

[62] Shao Yulin, *Shi Han Huiyilu* (My Mission to Korea) (Taipei: Zhuanji Wenxue Chubanshe, 1980), 56–57, 67–68; memorandum by Shao Yulin, "Guanyu Chaoxian wenti zhi baogao" (Report on the Korean Question), n.d., *WKP*, box 81; "Notes of a Conversation with Mr. James Dunn," 29 May 1945, "Notes of a Conversation with Mr. Wilhelm Morgenstierne," 29 May 1945, and "Notes of a Conversation with Mr. James Dunn," 30 May 1945, ibid., box 77; memorandum by Yang Yunzhu, "Lü Mei Hanqiao duli yundong yu Jinshan huiyi" (Independence Movement Among the Korean Nationals in the United States and the San Francisco Conference), 2 May 1945, ibid., box 79.

[63] Hu Chunhui, *Hanguo*, 122–123.

[64] Shao Yulin, *Shi Han Huiyilu*, 54–55, 66–67; Waijiaobu memorandum, "Tingzhan hou chuli Riben zhu fang'an"; secretariat of the Supreme Council of National Defense to Chiang, "Baogao" (Report) no. 749, 6 November 1944, *WKP*, box 79; Waijiaobu memorandum, "Fuzhu Hanguo duli fang'an" (Plan for Assisting Korean Independence), 25 March 1945, ibid., box 81.

An opportunity for forging a tripartite coalition regarding Korea seemed to come in September 1944, when the American and British governments sent separate but identical "draft questionnaires on Korea" to the Chinese government, suggesting that "studies of a factual nature be prepared and exchanged" between the Chinese and themselves.[65] This invitation resulted in a collaboration among the Supreme Council of National Defense, the National Military Council, and the Waijiaobu for drafting a response. In accordance with his diplomatic style after Cairo, Chiang Kai-shek approved the eventual report with these words: "In principle the whole text is usable, but we should not bring these points up before the other governments make their suggestions. We can properly let the Americans and the British know our stand after we at first give consideration to their opinions."[66]

All three agencies agreed that if China accepted President Roosevelt's trusteeship formula for Korea, the morale of the Korean partisans would be devastated. But, they reasoned, "in view of the reality," Chongqing did not seem to have any alternative other than agreeing to some kind of international supervision system for Korea. The Waijiaobu even suggested optimistically that an international regime in Korea might serve to check a Soviet scheme for Manchuria, though the other two agencies remained suspicious.[67]

Yang Yunzhu went to Washington to consult with the State Department. From 24 January to 14 February, the two sides held eleven meetings. Although the Americans and the Chinese agreed on certain general principles, they failed to clarify the key issue: the nature and form of an interim administration for Korea prior to Korean independence. The "in due course" clause of the Cairo Communiqué remained a mysterious factor in American–Chinese consultations. During the discussions, the Americans only briefly outlined their trusteeship idea and were reluctant or unable to offer any concrete plan. Still, Yang could sense the differences between the American formula and a Chinese plan held in his pocket. Yet, because Chiang only permitted the Chinese plan to be used as a counterproposal, Yang apparently never revealed that plan to his American counterparts.[68]

---

[65] "Oral Statement" and "Draft Questionnaire on Korea" that the Chinese government received from the U.S. government, n.d., *WKP*, box 79.

[66] Secretariat of the Supreme Council of National Defense to Chiang, "Baogao"; Chiang to Wang Chonghui, n.d., *WKP*, box 79.

[67] Chiang to Wang Shijie and Wang Chonghui, 16 October 1944, and enclosures, GRN 761 (National Military Council): file 147, DELD; Councilors Office of the National Military Council to Chiang, 19 October 1944, ibid.

[68] Memorandum by Yang Yunzhu, "Guanyu Gaoli wenti yu Mei waibu shangtao jingguo" (Report on the Consultation with U.S. State Department on the Korean Question), 10 April 1945, *WKP*, box 79; memorandum of conversation between Yang Yunzhu and State Department officials, 17 February 1945, *FRUS, 1945*, 6: 1020–1022.

Although it never reached the diplomatic arena, the Chinese plan serves as an illuminating historical document on the Chinese intentions about Korea after the Cairo Conference. Ever since the Cairo Conference, the Chinese government had tried to translate the "in due course" clause into tangible terms that would serve its interests. Militarily, this clause could mean a period of military occupation by the Allied forces, which, in the opinion of the Waijiaobu, might last for about five years. While the Chinese ground forces would assume responsibility for maintaining domestic order in Korea, the other Allies' air and naval forces could be deployed in readiness to defend Korea from external attack.[69] Remaining negative toward Washington's trusteeship formula for Korea, Chongqing developed an alternative formula. The program that Yang carried to Washington was entitled "Plan for Assisting the Independence of Korea." It contained an "ideal solution" of the Korean problem plus a secondary option. The most important components of the preferred solution were three: (1) the Allied responsibility for maintaining Korea's domestic order and national defense during the initial military occupation period; (2) the formation of Korean "provisional authorities" with full power to administer civil affairs in Korea soon after Japan's defeat; and (3) recognition and guarantee by the Allies of complete Korean independence and a formal Korean government following the conclusion of the occupation period.[70]

For Chongqing, the key to this solution was the coexistence of a Korean government and an Allied military authority in Korea from the very beginning of the occupation period. Chinese officials believed that Washington's trusteeship formula included no provision for such an authority and would therefore automatically delay Korea's complete independence. Yet, in view of the fact that Chongqing intended to transplant its own protégé, the KPG, back to Korea, the reference to "Korea's complete independence" in Chongqing's policy really meant China's prevailing influence. The Chinese formula also identified "in due course" with the occupation period and therefore rejected the trusteeship formula, which provided for postoccupation foreign supervision in Korea. Lastly, the international guarantee for Korean independence might be readily translated into the Western Allies' responsibility for China's security in Northeast Asia vis-à-vis the Soviet Union.

This would be the ideal solution, in Chongqing's view. However, if the American government were to insist that the Koreans lacked the ability to assume immediate self-government, KMT leaders were prepared to make

[69] Waijiaobu memoranda, "Sheli Taipingyang shang guoji zhanlüe didai" (Establishment of an International Security Zone on the Pacific), 7 June 1944, and "Tingzhan hou chuli Riben zhu fang'an," 7 June 1944, VHP, box 3.
[70] Shao Yulin, *Shi Han Huiyilu*, 38; secretariat of the Supreme Council of National Defense to Chiang, "Baogao"; memorandum by Yang Yunzhu, "Gaoli, Riben weiren tongzhidi ji wo guo shidi wenti."

a concession in reference to the third point listed earlier. The Chinese government would agree that *after* independence and *after* a formal government of Korea was recognized and guaranteed by the United Nations, a "temporary system of international assistance" should be established jointly by China, the United States, and Britain in Korea to assist the new Korean government. But this "assistance" should be limited to three years. As a concession to Washington's Big Four formula, Chongqing agreed that all these steps should be discussed and approved by China and the two Western powers. If the Soviet government were willing to join in, that would be welcome as well.[71]

Details of the assistance system were not included in the plan that Yang brought to Washington, but responsible Chinese officials had clear ideas about how it should be structured. In one of Ambassador Koo's dispatches to the Waijiaobu at the end of 1944, the formula was fully discussed. The chief goal of the system was to maintain China's dominant influence in Korea. Under this precondition, the advisory responsibilities in Korea could be divided among the Big Four. China would take charge of diplomatic and police affairs, the United States would guide financial and transportation matters, Britain would assume judicial responsibilities, and the Soviet Union could help with the public health needs of the Korean government. It would be even better if the other three governments did not insist on appointing their advisers and were willing to accept appointees from lesser states. In Ambassador Wellington Koo's opinion, because China and Korea were "as close as the lips to the teeth," China currently needed to act on Korea's behalf in international affairs and maintain military bases in that country. Such arrangements were necessary for China to discharge its international obligations at the end of the war, as well as to strengthen its own national defense. But at the same time, China's leading political responsibility in Korea must be supplemented by the Western Allies' major economic responsibility.[72]

The formulation of this assistance system idea indicated both the pragmatism of Chongqing's diplomacy and its tenacious pursuit to regain China's regional influence in East Asia. But in Chongqing's wartime planning for Korea, the new formula constituted just one stage of Chongqing's retreat before Washington's persistent policy of treating Korea as an international issue. The assistance system was not the final line of Chongqing's rear-guard fight. During the last year of the war, officials in Chongqing

---

[71] Memorandum by Yang Yunzhu, "Gaoli, Riben weiren tongzhidi ji wo guo shidi wenti"; Waijiaobu memorandum, "Fuzhu Hanguo duli fang'an."

[72] Koo to Waijiaobu, 1 December 1944, *WKP*, box 54. The metaphor of "the lips to the teeth" is another example of how certain traditional Chinese conceptions of territorial security may have influenced modern Chinese diplomacy. The first use by a Chinese statesman of this metaphor probably occurred in 655 B.C., and the story is recorded in the Confucian classic *Zuo Zhuan*.

themselves grew skeptical that their modified Korean policy would be acceptable to Washington. The Yalta Conference, which excluded the Chinese government, caused great anxiety among KMT leaders. After the conference, the Big Three publicized their agreements on postwar issues in Europe but ominously kept silent about issues in the Far East. In addition, the Western Allies' willingness to accept the Moscow-sponsored Lublin regime in Poland was viewed by KMT officials as a bad precedent for Korea. They feared that "a situation similar to the Polish politics" would likely ensue in Korea.[73]

Consequently, the question emerged as to whether the American trusteeship formula should be accepted as the last resort. Over this question, officials in Chongqing remained divided. The Waijiaobu argued that at the end of the war, China would be too weak to influence events in Korea; therefore, America's interest and presence in Korea should be encouraged. Chongqing should not be intransigent in responding to America's trusteeship plan. Officials in other agencies, such as the National Military Council, continued to worry about the implication of a Korean trusteeship for China's claim of sovereignty over Manchuria. Now some prominent KMT doctrinaire voices also joined the debate. The Chen brothers, Lifu and Guofu, held that as a revolutionary power, China had an obligation to support Korean independence and therefore should take decisive steps to recognize the KPG without too much anxiety about other countries' attitudes. Chongqing's Korea policy would remain muddled, and it would drift with events until the end of the war.[74]

---

[73] "Canzhao Kelimiya xuanyan shizuo chuli Riben, Riben fuyong ji Taipingyang jiefang quyu gangyao zhi niyi" (A Tentative Policy Outline on the Treatment of Japan, Japanese Dependent Areas, and Liberated Regions in the Pacific in Light of the Crimea Declaration), n.d. (1945), GRN 43 (Supreme Council of National Defense): file 287, DELD.

[74] Memorandum by Yang Yunzhu, "Gaoli, Riben weiren tongzhidi ji wo guo shidi wenti"; Councilors Office of the National Military Council to Chiang, 19 October 1944, GRN 761 (National Military Council): file 147, DELD; Hu Chunhui, "Chen Guofu yu Hanguo duli yundong" (Chen Guofu and the Korean Independence Movement), in Zhonghua Minguo Hanguo Yanjiu Xuehui, *Zhong Han Guanxi Shi Guoji Yantaohui Lunwen Ji, 960–1949* (Taipei: Zhonghua Minguo Hanguo Yanjiu Xuehui, 1983), 281.

9

Erosion of a partnership

In early January 1944, having returned from his summit meetings with Chiang Kai-shek and Joseph Stalin, President Roosevelt reported to the Pacific War Council with his usual optimistic tone, defining the meetings as "highly satisfactory." Alleging that he had reached agreements with the Chinese and Russians on all the major issues regarding postwar settlement in East Asia, Roosevelt's true enthusiasm concerned his first meeting with Stalin.[1] In retrospect, Roosevelt's separate meetings with Chiang and Stalin in late 1943 were two different points of departure. Afterward, American–Soviet cooperation continued to gain momentum in the direction set at Teheran, but the American–Chinese partnership experienced an anticlimax despite or partially because of the Cairo Conference. These two trends were typically reflected in Roosevelt's conduct of his last summit at Yalta in February 1945. On that occasion, he reached a secret understanding with Stalin over Asian problems without consulting and notifying the Chinese. In fact, in the last two years of the war, when the American government contemplated its postwar Asian policies in more concrete terms, there were serious questions about China's value as an ally in both war and peace.

The Chinese ally reevaluated

In 1944, there were two schools of thought among the China hands of the State Department, neither completely endorsing America's China policy as it stood. One group supported the wartime departure of the American government from its traditional China policy but was concerned about the discrepancy between the reality of China and Washington's inflated wartime definition of that country. At about the time of the Cairo Conference,

[1] Memorandum by Wilson Brown on the 36th meeting of the Pacific War Council, 12 January 1944, *RPMF*, box 168.

John C. Vincent observed: "We do not intend to be sentimentally generous and considerate with regard to China but we . . . must avoid a return to a pre-war attitude which was . . . patronizing at best, and disregardful of Chinese 'nationality'." Although he advocated an enhanced place for "Chinese nationality" in U.S. foreign policy, Vincent also cautioned against misconceptions of China from another extreme. Due to its internal weakness, he emphasized, China was not a first-class military and industrial power during the war and would be unlikely to become such a power after the war. In Vincent's opinion, Washington's policy of treating China as one of the Big Four "on moral and prestige ground" had actually resulted in a dilemma for China, whose "physical strength warrants classification only as a second-rate power." In other words, in Vincent's opinion, Washington did not yet have a proper China policy based on a realistic estimate of Chinese power, and its wartime political and financial investment in China lacked a sound basis.[2]

Stanley Hornbeck, an older China hand of the State Department, disagreed. He believed that the United States was capable, if willing, to alleviate China's poor physical conditions and help the Asian ally to develop in reality its wartime image as a great power. In mid-1944, in a memorandum to Secretary Hull, Hornbeck contended that the time had come for the U.S. government to reconsider its Europe-first strategy and to match its military policy to its political efforts in China. Hornbeck warned that despite America's adherence to the concept of China as one of the Big Four, its current lukewarm military effort in China was taking the risk of "letting China become a military and political nullity."[3]

The disagreement between Vincent and Hornbeck virtually implied agreement. After a few years of close encounters between the American and Chinese governments, both had come to realize that U.S. foreign policy must now come to terms with the military and political realities of China. Whereas Vincent urged bringing the paper-dragon kite of great-power China down, Hornbeck exhorted the U.S. government to empower that dragon and to make it fly on its own. Events in China in 1944 especially created a sense of urgency among American officials. In that year, the KMT regime's performance in resisting Japan's last offensive in the war, the *Ichigo* offensive, epitomized its profound moral, political, and military defects. According to Chongqing's own statistics, from early 1939 to late 1943, the Japanese army expanded its control of territories in the interior of China from 261 to 466 counties. From April to October 1944, Japan's drive to establish a transcontinental corridor from Manchuria to Indochina further contracted Chongqing's already meager economic base. Collapse of

[2] Memorandum by John C. Vincent, "Background and Brief Notes between China and the United States," n.d. (November 1943), *RDCA*, box 1.
[3] Hornbeck to Hull, 6 July 1944, *SHP*, box 380.

the KMT's moral leadership among the Chinese populace was exemplified in Henan, where peasants disarmed 50,000 government troops before the Japanese Army attacked. Having suffered from years of famine and the KMT regime's often callous treatment, these peasants regarded Japan's offensive as an opportunity for them to take things into their own hands. John Service of the U.S. embassy sent reports back to the State Department arguing that although the KMT government would probably not disintegrate completely due to recent events, the American government certainly needed to make some major policy readjustments. In Service's opinion, the policy of treating China as a great power was no longer justifiable, and Washington should use Chongqing's current crisis to push the KMT leadership into reforming its military and political policies. Service's suggestion was for Washington to stop its "mollycoddling" of Chongqing by scaling down military and financial aid.[4]

From a military perspective, planners of the Joint Chiefs of Staff reached a conclusion similar to Service's policy recommendation. The question they asked was whether Chongqing's military organization could be revitalized even with a substantial reinforcement of American aid. At the beginning of 1944, an answer was unmistakably provided by the Joint Intelligence Committee of the Joint Chiefs of Staff:

> Given adequate United Nations training and equipment and adequate leadership, a substantial number of Chinese divisions might at some later time be made into an effective fighting force.... However, we do not believe that for some time to come they would be able to carry out independent offensive operations against large scale resistance. While comparatively small forces can be so trained, to bring the present Chinese Army as a whole up to any reasonable standard of military efficiency would be an undertaking so vast that it could only be accomplished in a period of years.[5]

Accordingly, an attempt to revitalize the Chinese fighting forces through large-scale aid would be excessively expensive and unproductive.

Meanwhile, objections to sending American forces to the China theater were being forcefully voiced. In October 1944, in the wake of Chongqing's military debacle, Secretary of War Henry Stimson told President Roosevelt that "we should be absolutely inflexible in concentrating all the infantry power possible in the battle which Eisenhower is waging in Germany." Logically, such a strategy "made it absolutely impossible to consider using American troops for fighting the Japanese on the mainland of China." The

[4] Theodore H. White and Annalee Jacoby, *Thunder Out of China* (New York: Da Capo, 1980), 172–178; Ronald H. Spector, *Eagle against the Sun: The American War with Japan* (New York: Vintage, 1985), 365–367; Joseph W. Esherick, ed., *Lost Chance in China: The World War II Despatches of John W. Service* (New York: Random House, 1974), 131–136, 138–157.
[5] JIC 154/2, "China's Relations to the United Nations in the War Against Japan," 1 January 1944, *RJCS*, reel 13.

war in the Pacific, according to Stimson, could be won with naval and air forces. President Roosevelt readily agreed. General Albert Wedemeyer, successor to General Stilwell in the China theater, also agreed with this strategy. Early in 1945, Wedemeyer's "China Theater Outline of Far East Strategy" proposed that the war in the Far East should be conducted to eliminate the "dynamo of the enemy war effort" located in the Japanese archipelago, but to avoid large-scale operations by American ground forces in China.[6]

In the last two years of the war, even for the purposes of propaganda and psychological warfare, any attempt to assert that China was one of the great powers appeared farfetched. Illusions and high expectations about Chongqing among American leaders and officials disappeared quickly. It was no longer fashionable to view Chiang Kai-shek's China as one of the guardians of peace in the postwar years. Such a view, in the words of Colonel David Barrett, commander of the U.S. Army Observer Group in Yan'an, would mean "have sold ourselves down the river."[7] Planners in the State Department also shared this feeling. In the spring of 1945, the U.S. Army Air Force came up with a simpleminded plan suggesting that all the difficulties in America's China policy could be solved by helping Chongqing create a strong, modern air force. This naive plan was repudiated by State Department members of the new State–War–Navy Coordinating Committee (SWNCC). In their response, State Department officials emphasized that China had to stabilize itself first before it would be able to play a peacekeeping role in postwar East Asia. In their opinion, three conditions were found wanting in China: (1) internal political unity and stability; (2) the Chinese people's support for the KMT government; and (3) a sound economic and financial capacity to support modern armed forces. Until and unless these conditions were achieved, it would be unwise for the United States to commit itself either to a policy of helping the present KMT government develop a modern air force or to one of rearming China into a strong Asiatic power.[8]

The political implications of such comments were serious for the KMT regime. On the eve of the San Francisco Conference, expecting inter-Allied consultations on general postwar issues, the State Department further clarified its attitude in a comprehensive document concerning its China policy. Entitled "Policy with Respect to China," the document suggested that all current American relations with China be oriented to accomplish the short-term objective of America's Far Eastern policy, namely, the defeat of Japan. But the long-term goals of America's China policy had to await clarification

---

[6] Entry of 13 October 1944, *HSD*, 48 (reel 9): 146–147; JCS 924/13, "China Theatre Outline of Far East Strategy," 19 March 1945, *RJCS*, reel 13.

[7] David Barrett to Stilwell, 16 October 1944, *JSP*, box 28A.

[8] SWNCC 83: memorandum by Lt. General Barney M. Gilies, "Postwar Chinese Air Force," 21 March 1945, and C. W. McCarthy to Lovett, 2 April 1945, and JPWC report, "Postwar Military Policy with Respect to China," 25 April 1945, appendix c to enclosure b, *SWNCCF*, reel 10.

of the situation in China. Politically, the American government should
continue to support the KMT government of China, but at the same time
it should maintain "a degree of flexibility to permit cooperation with any
other leadership in China which may give greater promise of achieving
unity and contributing to peace and security in east Asia." The document
did not mention China as one of the Big Four. It merely observed that
diplomatically America would assist China, "as a nation [not the KMT
government], to attain [not maintain] a position of recognized equality
among the major powers." Economically, America was prepared to help
China build a well-balanced economy. But such assistance would depend
on what policies the Chinese government would follow and what actual
conditions affecting American trade with and in China would exist in the
postwar years.[9] Obviously, Hornbeck's domination of the department's
China policy had ceased and the Vincent line prevailed.

The State Department's stand was important because it was representative of a general attitude shared by leading officials in Washington, including President Roosevelt and his aides. In the last two years of the war, due
to the protracted KMT–CCP conflict; the difficulties in the Chongqing–
Washington relationship as reflected in the Stilwell affair; and Chongqing's
military disaster in 1944, few in Washington still cherished a rosy view of
Chiang Kai-shek's China. As a British diplomat observed in the summer of
1944, "the most arresting [development in Washington] is the growing
lack of enthusiasm for China, a fact which is striking indeed if compared
with the prestige that country enjoyed, say, six months ago. . . . The slump
in general Chinese stock is an accomplished fact and appears to be increas-
ing."[10] Chinese officials in the United States could not help but feel the
changed atmosphere. At about the same time, from Washington, H. H.
Kung reported sadly to Chiang Kai-shek: "Now most Americans believe
that China is not needed for defeating Japan. Other Allies also see us as
useless. This is an impression that I have got most sorrowfully by talking
to personalities of various circles."[11]

In 1944, President Roosevelt continued to receive reports on the dis-
tressing situation of the KMT regime. One source of such reports was John
Davies, who in late 1943 had met with the president as a member of
General Stilwell's staff at Cairo. On that occasion, Davies was struck by
Roosevelt's remark that if Chiang Kai-shek collapsed, the American government would support the most likely successor next in line. Before the
end of the year, Davies prepared an analysis of the KMT regime and sent
it to Harry Hopkins. In 1944, he continued to write letters to Hopkins
covering the conditions in China. Sharing John Vincent's feelings about

[9] Memorandum, "Policy with Respect to China," 18 April 1945, *RDCA*, box 10.
[10] H. G. Nicholas, ed., *Washington Despatches, 1941–1945: Weekly Political Reports from the British Embassy* (Chicago: University of Chicago Press, 1981), 405.
[11] H. H. Kung to Chiang, 17 August 1944, ZZSC, 3(1): 177.

American policy in China, Davies was more explicit than Vincent in criticizing the KMT regime and "the popular American misconception that Chiang Kai-shek is China." All of Davies's letters carried the same argument: the American government must not commit itself irrevocably to Chiang's regime, which enjoyed no popular support in China and was of slight use to America's war effort. In the short run, Davies argued, the KMT regime could make improvements only if it were pressured by a "stern bargaining" position of the American government. In the long run, the American government needed to consider the possibility that "China's future turns perhaps decisively on the [Chinese] Communists." Hopkins was impressed by Davies's analyses and was especially fond of his suggestion to send a military observers' mission to North China. He passed on some of Davies's letters to the president with his own endorsements.[12] Although his reaction to Davies's letters cannot be documented, President Roosevelt did persuade Chiang Kai-shek to allow an American military observers' mission to go to the Communist area in North China.[13]

Meanwhile, in his 1944 correspondence with Lieutenant Colonel Evans F. Carlson, Roosevelt revealed some of his feelings about the China question. The correspondence between Carlson and Roosevelt had started in the late 1930s when the president wanted the then Marine captain in China to report to him on developments in North China. In these early letters, Carlson praised the guerrilla warfare under the CCP leadership and excited Roosevelt's imagination about the feats of Chinese guerrilla fighters. In this period, Roosevelt had communicated with Carlson mostly through his personal secretaries and rarely expressed his own thoughts.[14] In 1944 Carlson was no longer in China, but he was still concerned about the situation there. In one letter to Roosevelt, Carlson requested the president to send him back to North China, where America could get "our most devoted support" and carry out the "ground work" for linking East and West. In another correspondence, he enclosed a letter addressed to himself and signed jointly by some top CCP leaders, again insisting that the Communist armies were "more trustworthy" and "useful" than the

[12] John P. Davies, Jr., *Dragon by the Tail: American, British, Japanese, and Russian Encounters with China and One Another* (New York: W. W. Norton, 1972), 280–299; Hopkins to Roosevelt, 2 February 1944, and enclosure: Davies to Hopkins, 23 January 1944, *HHP*, box 334; Hopkins to Roosevelt, 7 February 1944, and enclosure: Davies to Hopkins, 31 December 1943, ibid.; Hopkins to Roosevelt, 8 September 1944, and enclosure: Davies to Hopkins, 1 September 1944, ibid.; Davies to Hopkins, 22 October 1944, ibid.; Davies to Hopkins, 16 November 1944, ibid.

[13] War Department to AMMISCA, Chongqing, 9 February 1944, *HHP*, box 334; Michael Schaller, *The U.S. Crusade in China, 1938–1945* (New York: Columbia University Press, 1979), 181–182.

[14] Schaller, *U.S. Crusade in China*, 20–21; Kenneth E. Shewmaker, *Americans and Chinese Communists, 1927–1945: A Persuading Encounter* (Ithaca, NY: Cornell University Press, 1971), 102–106, 102 n. 53.

KMT units "in bringing to us the cooperation of the [Chinese] people when we commence military operations on the Asiatic mainland." In a direct response to Carlson, Roosevelt wrote:

> I think we are going through a transition period–especially the part relating to North China. I have done my best to keep some of the Chinese leaders from taking more positive action against the Eighth Route Army leaders, but it seems to go hard with the Generalissimo. I am sure, however, that the time will come when we will all want you back there. (Emphasis added)[15]

These words reflected Roosevelt's bewilderment about China. The president's remark on the "transition" in China evidenced his political acumen regarding the whole China question. Yet he was too cautious to act ahead of events. Although the Chongqing-centered policy would have to be modified, the president did not contemplate a sharp switch of American support from Chongqing to Yan'an. Roosevelt still wanted to waltz with Chiang for a while, but he was now prepared to invite Mao Zedong to join the dance as well. Beginning in the fall of 1944, Washington's new ambassador to China, Patrick Hurley, carried a mission for the president to mediate between Chongqing and Yan'an. Later, developments in China proved that the Chinese did not dance according to Washington's rhythm, nor did Ambassador Hurley really desire to change America's pas de deux with Chongqing. Nonetheless, Roosevelt believed that the reorientation of his China policy was significant. In March 1945, when questioned by Edgar Snow about America's policy between Chongqing and Yan'an, the president remarked: "Well, I've been working with two governments there, [and] I intend to go on doing so until we can get them together."[16]

President Roosevelt's revision of his earlier perception of China's international role was more substantial than the revision of his approach to China's domestic problems. Before his departure for the Yalta Conference in early 1945, Roosevelt told Secretary of State Edward Stettinius: "Our [China] policy was based on the belief that despite the temporary weakness of China and the possibility of revolutions and civil war, 450 million Chinese would someday become united and modernized and would be the most important factor in the whole Far East. China would someday assume the leadership in that area which the Japanese had [earlier] attempted to seize."[17] Still optimistic, this observation's two "somedays" are most

---

[15] Carlson to Roosevelt, 23 February and 28 October 1944 and enclosure: a letter to Carlson signed by Chu Teh [Zhu De], Chow [sic] En-lai [Zhuo Enlai], Yeh Chien-yin [sic] [Ye Jianying], and Nieh Yung-chen [Nie Yongzhen], 14 August 1944; *RPSF*, box 27; Roosevelt to Carlson, 2 March 1944, ibid.

[16] Edgar Snow, *Journey to the Beginning: A Personal View of Contemporary History* (New York: Vintage, 1972), 348.

[17] Thomas M. Campbell and George C. Herring, Jr., ed., *Diaries of Edward R. Stettinius, Jr., 1943–1946* (New York: New Viewpoints, 1975), 210.

illuminating. If the date for the emergence of China as a great power were to be indefinitely delayed, it seemed only logical for the American government to modify the Cairo decisions, which were based on the assumption that China was already a great power. The Yalta Conference would have such an effect. The diplomacy at Yalta will be discussed in the next chapter, but it is sufficient to say here that at Yalta, President Roosevelt decisively reversed the Cairo spirit by bypassing Chongqing and forging a new partnership with Moscow in Asian affairs. This is not to say that the president completely discarded the depreciated "China stock." He still wanted to secure whatever value remained in Chongqing as an ally in international politics. At Yalta, Roosevelt actually tried to accomplish this purpose by persuading Stalin to be another buyer of China stock. If he was partly successful, his success was achieved only by further reducing Chongqing's international stature.

The modification of Washington's perspective on and expectation of China in the last phase of the war had an immediate impact on the State Department's postwar foreign policy planning for East Asia. In 1942 and 1943, when the idea of making China a great power was still in fashion, the State Department's planning for East Asia had to proceed under its influence. Paradoxically, after the Cairo Conference attached a great-power emblem to the Chongqing regime, the planning staff of the State Department was no longer haunted by the ghost of great-power China. During the Cairo Conference, officials of the State Department were annoyed by President Roosevelt's indifference toward them, but otherwise they were basically satisfied with the Cairo decisions on postwar East Asia.[18] Cairo had the effect of formalizing the American position on certain postwar issues in East Asia and therefore enabled the planning operation in the State Department to conclude its search for guiding principles and move ahead to contemplate concrete policy measures.

Postwar control of Japan

The United States' post-Cairo planning for East Asia took the form of making preparations for the Allied civil affairs administration (CAA) of enemy-controlled territories. A principal issue involved the division of CAA responsibilities among the leading Allies. It was readily understood in the State Department that CAA responsibilities in the immediate postwar years would affect these powers' respective long-term influence on the Asian–Pacific region in significant ways.[19] In this regard, President Roosevelt's

---

[18] Hugh Borton, *American Presurrender Planning for Postwar Japan* (New York: Columbia University Press, 1967), 12–13.

[19] Major General J. H. Hilldring and Captain H. L. Pence to James Dunn, 18 February 1944, and enclosure, *FRUS, 1944*, 5: 1190–1194; CAC-100, 18 February 1944, and CAC-66a, 5 February 1944, *RHN*, box 109.

well-known idea about China's postwar role of policing Japan was immediately discarded. In early 1944, the American and British governments
agreed between themselves that Japan proper and the Central Pacific region,
including the Japanese Mandated Islands, the Bonins, and the Ryukyu
Islands, should come under the military and naval jurisdiction of the United
States for prosecuting the war and for postwar military government. Afterward, Chongqing's appeal for participation in a similar agreement with the
Western Allies met no favorable response in Washington.[20]

American planners had no difficulty in justifying America's predominant responsibility for making policies in postwar Japan. In the opinion of
the State Department, "the geographic position of the United States in
relation to Japan, and the military and financial resources of the United
States as well as events leading to the Pacific War," inevitably meant that
the military government in Japan must be of "dominantly American character." This position was not regarded in any manner as contradictory to
the American government's commitment to inter-Allied cooperation in the
postwar disposition of Japan, for American officials never construed the
commitment to mean equal sharing among the principal Allies of policymaking powers in regard to Japan.[21] Interestingly, in the last few months
of the war, American officials tended to view the British and the Chinese,
not the Russians, as America's most likely competitors in Japan. The State
Department anticipated Moscow's intentions to achieve influence in China
and Korea but not in Japan. Japan was nevertheless regarded as important
to the American–Soviet relationship at the global level. It must be secured
as America's power base in postwar East Asia vis-à-vis the Soviet power
that would probably be predominant in Europe.[22]

In view of the Soviet Union's neutrality toward Japan during most of
the Asian war, the U.S. government was able to avoid the issue of postwar
control of Japan when dealing with the Russians. Postwar treatment of
Japan was not on Roosevelt's agenda when he met with Stalin at Teheran.
Although the Yalta Conference decided in a secret agreement Soviet participation in the war against Japan, the agreement only mentioned some

[20] Memorandum from the State Department to the Joint Chiefs of Staff, 12 August 1944,
RDCA, box 11; the Joint Chiefs of Staff to the Secretary of State, 14 May 1944, and
enclosure, *FRUS, 1944*, 5: 1261–1262; CAC-66a, 5 February 1944, *RHN*, box 109.
[21] Memorandum from the Inter-Divisional Area Committee on the Far East, 13 March 1944,
FRUS, 1944, 5: 1202–1205; memorandum from the Office of Far Eastern Affairs, 18 April
1944, ibid., 1232; memorandum from the State Department to the President, 5 January
1945, *TSGR*, box 1.
[22] SWNCC 70/1/D: memorandum from the State Department, "National Composition of
Forces to Occupy Japan Proper," 1 May 1945, *SWNCCF*, reel 9; SWNCC 70/2: report
by the Subcommittee for the Far East, 23 June 1945, ibid.; Grew to Stimson, 28 June, and
enclosure, *FRUS, 1945*, 6: 578–579; "Capabilities and Intentions of U.S.S.R. in the Postwar Period," 5 January 1945, *OSSR*, reel 4.

territorial readjustments pertinent to Japan.[23] Moscow did not challenge America's exclusive responsibility for Japan until May 1945. At that time, Roosevelt's successor, President Harry Truman, sent Harry Hopkins to Moscow on a mission to learn Soviet leaders' intentions after the death of President Roosevelt. During Hopkins's visit, Stalin clearly indicated his interest in reaching some understanding with the Western Allies over postwar Japan, including occupation zones in Japan. In view of the established attitude of the State Department on the matter, Stalin's new interest was bound to meet resistance. Two months later, after a personal encounter with the Russians at the Potsdam Conference, President Truman found his own reason for not humoring the Russians. On that occasion, he was deeply disturbed by Stalin's intransigence on certain European issues. This led him to decide that he would not want to have a "joint setup with the Russians" in postwar Japan and that the projected American commander in postwar Japan must maintain complete control there.[24]

American planners considered the roles of other Allied governments in postwar Japan only when they came to the issue of burden sharing. State Department planners expected that postwar control of Japan would involve "long, difficult and costly processes, which the American people might support only grudgingly and impatiently." Therefore, American occupation policy toward Japan should at once prevent any other government's attempt to control postwar developments in Japan and limit the use of American forces to the minimum. The Joint Chiefs of Staff proposed to achieve this dual goal by effectively using U.S. air and naval forces in areas near Japan as substitutes for America's "preponderance of occupation forces" in Japan. In addition, the State Department still believed that America must avoid being blamed for all of Japan's ills and woes in the postwar years.[25] Therefore, planners in the State Department expected China, along with other powers, to participate in the Allied occupation of Japan.

It is not clear when or whether officials in the State Department ever learned of President Roosevelt's proposition to Chiang Kai-shek at Cairo about China's "leading role" in the Allied occupation of Japan. The role

---

[23] Memorandum, "Far East: (2) Inter-Allied Consultation Regarding Japan," n.d., *HHP*, box 169–171; Diane S. Clemens, *Yalta* (New York: Oxford University Press, 1970), 244–255.

[24] "Hopkins–Stalin Conference Record, Moscow, May 1945: Memorandum of 3rd Conversation at the Kremlin, 6 pm May 28," *HHP*, box 338; "Paraphrase of Navy Cable May 30, 1945: Top Secret and Personal from Hopkins for the Eyes of the President Only," ibid.; Harry S. Truman, *Memoirs by Harry S. Truman* (New York: Doubleday, 1955), 1: 412.

[25] "Far East: (2) Inter-Allied Consultation Regarding Japan," n.d., *HHP*, boxes 169–171; JCS 1398/2, "Size of U.S. Occupation Forces for Japan," 6 July 1945, *RJCS*, reel 4; SWNCC 70/3/D: memorandum from the State Department and the Joint Chiefs of Staff, 17 July 1945, *SWNCCF*, reel 9.

they were willing to assign to China in the occupation, however, was limited to the function of diversifying the racial components of the occupation forces so that the operation would not be construed as a white race's conquest of a yellow people. Despite Chongqing's hesitation about its role in the occupation, it is remarkable that American planners never doubted that the Chinese were eager to participate in the postwar control of Japan. Early in September 1944, when the Stilwell affair really became ugly, the Joint Chiefs of Staff informed General Stilwell that the Joint Chiefs and the State Department had agreed on a policy of joint administration by the Allies in postwar Japan. The Joint Chiefs instructed Stilwell to inform the Chinese government that China would be invited to participate in that operation.[26] It is not clear whether General Stilwell acted accordingly. The Joint Chiefs' directive certainly did not come at a good time.

Lack of communication between Washington and Chongqing on the occupation question did not prevent American planners from working out certain technical details unilaterally. When the war ended suddenly in mid-August 1945, the Joint War Plans Committee of the Joint Chiefs of Staff prepared a map to illustrate the American view of the Allied powers' respective military responsibilities at the end of the war. On the map the Asian–Pacific region was divided into four massive regions. A "British Empire Area" included India, Burma, Thailand, the southern half of Indochina, and territories in the Pacific south of the Philippines. Intentionally or inadvertently, American planners also included Tibet in the British area, though the region of Tibet was not marked in the map. A "China Area" included northern Indochina, Hong Kong, and China, with prominent exclusions. All of Manchuria would go to a "U.S.S.R. Area," along with the northern half of Korea roughly above the 40th north latitude; Taiwan was assigned to a "United States Area"; and Outer Mongolia and Xinjiang were to be decided. The "United States Area" virtually stretched from the Chinese to the American coasts of the Pacific Ocean in the western and eastern directions and verged on the Kamchatka Peninsula of the Soviet Far East in the north and the Dutch Indies in the south. Japan's home islands would, of course, be under America's total control. The U.S. forces and the Soviet Red Army would make no contact on the Asian continent except in Korea and possibly at the southern end of Manchuria. Notably, the map was not intended to predict what the actual military situation in Asia might be at the end of the war but rather was designed to propose how "areas of responsibility for execution of initial post-surrender tasks" should be arranged.[27]

[26] SWNCC 70/2: report by the Subcommittee for the Far East, 23 June 1945, *SWNCCF*, reel 9.
[27] JWPC 264/9, "Further Action as to Immediate Occupation of Japan and Japanese-Held Areas," 13 August 1945, *RJCS*, reel 5.

In this general context, the occupation of Japan would be carried out in three phases. U.S. officials expected that the first phase would last for about three months and would accomplish the primary disarmament of Japan. In this period, troops other than American might not be able to reach Japan; therefore, U.S. forces had to act unilaterally. During the second stage (about nine months), a portion of the American occupational forces would be replaced by troops of the other three leading Allies. In the third period (length undecided), the American forces would be reduced further. Despite its enormous manpower, which had often been mentioned by American leaders during the war, China was not expected to assume a larger share of the occupational duties than Britain and the Soviet Union. Such an allocation of occupation duties among the Big Four was a far cry from President Roosevelt's idea that China should be America's principal partner in postwar policing of Japan.[28]

In sum, by the end of the war, Washington's occupation policy regarding Japan consisted of four key points. First, because of its commitment to inter-Allied cooperation, the U.S. government would act in concert with the other leading Allies in all matters relating to the surrender and disarmament of Japan. Second, the other three Allies should be reminded of their obligation to participate in the military occupation of Japan and share the burdens of the operation. Third, the United States must exercise the "controlling voice" among the occupation forces in Japan. And, finally, Oriental elements should be present in the occupation forces and the Allied administrative body in Japan. On the eve of Japan's surrender, the SWNCC recommended the policy to President Truman for approval.[29]

Assigning only symbolic and menial functions to the other Allies in postwar Japan, American policy planners treated the postwar reform of Japan as the exclusive domain of the U.S. government. Since the Cairo Communiqué explicitly applied the principle of unconditional surrender to Japan, American planners obtained free rein in reshaping Japan according to their vision. Yet the Cairo Conference did nothing to clarify the meaning of that principle. At the beginning of 1944, the American government was prodded by the Russians for a meeting to define it. President Roosevelt demurred. In his own usage, the principle was good enough to carry two

---

[28] JWPC 385/1, "Ultimate Occupation of Japan and Japanese Territories," 16 August 1945, *RJCS*, reel 4; JWPC 385/5, 22 September 1945, ibid. In phase 1, the United States was expected to send 710,000 troops into Japan, including nineteen divisions and twenty-two air groups. In phase 2, the occupation forces would include 315,000 U.S., 175,000 Soviet, 135,000 British, and 60,000 Chinese troops. In phase 3, they would include 145,000 U.S., 100,000 Soviet, 65,000 British, and 60,000 Chinese troops. These figures would have to be modified in late September. The British were unwilling to supply more than one division, and the Russians also seemed reluctant to join the occupation under a non-Russian commander. The Chinese government was absorbed in its task of reoccupying the liberated territories in China, but for a while, it still agreed to send three divisions to Japan.

[29] SWNCC 21/3: memorandum for President Truman, 13 August 1945, *SWNCCF*, reel 3.

messages: (1) none of the Allied powers would make a separate peace with
the enemies, and (2) peoples of the vanquished Axis powers would have
to have confidence in the fairness of the Allies.[30] Planners in the State
Department felt that they had to go further by separating the unconditional surrender principle from conditions for peace. The principle should
be construed solely in military terms and viewed as a means to achieve the
total defeat of Japan. Such an interpretation would enable the Allies at
present to concentrate their attention on the military task and to consider
peace terms after the war ended. The State Department therefore chose to
construe the principle as meaning that the surrender instrument for Japan
should be in no sense contractual. The Japanese government should unilaterally declare its unconditional surrender, and after that, it should cease
functioning.[31]

American planners' insistence on complete submission by Japan did not
necessarily mean that they were preparing a severe peace for Japan. In the
last two years of the war, moderates in the State Department continued to
set the tone for U.S. planning for Japan. Therefore, the projected military
government in Japan was intended to take such action as was necessary to
safeguard the security of the occupation forces, but not to take measures
of a punitive nature needlessly humiliating to the Japanese people. On the
other hand, the military government would certainly be responsible for
enforcing necessary reforms in Japan.[32]

Interestingly, despite their confidence in America's formidable strength
and its new leading position in Pacific affairs, planners in the State Department did not seem certain that the United States would be able to change
Japan in the long run. Years after the Japanese surrender, Joseph Ballantine
recalled that during the war, he and some other officials in the State
Department had been confident about using examples, tutelage, and suggestions to educate the Japanese about the flaws in their traditional social
and political systems. These would be designed to induce the Japanese
to choose democratic reforms.[33] In the war years, however, such confidence was not always present in State Department officials' discussions

---

[30] Roosevelt to Hull, 17 January 1944, and Hull to Roosevelt, 14 January 1944, *RPSF*, box
74.
[31] CAC-267 Preliminary, 1 August 1944, *RHN*, box 114; PWC-284a, 13 November 1944,
SHP, box 125; Dooman to Dunn, 16 January 1945, *FRUS, 1945*, 6: 517.
[32] Memoranda by the Inter-Divisional Area Committee on the Far East, 22 March and 4
May 1944, *FRUS, 1944*, 5: 1213–1214, 1235–1238; PWC 116, 4 March to 9 May 1944,
OJ, 2-A-5 to 2-A-11; CAC-108, 9 March 1944, ibid., 2-A-31; PWC-113, 15 March 1944,
ibid., 2-A-32; PWC-115, 15 March 1944, ibid., 2-A-37; PWC-114m 21 March 1944,
ibid., 2-A-41; PWC-152, 1 May 1944, ibid., 2-A-51; PWC-296b, 19 May 1945, ibid., 2-
A-66; PWC-287a, 6 November 1944, ibid., 2-A-68; PWC-289a, 15 July 1944, ibid., 2-A-
72; PWC-290a, 15 August 1944, ibid., 2-A-75.
[33] "Ballantine Reminiscences," 15, Joseph W. Ballantine Papers, box 3.

of postwar policies toward Japan. For instance, after the Cairo Conference, at one such meeting, Harley Notter noted how different the current discussion was from that of 1918, when President Wilson had assumed that democracy could prevail throughout the world. He remarked: "But now the members [of the meeting] did not believe something could be done to influence Japanese politics."[34]

Such a pessimistic view of a democratic future for Japan permeated the minds of Japanese specialists in the State Department, who tended to emphasize the peculiarity of Japanese institutions. These officials adhered to an elitist approach to the Japanese question and were not tempted to follow President Wilson's example of making a direct appeal to the people, as he had done in Germany at the end of World War I. The issue of the Japanese imperial house remained a prime example in this regard. In these officials' opinion, for the purpose of concluding the war, the Japanese emperor still held a sacred position in the minds of all Japanese, and he was the only person in Japan who could stop the fanatical militarists and arrange to accept a surrender. For the sake of the Allied military government in postwar Japan, the name of the Japanese emperor could also be invoked to achieve cooperation from Japanese civil officials and pacify the Japanese population. If the long-term objective of transforming the Japanese national character was ever to be attained, the process of democratization should not start "from the ashes of the old system." Reshaping of the Japanese political system would have to come under the leadership of an elite group in Japan, but not through an immature popular revolution, which would probably happen if the emperor were removed.[35]

The so-called Japan hands in the State Department shied away from the conception of "revolution" that was often invoked by Chinese officials' statements regarding Japan. Yet, strangely enough, although they believed that "the Chinese attitude would not be a determining factor in the position of the United States on the question of the emperor," these American officials chose to interpret Chongqing's attitude toward the issue as in concert with theirs. Nor did opponents of the experts' judgment in the State Department invoke any Chinese insights. Breckinridge Long, Dean Acheson (both Assistant Secretaries of State), and Hornbeck did not necessarily agree with each other on whether the emperor should be removed by forces from outside Japan, but they felt that the Japan hands' stand on the matter was too conciliatory, bordering on appeasement of Japan.

[34] T-58, 3 December 1943, *OJ*, 1-C-8.
[35] Joseph E. Grew, *Turbulent Era: A Diplomatic Record of Forty Years, 1904–1945* (Boston: Houghton Mifflin, 1952), 2: 1406–1407; PWC-145 and PWC-146, 26 April 1944, *RHN*, box 142; T-58, 3 December 1943, *OJ*, 1-C-8; 22nd meeting of PWC, 21 April 1944, *SHP*, box 123.

They could not imagine the United Nations associating themselves with the notorious imperial institution in Japan for the purpose of creating democracy and peace. Such an association, they feared, would in reality perpetuate that institution and could commit American forces to preventing a much needed revolution in Japan.[36]

These views were supported by an officer from the field. John Emmerson had specialized on Japan by working on Ambassador Grew's staff in prewar Tokyo, and in 1944 he was detailed to General Stilwell in the China–India–Burma theater. Whereas the Japan specialists in Washington based their policy suggestions mainly on their knowledge of Japan gained in the prewar period, Emmerson derived his conclusions from his experience of working with Japanese prisoners of war and Japanese antiwar activists in China. He saw successful cases in China of changing Japanese war prisoners' attitudes through reeducation programs. These convinced Emmerson that although the Japanese emperor might be useful to the Allies in the first days of Japan's surrender, the key to a positive Japanese policy was to "speak directly to the people of Japan." In his dispatches sent to Washington, Emmerson especially recommended "the long experience and the intelligence of the Japanese People's Emancipation League organized by the Chinese Communists."[37]

Emmerson's policy dispatches reached the State Department and, through John Davies, went to Harry Hopkins. To Emmerson's peers in the State Department, his suggestions appeared radical. The White House kept silent in the debate. Hopkins's personal view on postwar Japan diverged from both Emmerson's and the Japan hands' in the State Department. In February 1945, he wrote an article for *The American Magazine* entitled "Tomorrow's Army and Your Boy." The article included this passage: "I have no doubt that powerful forces in Germany and Japan are preparing even now for their next attempt to conquer us. We will try to keep them impotent, but only a perpetual army of occupation would be able to prevent them from rearming eventually." Hopkins's was a pre-cold war effort to prepare the American public for their country's long-term responsibility for international security. His argument regarding "perpetual"

[36] PWC-147, 4 April 1944, *OJ*, 2-C-9; minutes of the 24th and 25th meetings of the Department of State Committee on Postwar Programs, 26 and 27 April 1944, *SHP*, box 122; F. L. Israel, ed., *The War Diary of Breckinridge Long: Selection from the Years 1939–1944* (Lincoln, NE: University of Nebraska Press, 1966), 340; Dean Acheson, *Among Friends: Personal Letters of Dean Acheson* (New York: Dodd, Mead, 1980), 55; Acheson, *Present at the Creation: My Years in the State Department* (New York: W. W. Norton, 1969), 112–113; Hornbeck to Hull, 24 April 1944, *SHP*, box 380.

[37] John K. Emmerson, *The Japanese Thread: A Life in the U.S. Foreign Service* (New York: Holt, Rinehart & Winston, 1978) 26–53, 76–125, 169–176, 180, 190–203; Davies to Hopkins, 5 September 1944, and enclosed memorandum by Emmerson, 18 August 1944, *HHP*, box 334; Davies to Hopkins, 11 October 1944, and enclosed memorandum by Emmerson, 6 October 1944, ibid.

antagonism with Japan lent support neither to the elitist nor to the mass line of reforms in Japan.[38]

The American government's public stance on an unconditional surrender policy and the State Department planners' secret advocacy of retaining the Japanese emperor proved a most unfortunate contradiction in U.S. policy toward Japan at the end of the war. The conclusion of the Pacific war has been subjected to careful scholarly examinations. It is sufficient to say here that after the unconditional surrender policy pushed the war in the Pacific to its bitter end, which included the use of the atomic bomb, the Allies accepted a principal condition that the Japanese government had sought for some time for stopping the fight: the retention of the emperor.[39] Participants in the State Department's policy planning for Japan were not blind to the contradiction. In the postwar years, Hugh Borton admitted that despite the unconditional surrender policy, the State Department had been making preparations for an "indirect occupation" of Japan, meaning an occupation carried out through the Japanese imperial house. Ballantine also believed that by agreeing not to remove the emperor forcefully, the Allies ended the war with Japan through a "contractual agreement," the antithesis of the very conception of unconditional surrender.[40]

In the post-Cairo years, the State Department's planning for an economic policy toward Japan continued to struggle to find a balanced approach that would be adequate for rendering Japan harmless and at the same time not unreasonably severe. A moderate orientation had already been systematically argued before Cairo, but an eclectic economic policy toward Japan was still difficult to formulate in the last two years of the war. Although radical arguments for reducing Japan to an agrarian state continued to be made, the mainstream view was that excessive economic restrictions on Japan would probably be counterproductive. Most department planners involved in the matter believed that the basis of Japan's military aggression was not its industrial structure, but rather an "empire self-sufficiency" system that consisted of Japanese overseas possessions

---

[38] Emmerson, *Japanese Thread*, 176; Davies to Hopkins, 5 September and 11 October 1944, HHP, box 334; an article by Hopkins, "Tomorrow's Army and Your Boys," and the release by *The American Magazine*, "Perpetual Occupation of Axis Countries Proposed by Hopkins," 2 February 1945, RPOF 4117.

[39] Michael Schaller, *The American Occupation of Japan; the Origins of the Cold War in Asia* (New York: Oxford University Press, 1985), 9–18; Grew, *Turbulent Era*, 2: 1421–1440; James F. Byrnes, *Speaking Frankly* (New York: Harper, 1947), 204–210; entries of 2 and 24 July 1945, HSD, 52 (reel 9): 5–10, 38–39. For two detailed discussions of the conclusion of the Pacific war, see Robert J. C. Butow, *Japan's Decision to Surrender* (Stanford, CA: Stanford University Press, 1954), and Leon V. Sigal, *Fighting to a Finish: The Politics of War Termination in the United States and Japan, 1945* (Ithaca, NY: Cornell University Press, 1989).

[40] Borton, *American Presurrender Planning*, 15; "Ballantine Reminiscences," 16, Ballantine Papers, box 3.

enabling Japan to maintain an "autarkic independence in war essentials." This system would dissolve after the implementation of the Cairo territorial regulations. Deprived of its imperial territories and put under imports control, Japan would be blocked in developing offensive military strength. After this security goal was achieved, these officials believed, Japan should be allowed to develop a healthy, balanced economy.[41]

Disagreement between the hard-liners and the moderates focused mainly on what economic policy would be most effective in preventing Japan from again becoming a *military* threat, but the possibility of a Japanese challenge in a purely *economic* sense hardly occurred to American planners. It should be remembered that the economically weak Chinese paid close attention to the issue of reversing the economic imbalance between China and Japan. The American attitude can be illustrated in the following example. In early 1945, at a State Department meeting, a question was raised with regard to the exact meaning of Japan's being prevented from reviving its system of "nationalistic or imperialistic economic self-sufficiency." Should this policy, it was asked, also mean that Japan should be prohibited from developing an automobile industry supported by high tariff barriers? The participants of the meeting agreed that Japan should be allowed to achieve self-sufficiency, particularly in nonmilitary industries.[42]

In the State Department's post-Cairo planning, the importance of China and Japan continued to be viewed separately in both political and economic terms. In the spring of 1945, a State Department document summarized U.S. foreign policy toward postwar East Asia. The document reiterated America's policy of making China a "bulwark of peace in the Far East," suggesting that after it regained territorial integrity, China would have an opportunity to achieve economic and industrial modernization. Yet, the document did not try to predict how long it would take China to achieve this goal. There was not even the slightest hint that in the postwar years China would be able to replace Japan as the economic stabilizer in East Asia. As for Japan, the document was opposed to any reparations claims that might hinder America's long-term objective of reintegrating Japan into the community of nations. According to the document, "it would be unrealistic to assume that the just claims of countries ravaged by Japanese aggression could be taken as a measure of collectible reparation."[43] Faced with the choice between adequate compensation for the victims of Japan's aggressions and salvage of Japan from economic destruction, State Department planners opted for the latter.

[41] CAC-194, 30 April 1944, *RHN*, box 111; CAC-165 Preliminary, 15 April 1944, ibid., box 110.
[42] CAC-165 Preliminary, 15 April 1944, *RHN*, box 110; CAC-194, 30 April 1944, ibid., box 111; IDACFE meeting No. 188, 16 February 1945, *OJ*, 2-B-169.
[43] PR-2 Preliminary, 6 March 1945, *RHN*, box 119.

Territorial readjustment

The Cairo decisions on territorial readjustment in East Asia caused confusion as much as they provided direction. Before Cairo, American planners had sought a time and a geographical criterion for disposing of the Japanese territorial possessions. But the Cairo Communiqué only mentioned 1914 as a date for territorial settlement. Territories like the Kuriles, the Ryukyu Islands, and South Sakhalin, all acquired by Japan before 1894, were left out. This situation did not help the Cairo document win much respect in the State Department. In Hornbeck's opinion, the document must have been drawn up in haste. Therefore, it would be unwise for planners in the State Department to attach much importance to its phraseology.[44]

In the State Department's post-Cairo planning for Taiwan, the Cairo promise of restoring China's sovereignty on the island did not limit the planners' search for a solution that could best serve American interests. Although the State Department supported the Cairo decision on China's sovereignty in Taiwan, more important for its planners were the questions of when and how Taiwan should reunite with China. After Cairo, these questions were at first raised by the Navy and War departments. Certain military planners were antagonized by the Cairo decision. They believed that Taiwan should be treated separately from China as a geographical, strategic, and economic unit. In their opinion, Taiwan's strategic location on the Western Pacific rim was too important to be considered merely as an adjunct to the Asian continent. Its economic and technological developments were also too far ahead of those in the Chinese mainland provinces to be reintegrated smoothly into China. These military planners were so annoyed by the State Department's subscription to the Cairo decision that they named State Department officials "China firsters."[45]

That was a misnomer. In mid-1944, the State Department and the Joint Chiefs of Staff agreed on a map depicting important strategic bases in the Pacific, a matter approved by President Roosevelt. The map classified bases into two color groups – blue bases under America's direct control and black bases under international control. On the map, the Bonins, the Izu Islands, and the Japanese Mandated Islands were colored blue. Those colored black included the Kuriles, the Ryukyu Islands, Taiwan, some former Dutch

---

[44] T-58, 3 December 1943, *OJ*, 1-C-8.
[45] Memorandum of conversation between Commander Tuck and Commander Shears of the Office of the Chief of Naval Operations and State Department officials, 20 December 1943, U.S. State Department, Central Files: China: 740.00119 Pacific War/34; PWC-199, 27 March 1944, and PWC-200, 2 June 1944, *RHN*, box 143; JPS, "Seizure and Occupation of Formosa," 8 September 1944, *RJCS*, reel 11; George H. Kerr, *Formosa Betrayed* (Boston: Houghton Mifflin, 1965), 19–22.

islands, the Japanese home islands, Korea, and certain locations along the east coast of China.[46] The classification of these projected base sites would change, and the meaning of "international control" was yet to be defined. It was nevertheless significant that American military and civilian planners agreed on the notion that an "extensive overseas basing system was a legitimate and necessary instrument of U.S. power, morally justified and a rightful symbol of the U.S. role in the world." They had no disagreement on Taiwan's inclusion in the basing system. But planners in the State Department believed that the goal could be achieved without compromising America's general political relations with the Chinese government. In other words, after Cairo they continued to be confident that strategic bases in Taiwan could be obtained by the United States after the island went to China.[47]

Had officials in Chongqing known the content of the State Department's CAA planning for Taiwan, they would have regarded the "Chinese firster" accusation as a bad joke. In 1944, a controversy between General Douglas MacArthur and Admiral Ernest King was unfolding over the strategic priorities between the Philippines and Taiwan. The State Department's pre-Cairo assumption that U.S. forces would conquer Taiwan had to be tested against the result of that debate.[48] Yet a conviction persisted in the State Department that whether or not U.S. forces conquered Taiwan before the Japanese surrender, the United States must assume responsibility for the interim military government on the island pending its restoration to China. American officials had always doubted the KMT regime's ability to liberate Taiwan by itself; now they also began to believe that at the end of the war, the Chinese government would continue to be impotent and therefore unable to establish effective control over that island.[49]

According to the Cairo decision, American planners nonetheless felt obliged to consider the Chinese government as a principal partner of the projected U.S. military authority in Taiwan. But Chinese participation must be conditioned in such a way that would facilitate, not restrict, the U.S. occupation authority. In the department's CAA plans for Taiwan, an "advisory part" was carefully reserved for China. To show the Chinese government that its sovereignty would be respected, the American government would not discuss policy issues regarding Taiwan with any Chinese

---

[46] Meeting No. 93 of IDACFE, 30 June 1944, *OJ*, 2-B-74; meeting No. 170 of IDACFE, 30 November 1944, ibid., 2-B-151.

[47] CAC-152, 20 April 1944, *RHN*, box 110; James R. Blaker, *United States Overseas Basing: An Anatomy of the Dilemma* (New York: Praeger, 1990), 28.

[48] Ronald H. Spector, *Eagle Against the Sun: The American War with Japan* (New York: Vintage, 1985), 418–420; Grace P. Hayes, *The History of the Joint Chiefs of Staff in World War II: The War against Japan* (Annapolis, MD: Naval Institute Press, 1982), 603–624.

[49] CAC-171, 20 April 1944, and PWC-197, 8 May 1944, *RHN*, box 110.

or Taiwanese groups that did not have Chongqing's approval. Other devices were proposed for appeasing Chongqing's sensitivity, such as giving consideration to Chinese plans, seeking advice from the Chinese government, and using Chinese personnel by the American military authority in Taiwan.

On the other hand, limits were set for this U.S.–Chinese partnership. For instance, no Chinese military mission should be invited to join American forces during or after the invasion of Taiwan lest such an invitation be misinterpreted by Chongqing as an American policy for a joint Sino–American military government on the island. In matters concerning personnel, the American military authority should exercise the right to use the Taiwanese without Chongqing's prior consent and also have complete control over mainlanders' entry into Taiwan. American planners wanted to prevent "overstaffing at high levels" of the civil administration in Taiwan by persons recommended by the Chinese government. Certainly the U.S. occupation authority in Taiwan should not work through a Chinese "subgovernment." Most important, the State Department suggested that during the entire transitional period, the policy of the American military government should be oriented to meet Taiwanese interests as distinct from Chinese interests. Only in some long-term administrative matters, such as the educational system, the military government could consider measures in accord with Chinese policies, provided that "those policies are in accord with American ideals and with international law." Among those so-called short-term matters, where "Taiwanese interests" should surpass Chinese interests, were the legal system, land tenure, and the monetary system. Planners in the State Department had the same concern as Chinese planners about postwar stability in Taiwan. Interestingly, both believed that these existing institutions in Taiwan would be able to function better for that purpose than corresponding Chinese systems on the mainland.[50]

As mentioned earlier in this study, it had been a foregone conclusion in the State Department even before the Cairo Conference that the Chinese government would have to receive Taiwan from an American occupation authority. After Cairo, American planners continued to consider the timing and conditions for eventually transferring the island back to China. In May 1944, a principle was adopted that the transfer should be done en bloc. In other words, the Chinese government would not be given any governmental function to perform in Taiwan until the moment it took over all functions at the same time. In the State Department's view, the "timing might depend on whether large-scale civil disturbances would occur in China before the final transfer of sovereignty from Japan to China."[51]

[50] PWC-184a, 28 June 1944, *RHN*, box 124; CAC-292 Preliminary, 7 September 1944, and PWC-300, 27 September 1944, ibid., box 114; PWC-195, 15 May 1944, PWC-186, 8 May 1944, PWC-193, 5 May 1944, and CAC-166, 7 April 1944, ibid., box 110.
[51] PWC-195, 15 May 1944, *RHN*, box 110.

Like planners in the military branches, State Department officials did not want the strategically important Taiwan to become politically volatile, and they were preparing the American government to postpone the implementation of the Cairo decision in the event of a Chinese civil war.

Planners in the State Department were also resourceful enough to conceive a legal basis for a prolonged American occupation of Taiwan. At first, they considered a plan by which the sovereignty of Taiwan would remain with Japan until it was transferred to China by "legal means." That would allow American forces to occupy the island as a former enemy territory. Further deliberations concluded that temporary retention of Japan's sovereignty would not be necessary. It was suggested that on occupation of Taiwan, the United Nations might "take title to the area through a declaration of annexation." The formula eventually adopted by the State Department was ambiguous: "[Our] military administration of civil affairs in Formosa will continue until such time as Chinese sovereignty in Formosa is restored."[52]

Due to the Navy and the War departments' objections on security grounds, the State Department never informed the Chinese government of American CAA plans for Taiwan. The Chinese government was aware that a large-scale preparation for Taiwan was in progress in the United States. Taiwanese partisans in Chongqing also urged the KMT regime to reach an understanding with Washington before it was too late. But the KMT leadership seemed satisfied with the prospect of receiving the island from American forces, thus sparing itself the trouble of military conquest and initial military occupation. There is no evidence that after Cairo the Chinese government was ever worried about any American scheme for Taiwan.[53] Early in 1945, Tao Xisheng, one of Chiang Kai-shek's personal secretaries and the ghost writer of Chiang's *China's Destiny*, told an American foreign service officer that at the end of the war, the Chinese government might have neither the popular support in Taiwan necessary for a smooth civil administration nor a navy powerful enough to protect the island. Therefore, an interim American protectorate over Taiwan would be welcomed by the Chinese government. To reinforce his point, Tao revealed that Chiang himself had not wanted Taiwan to be considered part of China in the map attached to his *China's Destiny*.[54] Without other evidence, it is difficult to evaluate the significance of Tao's overture. It could either be a trial balloon from Chiang to test the American intention or an unauthorized endeavor by Tao himself.

Ironically, events in Taiwan at the end of the war defied planning so far

[52] Minutes of the 50th meeting of the Postwar Program Committee, 13 June 1944, and PWC-254, 28 June 1944, *SHP*, box 122.

[53] Minutes of the 50th meeting of the Postwar Program Committee, 13 June 1944, *SHP*, box 122; Kerr, *Formosa Betrayed*, 12–15.

[54] Memorandum by John S. Service, 19 February 1945, *RDCA*, box 9.

as the State Department's work was concerned. Although the State Department's wartime plan for Taiwan at best envisioned only a limited partnership with China, at the end of the war it was the impotent KMT regime, not U.S. forces, that took full control of the island. In October 1944, America's military strategy in the Pacific was decided in favor of the Philippine priority. This meant that Taiwan would be bypassed by American forces. Consequently, America's CAA planning for Taiwan began to disintegrate slowly. In 1945, the Allied military and diplomatic efforts focused on areas close to Japan's power bases in the northwestern Pacific and Northeast Asia. Taiwan was not even on the agendas of the Yalta and Potsdam conferences.[55] For the moment, American planners did not know what to do with Taiwan. In March 1945, the staff of the SWNCC listed CAA for Taiwan as one of the issues to be decided. After the Japanese surrender, the SWNCC finally came to the conclusion that "due to recent developments," CAA for Taiwan should be removed from its agenda.[56] Allegedly, in early 1945 President Roosevelt decided that Taiwan should be returned to China immediately after Japan's surrender. But he did not communicate the idea to the State Department, and therefore no changes in the State Department's plan for Taiwan were made accordingly.[57] The demise of the State Department's plan for Taiwan was purely a result of America's military strategy in the Pacific in the last stage of the war. The true beneficiary of this development was the KMT regime. From 1945 to 1949 the KMT regime consolidated its control of the island, and after losing the mainland to the Chinese Communists in the Chinese Civil War, Chiang Kai-shek did not encounter an American military authority in Taiwan that might have denied him a haven.

Compared with the case of Taiwan, the State Department's planning for the Ryukyu Islands was more consequential. Although listed as a black base area in America's strategic planning, the Ryukyus were not regarded as strategically important by American military planners.[58] Therefore the State Department contemplated the status of these islands almost entirely in a political context. In June 1945, after American troops successfully invaded Okinawa, the largest island of the Ryukyu archipelago, the future of these islands was placed at the disposal of the U.S. government. After the Cairo Conference, the State Department's attitude was that unless

---

[55] Kerr, *Formosa Betrayed*, 31; "Briefing Book Paper No. 606: Soviet Support of the Cairo Declaration," n.d., *FRUS: Berlin*, 1: 927.
[56] SWNCC 68: report by the Subcommittee for the Far East, 19 March 1945, *SWNCCF* reel 9; SWNCC 68/1: note by the secretaries of SWNCC, 28 September 1945, ibid.; SWNCC 69/2: note by secretaries of SWNCC, 25 August 1945, ibid.
[57] Joseph W. Ballantine, *Formosa: A Problem for United States Foreign Policy* (Washington, DC: Brookings Institution, 1952), 56–57.
[58] Memorandum of conversation among Admiral Train, Captain Ruble, Blakeslee and Borton, 18 October 1944, *OJ*, 2-B-151.

Chongqing forcefully pressed its claim over the Ryukyus or the residents
of these islands themselves favored a return to China, the Ryukyus should
remain under Japanese sovereignty. In the opinion of the State Department, if turned over to China, the Ryukyu Islands would likely become a
liability to the Chinese government. For one thing, the already staggering
Chinese economy could not afford a navy strong enough to protect these
islands. For another, to a great extent, the local population had been
culturally "Japanized." They would constitute a potential ethnic problem
for the Chinese government. Planners in the State Department adopted this
seemingly pro-Japanese stand with an understanding that Japan, being
deprived of Taiwan and the Mandated Islands, would not be able to turn
the Ryukyus alone into a strategic stronghold threatening peace in the
Pacific.[59]

In the evolution of the U.S. policy toward Korea, the Cairo Conference
concluded a period of exploring principles but did not initiate another for
formulating operational policies. Early in April 1944, London unexpect-
edly urged Washington to translate the Cairo decision on Korea into tangible terms. The British Embassy in Washington sent a questionnaire on
Korea to the State Department, trying to hammer out an Anglo–American
interpretation of the Cairo Declaration on Korea. But the Americans suggested that the Chinese ought to be included as well in any further discussion of Korea. This led to the Yang Yunzhu mission to Washington, as
discussed in the previous chapter.[60]

The invitation extended to Chongqing was more a symbolic manifesta-
tion of Washington's policy of treating China as an ally and a tactic to
tackle the British than a serious call for Chinese opinion on Korea. Actually, the State Department believed that because of the Cairo Conference,
Chongqing would be more manageable than before on the Korean question. In June 1944, when Vice-President Henry A. Wallace was on his way
to China, the State Department expected that the Korean question might
be stirred up by his visit in Chongqing. But its directive to Ambassador
Gauss confidently stated: "In the circumstances of the Cairo Declaration
it would seem that the Chinese would hardly be likely to act in the matter
of Korean recognition without prior consultation with the parties to that
instrument." In February 1945, Shao Yulin, an official of the Waijiaobu
and personal adviser to Chiang Kai-shek, told Ballantine in Washington
that his government had no official relation with any Korean group and
was in complete agreement with the American government on withholding
recognition from the KPG at present. This information further confirmed

[59] CAC-307 Preliminary, 7 October 1944, *OJ*, 2-A-96; meeting No. 149 of IDACFE, 10
October 1944, ibid., 2-B-130; ISO-253, 2 April 1945, *RHN*, box 167.
[60] P. H. Gore-Booth to Harley A. Notter, 4 April 1944, G. B. Sansom to J. W. Ballantine,
16 and 28 June 1944, and memorandum of conversation between George Sansom and
Ballantine, 17 July 1944, *RHN*, box 19.

the State Department's judgment.[61] At about the same time, Yang Yunzhu's mission to Washington revealed the posture adopted by the Chinese diplomats on Korea: unless asked by Washington, the Chinese government would keep its thoughts to itself. After the encounter with President Roosevelt at Cairo, Chiang, worried about being construed as ambitious and expansionist, chose a policy of silent dissent in dealing with Washington. But this only resulted in American officials' believing that the Chinese government now acquiesced in the U.S. formula.

During the last two years of the war, the State Department's planning for Korea did result in itemizing the trusteeship formula to a certain degree. Two postwar periods were contemplated. One was the period of military government in Korea right after the Japanese surrender. It was to be followed by another, the trusteeship period preceding Korea's complete independence. Chinese participation in both was expected. Despite the unmistakable military weakness of Chongqing, the State Department planning staff still assumed that at the end of the war the Chinese government would be able to dispatch troops to China's neighboring areas, including Korea and Indochina. Therefore, China, along with Britain, was expected to participate in the reconquest of Korea and in the ensuing Allied military government in that country.[62]

The U.S. government's open pledge for Korean independence at Cairo stimulated the State Department's effort to match the means of policy with American objectives in Korea. A new element in the post-Cairo planning for Korea was a positive consideration of America's military role in reconquering that peninsula. To guarantee the implementation of U.S. policy in Korea, the State Department planning staff argued in early 1944, American troops would have to constitute a substantial portion of the liberation forces in Korea, and the other powers' representation in the projected occupation authority should not "be so large as to prejudice the effectiveness of American participation in CAA." Yet such a projection was not supported by the U.S. military strategy for the Pacific. In 1944, the issue of Soviet entry into the Pacific war was under consideration in Washington. American strategists expected the Red Army to operate in Manchuria and North China, assisting America's main effort to defeat Japan in the Pacific. But Korea was either overlooked or left to uncertainty.[63] The evolution of the State Department's planning was nevertheless significant. Before Cairo, China and the Soviet Union had been regarded as

---

[61] Hull to Gauss, 12 June 1944, *FRUS, 1944*, 5: 1295; memorandum of conversation between Shao Yulin and Ballantine, 5 February 1945, *FRUS, 1945*, 6: 1018–1020; Dunn to Hurley, 20 February 1945, ibid., 1022–1023.

[62] CAC-128, 29 March 1944, *RHN*, box 109.

[63] CAC-66a, 5 February 1944, ibid.; United States Department of Defense, *The Entry of the Soviet Union into the War Against Japan: Military Plans, 1941–1945* (Washington, DC: G.P.O., 1955), 28–45 (hereafter cited as *Entry of the Soviet Union*).

two powers that, more than any other Allied government, would have great interests and influence in postwar Korea. U.S. policy toward Korea had then aimed at preventing rivalry between the two in Korea. After Cairo, although the policy objective remained the same, the State Department came to believe that U.S. foreign policy in Korea would be valid only if the United States itself became the leading influence in that country.

With regard to the trusteeship period following the initial stage of the occupation, the planning staff of the State Department did not make substantial progress. Despite the omission of the trusteeship formula in the Cairo Declaration, the State Department interpreted that document as an endorsement of its standing preference for an interim international regime in Korea prior to its full independence. Never taking seriously Chongqing's passivity toward the trusteeship solution, American policymakers turned their attention to convincing the Russians of the advantage of their Korea policy. This was achieved at Yalta by an oral understanding between Roosevelt and Stalin. They agreed that the United States, China, the Soviet Union, and probably Great Britain should be included in the international supervision of Korea before its independence. They also made a special point that in this period no foreign troops should be stationed in Korea. The two disagreed only on the length of the trusteeship. Roosevelt suggested a period of twenty to thirty years, but Stalin preferred a briefer one. Although again the State Department was not consulted, the president once more achieved the goal that the political strategists in the State Department had been pursuing: Soviet consent to an international trusteeship in Korea. Yet the president also disappointed the State Department on one vital issue. Taking into account the prospect of Soviet entry into the war against Japan, planners in the State Department believed that it was important for the American and Soviet leaders to discuss carefully "the question of which countries should participate in the military occupation of Korea." In agreeing on the nonmilitary nature of the international trusteeship, Roosevelt and Stalin somehow completely evaded the issue of the occupation period that would precede and affect the implementation of the trusteeship formula in Korea.[64]

The discrepancy between political objectives and military means would prove a vital weakness in Washington's postwar policy regarding Korea. Although officials in the State Department recognized that the U.S. military presence in Korea would be a sine qua non for the success of the American policy, American military planning in the Pacific followed its own logic. Early in 1945, when American strategists did begin to consider

---

[64] PWC-124a, 4 May 1944, *RHN*, box 109; "Briefing Book Paper: Inter-Allied Consultation regarding Korea," n.d., *FRUS: The Conferences at Malta and Yalta, 1945*, 358–361 (hereafter cited as *FRUS: Malta and Yalta*); Bohlen minutes of Roosevelt–Stalin meeting, 8 February 1945, ibid., 770.

the importance of Korea for future military operations, they saw it as one of the strategic links forging a "Japanese citadel." In April 1945, the U.S. Joint Chiefs of Staff believed that by controlling this "citadel" first, a campaign of bombardment and blockade against Japan could be conducted to pave the way for the final invasion. The disadvantage was that such a campaign in peripheral areas might prove time-consuming and costly, and therefore might delay the invasion of Japan proper. After Okinawa was conquered with heavy American casualties, U.S. strategists believed that an adequate forward base was secured from which the invasion of the Japanese home islands could be launched. Consequently, the need to conquer Korea before the invasion disappeared.[65] In June and early July, the State Department prepared a series of "briefing book papers" for the coming Potsdam Conference. With regard to Korea, these papers only restated the principle of international trusteeship and emphasized that, to be successful, such an arrangement ought to be *preceded* by a joint military effort by the major Allies to liberate Korea. But American military leaders were not prepared to discuss such efforts with the Russians at Potsdam. When questioned by the Russians about the timing of the U.S. military operation against Korea, General George C. Marshall replied that the issue could not be decided until the early results of the American invasion of Japan were stabilized.[66]

When the war continued, the Truman administration maintained the policy calling for an international trusteeship for Korea. The Korean issue in Asia was not perceived as having ominous implications for U.S.–Soviet relations, as did the Polish issue in Europe. Even those in the American government who in 1945 were determined to regard the Soviets as a new potential enemy could not think of an alternative to trusteeship in Korea. In May, Acting Secretary of State Joseph Grew was worried about the danger of a Soviet–Western confrontation after the war. He was especially concerned with the possible consequences of the Soviet entry into the Pacific war. Grew did not believe that the United States should implement the Yalta agreement on the Far East without attaching some new conditions to it. One of these was that Moscow must definitely accept a Big Four trusteeship as the only authority for selecting a temporary Korean government. He did not know that this "new condition" had been agreed on orally by Roosevelt and Stalin at Yalta. Grew's overture for revising the Yalta agreement is nevertheless instructive. It points to the fixed conception of Korea among American policymakers. Also unchanged was Washington's determination to arrest Chongqing's anti-Soviet tendency on the

---

[65] Hayes, *Joint Chiefs of Staff*, 551, 658, 702–703, 713; *Entry of the Soviet Union*, 61–68.
[66] "Briefing Book Paper No. 252: Interim Administration for Korea and Possible Soviet Attitude," n.d., *FRUS: Berlin*, 1: 311–313; "Briefing Book Paper No. 605: Form of Soviet Military Participation," n.d., ibid., 924–926; tripartite military meeting, 24 July 1945, ibid., 2: 351–352.

Korean issue. Observing the Soviet leaders at close range, George Kennan believed that the leaders in Chongqing were paranoid in fearing a Soviet conspiracy about Korea. He did not see any evidence suggesting that Moscow intended to organize a Korean movement within Soviet borders as an instrument of expansion. Instead, Kennan suggested that the KMT leadership pay attention to the Korean group in the Chinese Communist area. In July, a planning committee of the State Department reiterated the department's standing conviction that it would be unwise for the United States to support the Chinese approach for using the KPG as a countervailing political force against the Soviet Union. If there really was a danger of a Soviet-sponsored Korean government, the committee reasoned, the "best antidote" would not be the Chinese-sponsored KPG, but rather cooperation between the other three Allies and Moscow.[67]

What American policymakers did not know at the time was that the Russians had already begun to retreat from the stand they took at Yalta on trusteeship in Korea. During the Sino–Soviet negotiations in Moscow from July to August, which were held as a corollary of the Yalta Agreement, Stalin complained to T. V. Soong that although he and Roosevelt had agreed on trusteeship in Korea as a prelude to independence, the current American leadership was more receptive to the British view, seeing trusteeship as a step toward colonization. He also asserted that no binding decision regarding Korea had been reached at Yalta.[68]

Given the increasingly tense U.S.–Soviet relations in Europe and the dramatic situation in East Asia during the final days of the Pacific war, Washington could no longer hope that harmonious cooperation with the Soviet Union would emerge in postwar Korea. Nevertheless, trusteeship was not abandoned. It only changed from a vehicle for Big Four cooperation into one of the thorny issues in the emerging Soviet–American rivalry. It also became clear to Washington that the policy must be supported with military force. On 10 August, angered by Soviet behavior during the Sino–Soviet negotiations in Moscow, Ambassador Averell Harriman suggested to President Truman that American troops land at Dalian (Dairen) and in Korea if Japan surrendered before the Russians could occupy these areas. "I cannot see," the ambassador remarked, "that we are under any obligation to the Soviets to respect any zone of Soviet military operation." Earlier, the Joint Chiefs of Staff had already considered the Korean port city of Pushan as one of the preferred strategic points in the Far East for America to control on Japan's surrender. Now, with the president's

[67] Grew to Stimson, 12 May 1945, and minutes of the Committee of Three meeting, 15 May 1945, *OJ*, 5-B-7; entry of 15 May 1945, *HSD*, 51 (reel 9): 128; Kennan to the Secretary of State, 17 April 1945, *FRUS*, 1945, 6: 1026–1027; meeting No. 215 of IDACFE, 31 July 1945, *OJ*, 2-B-196; Grew, *Turbulent Era*, 2: 1445.

[68] "Notes taken at Sino–Soviet conferences, Moscow, 1945": minutes of Soong–Stalin meeting, 2 July 1945, *VHP*, box 2.

approval, Joint Chiefs of Staff planners treated Harriman's proposal as a "matter of urgency" and set a timetable for the race to Dalian and Korea. Also on 10 August, the War Department instructed General Wedemeyer in China to provide American assistance to the Chinese government for the purposes of recapturing Chinese territories from Japanese occupation and sending Chinese troops to Korea and Japan. In an ensuing discussion between Wedemeyer and Chiang Kai-shek, the two agreed that Chinese troops' timely control of Pushan would be able to prevent the Russians from establishing themselves or a Korean Communist regime on that peninsula.[69] Chiang Kai-shek must have been delighted by the reorientation of Washington's Korea policy. But the idea of using Chinese troops in Korea to counter the Red Army proved to be wildly optimistic about Chongqing's ability. Soon it became clear that the Allied occupation of Korea had to begin without Chinese and British participation. The two countries' forces would have to be introduced into the southern half of Korea whenever conditions permitted.

Thus, by the end of the war, Washington's Korea policy was no longer based on Big Four cooperation. Under the name of trusteeship, American policymakers sought to organize an ABC entente for the purpose of checking the Russians. It was ironic that during most of the war this goal had been sought by Chongqing but rejected by American leaders. Now the Americans felt it necessary to embark on such a policy but the impotent Chinese were unable to lend any assistance. The State Department's expectation that the Soviets would be the predominant military influence in Korea was realized when the Red Army poured into that peninsula during the second half of August 1945. Under the circumstances, American policymakers improvised a two-zone occupation arrangement for the purpose of containing the Russians in Korea. But the implementation of this scheme would have to rely on Moscow's willingness to confine its own military advance to the area north of the 38th parallel.[70]

When the war ended in Asia and the Pacific in mid-August 1945, the wartime planning by both the American and Chinese governments for Korea proved futile. The American and Chinese policies toward Korea had

---

[69] Harriman to Truman, 10 August 1945, *FRUS, 1945*, 7: 967; Albert C. Wedemeyer, *Wedemeyer Reports!* (New York: Henry Holt, 1958) 344–345; Herbert Feis, *The China Tangle: The American Effort in China from Pearl Harbor to the Marshall Mission* (Princeton, NJ: Princeton University Press, 1953), 337; Wedemeyer to Marshall, 10 July 1945, *RCT*, box 1539; *CSYZ*, 38: 196; Charles F. Romanus and Riley Sunderland, *United States Army in World War II: China–Burma–India Theater: Time Runs Out in CBI* (Washington, DC: G.P.O., 1959), 389–391.

[70] SWNCC 21: JCS 1467/1, 13 August 1945, *SWNCCF*, reel 3; draft memorandum by Dunn to the JCS, n.d., *FRUS, 1945*, 6: 1037–1039; JWPC 264/9, "Further Action as to Immediate Occupation of Japan and Japanese-Held Areas," 13 August 1945, and JWPC 385/1, "Ultimate Occupation of Japan and Japanese Territories," 16 August 1945, *RJCS*, reel 4.

some features in common. Both contained paternalism of their own types, both took the Soviet Union as the potential threat to their objectives in Korea, and both relied heavily on diplomatic maneuvers to commit the other Allied governments to their solutions for the Korean issue. Otherwise, the Americans and the Chinese pursued different objectives. Whereas Chongqing's Korea policy was regional and saw that country as a key to China's postwar security, Washington's was global and treated Korea as a testing ground for President Roosevelt's version of a new world orchestrated harmoniously by the great powers. On the matter of Korea, both Chiang Kai-shek and Franklin D. Roosevelt practiced power politics by following different rules. From a weak position, Chiang resorted to the old approach of Chinese diplomacy of using one barbarian state to check another, hoping American interests could be played against Soviet schemes in Korea. By contrast, Roosevelt tried to cement the leading Allies' cooperation in the postwar years through equitable readjustment of interests among themselves. Trusteeship for Korea was designed for such a purpose. Yet, even before the conclusion of the war, leaders in Chongqing and Washington realized that their policies for Korea were doomed because neither was well prepared to deal with the Soviet military power in Northeast Asia.

10

The Manchurian triangle

Ever since the Chinese–Japanese confrontation escalated into a conflict in the Pacific, Chiang Kai-shek had had feared that the Russians might reap the third party's benefit from the Asian tussle. During the last two years of the war, when the American government worked for Soviet participation in the war against Japan, Chiang saw his fear materializing. Manchuria, where the Japanese militarists had started the Asian crisis, was again destined to occupy the center of Asia's international scene due to its strategic importance for any Soviet military action against Japan. As the Japanese Empire ebbed, rivalry over the future of Manchuria began in earnest within the anti-Axis coalition. Inter-Allied Manchurian diplomacy began right after the Cairo Conference, and its two decisive stages, played out separately in Yalta in February 1945 and in Moscow in July and August of the same year, eventually created a new triangular relationship among Washington, Chongqing, and Moscow. The immediate objective of these diplomatic undertakings was Soviet entry into the war against Japan, but the governments involved also sought to readjust their long-term interests in Manchuria and China.

Chongqing's effort to enlist American support

Chongqing was not well prepared for the new round of competition for Manchuria. The Cairo decision on Manchuria in favor of China's sovereignty did not encourage any substantial progress in Chongqing's post-conference policy preparation for recovering the region. Chinese military authorities never developed a plan for reconquering the area. In the last year of the war, mainly due to General Wedemeyer's efforts, the only counter-offensive strategy developed by the Chinese government was for seizing certain ports along the southeastern coast of China. The purpose was to open more routes for Allied aid to Chiang Kai-shek's government in the

south. Japan's sudden surrender in August, however, did not give even
this plan a chance.[1] In July, foreseeing the inevitable postwar competition between the KMT and the CCP in northeastern China, General Wedemeyer tried in vain to persuade leaders in Washington to supplement the
Yalta arrangement with a Big Four agreement on Chongqing's right to occupy the southern half of Manchuria *after* Japan's capitulation. After Japan
surrendered, without such an international guarantee, Chiang and Wedemeyer had to work frantically to find ways of shipping KMT troops to
North China and Manchuria as quickly as possible.[2]

Chongqing's lack of military planning for reconquering Manchuria may
be explained by its wartime confinement in southwestern China. At the
same time, the fragmentary nature of KMT politics stalled Chongqing's
political planning for the region. In May 1944, the Central Committee of
the KMT adopted a general principle stipulating that after Japanese-
occupied areas were liberated, the former provincial and local governments in these areas should be restored. This regulation ensured that those
Chinese officials who had fled their offices in advance of the Japanese
offensive would resume their prewar positions. But this principle could not
be applied readily to the northeastern provinces. Before Japan seized Manchuria in the early 1930s, the KMT government had asserted its authority
in Manchuria only through Zhang Xueliang, the "Young Marshall." Since
the Sian Incident of 1936, Zhang had remained Chiang's prisoner. Now
Chiang could not possibly consider returning the Young Marshall to his
old power base after the war ended. Also, within the KMT Central Committee, it was believed that the Japanese model of many smaller provinces
was more effective than the old Chinese system. Given the fact that the
authority of Chiang Kai-shek's regime had always been based on a delicate
balance of power among the provinces and between the central and local
governments, the future government structure in Manchuria became an
especially difficult question. Without Zhang Xueliang, the territory constituted a power vacuum in KMT politics that caused tense competition among
various contenders. Although in the spring of 1944 an "Investigation
Committee on the Northeast Provinces" was established in Chongqing, the
KMT regime's indecision about the administrative structure for Manchuria
continued into the postwar years.[3]

---

[1] "Fangong jihua" (Plans for Counteroffensive), n.d., ZZSC, 2(3): 597–602.
[2] Wedemeyer to Marshall, 10 July 1945, RCT, box 1539; minutes of [American–Chinese]
Combined Staff Meetings, no. 107, 13 August 1945, minutes no. 110, 18 August 1945, and
minutes no. 111, 20 August 1945, ibid., box 1550.
[3] GW, 80: 19–20, 363–369; "Juwu huiyi beiwanglu" (Memoranda on the Meetings of the
[Central Planning] Board), 27 March 1944, HSP, box 1; "Haisang ji," 5: 6, ibid., box 2;
Information Series No. 124A, 6 May 1944, RDCA, box 7; Wu Huanchang, "Kangzhan
shengli hou jieshou Dongbei de huiyi" (Reminiscences on the Takeover of the Northeast
After the Victory of the War of Resistance), ZW, 24 (1974): 2: 33–39; Tian Yushi, "Dongbei

To the KMT regime, the international aspect of the Manchurian question was more frightening than its internal complications. Officials in Chongqing feared that after engaging the Japanese forces in Manchuria, the Soviet Red Army might make contact with the CCP or, even worse, establish a ring of satellite states in Northeast Asia consisting of Manchuria, Mongolia, Korea, and Japan.[4] At Cairo, Chiang Kai-shek had failed to maneuver President Roosevelt into accepting an arrangement between China and the Western Allies for preventing any country from entering the Pacific war in its final stage to reap a victor's benefit. In the last two years of the war, with greater anxiety than before, KMT leaders watched Washington's policy moving in the direction opposite to their wishes. Across the Pacific, in attempting to enlist the Soviets in the Asian conflict, American leaders tended to think that Chongqing was paranoid with regard to Soviet intentions in the Far East. They were also becoming less and less patient with the poor performance of the KMT regime in the war. In October 1944, Harry Hopkins complained to Ambassador Koo that President Roosevelt was the only leader among the heads of the Big Three who promoted China's great-power status, but the Chinese government had let him down. A month later, the president himself told H. H. Kung that in the past he had had great hopes that China's enormous manpower could make a decisive contribution to the defeat of Japan, but that now he was troubled by China's demonstrated inadequacies as a military partner in the war. Chiang Kai-shek was shocked by rumblings like these. He believed a "sudden change" had occurred in America's China policy. The reason, he speculated, was that President Roosevelt was now being surrounded by a group of "pro-communists."[5]

Chiang Kai-shek and his associates were not blind to the connection between American leaders' devaluation of Chongqing's military performance and their new eagerness to encourage the Russians to enter the Pacific war. The meaning of this development to China was further clarified in late 1944, when Ambassador Koo talked to Admiral William D. Leahy, President Roosevelt's Chief of Staff. Ambassador Koo reported to Chiang Kai-shek that Washington might have already invited the Russians to join the Pacific war but wanted China to pay a price in Manchuria. Thus, the Manchuria question seemed to become a copy of the Shandong question

jieshou san nian zaihuo zuiyan" (Reminiscences on the Disastrous Three Years of Taking Over the Northeast), ZW, 35 (1979): 6: 23–24; Chang Cheng et al., *Xiandai Dongbei Shi* (Modern History of the Northeast) (Ha'erbin: Heilongjiang Jiaoyu Chubanshe, 1986), 399.
4 Chennault to Roosevelt, 19 April 1944, FRUS, 1944: China, 59; Xu Shuxi to Soong, 24 January 1944, TSP, box 30.
5 Kung to Chiang, 27 June 1944, ZZSC, 3(3): 307–308; "Notes of a Conversation with H.H. [Hopkins]," 10 October 1944, WKP, box 77; Kung to Chiang, 16 November 1944, ZZSC, 3(1): 202–203; CZM, 13: 149.

during World War I. Only this time, Japan was the power to be ousted from China and the Soviet Union would be rewarded.[6]

To avert such a crisis, during that year some Chinese officials contemplated a readjustment of Chongqing's own policy. One option suggested by some in the Waijiaobu was that the Chinese government reorganize its military effort drastically in order to expedite an early victory over Japan. In that case, Russia might be prevented from entering the war or, at the very least, the KMT regime might be able to achieve a better strategic position for restraining the Soviet influence in North China and Manchuria. A political option was voiced by Sun Ke. A proponent of improving Chinese–Soviet relations, Sun nevertheless feared that Soviet participation in the war against Japan would result in a CCP–Soviet military collaboration in Manchuria and North China. In Sun's opinion, that dire situation could be prevented only if Chongqing was willing to reach a settlement with Yan'an quickly.[7] But neither of these alternatives was favored by the top leaders in Chongqing, who were seeking a means of dealing with the imminent prospect of Soviet entry into the war without any drastic change in the government's current military and political orientations.

Despite his abortive effort at Cairo, Chiang Kai-shek persisted in seeking a solution in Washington. During the first half of 1944, Chiang at first used incidents along the border between Outer Mongolia and Xinjiang as evidence of Moscow's sinister intentions toward China, trying to motivate American leaders to take diplomatic action on China's behalf. When this line proved ineffective, Chiang had to reconsider his confrontational posture toward the Russians.[8] When Vice-President Henry A. Wallace visited Chongqing in the summer of 1944, Chiang Kai-shek expressed his readiness to improve relations with the Russians if the American government agreed to sponsor a Sino–Soviet conference. Wallace did not give Chiang any encouragement. He told Chiang that although President Roosevelt was anxious to help solve the KMT–CCP difficulties in China in order to remove any hidden danger of a Chinese–Soviet conflict, the president was unwilling to act as a mediator between Chongqing and Moscow. Although afterward Roosevelt gave Chiang an ambiguous promise to reconsider America's mediating role between Chongqing and Moscow, he still emphasized that a working agreement between the KMT and the CCP ought to precede any Sino–Soviet negotiation. Insisting on the last point, Roosevelt

---

[6] "Notes of a Conversation with Admiral L. [Leahy]," 10 October 1944, *WKP*, box 77; Koo to Chiang, 9 November 1944, ibid., box 57. During World War I, to reward Japan's belligerence against the "Central Powers," the Western Allied powers agreed to support Japan's claim to the German sphere of influence in Shandong of China.

[7] Xu Shuxi to Soong, 24 January 1944, *TSP*, box 30; Gauss to Hull, 4 July 1944, *FRUS, 1944: China*, 113–115.

[8] *CSYZ*, 37: 277; John W. Garver, *Chinese–Soviet Relations, 1937–1945: The Diplomacy of Chinese Nationalism* (New York: Oxford University Press, 1988), 199–204.

agreed with the State Department that a KMT–CCP rapprochement was needed to improve the atmosphere between Chongqing and Moscow and to soften the Russian leaders' attitude toward the KMT regime.[9] At one point, Roosevelt hinted to H. H. Kung and Wellington Koo how negotiations with the Russians should be conducted. The president said that if he were in the position of the Polish Prime Minister, he would swallow his pride and try to reach a settlement with the Russians. The two Chinese officials did not miss the message in these words.[10]

Chongqing also tried other ways to circumvent Washington's reluctance to become involved in the Sino–Soviet entanglement. In December 1944, the Waijiaobu asked the American government for copies of agreements between the United States and European governments regarding administrative affairs in liberated Europe. Although these agreements could serve as models for Chongqing's own similar agreements with any Allied powers that might liberate Chinese territories from Japanese occupation, they would be particularly useful for an agreement with the Soviet government over Manchuria. Before the State Department was able to grant Chongqing its request, however, the War and Navy departments demurred. They argued that since the U.S. government was not prepared to use large-scale forces in China, it had no interest in the matter of Chongqing's civil administrative agreements.[11]

While avoiding entanglement with the Chinese–Soviet difficulties, the American government threw itself into the job of finding a solution for the KMT–CCP rancor. Washington wanted such a solution to pave the way for Chongqing's negotiations with the Russians. Yet, the effort had a faulty start. With regard to Yan'an, Chiang Kai-shek could ignore critics like Sun Ke, but he had to take Roosevelt's counsel seriously. The Stilwell affair helped Chiang to get out of his dilemma. That affair ended with a major personnel change in America's leading officials in China. In November, Patrick J. Hurley took charge of the U.S. Embassy in Chongqing and General Albert C. Wedemeyer replaced Stilwell as Chiang's American chief of staff. These changes in personnel were regarded by Chiang and his officials as reassuring. Hurley's and Wedemeyer's amiable approach toward the KMT regime, however, proved detrimental to the ambassador's mediation effort between Chongqing and Yan'an. Soon T. V. Soong told his American contacts that Chongqing's position in dealing with Yan'an

[9] *The China White Paper, August 1949* (Stanford, CA: Stanford University Press, 1967. Originally issued as *United States Foreign Relations with China: With Special Reference to the Period of 1944–1949* by the U.S. State Department), 549–560 (hereafter cited as *White Paper*); State Department memorandum for the Secretary of State, n.d. (July 1944), *FRUS, 1944: China*, 484–485.

[10] *RWK*, 5(E): 681.

[11] SWNCC 83: Secretary of State to Secretaries of War and Navy, 15 December 1944, and Secretaries of War and Navy to Secretary of State, 17 January 1945, *SWNCCF*, reel 10.

had grown significantly stronger because of the recent change in Washington's China policy. Therefore, there was no further need for the KMT government to reach an early settlement with the CCP.[12]

KMT leaders believed that in Ambassador Hurley they had finally found the right person to present their views to Washington. This development also rekindled their hope of enlisting America's active support for Chongqing's diplomacy with Moscow. At the beginning of 1945, a new optimism was reflected in instructions of the Waijiaobu to its overseas diplomatic missions that within the year they should take the initiative in creating a "general intimate atmosphere" between China and the Soviet Union.[13] On 4 February, Ambassador Hurley reported to the State Department that the Chinese and Soviet governments had agreed on a Chinese mission to Moscow. T. V. Soong would lead the mission in late February or early March. Chiang Kai-shek wanted Washington's full cooperation in this undertaking. For this purpose, he asked Hurley to send a tentative agenda to Washington for Soong's negotiations with the Russians. According to the agenda, Soong should discuss general cooperation between the two governments, Soviet participation in the war against Japan, Sino–Soviet relations in Korea and Manchuria, postwar economic problems, and border disagreements between the two countries.[14]

The State Department remained skeptical. In an instruction to Hurley, Acting Secretary of State Joseph Grew reminded the ambassador that the U.S. government's policy was not to act either as an adviser on China's policy toward Soviet Russia or as a mediator between the two countries. Chongqing should make its own decisions on the agenda, and, the instruction continued, "we ought not take it upon ourselves to place a caveat upon or to sponsor discussion of any particular question." Grew also called Hurley's attention to President Roosevelt's earlier communication with Chiang Kai-shek calling for a KMT–CCP settlement prior to any Sino–Soviet conference.[15]

Nevertheless, when Chongqing was about to make a determined diplomatic move, the State Department was unable to remain indifferent. A commentary on the Chinese agenda was therefore drafted by the State Department's Division of China Affairs. Perhaps for the purpose of correcting

---

[12] Joseph W. Alsop to General Robert B. McClure, 30 December 1944, *RCT*, box 1542; Michael Schaller, *The U.S. Crusade in China, 1938–1945* (New York: Columbia University Press, 1979), 197–198, 217–218; Tang Tsou, *America's Failure in China, 1941–1950* (Chicago: University of Chicago Press, 1963), 182–183, 246–247; O. Edmund Clubb, *China and Russia: The "Great Game"* (New York: Columbia University Press, 1971), 341.

[13] Soong to Koo, 29 December 1944, *WKP*, box 68.

[14] *White Paper*, 92; Grew to Stettinius, 5 February 1945, *FRUS: Malta and Yalta, 1945*, 952–953.

[15] *White Paper*, 93–94.

Hurley's attitude, this opinion was also despatched to the American embassy in Chongqing. Generally speaking, State Department officials did not believe that the time was opportune for a direct Sino–Soviet conference. There was still no KMT–CCP working agreement in China, nor had the KMT's leadership abandoned its antagonism toward the Soviet Union. The Chinese government also had not selected the right items for its agenda. For instance, the Chinese probably would be unable to cope with the delicate issue of Soviet entry into the Pacific war. Certain territorial problems could not be properly addressed in a bilateral conference. Last but not least, the Chinese agenda ignored a vital problem in the Chinese–Soviet relationship: the Soviet attitude toward the KMT–CCP cleavage in China.[16]

The State Department's formula

The State Department's ideal conditions for a Sino–Soviet conference would never emerge. But such a conference failed to take place in the early months of 1945 not because Chongqing was discouraged by the State Department's rebuttal to Hurley's offer to help. Rather, the Sino–Soviet negotiations were delayed by President Roosevelt's conduct of U.S. foreign policy at Yalta, which convinced Stalin that the originally scheduled meeting with T. V. Soong could be postponed to Moscow's advantage. At Yalta, President Roosevelt not only agreed to help Russia gain privileges in Manchuria as part of the price for its entry into the Pacific war, but also volunteered to break the news to the Chinese government when the Soviet Red Army was ready for the war in Asia. Under the circumstances, Stalin might feel that there was no need for him to rush into a dialogue with Soong about the conditions leading to a Sino–Soviet rapprochement, which were already included in the Yalta Agreement on the Far East. Instead, a meeting with the Chinese could be postponed to a later time when the Soviet government was able to summon enough military and diplomatic resources to impose the Yalta Agreement on the Chinese government.[17]

The Yalta secret accord among the Big Three was a landmark of U.S. foreign policy in East Asia. Within the fifteen months between Cairo and Yalta, China's image as a great power had faded away in Washington. At Yalta, President Roosevelt redefined his military and political strategies for East Asia and helped to transform the previously uncertain and evasive Soviets into an imposing cornerstone of a new postwar order in the Asian–Pacific region. But it would be misleading to suggest that the Yalta diplomacy was basically an impromptu act executed by President Roosevelt.

[16] Grew to Hurley, 12 February 1945, *GRCE*, box 1.
[17] Bohlen minutes of Roosevelt–Stalin meeting, 8 February 1945, *FRUS: Malta and Yalta*, 769–770; Harriman memorandum of conversations with Soviet leaders, 10 February 1945, ibid., 894–895; Grew to Stettinius, 9 February 1945, ibid., 961.

The president's contribution granted, the Yalta accord was also a logical result of the year-long search by the American government for an alternative or supplement to the Cairo formula. Any critique of the Yalta diplomacy would be inadequate without looking into the policy planning for Manchuria in the State Department during the preceding months.

In 1944, planners in the State Department held it an "unlikely assumption that American Army forces will occupy Manchuria or have a large share in such occupation." Thus, they contemplated a U.S. military authority in Manchuria only to meet an improbable contingency. They foresaw a KMT–CCP rivalry in Manchuria but firmly believed that American armed forces in the region, if any, must not become involved. They also made the Liaodong Peninsula an exception to the Cairo decision on Manchuria, reasoning that the Guandong Leased Territory had a unique legal status and that the U.S. Navy might want to occupy Dalian (Dairen) and Port Arthur, both located in the Liaodong Peninsula, for a considerable period after the war. It should be recalled that at Cairo, despite his desire for an American military presence in southern Manchuria, Chiang Kai-shek had discussed the status of the Liaodong Peninsula with Roosevelt precisely in order to prevent the view that Liaodong was separate from the rest of Manchuria.[18]

In the State Department's judgment, a Chinese reconquest or a Soviet occupation of Manchuria was more likely to take place than the establishment of a U.S. military authority there. Ideally, the Chinese themselves were the force to drive the Japanese out of Manchuria, and the war could then be won without Russian assistance. Harry Hopkins shared this view and once related it unequivocally to T. V. Soong. But in 1944, only a few officers in the U.S. government, such as Stanley Hornbeck, still believed that this scenario was possible. In the summer, for the first time, the Joint Chiefs of Staff adopted the view that Soviet participation in the Pacific war would mean a Soviet drive into Manchuria and that the American government should formulate its own policy accordingly.[19] Yet, this anticipation did not offer planners in the State Department any clue to Soviet intentions regarding that area. After the Cairo Conference, American planners were actually bewildered by the absence of any Soviet dimension to the Cairo decisions on postwar East Asia. Mainly speculating, they agreed that the Soviet policy in East Asia would be based on security considerations and that the Russians would probably enter the Pacific war for the purpose of

---

[18] CAC-119 Preliminary, 14 March 1944, *RHN*, box 109; PWC-136a, 9 May 1944, *SHP*, box 124.

[19] "Note on Conversation with Mr. Harry Hopkins on September 5, 1943," *TSP*, box 29; Hornbeck to Hull, 15 August 1944, *SHP*, box 380; United States Department of Defense, *The Entry of the Soviet Union into the War Against Japan: Military Plans, 1941–1945* (Washington, DC: G.P.O., 1955), 1–29, 38–44 (hereafter cited as *Entry of the Soviet Union*).

achieving full representation in any postwar settlement for that region. But judgments varied in the State Department on whether the Soviet government would want to control Manchuria directly in order to implement its policy objectives in East Asia.[20]

Such confusion could have been avoided had the White House and the State Department communicated better with each other. One year after the Teheran Conference, where he had only mildly expressed his interest in Manchuria, Stalin was quite frank about his intentions in Northeast Asia. In December 1944, using a map, Stalin disclosed to Ambassador Harriman that at the end of the war the Soviets wanted to recover the Kurile Islands and the southern half of Sakhalin, to lease the southern half of the Liaodong Peninsula and the Chinese Eastern Railroad, and to legalize the independent status of Outer Mongolia. He also made it clear that these demands were political conditions for Soviet entry into the war against Japan. In his ensuing report to President Roosevelt, Harriman pointed out that Stalin's desire for the Soviets to lease southern Liaodong, including Port Arthur and Dalian, was not in concert with the president's own concept at Teheran calling for an international free port in Manchuria. Harriman also seriously doubted that Stalin's pledge to respect China's sovereignty in Manchuria meant anything in practice if the Russians wanted to control the Chinese Eastern Railroad. This information and Harriman's alarming comments could have helped put the State Department's planning for the Yalta Conference on a less speculative course. But Harriman had sent his "personal and top secret" report only to the president through U.S. Navy channels.[21] Consequently, although the State Department was prepared to qualify China's sovereignty in Manchuria in the unlikely event of *American* occupation of that region, it failed to provide any advice to President Roosevelt on the extent to which the *Russians* could be allowed to do the same thing.

Instead, before the Yalta Conference, the State Department's attention focused on Moscow's intentions concerning China's domestic politics. Available evidence in this respect, however, did not suggest to the planning officials that Moscow was scheming against the KMT government. The

[20] T minutes 58, 3 December 1943, *OJ*, 1-C-8; Hornbeck to Hull, 5 May 1944, *SHP*, box 380; Koo to the Waijiaobu, 24 June 1944, *WKP*, box 68; "Notes of a conversation with Dr. Stanley Hornbeck," 5 September 1944, ibid., box 77; John M. Blum, ed., *The Price of Vision: The Diary of Henry A. Wallace, 1942–1946* (Boston: Houghton Mifflin, 1973), 332.
[21] Harriman to Roosevelt, 15 December 1944, *FRUS: Malta and Yalta, 1945*, 378–379. Secretary Hull resigned from his post in November 1944 with the impression that the Russians would join the fight against Japan with no strings attached. His successor, Edward R. Stettinius, Jr., was informed of the Soviet demands only after President Roosevelt discussed these matters with Stalin at Yalta. See Cordell Hull, *Memoirs of Cordell Hull* (New York: Macmillan, 1948), 2: 1310; Edward R. Stettinius, Jr., *Roosevelt and the Russians: The Yalta Conference* (Garden City, NY: Doubleday, 1949), 92.

Soviet government not only renounced categorically any intention of opposing the KMT regime by assisting the CCP, it also expressed support for the leading role of the United States in stabilizing the Chinese situation. According to reports of the Office of Strategic Services (OSS), contact between Moscow and the CCP in Yan'an was minimal. The OSS also did not believe that there was any policy coordination between the two because the CCP leadership showed no knowledge of Moscow's postwar policy in East Asia. For instance, they were even unaware of the Soviet intention to enter the Pacific war.[22]

Consequently, by the time of the Yalta Conference, the State Department not only accepted the military necessity of the Soviet entry into Manchuria, it also tended to view Moscow as an important partner able to assist America's political efforts in China. In its policy recommendations to President Roosevelt for the Yalta Conference, or the briefing book papers, the State Department called for the discarding of the old "preventive" and "self-denying" policies of the prewar period such as the "Open Door" in China and the "Washington treaties" in the Pacific. These should be replaced by a positive strategy of helping China develop its own capability to withstand foreign encroachment and making an active contribution to a new, peaceful order in the Asian–Pacific region. In the State Department's opinion, although the United States would inevitably take the lead in helping China, its policy goals in China could not be achieved without support from Great Britain and the Soviet Union. The rationale for such a China policy was as follows: an effective postwar control of Japan would be attainable only through Big Four cooperation, in which China's role could not be neglected; but such cooperation would not materialize unless the Big Three, acting in concert, helped China.[23] In this manner, China's role at Cairo as America's principal partner in dealing with Japan was transformed into one at Yalta as a problem for the Big Three to solve together.

The State Department also took the view that cooperation between Chongqing and Moscow was the "sine qua non for peace and security in the Far East." The American government must work on both the Chinese and Soviet sides. But time was running out. The KMT regime was horrified

[22] Harriman to Hull, 22 June 1944, *FRUS, 1944: China*, 799–800; memorandum by OSS, 8 January 1945, *RDCA*, box 8; "Capabilities and Intentions of U.S.S.R. in the Postwar Period," 5 January 1945, *OSSR*, reel 3. Yan'an would soon learn of Moscow's intention to enter the war against Japan. What the CCP leadership did not know in advance was when and where the Soviet Red Army would act. See Shi Zhe, *Zai Lishi Juren Shenbian: Shi Zhe Huiyilu* (Beside Historical Giants: Memoirs of Shi Zhe) (Beijing: Zhongyang Wenxian Chubanshe, 1991), 217.

[23] State Department to U.S. Embassy, Chongqing, 8 February 1945: enclosures no. 2 and no. 3, *GRCE*, box 1; "Political Memoranda for the Yalta Conference, Feb. 45: Far East: (1) China," *HHP*, boxes 169–171.

by the prospect of a Soviet military presence in Manchuria. Wei Daoming, Chongqing's ambassador in Washington, told the State Department on one occasion that the Chinese government was prepared to take necessary actions to prevent the Russians from making contact with the CCP in North China. Considering Chongqing's military failures in North China, Wei was obviously bluffing. But the statement was still disturbing to officials in the State Department. Once the Russians entered the Asian conflict via Mongolia, out of military necessity if not for other reasons, they would almost inevitably make contact with the CCP, the strongest Chinese military group nearby.[24]

To avert a possible political crisis between the KMT regime and the Soviet government, the State Department believed, the best solution was a unified command of the KMT and the CCP forces either through a KMT–CCP agreement or "an overall American command of Chinese forces." But after the Stilwell affair, American command of all Chinese forces appeared unlikely. Ambassador Hurley's matchmaking between Chongqing and Yan'an was not working either. Consequently, the bottom line recommended by the State Department planners was to "lend no support to a policy by the Chinese Government which might impede Russian military action against Japan." The work on the Soviet side appeared easier. The American government should convince Soviet leaders that America's policy in China was to create a Chinese power friendly to all of its neighbors. The policy would in no sense threaten Soviet security. As for Russian commercial interests in Manchuria, the State Department recommended a favorable attitude on the part of the American government as long as the Chinese and Soviet governments were able to reach some arrangements between themselves.[25]

In sum, by the time of the Yalta Conference, the State Department's policy recommendations on East Asian problems took the Soviet Union as an important party to the power configuration in Northeast Asia. To accommodate the Soviet power in the region, the State Department recommended that American conferees at Yalta support legitimate Soviet interests there. It should be recalled that ever since the Pacific war began, American leaders had expected that some sort of general agreement between Chongqing and Moscow would have to be worked out. During the better part of the war the subject repeatedly arose, only to be shelved in American–Chinese diplomacy. By early 1945, the situation had changed. Now the whole issue was dictated by the prospect of Russia's entry into the Asian war, which would make it the most powerful military influence

---

[24] Hull to Gauss, 3 May 1944, *FRUS, 1944: China*, 784–785; Clubb, "American Policy with respect to Sino–Soviet Relations," 19 May 1944, ibid., 785–793.

[25] Secretary of State to U.S. Embassy, Chongqing, 8 February 1945, enclosures nos. 1, 2, 3, and 5, *GRCE*, box 1.

in Northeast Asia. Manchuria became an area where the foundation of the Big Four's postwar cooperation in East Asia would rest. Although Washington continued to persuade the Chinese government to adopt a rational stand in its Russia policy, America's direct diplomacy with the Soviets over East Asia would now take the driver's seat.

The deal at Yalta

At Yalta, President Roosevelt told Secretary of State Edward Stettinius that the discussion with the Russians on the Far Eastern issues was primarily a military matter. This was an understatement bordering on a coverup. The president wanted to reach a "thorough-going understanding" with the Soviet government on both military and political problems in East Asia while keeping the State Department out of the delicate negotiations.[26] The Yalta Agreement on the Far East was a *quid pro quo* device in which the Soviet government committed itself definitely to participating in the Pacific war within three months after the defeat of Germany. In return, the Western Allies agreed to Russia's "political conditions" for doing so.

Having met with Stalin once at Teheran and been privy to the Stalin–Harriman conversation in late 1944, President Roosevelt was prepared to listen to Stalin's demands in East Asia. None of these demands was rejected at Yalta. South Sakhalin and the Kurile Islands would be transferred to the Soviet Union without qualification. The status quo of Outer Mongolia would be maintained without any definition of that term. The old tsarist right to control the Chinese Eastern and the South Manchurian railroads would be partially restored to the Soviet government in the form of Soviet–Chinese joint management. Only in the matter of Soviet interest in a warm-water port did Roosevelt and Stalin articulate different preferences. Observing a similarity between the Russian demand for a warm-water port in Manchuria and the Chinese–British controversy over Hong Kong, the president preferred an international solution – a free port. Yet, in the final agreement, the Western leaders agreed to a Soviet leasehold of Port Arthur and also to ambiguous wording on Soviet "preeminent interests" concerning Dalian and the railroads in Manchuria. Roosevelt did make one general reservation in the agreement: the decisions concerning China should not be regarded as final without the consent of the Chinese government. But the accord also stated that "the President will take measures in order to obtain this concurrence on advice from Marshall Stalin" and that "the Heads of the three Great Powers have agreed that these claims of the Soviet Union shall be unquestionably fulfilled after Japan has been defeated." These sentences tended to render the president's reservation

[26] Stettinius, *Roosevelt and the Russians*, 92; Robert E. Sherwood, *Roosevelt and Hopkins: An Intimate History* (New York: Harper, 1948), 843–844.

meaningless. To complete the accommodation of the Soviet power in Northeast Asia, Roosevelt and Stalin also reached an oral understanding on international trusteeship for Korea. In any case, Korea would be the last territory to be liberated from Japan by the Allied forces, and for the moment, the Yalta conferees preferred not to trouble themselves with the details regarding that area.[27]

When the content of the secret Yalta accord was disclosed to the Chinese government a few months later, its meaning was clear: the agreement confronted the Chongqing regime with Big Three unity endorsing the Soviet scheme in Manchuria and Outer Mongolia, a situation not unfamiliar to the Chinese in their modern foreign relations. But for American leaders, the Yalta diplomacy bore no resemblance to the old treaty powers' common front vis-à-vis China. As indicated in the State Department's preconference deliberations, as well as in the president's negotiations at Yalta, American policymakers believed that accommodation of Soviet interests in Northeast Asia was needed for both military and political purposes. The political significance of the Yalta accord was reflected in Stalin's promise to conclude a pact of friendship and alliance with Chiang Kai-shek's government. Therefore, from the American leaders' point of view, the KMT regime was paying a price in Manchuria not merely for Soviet participation in the war but also for Moscow's much needed goodwill.[28] In other words, the Yalta diplomacy was a Big Three intrigue for making the Big Four scheme work.

That was a conclusion that leaders in Chongqing were unable to reach easily. During the Yalta Conference, kept completely in the dark, Chiang Kai-shek suspected that the American government might strike a deal with the British and the Russians at the expense of China. He feared that a period of trial for the foreign policy of his government was just beginning.[29] After the Yalta Conference, Chiang first learned from the Chinese Embassy in Moscow that at Yalta the Russians had demanded reinstatement of tsarist privileges in Manchuria. Soon, in mid-March, Chiang received a report from Ambassador Wei Daoming on his recent conversation with President Roosevelt. Roosevelt had talked to Wei "informally" about some of the understandings at Yalta. According to the president, at Yalta the Russians had indicated a "more positive" attitude than before toward joining the war against Japan. Without mentioning any American commitment at Yalta, Roosevelt disclosed Stalin's demands regarding Outer

---

[27] Bohlen minutes of Roosevelt–Stalin meeting, 8 February 1945, *FRUS: Malta and Yalta,* 766–771; Harriman memorandum of conversations with Soviet leaders, 10 February 1945, ibid., 894–897; "Agreement Regarding Entry of the Soviet Union into the War Against Japan," 11 February 1945, ibid., 984.

[28] Ibid., 771; Robert Dallek, *Franklin D. Roosevelt and American Foreign Policy, 1932–1945* (Oxford: Oxford University Press, 1979), 519.

[29] *CZM,* 1: 34, 13: 176.

Mongolia, the South Manchurian Railroad, and Port Arthur. The president hastened to reassure Wei that the Soviet demand for maintaining the status quo of Outer Mongolia recognized China's sovereignty in that territory and therefore would not cause any problem. China's sovereignty over the railroads in Manchuria would also not be compromised because the Russians were willing to use these lines under certain conditions of "trusteeship." This might conceivably mean a tripartite commission including railroad experts from China, the Soviet Union, and probably the United States. As for Port Arthur, the president mentioned Stalin's demand for a Soviet leasehold but concealed his own agreement to this demand. He merely said that he had suggested that Stalin discuss the issue with the Chinese government. In the end, President Roosevelt did not forget to mention that although the issue of the Chinese Communists had not been discussed at Yalta, Stalin's general attitude toward Far Eastern problems had been "reasonably good." If President Roosevelt intended to placate Chongqing by misrepresenting the Yalta accord, he was aided in this regard by the incompetent Chinese ambassador. In his report to Chiang, Ambassador Wei made it sound as if the idea of Russia's leasing of Port Arthur was not a demand from Stalin but merely advice given by the president for Chongqing to consider at its own discretion.[30]

President Roosevelt's true motive in leaking the information about Yalta to the Chinese government cannot be documented. From late February to early March, Ambassador Hurley was in Washington. He managed to persuade President Roosevelt to let him see the content of the Yalta agreement. Later, Hurley would claim that he was shocked by that document and felt it was a betrayal of China's interests. Allegedly, Hurley convinced the president that the agreement must be "ameliorated."[31] President Roosevelt's conversation with the Chinese ambassador was anything but an effort to ameliorate the Yalta accord. It was more like a step toward gradually conditioning the minds of the KMT leaders to accept it. Yet, after talking to Hurley, Roosevelt may have sensed how difficult his task would be in persuading the Chinese to swallow the bitter fruit of Yalta. In talking to Wei, he may have wanted to inform leaders in Chongqing of the Yalta agreement piece by piece and give them time to digest it. The briefing session may also have been intended to impress on Chongqing that although China had not been invited to Yalta, the American government had not done anything to harm Chinese interests.

If this was Roosevelt's purpose, he failed. Startled by the news of a

[30] Wei Daoming to Chiang, 12 March 1945, ZZSC, 3(2): 542–543; CZM, 13: 178; RWK, 5(E): 841.

[31] Don Lohbeck, *Patrick J. Hurley* (Chicago: Henry Regnery, 1956), 366–368; Russell D. Buhite, *Patrick J. Hurley and American Foreign Policy* (Ithaca, NY: Cornell University Press, 1973), 203–207; James M. Burns, *Roosevelt: The Soldier of Freedom* (New York: Harcourt Brace Jovanovich, 1970), 589–590. These studies have different opinions on the credibility of Hurley's retrospective story.

possible U.S.–Soviet deal over Chinese territories, KMT leaders were especially apprehensive about the impact of such a deal on the KMT–CCP relationship. After receiving Wei's report, Chiang Kai-shek summoned his top advisers to discuss the situation. At first, Chiang was unwilling to accept the ominous implication of the report. He still hoped that American troops would be able to land in southern Manchuria earlier than the Russians. Also, he did not think that Moscow, insidious as it might be, would take the risk of offending the whole Chinese nation by supporting a Chinese Communist puppet government in Manchuria. But others present pointed out that Washington had never been unequivocal about its policy in Manchuria, and it might not be willing to act for China's sake. Moreover, operating by land, the Russians would probably be able to reach Manchuria faster than the Americans. An argument was also made that, unlike the Manchus, the CCP was not an alien group in China, and a CCP regime in Manchuria backed by the Soviets would have a meaning to China's politics totally different from that of the Manchukuo regime. Yet these officials could not find a way out of the predicament other than suggesting that they continue to plead for American support.[32]

After the meeting, Chiang still did not know how to instruct Ambassador Wei to proceed. In the second half of March, Chiang twice talked to Ambassador Koo, hoping to learn the opinion of this veteran in China's diplomatic struggle. Koo commented that President Roosevelt seemed to have agreed at Yalta to a policy of asking China to abandon its struggle for abrogating the unequal treaties and recovering the lost territories. Such a policy had to be rejected by the Chinese government. To encourage Chiang Kai-shek to hold firmly against the new tendency in Washington's policy, Koo remarked that although President Roosevelt might be offended by China's negative response, the United States was a democratic country and its public opinion would eventually act against a policy of selling out the Chinese ally. But Koo's suggestion that Chiang act in contradiction to President Roosevelt seemed more troubling to Chiang than anything else. Chiang kept stating his disbelief that the president should fail to see the disadvantage to China in the Soviet demands. Afterward, Koo did not think that he had convinced Chiang.[33]

Disheartened by Chiang's indecisiveness, Ambassador Koo took on himself the task of persuading American leaders to change their policy. In a conversation with Admiral Leahy on 11 April, the ambassador protested that the Soviet scheme for Manchuria would rekindle the old rivalry among foreign powers to control that territory and again make China an object of foreign powers' conspiracies to seek spheres of influence. Leahy's response was cynical: the Russians had asked for very little, and they would march into Manchuria to take whatever they wanted. He also told the ambassador

[32] "Haisang ji," 3(2): 2–4, *HSP*, box 2.
[33] *RWK*, 5(E): 864–866, 869–872.

that if China was discontented, it could seek supportive friends, whatever countries they might be, at the peace table after the war.[34]

Koo's and Chiang's attitudes constitute a revealing contrast. The former was a career diplomat who had spent his adult life trying to restore China to its full nationhood. The latter was a politician who had reached his paramount position in Chinese politics by following a road filled with conspiracies, convenient alignments, and ruthless power calculations. In these two minds, the national interests of China meant very different things. Whereas Chiang's principal concern was to secure American support in his struggle against both the Soviets and the CCP, Koo did not want to compromise China's sovereignty for political expedience. From his experience, Koo had learned that the traditional approach of Chinese diplomacy, using barbarians to control barbarians, had never worked to China's advantage. Once he became aware of Chiang's notion of inviting the Americans to Port Arthur in order to stop the Russians, Koo believed that a wrong decision on this matter might lead to a diplomatic catastrophe that would push China back to its dire condition prior to 1900.[35]

Chiang had no intention of changing his orientation now, nor did he wait passively. T. V. Soong, after a period of falling out of Chiang's favor, again became the most useful person who Chiang hoped could reach President Roosevelt. Even before he received the report from Ambassador Wei, Chiang wanted Soong to make a quick trip to Washington to discuss with President Roosevelt "certain most important and secret matters . . . on which the speedy prosecution of the war and improved international relations depend." In early March, Soong at first made a request through Hurley for an immediate audience with the president. It was rejected by the State Department on the ground that should Roosevelt receive a foreign minister before the San Francisco Conference of the United Nations, all others would make the same request. Roosevelt then agreed to talk to Soong "as a friend" just prior to the conference in April. Desperate, Soong turned to Hopkins to arrange an earlier meeting with the president. In his letter to Hopkins, Soong said that leaders in Chongqing felt that "never has it been so important that we obtain the President's advice now about our joint strategy, and this includes our relations with Soviet Russia, the Communists, and plans we have for dealing as best we can with our desperate economic problems." Soong must have been very conscious of the unflattering image among American officials of the KMT regime as a loan seeker, for he made an unusual promise: "I would not come to ask for a loan or for embarrassing decisions but to consult the President and his top advisers with, we believe, the future of China and Asia at stake." With these words, Soong cast aside the usual concern about dignity in Chinese diplomacy and

[34] Ibid., 872; "Notes of a Conversation with Admiral Leahy, 4/11/45," *WKP*, box 77.
[35] *RWK*, 5(E): 867–868.

showed the unprecedented disturbance in Chongqing's official circles caused by the Yalta Conference. But at that moment, Hopkins was confined to his sick bed in Rochester, Minnesota, unable to do anything to help Soong.[36]

On 15 March, President Roosevelt sent a message to Chiang Kai-shek, which proved to be his last communication with the KMT leader. In the message the president tried to persuade Chiang to see the advantage of including some CCP or third-party members in the Chinese delegation to the San Francisco Conference. Otherwise, except for expressing his sympathy toward Chiang, who faced "various problems," Roosevelt did not mention a word about Sino–Soviet relations. On 6 April, Chiang Kai-shek himself wrote to Roosevelt requesting that the president grant an audience to Soong. It was a time when Roosevelt was physically slipping away and mentally preoccupied with the forthcoming conference in San Francisco. Soong's name did not appear among those received by the president during the last week of his life. On 12 April, President Roosevelt died of a massive cerebral hemorrhage.[37]

Consumed by anxiety, Chiang Kai-shek at once feared that because of Roosevelt's untimely demise, in the future his government would have to deal with the British and the Russians in the absence of any reliable ally. Then some comforting news came from abroad. T. V. Soong reported that Harry Hopkins had guaranteed to him that the new president would continue President Roosevelt's foreign policy and would not let China fall under Communist or Soviet influence. According to Hopkins, at Yalta the Russians had only wanted to make an arrangement with China to recover their interests in Port Arthur and the Manchurian railroads, but not to control the northeastern provinces of China. Ambassador Koo also reported to Chiang that President Truman never trusted anyone with Marxist tendencies, and allegedly his first three days in the White House had already forced the Russians to adopt a more reasonable foreign policy. After further discussion with Hurley, Chiang became somewhat relaxed and thought that "to the danger of Russian seizure of the northeastern provinces, the United States seems to begin to pay closer attention."[38]

Truman takes charge

"Closer attention"? Maybe. But, like its predecessor, the Truman administration had no intention of promoting military containment in Manchuria as

---

[36] Mrs. Soong to Hopkins, 12 March 1945, and enclosure: T. V. Soong to Hopkins, 10 March 1945, *HHP*, box 334.

[37] Stettinius to Atcheson, 15 March 1945, *FRUS, 1945*, 1: 121; Chiang to Roosevelt, 6 April 1945, *RPPF* 2907; Jim Bishop, *FDR's Last Year, April 1944–April 1945* (New York: Pocket Books, 1975), 740–798.

[38] *CZM*, 13: 180–181; Soong to Chiang, 15 April 1945, *ZZSC*, 3(2): 544–545; Koo to Chiang, 15 April 1945, *WKP*, box 82.

a way of checking the Soviet influence. Late in April, on reviewing America's strategy in the Pacific, the Joint Chiefs of Staff finally stated their belief that Soviet entry into Manchuria according to the Yalta arrangement might create difficulties for implementation of the Cairo decision on China's sovereignty in the area. The Joint Chiefs of Staff therefore recommended sending a token American force into Manchuria.[39] But this notion was dismissed by the SWNCC. Its Subcommittee on the Far East believed:

> Use of American forces to influence the settlement of China's internal diffi-
> culties and to check the expansion of Soviet influence in the Far East would
> be unlikely to succeed in those purposes, might be extremely costly in American
> lives and resources, and, through its effect on American–Soviet relations,
> might do irreparable injury to the cause of world peace.

This was almost the end of Chiang's master plan for using the Americans to check the Russians in Manchuria.[40]

The U.S.–Soviet relationship did indeed come under close review soon after Harry S. Truman took charge of the White House. The growing difficulties with the Russians on the issue of Poland were especially irritating to the new president. At the same time, Ambassador Harriman and George Kennan in Moscow warned against taking the Soviet leaders' words about China at face value. Kennan thought it especially unfortunate that in the current American foreign policy there was "an undue reliance on Soviet aid or even Soviet acquiescence in the achievement of our long term objectives in China." Secretary of State Stettinius cautioned the chimerical Ambassador Hurley that when Russia became active in the Asian war or if the internal disunity in China continued, Moscow might reconsider its current policy of supporting the American effort in China. Therefore, the ambassador should put additional pressure on Chiang Kai-shek for an early reconciliation with the CCP.[41]

Although this advice indicated a departure by the State Department from its earlier attitude toward the Soviet Union, America's Yalta commitment was not relinquished. Joseph Grew did make a serious effort to modify that commitment without success. Privately convinced that the Soviet Union was pursuing a policy of expansion and that "a future war with Soviet Russia is as certain as anything in this world can be certain," Grew had no faith in the system constructed at Yalta.[42] In a memorandum

[39] *Entry of the Soviet Union*, 67–68.
[40] "Ballantine Diary," 261, Ballantine Paper, box 1; SWNCC 67/1: draft report by Subcommittee for the Far East, "Manchuria Military Government: Extent and Conditions of U.S. Participation," 11 July 1945, *SWNCCF*, reel 9.
[41] Harry S. Truman, *Memoirs of Harry S. Truman* (New York: Doubleday, 1955), 1: 35–38; memorandum of conversation between Harriman and Stanton, 19 April 1945, *RDCA*, box 8; *White Paper*, 94–98.
[42] Joseph E. Grew, *Turbulent Era: A Diplomatic Record of Forty Years, 1904–1945* (Boston: Houghton Mifflin, 1952), 2: 1444–1446.

of 12 May addressed to Secretary of War Stimson, Grew, in his capacity as Acting Secretary of State, questioned whether the whole concept of the Yalta agreement, including the Soviet entry into the Pacific war, should be reconsidered. He also questioned what policy the United States should adopt in the eventuality of Soviet Russia's demand for participation in the occupation of Japan. Grew proposed that the Yalta accord on Asia be supplemented by four conditions. First, Moscow should cooperate with the American effort to unify China under Chiang Kai-shek's leadership, and the unification of China should be made a precondition for the American government to approach Chongqing to obtain its endorsement of the Yalta accord. Second, Moscow must adhere unequivocally to the Cairo decisions with regard to the return of Manchuria to China and the future status of Korea. Third, the Soviet government should accept definitely that Korea would be placed under a Big Four trusteeship solely responsible for selecting a temporary Korean government. Finally, Russia should grant American commercial airplanes emergency landing rights on certain islands of the Kuriles.[43]

Three days later, the secretaries of State, War and the Navy had a "pretty red hot" meeting on the issues raised by Grew. Ambassador Harriman was also present due to his firsthand knowledge of President Roosevelt's policy at Yalta. Harriman pointed out that the Soviets had broken every agreement made at Yalta except the main one relating to their entry into the Pacific war. He told those present that Roosevelt and Stalin had reached oral agreements concerning a coalition government in China under Chiang Kai-shek and a trusteeship for Korea. This information seemed to render part of the Grew memorandum superfluous. But more important was Stimson's concern about the war in Asia. Viewing Grew's notion as premature, he suggested delaying consideration of the subject until July, when the president might want to discuss it personally with Stalin at another summit of the Big Three. Still waiting for the news about the "S-1 secret," or the atomic bomb, Stimson argued that "it seems a terrible thing to gamble with such big stakes in diplomacy without having your master card in your hand." Those at the meeting concurred.[44]

A week later, when Stimson gave his formal reply to Grew, it proved that the War Department, with or without the "master card" in its hand, wanted the deal made at Yalta to be carried out. The War Department believed that the Yalta accord on the Far East had conceded to the Russians only things within their reach, and that only at an unacceptable cost in American lives could the United States establish control over the territories concerned. In addition, although Soviet belligerency in the Pacific

---

[43] Grew to Stimson, 12 May 1945, *OJ*, 5-B-7.
[44] Minutes of a meeting of the Committee of Three, 15 May 1945, ibid.; entry of 15 May 1945, *HSD*, 51 (reel 9): 128.

war was no longer necessary for defeating Japan, it was still desirable for the purposes of shortening the war and saving American lives. Consequently, from the military point of view, a complete understanding with Russia on the Far East remained necessary. Diplomatically, the War Department did not believe that the proposed recycling of the Yalta agreement would be able to produce a better arrangement.[45]

While the Western–Soviet understanding concerning European affairs was collapsing, the secret Yalta accord regarding East Asia remained intact. In late May, Harry Hopkins had recovered physically and felt well enough to undertake a mission for Truman to Moscow. One purpose of the mission was to obtain confirmation from Stalin that the Yalta accord remained operational. During his conversation with Hopkins and Ambassador Harriman, except for showing some interest in postwar arrangements in Japan, Stalin maintained his position taken at Yalta. He made a "categorical statement" reaffirming his support of America's policy in China. Noteworthy was Stalin's pledge to Hopkins that the Red Army would enter the Asian war through Manchuria no later than 8 August, a promise Stalin was to keep precisely. He also told the Americans that he was ready to talk with T. V. Soong about the Yalta proposals in early July. Harriman wanted to know what attitude Moscow would take if the KMT and the CCP did not unify themselves by the time Soviet troops entered Manchuria. Stalin asserted that his government had no intention of interfering with Chinese sovereignty in Manchuria or any other part of China. The ambassador was not satisfied and pressed further, asking whether Soviet troops in Manchuria would allow Chiang Kai-shek to organize the civil administration there. To this Stalin responded: "Chiang could send his representatives to set up the Kuomintang regime in any areas where the Red Army were [sic]."[46] Apparently Stalin did not want to give the American government any excuse to retreat from the Yalta accord. Now it was Washington's responsibility to obtain Chongqing's consent to that arrangement.

The mood in Chongqing was somber. After the Soviet government renounced its neutrality treaty of 1941 with Japan on 5 April 1945, the Chinese government believed Soviet occupation of Manchuria was imminent. Having failed to get Washington's promise to land American troops in southern Manchuria, Chiang instructed his generals to be prepared to encounter the Russians, who might seize Manchuria in the name of fighting the Japanese.[47] In practice, Chiang's instruction only prepared KMT officials mentally for the inevitable. Afterward, the KMT regime remained to maneuver only on the diplomatic front. In an April report to Chiang

---

[45] *Entry of the Soviet Union*, 61–68, 70–71.

[46] "Hopkins–Stalin Conference Record, Moscow, May 1945: Memorandum of 3rd Conversation at the Kremlin, 6 pm May 28," *HHP*, box 338.

[47] *CZM*, 13: 183.

Kai-shek, the Waijiaobu suggested that the current Chinese–Soviet relationship had become exceedingly complicated and a definite Chinese policy was difficult to formulate. Still, it proposed to take advantage of the San Francisco Conference of the United Nations to launch a diplomatic offensive. Although that conference would focus on general peace issues, the Chinese government might well present to the American leaders the Chinese–Soviet relationship as an issue vital to world peace. Washington should become acquainted with the Chinese anxieties about the Soviet intentions in Manchuria and Xinjiang. The Waijiaobu believed that American assistance should be sought as a condition for frank negotiations between China and the Soviets. To show the sincerity of the Chinese government, the Americans ought to be informed that in exchange for Moscow's understanding and good faith, Chongqing was prepared to make certain "extraordinary concessions" to the Russians, including favorable consideration of Soviet commercial interests in Manchuria and Xinjiang, as well as a high degree of autonomy for Outer Mongolia. The Waijiaobu also prepared two draft agreements to show to American leaders, one on Sino–Soviet long-term cooperation and another on civil affairs in liberated Chinese territories.[48]

As indicated earlier in this study, by the time of the San Francisco Conference, the Chinese government had found many subjects pertinent to postwar East Asia that it wished to discuss with the American government. Yet Chiang Kai-shek's preference for a passive posture at San Francisco accomplished nothing. Only in his conversations with President Truman in Washington was T. V. Soong able to voice Chongqing's concern about the Soviet Union. On 19 April, Soong was at last received by President Truman. On this occasion, Soong told the president that he would go to Moscow to negotiate with Stalin after the San Francisco Conference, which Truman urged Soong to do as soon as possible. But to Soong's complaint about the Soviet demands in Manchuria, which, in Soong's opinion, would push China back to the "old system of leased territories and spheres of influence," Truman only "nodded all the time" and offered no definite response.[49]

There is a question as to how well Truman was prepared for his meeting with Soong. According to Truman's memoir, on 22 April he held a special meeting with some State Department officials to prepare himself for his first meeting with Soviet Foreign Minister Molotov. No such session was conducted for his first meeting with T. V. Soong. Two days before the Truman–Soong meeting, in advising Truman to receive Soong for "a few minutes," Secretary of State Stettinius regarded the audience only as a matter of protocol. Aside from the atomic bomb, the Yalta agreement on the Far East was another secret within the American government, and

[48] Chiang to Soong, 3 April 1945, and enclosures, *WKP*, box 81.
[49] Truman, *Memoirs*, 1: 81; *RWK*, 5(E): 836.

therefore President Truman was almost on his own to absorb its significance. Truman's diary entry of 14 April indicates that on that day he
discussed with Hopkins before and over lunch the "whole history of the
Roosevelt Administration [from] 1933 to date–[with] particular emphasis
on the foreign visits on which the President had taken Harry Hopkins,"
including the Yalta Conference. From this one-and-a-half-hour discussion,
Truman could obtain only limited assistance from Hopkins. His reaction
to Soong's statements certainly did not indicate any thorough understanding of his predecessor's policy with regard to Sino–Soviet relations.[50]

In late April, from a State Department memorandum, perhaps for the
first time, President Truman learned about the State Department's views
on the China policy. Yet this document was not informed by the Yalta
accord, and therefore it was useless for advising Truman on particular
issues between China and Russia as they were addressed by the Yalta
diplomacy. On 14 May, Soong and Truman had another meeting. Grew
also attended. In the conversation Soong's approach was rather deceptive,
and Truman, still trying to grasp America's Asian policy, was apparently
misled. For instance, Soong pressed for more American aid but justified
this request on the ground that the "brunt of driving out Japanese forces
from China" fell on China. Informed officials in both Chongqing and
Washington knew that the United States was giving aid to Chongqing for
certain reasons, but not because of the expectation that the KMT regime
would be able to drive Japan out of China. Using a map, Soong also
showed Truman the locations of Taiwan and Manchuria, saying that in
accordance with the Cairo decisions, both territories should be returned to
China in the event of American landings. Thus Soong implied that under
the Cairo Communiqué the American government had an obligation to use
force to restore these territories to China. Truman concurred with Soong's
statement, not knowing what he promised. His consent to this point would
later require qualification by the State Department. After talking at some
length about Chongqing's concern about Moscow's attitude toward the
CCP, Soong suggested that he return to Washington immediately after his
meeting with Stalin. The "political implications" of such an arrangement,
Soong contended, would be helpful to his negotiations with the Russians.
Truman was again willing to agree but was stopped at this point by Grew.
Truman explicitly expressed his disagreement with Soong only once when
the latter suggested a regional security pact for the Pacific. Soong himself
had no illusions about this meeting with Truman. Taking Truman's attitude to be generally sympathetic, Soong nevertheless believed that he had

---

[50] Truman, *Memoirs*, 1: 90–91; Stettinius to Truman, 17 April 1945, *RPPF* 2907; Robert
H. Ferrell, ed., *Off the Record: The Private Papers of Harry S. Truman* (New York: W.
W. Norton, 1980), 18–19; W. Averell Harriman and Elie Abel, *Special Envoy to Churchill
and Stalin, 1941–1946* (New York: Random House, 1975), 446–447.

been unsuccessful in gaining the president's positive commitment. After all, he could not carry out a mission for Chiang in Washington without being a loan seeker. Later, Soong admitted to Ambassador Koo that he had to solicit more loans from the U.S. government, something that he had earlier promised to Hopkins not to do. Soong believed that this had prevented him from focusing his mission on the Soviet threat in China.[51]

On 21 May, without President Truman's authorization, Ambassador Hurley leaked the contents of the Yalta accord to Chiang Kai-shek. On that occasion, Hurley also told Chiang that he had returned from Washington via the Soviet Union, where he had talked to Stalin. Stalin had stressed to Hurley that before the American government officially informed Chongqing of the Yalta agreement, he would not discuss that matter with the Chinese even if T. V. Soong came to Moscow.[52] This meant that Chongqing would have no choice but to negotiate with Moscow within the framework of the Yalta accord. After Hurley's disclosure, the sense of crisis in Chongqing became even more intensified. Three days later, when talking to Hurley again, Chiang indicated that China's negotiations with the Soviets would hinge on whether American troops were going to land in southern Manchuria. Either ignorant of the American military policy in the Pacific or anxious to console his Chinese host, Hurley misleadingly reassured Chiang on this matter.[53]

At the same time, Chiang instructed T. V. Soong in San Francisco to have an urgent meeting with Wellington Koo and Wang Chonghui, both members of the Chinese delegation to the conference. In late May, the three discussed the crisis several times, but they could not agree on how the Chinese government should act. Koo saw only two ways for the Chinese government to avoid diplomatic humiliation in Moscow. One was to "temporize": Chongqing could ignore the American–Soviet understanding and delay Soong's mission to Moscow in the hope that the United States and China would be able to defeat Japan before the Soviet entry into the war. Another was to bring the CCP into the government, which would put Yan'an in a position to share with the government the responsibility for whatever decisions it made in relation to the Soviet Union. This gesture might also reassure Moscow about China's goodwill and thus persuade the Russians to retreat from their Yalta demands in Manchuria. By taking these courses, Koo hoped, the KMT regime would be able to reduce its

[51] Memorandum by the Division of Far Eastern Affairs, 18 April 1945, *FRUS, 1945*, 7: 93–95; memorandum of conversation between Truman and Soong, 14 May 1945, ibid., 101–103; Dooman to Dunn, 4 July 1945, ibid., 126; Truman, *Memoirs*, 1: 81, 297–298; Grew, *Turbulent Era*, 2: 1460–1461; *RWK*, 5(E): 836; Soong to Hopkins, 8 May 1945, *HHP*, box 220.

[52] Truman, *Memoirs*, 1: 296–297; Wang Shijie to Soong, 22 May 1945, *ZZSC*, 3(2): 546–547; *White Paper*, 94–96.

[53] *CZM*, 13: 186.

dependence on Washington and regain diplomatic initiatives. Wang made
no particular suggestion for action, but he doubted that the Soviet Union,
an exceedingly ambitious power, would under any circumstances give up
its demands in China. Soong also did not think that Chiang would favor
the idea of admitting the CCP into the government. In fact, at the time,
Soong's opinion on the Soviet–CCP question was the opposite of Koo's.
Soong hoped that a rapprochement between Chongqing and Moscow would
result in the latter's abandonment of the Chinese Communists, thus strengthening the government's position in dealing with them.[54]

On 26 May, Soong reported to Chiang the inconclusive discussion. In
relating Koo's suggestions, he simply omitted the one for accommodating
the CCP. Soong told Chiang that Roosevelt's policy at Yalta had origin-
ated in his disillusion with Chongqing's military ability, but that in his
recent conversations with American leaders in Washington, Soong had
obtained an impression that the Truman administration would not abandon China. Secretary of State Stettinius had especially promised Soong that
in Moscow Hopkins would emphasize China's sovereignty in Manchuria
and that President Truman would invite Soong to discuss a "Chinese–
American orientation" to deal with the Russians soon after Hopkins returned from his Russian mission.[55] Thus, betting on the American leaders'
change of minds, Soong negated Koo's tactic of passive resistance against
Yalta and recommended to Chiang that the KMT regime continue to
coordinate its diplomacy with Washington.

The Hopkins mission to Moscow only proved that the Yalta understanding on the Far East between the American and Soviet governments
would not crack. By this time, it had become clear that among the leading
Allies, only Chongqing wanted to alter the Yalta formula. But Chiang and
his entourage still entertained an illusion that this could be done with the
help of the American government. On 9 June, to implement the procedure
decided at Yalta, President Truman, on receiving Stalin's signal, formally
informed T. V. Soong of the Yalta agreement. The president also instructed Hurley to hold a conversation with Chiang in Chongqing on the
same subject.[56] Now the door was open in Moscow for KMT leaders to
proceed with their negotiations in Moscow, but the door was closed in
Washington for Chongqing's scheme to alter the American commitment at
Yalta.

[54] Soong to Chiang, 26 May 1945, ZZSC, 3(2): 548–549; RWK, 5(E): 838–842; Wang
Shijie, *Wang Shijie Riji* (Diaries of Wang Shijie) (Taipei: Zhongyang Yenjiuyuan Jindaishi
Yenjiusuo, 1990), 5: 109.
[55] Soong to Chiang, 26 May 1945, ZZSC, 3(2): 548–549.
[56] Soong to Chiang, 9 June 1945, and appendix, ZZSC, 3(2): 555–557; Hurley to Chiang,
15 June 1945, ibid., 567–568; Truman, *Memoirs*, 1: 298–300; Grew, *Turbulent Era*, 2:
1465–1466.

KMT leaders continued to strive for the modification of the Yalta accord before Soong went to Moscow. In June, Soong again talked a few times with President Truman in Washington, and Chiang also conversed with the American and Soviet ambassadors in Chongqing. They were eager to clarify three issues with the American and the Soviet governments. First, the lease involving Port Arthur was absolutely unacceptable, and China could only agree to some international or Sino–Soviet joint utilization of that port. Second, the meaning of maintaining the status quo in Outer Mongolia in the Yalta accord was not clear. The Chinese government wanted to exclude the issue from the agenda for the coming Moscow conference. Third, Chongqing hoped to clarify the vague wording in the accord about Soviet "preeminent interests" in Dalian and the Manchurian railroads, as well as internationalization of the port of Dalian. All these overtures were made in vain. After they had confirmed to each other their commitment to the Yalta arrangement, neither Washington nor Moscow was willing to make any change for the sake of China.[57]

Under pressure from both Washington and Moscow, the KMT regime habitually resorted to the old barbarian management tactic. In their conversations with President Truman and Ambassador Hurley in June, T. V. Soong and Chiang Kai-shek continued to try to commit the American government to a military occupation in southern Manchuria or to an international regime for Port Arthur. Chiang even suggested to Hurley that the projected bilateral negotiations between China and the Soviet Union be enlarged into a quadruple conference also including the Americans and the British.[58] With Soviet Ambassador Appolon A. Petrov, however, Chiang Kai-shek used other rhetoric. In a conversation held on 3 June, Chiang suggested to Petrov that the Manchurian question provided a "second chance" for close Chinese–Soviet cooperation. Recalling a time after World War I when the Soviet Union had been the first foreign power to renounce tsarist privileges in China, Chiang now disingenuously invited the Soviet government to help China regain Manchuria. He predicted that China and the Soviets had a good opportunity to achieve cordial cooperation similar to the KMT–Moscow alliance in the early 1920s. But according to Chiang, this new cooperation would have a much larger scope, including Sino–Soviet understandings on postwar affairs in East Asia. After receiving Hurley's formal notification of the Yalta agreement, Chiang further told Petrov that the problems concerning China and the Soviet Union should

[57] Minutes of Chiang–Petrov conversation, 12 June 1945, ZZSC, 3(2): 558–562; Soong to Chiang, 13 June 1945, ibid., 563–564; minutes of conversation between Soong and Hopkins, 13 June 1945, ibid., 565–567, ibid.; Truman, *Memoirs*, 1: 300–301.
[58] Grew, *Turbulent Era*, 2: 1466–1468; Hurley to Hull, 15 June 1945, GRCE, box 1; CZM, 1: 43.

be discussed directly by the Chinese and the Soviet governments, and that America's consent or objection did not really matter.[59]

This double-talk with the Americans and the Russians certainly did not mean that the Chinese government was wavering between Washington and Moscow.[60] Chongqing's two-pronged maneuver with the Americans and the Russians did not reflect any fundamental readjustment of its foreign policy. The KMT leaders' desire to gain American support for their dealing with the Russians was fundamental. Chiang's rhetoric for cultivating Soviet good feelings was merely an opportunistic tactic. After the Yalta Conference, the KMT regime found itself precariously positioned under a falling Soviet sledgehammer, and its diplomacy was first and foremost aimed at making American policy a protective buffer that would be able to alleviate the smash. But when KMT leaders sensed that Washington's policy was more like an anvil underneath them, they wanted to try everything that could possibly soften Moscow's attitude.

Ambassador Koo did not think the Chinese government needed to be caught in such a predicament. At San Francisco he advised T. V. Soong that if he was not prepared to make embarrassing concessions to Soviet demands, the best policy was not to go to Moscow at all. Why, he asked, could not China wait until the end of the war? Koo's consistent objection to submitting the Chinese diplomacy to the Yalta accord motivated Soong to invite the ambassador three times in June to join his mission to Moscow. Aware of the distance between his own views and those of Chiang Kai-shek, Koo doubted that Chiang would want him to go. If Chongqing's policy was to make concessions, Koo wondered whether his presence in Moscow might be embarrassing, not helpful, to Soong.[61]

Chiang Kai-shek needed the Moscow negotiations to achieve a general political understanding with Stalin. A legal settlement between the two sides on territories and other rights was itself secondary and permissive of flexible bargaining. Therefore, he was not disposed to include seasoned diplomats like Koo in the mission to Moscow. He wanted the Moscow conference to appear like a meeting between two friendly revolutionary governments, without the burden of diplomatic formalities. Soong's leadership of the mission would represent authority from Chiang himself. To add a further personal touch, Chiang Kai-shek sent his son, Jingguo, to accompany Soong. At least on this point, Stalin was in agreement with Chiang. Koo was a familiar figure to the Soviet diplomatic circle from the difficult Sino–Soviet negotiations over Outer Mongolia and Manchuria in the 1920s. Stalin specified to Chongqing that he did not desire to see Koo

---

[59] Minutes of Chiang–Petrov conversation, 3 June 1945, ZZSC, 3(2): 549–552; minutes of Chiang–Petrov conversation, 26 June 1945, ibid., 569–571.

[60] For a different view, see Garver, *Chinese–Soviet Relations*, 210.

[61] *RWK*, 5(E): 840–841, 872, 5(A): 852.

in Moscow, and his excuse was that Koo could not represent Chiang's authority as convincingly as Soong.[62] Given Chiang's political maneuvering, Koo would have been an irrelevant envoy, and with Stalin's territorial ambitions in China, Koo would have been a tough negotiation partner. Symbolically, the rejection of Koo by both Chiang and Stalin forecast the course and results of the Moscow negotiations.

[62] Minutes of Chiang–Petrov conversation, 3 June 1945, ZZSC, 3(2): 552; Soong to Chiang, 13 June 1945, ibid., 567; minutes of Chiang–Petrov conversation, 26 June 1945, ibid., 571. For Koo's role in the Sino–Soviet negotiations in the 1920s, see Aitchen K. Wu, *China and the Soviet Union: A Study of Sino–Soviet Relations* (New York: John Day, 1950), 148–156, 287, 347–359; Peter S. H. Tang, *Russian and Soviet Policy in Manchuria and Outer Mongolia, 1911–1931* (Durham, NC: Duke University Press, 1959), 141–143, 150–153.

11

Bargaining at Moscow

On 30 June 1945, T. V. Soong and his retinue, aboard a specially chartered American airplane, landed in Moscow. Soong was to start his mission in the Soviet capital without much hope of prevailing over the Russians. Bargaining with Stalin, begging for American support, and waiting constantly for clarification of policies from Chongqing together would drive Soong to the verge of mental and physical collapse. In mid-July, after returning to Chongqing from the first round of negotiations, Soong complained to Ambassador Hurley: "I am a broken man. I am personally ill from overstrain and overwork."[1] It took one and a half months and thirteen difficult sessions, with an interruption during the Potsdam Conference, for the conferees in Moscow to conclude their negotiations. In the end, Soong did not attach his signature to the new agreements between the Chinese and Soviet governments. That formality was performed by Wang Shijie, who succeeded Soong as foreign minister during the Potsdam interval. This substitution was not a trivial matter. It reflected the KMT government's awkward position in concluding the agreements with Moscow. T. V. Soong must have remembered how the Shandong question in 1919 had caused nationwide protests in China. He did not want to become a scapegoat for Chiang Kai-shek's policy in the Moscow negotiations, which resulted in humiliating concessions to Soviet demands in Manchuria and Outer Mongolia.[2]

---

[1] Hurley to the Secretary of State, 29 July 1945, *FRUS: Berlin*, 2: 1246.
[2] Scholarly exploration of the meaning of the Moscow negotiations is only a recent development. Two different views have emerged. Relying principally on an incomplete set of Chinese records of the negotiations published in *Zhonghua Minguo Zhongyao Shiliao Chubian* (ZZSC), John W. Garver, *Chinese–Soviet Relations, 1937–1945: The Diplomacy of Chinese Nationalism* (New York: Oxford University Press, 1988), 214–230, depicts Chiang Kai-shek as a determined nationalist leader whose diplomatic skill during the Moscow conference saved China from losing more rights to the Soviets. Odd Arne Westad's *Cold*

The significance of the Moscow negotiations is neither a mere footnote to the Yalta diplomacy among the Big Three nor an indicator of the breakdown of the Yalta understanding. From the outset of the Soong–Stalin conference, all three governments in Chongqing, Moscow, and Washington understood that it was held as a sequel to the Big Three summit at Yalta. Although U.S.–Soviet relations in Europe turned cold soon after Germany surrendered, the war and inter-Allied relations in Asia maintained their own momentum. No longer anxious to have the Soviet Red Army enter the Asian conflict, policymakers in Washington nevertheless did not want to breach their relations with Moscow over Asian problems. During the Chinese–Soviet negotiations, the American government at first adopted the position of a concerned patron, probably assuming that the Chinese in Moscow would automatically complete the necessary procedure of formalizing the Yalta agreement. Only later, when the Russians increased their pressure on the Chinese, did Washington become worried that Stalin might be able to modify the Yalta accord to his advantage. But it was too late for the American government to influence the course of the negotiations, except for making some oral representations to Moscow through its ambassador.

Like the Americans, the Russian leaders expected a quick deal with the Chinese, hoping that the talks could conclude within a week.[3] This way they would have been able to come to the Potsdam Conference and focus on difficulties between themselves and the Western powers over Europe. But the Moscow negotiations were protracted because Chongqing and Moscow had different interpretations of the Yalta accord. The Chinese retreated from their original stand only bit by bit. Without question, having its peerless military strength in Northeast Asia in the final stage of the war, the Soviet government probably could not have been prevented by any other force from taking what it wanted in Manchuria. Yet, aside from its interest in that region, Moscow also needed a lawful arrangement with Chongqing for its postwar relations with both China and the United States. This purpose was facilitated by Chongqing's partisan concern about the Chinese Communists and also by Washington's hesitant policy.

In negotiations with the Soviet government, the KMT regime was in an

---

War and Revolution: Soviet–American Rivalry and the Origins of the Chinese Civil War, 1944–1946 (New York: Columbia University Press, 1993), 31–56, has access to a complete set of minutes of the negotiations kept by Hu Shize (Victor Hoo), then Chinese Vice-Minister of Foreign Affairs and a member of the Chinese delegation. Westad's focus on the KMT–CCP struggle has led to his hasty conclusion that Chiang concluded the new treaty with the Soviets mainly to strengthen his position in China against the Chinese Communists. The treatment of the subject presented here aimed at revealing the dual nature of the KMT foreign policy. In other words, when dealing with the Soviets and any other foreign government, Chiang Kai-shek was a mixture of nationalist leader and partisan politician.

[3] Soong to Chiang, 13 June 1945, ZZSC, 3(2): 566.

awkward position as both a national and a partisan government. As a national government, Chongqing felt obliged to fulfill China's national aspirations, as reflected in many of its own plans and statements on China's war and peace aims. However, as a partisan government that had survived various civil and foreign conflicts by pragmatic or even opportunistic calculation of political forces within and without China, the KMT regime logically treated its relationship with Moscow as part of its political strategy against the Chinese Communists. When China remained divided politically, the KMT government could not avoid facing a choice between national sovereignty and political expedience in its negotiations with Moscow. The task became further complicated because of the existence of the Yalta precedent. The change of leadership in the White House early in the year did not help at all in Chongqing's effort to learn Washington's intentions in Asia at the time. T. V. Soong's task was difficult not only because of the high-handed diplomacy of the Soviet government, but also because of Washington's ambivalent attitude and Chiang Kai-shek's control from afar.

First round: diplomacy of quid pro quo

When Soong and Stalin first greeted each other on 30 June, both exuded cordiality. Soong expressed his desire to talk with the Soviet leaders in "perfect frankness without the usual politeness of diplomatic ways." Stalin expressed his "full support" of his guest's desire and professed confidence in the success of Soong's mission.[4] Yet, two days later, when the first formal session began, the Chinese were shocked by the candor of the Soviet demands. Despite their knowledge of the Yalta accord, this was the first time they heard the Soviet leader's interpretation of that document. Soong at first tried to proceed with a point-by-point discussion of the Yalta agreement, suggesting that the first item of the agreement, Outer Mongolia, be placed "in abeyance." This provoked a long rebuttal from Stalin, who contended that his country must emerge from the war with a strengthened strategic position in East Asia toward Japan. His reason for granting Outer Mongolia independent status was to enable Russia to incorporate this region into its defense system. By the same token, according to Stalin, Soviet demands for Port Arthur, the Manchurian railroads, and Dalian (Dairen) were all made out of concern for Russia's security during the postwar years. Knowing of Chongqing's potent objection to a Russian leasehold of Port Arthur, Stalin shrewdly agreed to consider other alternatives, provided that the resultant arrangement could guarantee Soviet control of that port. Stalin explained to the Chinese the meaning of Soviet

---

[4] "No. 1. Meeting between Marshall Stalin and Dr. Soong. June 30, 1945," *VHP*, box 2.

"preeminent interests" regarding Dalian and the railroads: Russia should have the right to administer Dalian for forty years and ownership of the railroads for forty-five years. In addition, Soong received the disturbing impression that Moscow's attitude toward the CCP issue was by no means as wholesome as the Americans had assumed. Although Stalin agreed that China could have only one government under the leadership of the Kuomintang, he advised Soong that the KMT regime might well benefit from accommodating the Communists and liberals. From Chongqing's point of view, such advice from Stalin was a dangerous sign.[5]

After the first meeting, the Chinese delegation devoted five days to appraising the Soviet demands and consulting Chongqing for counterproposals. The issue of Mongolian independence caused the greatest concern within the Chinese delegation. In his report to Chiang, Soong proposed a few alternatives that might satisfy the Soviet concern with security while retaining Outer Mongolia under Chinese sovereignty. Preparing for the worst, Soong also suggested the possibility of breaking off the negotiations if the Russians persisted with their demand for Mongolian independence.[6] Chongqing had not expected that talks with Moscow might founder on this problem. On 5 July, Chiang held an emergency meeting with a dozen KMT high officials to discuss the crisis. Opinions expressed by the participants ranged from granting Mongolia independence to opposing any compromise, even at the cost of breaking off the Moscow negotiations. Yet, to the KMT regime, the stakes were too high to allow the Moscow Conference to collapse at the first sign of frustration. General Xiong Shihui, then in charge of the Central Planning Board, proposed a quid pro quo approach. Xiong argued that, unable to ignore the Yalta agreement and to find a better way to prevent the Soviets from supporting the CCP, Chongqing must continue its negotiations with the Russians. Therefore, China's sovereignty in Outer Mongolia would have to be sacrificed in return for the Soviet leaders' promise to discontinue support for the CCP. After making such a concession, the Chinese government ought to insist that the future Chinese–Mongolian boundary be drawn in accordance with the Chinese map. The next day Wang Shijie also advised Chiang that since Outer Mongolia had already left China for some twenty years, China's agreement

---

[5] "Notes Taken at Sino–Soviet Conferences, Moscow, 1945: 2 July, 1945," ibid. (hereafter cited as "Moscow Notes" and dates).
[6] Two cables from Soong to Chiang, 3 July 1945, and Soong to Chiang, 4 July 1945, ZZSC, 3(2): 591–593. Probably at about this time, Chiang Kai-shek instructed his son, Jingguo, to hold a private discussion with Stalin with regard to Outer Mongolia. Jiang Jingguo later alleged that on this occasion, Stalin admitted that Soviet control of Outer Mongolia was a preventive measure against Japan or a "third power." Stalin did not deny that this "third power" might be the United States. Jiang Jingguo's allegation cannot be verified by other sources. See Jiang Jingguo, *Fuzhong Zhiyuan* (A Long Journey with a Heavy Burden) (Taipei: Youshi Shudian, 1960), 64–67.

on its postwar independence in exchange for Soviet respect for Chinese sovereignty in Manchuria would not be a bad deal. After further consultation with some senior figures of the KMT party, Chiang finally made up his mind. In his own words, a compromise of mere "formality" (China's nominal sovereignty over Outer Mongolia) was worthwhile if it could save China from "national calamities" (Communist rebellion supported by the Soviet Union).[7]

While leaders in Chongqing were reaching a decision on relinquishing China's sovereignty over Outer Mongolia, in Moscow T. V. Soong also sought support from Ambassador Harriman, who remained in the Soviet capital. Ambassador Harriman's attitude regarding the Mongolia issue was at best apologetic. He told Soong that at Yalta, President Roosevelt had never considered the question and had not known of China's negative stand on Mongolian independence. Meanwhile, Stalin's interpretation of the Yalta agreement on Dalian and the railroads caused Harriman serious concern.[8] In reality, the American policy toward Mongolia was not as innocent as Harriman was intimating. Indeed, Outer Mongolia did not feature in the State Department's agenda for the Yalta Conference, but President Roosevelt had been aware of the State Department's stand on the issue. In the spring of 1944, in an effort to arouse President Roosevelt's wariness toward the Russians, Chiang Kai-shek called his attention to a recent event in Xinjiang, where Chinese troops had allegedly been attacked by Soviet airplanes based in Outer Mongolia. At the time, Roosevelt was concerned about the deterioration of the Chinese–Soviet relationship and intended to "be a little bit more definite with Chiang," meaning to give him some reassurance. But the State Department advised against such a response. Secretary Hull advised the president that the Soviet government held a dual policy both recognizing Chinese sovereignty over Outer Mongolia and treating that area as an independent state. In Hull's opinion, the U.S. government should not become entangled in the dispute between China and the Soviets. As a result, Roosevelt's response was to ask Chiang ambiguously to place the matter "on ice until the end of the war . . . without anyone abandoning any sovereignty or right."[9] In fact, the planning staff of the State Department had long believed that if the U.S. government had to take a stand on the issue publicly, it should support Mongolian independence. At Yalta, Secretary of State Stettinius had also interpreted President Roosevelt's acceptance of the status quo of

[7] "Haisang ji," 3: 5–7, *HSP*, box 2; Wang Shijie, *Wang Shijie Riji* (The Diaries of Wang Shijie) (Taipei: Zhongyang Yenjiuyuan Jindaishi Yenjiusuo, 1990), 5: 117–118; Garver, *Chinese–Soviet Relations*, 218.

[8] Soong to Chiang, 3 July 1945, *ZZSC*, 3 (2): 591.

[9] "Political Memoranda for the Yalta Conference, Feb. 45: China," *HHP*, box 169–171; *CSYZ*, 37: 277; Roosevelt to Hull, 7 April 1944, Hull to Roosevelt, 7 April 1944, and Roosevelt to Chiang, 8 April 1944, *RPMF*, box 10.

Outer Mongolia as an acquiescence in the continuance of Soviet actual control.[10]

Now, after receiving Harriman's account of his conversation with Soong, President Truman and his Secretary of State, James F. Byrnes, instructed the ambassador that the American government did not want to interfere with the Moscow negotiations by providing an official interpretation of the Yalta agreement. But he could "informally" advise Soong that America's view on the Yalta provision regarding the status quo of Outer Mongolia recognized China's practically unexecuted de jure sovereignty. Evasive on the Mongolia issue, Truman and Byrnes shared Harriman's concern about Soviet intentions in Manchuria. They instructed Harriman to choose an appropriate time to ask the Moscow conferees to include in their final agreement the equal right of all peace-loving nations to use the port facilities of Dalian and to participate in the transportation privileges on the railroads.[11] Thus, in the changed atmosphere of the inter-Allied relationship, Roosevelt's still optimistic "Manchurian triangle" was inconspicuously superseded by the traditional open door policy. During the Sino–Soviet negotiations, Washington would continue to adhere to this stand. It should be remembered that not long before, on the eve of the Yalta Conference, the State Department had argued for abandoning the open door as an anachronism. But President Roosevelt's cavalier handling of China's interests at that conference, and the changed atmosphere between the United States and the Soviet Union on the eve of peace, led Roosevelt's successor to refurbish that antique.

On 6 July, Chiang's instructions arrived in Moscow. Chiang made it clear that China's future hinged on the Mongolia and Manchuria questions, but in different senses. Soong was instructed to insist on China's full sovereignty in Manchuria. Otherwise, he was authorized to make a concession to the Soviet demand regarding Mongolia, provided that the concession induced the Soviets to support Chongqing's position with regard to Manchuria, Xinjiang, and the CCP. Soong was dubious that Chongqing's goal of *full* sovereignty in Manchuria would be attainable even with the sacrifice of Outer Mongolia. He immediately asked Chongqing whether some flexibility on Manchuria could be allowed. The next day, Chiang sent two more dispatches to Soong, ordering him not to go further than the "maximum sacrifice" regarding Outer Mongolia and to break off the negotiations in the face of Soviet intransigence.[12] Apparently, Chiang

---

[10] CAC-297, 23 October 1944, *RHN*, box 115; Thomas M. Campbell and George C. Herring, Jr., *The Diaries of Edward R. Stettinius, 1943–1946* (New York: New Viewpoints, 1975), 225.

[11] Harry S. Truman, *Memoirs by Harry S. Truman* (New York: Doubleday, 1955), 1: 350–353.

[12] Two cables from Chiang to Soong, 6 July 1945, Soong to Chiang, 6 July 1945, and two cables from Chiang to Soong, 7 July 1945, ZZSC, 3(2): 593–597.

264 *A partnership for disorder*

Kai-shek also began to doubt that reconciliation with the Russians was attainable at a reasonable price.

When the Chinese and the Russians met again late in the evening of 7 July, Soong tried once again to reason with Stalin before making a deal over Outer Mongolia. He argued that the Soviet scheme for the territory was not in concert with the Yalta agreement. Unfortunately, since China had not been a party to the Yalta Conference, Soong was unable to talk about the "real" meaning of that agreement as authoritatively as Stalin. Then Soong had to change to another line, contending that by giving up such a large territory, the KMT regime would collapse under the pressure of internal opposition. Stalin was not moved. He reassured Soong that even the CCP would not be able to overthrow the central government if the latter concluded an alliance with the Soviet Union. The two sides parted coldly that night, and the future of the conference seemed in serious doubt.[13]

The impasse over Outer Mongolia ended two days later due to Chiang's change of mind on Soong's request for a more flexible stand in Manchuria. Now Chiang agreed to qualify China's full sovereignty over Manchuria by accepting Soviet practical control of Port Arthur as a naval base and additional Russian responsibility for the management of the Chinese Eastern Railroad.[14] When the new instructions arrived in Moscow, Soong gained some confidence in Chiang's quid pro quo formula involving the sacrifice of Outer Mongolia. At the same time, Harriman convinced Soong that the American government could do little for the Chinese in their negotiations with the Russians. According to Harriman, America's own intention to occupy islands in the vicinity of Japan prevented Washington from helping China resist the Soviet demand for control of Port Arthur. He also suggested that China might be well advised to allow the Russians to participate in the administration of Dalian and the railroads. Offering a piece of general advice, Harriman exhorted Soong that no permanent solution should be sought with the Russians, and that the current task of the Chinese government was to establish a compromise with Moscow as a legal restraint on Soviet influence in Manchuria.[15]

These developments convinced Soong that further stumbling over Outer Mongolia would not greatly improve his bargaining position. When he resumed his nocturnal discussions with Stalin on 9 July, Soong decided to make some progress with the Russians. Soong presented Chiang's "sacrifice" of Outer Mongolia to Stalin, in Soong's words, "on the altar of perpetual friendship between China and the U.S.S.R." In return, the Chinese asked the Soviet leaders to support their stand on several issues: (1)

[13] "Moscow Notes," 7 July 1945, *VHP*, box 2.
[14] Two cables from Chiang to Soong, 8 and 9 July 1945, *ZZSC*, 3(2): 605, 606–607.
[15] Soong to Chiang, 9 July 1945, ibid., 608–609.

Sino–Soviet joint use of Port Arthur; (2) Dalian as an open port; (3) Chinese ownership but Sino–Soviet joint operation of the Manchurian railroads; (4) Sino–Soviet cooperation in eliminating trouble in Xinjiang; (5) Soviet moral and material support only to the central government vis-à-vis the CCP; and (6) Mongolian independence achieved through a plebiscite and China's recognition only after the defeat of Japan. If Stalin was pleased that he had prevailed over the Chinese, he did not betray a sign. He did not give Soong any reason to believe that China's sacrifice of Outer Mongolia would oblige the Soviet government to make any reciprocal gestures. As a face-saving gesture to Chongqing, Stalin agreed to delay the final settlement of the Mongolia issue until the end of the war. But he would not satisfy Soong's other demands so easily. Even the Mongolia question was not closed. Soong conveyed Chiang's desire that the "area of Outer Mongolia should conform [to the] former area set out in our maps," but when pressed by Stalin, Soong admitted that the Chinese delegation was not equipped with such a Chinese map.[16] The door for further disagreement was thus left open.

Chiang's quid pro quo formula gave up Outer Mongolia but obtained no clear advantages in the other matters. Stalin had no objection to China's full sovereignty in Manchuria as long as Russian control of Port Arthur and Sino–Soviet "joint possession" of the railroads could be secured. With regard to the CCP issue and the Xinjiang question, Stalin remained evasive. When Soong pleaded for Soviet help in resolving the Communist problem in China, Stalin asked almost playfully: "You want us to disarm [the] communists?" Then he praised the CCP as "good patriots" and suggested that the KMT regime find a political solution to the CCP issue. This attitude confirmed Soong's earlier apprehension that Patrick Hurley had misinformed Chongqing about the Soviet Union's unconditional support of the KMT in China's internal politics. Regarding Chongqing's concern about the rebellious situation in Xinjiang, Stalin advised Soong that the Chinese government should grant "rights" to the indigenous ethnic groups. Otherwise, he rejected Soong's allegation that the rebels in Xinjiang were using weapons smuggled in from the Soviet Union.[17]

Despite the vast distance remaining between the two sides, after the 9 July session T. V. Soong sent an optimistic report to Chiang Kai-shek. Asserting that "the major issues had been approximately settled," Soong nevertheless asked Chiang to allow him more latitude to maneuver with

---

[16] "Moscow Notes," 9 July 1945, *VHP*, box 2.

[17] Ibid.; Soong to Chiang, 1 July 1945, *ZZSC*, 3(2): 575. In November 1944, an "East Turkestan Republic" was established in Xinjiang to challenge the KMT government. See Linda Benson, *The Ili Rebellion: The Moslem Challenge to Chinese Authority in Xinjiang, 1944–1949* (Armonk, NY: M. E. Sharpe, 1990).

the Russians, especially concerning Dalian and the railroads.[18] It was at this moment that Ambassador Harriman became concerned about Soong's judgment. In Harriman's view, he seemed easily satisfied by Stalin's vow of Soviet support for Chongqing's sovereignty in Manchuria and appeared willing to make excessive concessions there, regardless of America's open door doctrine. In fact, Soong expressed optimism about the results of the 9 July session only to conceal his apprehension that the negotiations with the Russians could not be concluded before the Potsdam Conference. Fearing that Potsdam might become a second Yalta, Soong wanted to convince both Chongqing and the Americans that he was on the verge of success and that he only needed a little more freedom of action to wind up his business in Moscow.[19]

Negotiations during the next three days proved that Soong's goal was unattainable. In these discussions the Mongolian question no longer constituted the overwhelming obstacle, mainly because Soong overlooked Chiang's demand that the Chinese–Mongolian border be clearly defined prior to China's agreement to the independence of Outer Mongolia. He simply accepted Stalin's suggestion not to include the border question in their discussion. As for concrete arrangements for the railroads, Port Arthur, and Dalian, despite Soong's statement that a final agreement was close, the difficulties seemed insurmountable. No longer insisting on Soviet ownership of the railroads, the Russians refused to accept any solution short of having the predominant position in the management of the Chinese Eastern Railway and the South Manchurian Railway. The Russians also raised new issues concerning branch lines and auxiliary enterprises. In the two ports, the Russians demanded clear and direct control, disregarding the Chinese formulas for a joint military commission in Port Arthur and for a commercial arrangement favorable to Russia in Dalian, which Chongqing believed would both serve Russia's practical needs and maintain the image of the Chinese government as the sovereign authority. Another deadlock was thus reached. Stalin could no longer delay his journey to Potsdam, and Soong also intended to use the interval to return to Chongqing for further instructions. In order to keep the door open for further negotiations, the conferees agreed not to reveal the impasse to the outside world.[20]

Interestingly, Stalin was emphatic that the content of the Moscow negotiations must not be leaked to Yan'an, saying that according to his information, Sun Ke was conducting "very bad" communications with the CCP regarding the negotiations. Stalin's admonition is indicative of the

[18] Soong to Chiang, 9 July 1945, ZZSC, 3(2): 609–610.
[19] Ibid.; W. Averell Harriman and Elie Abel, *Special Envoy to Churchill and Stalin, 1941–1946* (New York: Random House, 1975), 483.
[20] "Moscow Notes," 10, 11, and 12 July 1945, VHP, box 2; Chiang to Soong, 11 July 1945, and Soong to Chiang, 11 July 1945, ZZSC, 3(2): 621–622.

state of his relations with the CCP. Not only was there at the time no policy coordination between Yan'an and Moscow, but Stalin apparently feared Yan'an's unfavorable reaction to the Moscow negotiations. The CCP's criticism of the KMT's concessions at Moscow might either have forced Chongqing to harden its stand in the negotiations or prompted Chiang to forge a united front with Yan'an in dealing with the Russians. Stalin was not disposed to deal with either situation. Up to this point, Stalin had benefited from the KMT–CCP antagonism, and he intended to retain that advantage. But Stalin's concern proved to be unnecessary. As mentioned before, Chongqing had never seriously considered the alternative of uniting with the CCP in dealing with the Soviets.[21]

Potsdam interlude: diplomacy of ambiguity

The Potsdam Conference dealt with many subjects, but its significance to Sino–Soviet negotiations was not well known at the time. The legal basis for American interference in the Moscow deadlock was the Yalta agreement. But after the first round of the Moscow negotiations ended, the relationship between the Yalta accord and the Soong–Stalin negotiations became blurred. The Russians successively added new items to their list of demands, using the Yalta agreement to support their demands only when this was convenient. Not present at Yalta and not even provided with an official interpretation of the Yalta accord by the American government, the Chinese did not find much advantage in citing the Big Three summit. At one point, when Molotov pressed Soong for concessions over Dalian and the railroads by citing the Yalta wording for Soviet "pre-eminent interests," Soong found himself arguing: "Yalta is not sacred."[22] Now that their bilateral talks had reached a stalemate, the Chinese and the Russians thought that American influence might help their respective causes.

Before his departure for Chongqing on 14 July, T. V. Soong told Harriman that China had already made "maximum concessions" and that his hope now lay in President Truman's ability to persuade Stalin to accept the Chinese position. In fact, Soong made Truman's interference on China's behalf a precondition for his return to Moscow. At the same time in Chongqing, Chiang Kai-shek also pleaded for help from President Truman. In a message, Chiang informed Truman that China had not only gone to the limit in trying to accommodate the Yalta formula, but had already gone beyond it on the Mongolian issue. Chiang asked the president to impress on Stalin China's reasonable stand so that the Soviet leader would no longer insist on further Chinese concessions. Meanwhile, he told Soviet Ambassador Petrov that China's "independent foreign policy" would not

---

[21] "Moscow Notes," 12 July 1945, *VHP*, box 2.
[22] "Moscow Notes," 10 July 1945, ibid.

be affected by any decisions concerning China that might be made at Potsdam.[23]

At the time, there was some opinion within the American government in favor of active U.S. interference in the Moscow stalemate. On 13 July, at the suggestion of Harriman, Under Secretary of State Joseph Grew sent to James F. Byrnes, the new Secretary of State who was accompanying President Truman to Berlin aboard the U.S.S. *Augusta*, a memorandum entitled "Interpretation of the Yalta Agreement." The document suggested a policy very close to Chiang Kai-shek's quid pro quo formula. It supported Chinese recognition of Mongolian independence in return for Soviet support of the KMT regime's control over Manchuria and Inner Mongolia, believing that only American diplomatic action, in the form of official clarification of the American commitment in the Yalta agreement, could prevent the Russians from achieving predominant control over Dalian and the Manchurian railroads.[24] During the Potsdam Conference, this policy was argued forcefully by John Carter Vincent, who was then chief of the Division of China Affairs and a member of the American delegation. Between 17 and 19 July, he produced four memoranda reviewing in detail the status of the Sino–Soviet negotiations. Vincent believed that at Moscow "a bargain is being made on the basis of a bargain made at Yalta" and that the Moscow discussion as it stood constituted "in the main retrogress." The Moscow negotiations were being used by the Soviet leaders to lay the foundation for a Russian sphere of influence in Manchuria and were thus endangering important American interests in Northeast Asia. Due to its commitment to the Yalta agreement, Vincent pointed out, the U.S. government could be neither completely negative nor indifferent to the Sino–Soviet talks. Vincent's advice was for the U.S. government to support the current Chinese stand in Moscow and prevent the situation from worsening. The American government should also adopt a long-term perspective on the Yalta agreement and the Sino–Soviet treaty in the making, both of which should be viewed as expedients to be liquidated as soon as conditions permitted.[25]

But Vincent did not recommend transforming the bilateral talks in Moscow into a tripartite bargaining process including the Americans. On 23 July he devised a draft protocol as the instrument of American interference, which could be included in the final documents of the Potsdam Conference to curb the Russians in Manchuria. Accordingly, the Soviet

---

[23] Two cables from Harriman to Truman and Byrnes, 12 and 13 July 1945, *FRUS: Berlin*, 1: 862–864; Hurley to Byrnes and Harriman, 19 July 1945, and Hurley to Truman and Byrnes, 20 July 1945, ibid., 2: 1224–1227; Harriman memorandum on the Soong–Stalin talks, 18 July 1945, ibid., 2: 1239; minutes of Chiang–Petrov conversation, 19 July 1945, ZZSC, 3(2): 639.

[24] Grew to Byrnes, 13 July 1945, *FRUS: Berlin*, 1: 864–872.

[25] Russell to Byrnes, 20 July 1945, and attachment 1, ibid., 2: 1227–1237.

Union should grant full recognition to the "sovereignty of the Government of China in Manchuria." Then both the Chinese and Soviet governments should pledge to adhere to "the principle of equality of opportunity which underlies the historic 'open door' policy," ensuring the accessibility of Dalian and the Manchurian railroads to all interested nations. Vincent believed that such a document could help the Chinese in Moscow: "The Chinese are in no position to bargain . . . [and] our interpretation of the Yalta commitments is for them controlling." At Potsdam, Vincent had the support of Ambassador Harriman and Secretary of War Stimson, who also urged President Truman to clarify with Stalin America's attitude toward the Manchurian question.[26]

Although also concerned with the Russians' aggressive attitude toward the Manchurian question, President Truman and Secretary Byrnes did not seem to share the view that the predicament of the Sino–Soviet talks warranted active interference by the American government. When Truman and Stalin first met on 17 July, the Soviet leader briefed the Americans about the status of the Moscow negotiations. He reassured the president that the Soviet government would respect Chiang Kai-shek's government as the sole sovereign authority in Manchuria. He also insisted that the Soviet demand for pre-eminent interests with regard to the railroads and Dalian was in no sense contradictory to the American desire for Dalian as a free port or to American interests in the railroads. Truman seemed satisfied with this pledge and remarked: "It would then follow the Open Door policy." Secretary Byrnes wanted to hear from Stalin that arrangements in Manchuria would be in strict accordance with the Yalta agreement. To this Stalin responded by asserting that actually the Soviet stand in the Moscow negotiations had been more liberal or less demanding than at Yalta. He put the blame for the obstacles in the Moscow negotiations completely on the Chinese government, saying: "Chongqing did not understand horse trading; they were very slow and tried to wangle every little thing. They did not seem to be aware of the big picture." Truman and Byrnes did not comment on the Chinese–Soviet differences but merely reiterated that America's dominant interest lay in Dalian as a free port. That closed the discussion of the Sino–Soviet negotiations, and the subject would not be mentioned again during the Potsdam Conference.[27]

Truman's satisfaction with the Moscow negotiations is shown in a letter to his wife on the day after his meeting with Stalin: "[A] start has been made and I've gotten what I came for – Stalin goes to war August 15 with no strings on it. He wanted a Chinese settlement – and it is practically

---

[26] Vincent to Dunn, 23 July 1945, ibid., 2: 1241–1243; Harriman to Byrnes, 28 July 1945, ibid., 2: 1243–1244; Stimson to Truman, 16 July 1945, ibid., 2: 1223–1224.

[27] Bohlen notes of Truman–Stalin meeting, 12 July 1945, ibid., 1: 43–47; Bohlen memorandum on Truman–Stalin meeting of 17 July 1945, 28 March 1960, ibid., 2: 1585–1587.

made – in a better form than I expected. Soong did better than I asked him." After his meeting with Stalin, Truman also told Stimson that he had just "clinched the Open Door in Manchuria."[28] Yet, what still worried Truman was the attitude of Chongqing. According to Admiral Leahy's recollection, when Truman and Byrnes told him about their meeting with Stalin, they felt that without further radical concessions by the Chinese government, a Sino–Soviet agreement could not be reached. In that case, Stalin would enter the Pacific war to satisfy Soviet demands and ignore Chongqing's disposition completely.[29]

Vincent's resorting to the open door device at Potsdam was a remarkable retreat from the State Department's advice to President Roosevelt before Yalta against relying on the prewar norms of U.S. policy in China. Although they now saw no better means than the old device for securing America's interests in Manchuria, China specialists in the State Department also realized that, as in the 1930s, the open door policy would not work in Manchuria if the American government failed to lend meaningful support to the Chinese government. Yet their recommendation for revitalizing the open door approach was only partially accepted by Truman and Byrnes, the latter enjoying Truman's trust "implicitly" but carrying "the State Department on his cuff" at Potsdam.[30] The Truman–Byrnes team mentioned the open door principle to Stalin and then came away satisfied with the Soviet leader's oral endorsement. But they ignored Vincent's warning that "the Chinese are in no position to bargain" with the Russians and that therefore the open door principle could only be substantiated by a strong American stand.

On 23 July, President Truman approved a telegram to Chiang Kai-shek drafted by Secretary Byrnes, replying to Chiang's message of 20 July that pleaded for American support in the Sino–Soviet negotiations. The telegram was straightforward:

> I asked that you carry out the Yalta agreement but I had not asked that you make any concession in excess of that agreement. If you and Generalissimo Stalin differ as to the correct interpretation of the Yalta agreement, I hope you will arrange for Soong to return to Moscow and continue your efforts to reach complete understanding.[31]

The first sentence seemed to disapprove of Chongqing's relinquishing Outer Mongolia and to caution against any further concessions. But then, since

[28] Robert H. Ferrell, ed., *Dear Bess: The Letters from Harry to Bess Truman, 1910–1959* (New York: W. W. Norton, 1983), 519; entry of 17 July 1945, *HSD*, 52 (reel 9): 23.
[29] Entry of 17 July 1945, "William D. Leahy Diaries," 109, William D. Leahy Papers (microfilm), reel 4.
[30] Ferrell, *Off the Record: The Private Papers of Harry S. Truman* (New York: Penguin, 1980), 348; "Reminiscences of Joseph Ballantine," 17, Ballantine Papers, box 3.
[31] Truman to Hurley, 23 July 1945, *FRUS: Berlin*, 2: 1241.

no American support was offered for the Chinese stand in the negotiations, the demand for the KMT regime to reach a "complete understanding" with the Russians could only have the effect of pressing Chongqing to make further concessions.

It is not surprising that afterward Truman and Byrnes interpreted differently the meaning of this contradictory message. After despatching the cable, Byrnes told British Prime Minister Winston Churchill that he had just advised the Chinese "not to give way on any point to the Russians, but return to Moscow and keep on negotiating pending further developments." By "pending future developments," Byrnes implied that an American ultimatum to, or atomic bombing of, Japan might result in an early Japanese surrender and thus prevent Russian entry into Manchuria. Churchill inferred accordingly that the Americans were no longer eager to have Russian participation in the war against Japan.[32] In his memoirs, Byrnes suggests that both President Truman and he himself were motivated by a fear of immediate Soviet entry into the Pacific war as a result of Chinese refusal to resume the negotiations in Moscow.[33] Yet, if Byrnes really intended to ask the Chinese to resist Soviet pressure, he failed completely to understand the situation that Chongqing was facing: without American assistance to modify the Soviet demands, the Chinese government would have to make a choice between capitulation in Moscow and withdrawal from the negotiations.

But afterward, President Truman insisted that at Potsdam he still viewed a Sino–Soviet agreement as the precondition for Soviet participation in the war against Japan. In January 1946, President Truman wrote a memorandum to Byrnes, pointing out: "At the time [of Potsdam] we were anxious for Russian entry into the Japanese War." In his memoirs, Truman also states: "As our forces in the Pacific were pushing ahead, paying a heavy toll in lives, the urgency of getting Russia into the war became more compelling.... That was one of the compelling reasons that would take me out of the country to a meeting with Stalin and Churchill. And this is why we were urging the Chinese and the Russians to conclude an accord on the basis of the Roosevelt, Churchill and Stalin agreement at Yalta."[34]

Perhaps both Byrnes and Truman were telling the truth about their own intentions at Potsdam. If this is the case, the lack of full discussion and

[32] Byrnes–Churchill conversation, 23 July 1945, ibid., 276; Michael Schaller, *The U.S. Crusade in China, 1938–1945* (New York: Columbia University Press, 1979), 256; Martin J. Sherwin, *A World Destroyed; the Atomic Bomb and the Grand Alliance* (New York: Knopf, 1975), 227.

[33] James F. Byrnes, *Speaking Frankly* (New York: Harper, 1947), 205; Byrnes, *All in One Lifetime* (New York: Harper, 1958), 290–291.

[34] Herbert Feis, *The China Tangle: The American Effort in China from Pearl Harbor to the Marshall Mission* (Princeton, NJ: Princeton University Press, 1953), 325; Truman, *Memoirs*, 1: 349.

common understanding of the Sino–Soviet talks between the president and his Secretary of State is remarkable. Their difference may have reflected the hesitation of American policy on the issue of Soviet belligerency in the Pacific war at the time of the Potsdam Conference. Although the deteriorating relationship between the Western Allies and Russia in Europe caused serious doubt within the American government as to the wisdom of supporting Soviet belligerency in the Pacific war, a negation of the Yalta understanding on this matter would involve too many uncertainties. American policymakers had to ask themselves whether the atomic bomb alone could bring about an early surrender of Japan; whether the Japanese forces in Manchuria would stop their resistance automatically once their home islands were crushed; what would be the effect on the general relationship with the Russians if the U.S. government rescinded the Yalta agreement; and whether the Russians could really be prevented from entering the war in East Asia.

When American leaders arrived in Berlin, they did not have definite answers to these questions. The policy that eventually emerged at Potsdam on Soviet belligerency in the Asian conflict was a cautious approach: as long as the war with Japan continued and the Western Allies themselves had no intention of assuming military responsibility for liquidating Japanese forces in Manchuria, American policymakers did not want to risk a rupture with the Russians by openly repudiating the Yalta accord. On the other hand, by the time of the Potsdam Conference, American policymakers were no longer as eager as they had been at Yalta to urge the Russians to enter the Pacific war.[35] Therefore, no matter how different their ideas about Soviet belligerency in Asia were, Truman and Byrnes must have agreed on one thing: they themselves must not confront Stalin with East Asian complications. Otherwise, they sent their message to Chiang Kai-shek for different purposes. The president wanted Chongqing to play out its role as prescribed by the Yalta formula and reach an agreement with the Russians. Byrnes gambled wishfully, assuming that the Chongqing regime was tough enough to withstand Soviet pressure and skillful enough to play a game of temporization in Moscow, thus arranging a slow death for the Yalta agreement.

Truman's message to Chiang had only one effect on the Chinese government. To KMT leaders it was a perfunctory, evasive, and even callous response to their plea for help. When T. V. Soong returned to Chongqing, he apparently hoped that by playing a game of procrastination with the Russians, he would give the Americans time to intervene. But now he

---

[35] Stimson to Truman, 16 July 1945, *FRUS: Berlin*, 2: 1265–1267; Leahy to Truman, 16 July 1945, ibid., 2: 1324; U.S. Department of Defense, *The Entry of the Soviet Union into the War Against Japan: Military Plans, 1941–1945* (Washington, DC: G.P.O., 1955), 91–92; Truman, *Memoirs*, 1: 444–446; Byrnes, *All in One Lifetime*, 297–298; "Oral history interview," 22, Eugene H. Dooman Papers, box 2; Walter Millis, ed., *The Forrestal Diaries* (New York: Viking, 1951), 73; Sherwin, *A World Destroyed*, 193–237.

realized that he had failed and that the Americans did not want to help Chongqing get out of the trap in Moscow. This led Soong to decide to desert his mission in order to save his own political future. After Truman's message arrived in Chongqing, Soong told Wang Shijie that he intended to resign as Foreign Minister and hoped that Wang could be his successor to finish the job in Moscow. When Chiang himself asked Wang to take Soong's place, he expressed displeasure about Soong's fear of being blamed in the future for giving up Outer Mongolia. This made Wang feel unable to evade the responsibility imposed on him. But now he became concerned about whether the concession over Outer Mongolia would be rewarded with Soviet abstinence in Manchuria.[36] Ambassador Hurley, however, was vehemently opposed to Soong's default of his duty, lest the whole negotiations be damaged. Hurley made his protest to Chiang and eventually accepted a compromise: Soong would be allowed to resign, but he must go back to Moscow with Wang Shijie, the new Foreign Minister. Reluctantly Soong agreed to go back, but he also made it clear to Wang that Wang would have to sign the final agreements with the Russians.[37]

Chiang Kai-shek had no other choice but to send his representatives back to Moscow. On 4 August, in a conversation with Ambassador Petrov, Chiang made some conciliatory remarks about his appreciation of Stalin's concern for Soviet security in Manchuria. He hoped that the Soviet government could give reciprocal consideration to China's concern with maintaining its sovereignty in the same territory. To impress the ambassador with his sincerity, Chiang expressed his wish to visit Moscow personally after the conclusion of the Sino–Soviet treaty.[38] The next day, T. V. Soong and Wang Shijie left for Moscow. Hurley reported to Byrnes that "notwithstanding Dr. Soong's personal attitude and the various precautions he has taken to avoid personal responsibility, we are convinced that the Generalissimo is demanding that an amicable agreement be reached immediately with the Soviets on the basic essentials of the Yalta decisions though not in the words of the document."[39] Byrnes thus harvested an unexpected result from his telegram drafting: the Chinese government did not take the message of 23 July as a signal for putting up further resistance in Moscow; instead, it felt compelled to pay a higher price than it was willing in order to achieve a settlement with the Soviet government.

Second round: diplomacy of military pressure

Soong and Wang arrived in Moscow in the afternoon of 7 August. Inasmuch as the plan for inviting American interference on China's behalf had

---

[36] Wang Shijie, *Wang Shijie Riji*, 5: 130–131; Garver, *Chinese–Soviet Relations*, 224.

[37] Hurley to Byrnes, 29 July 1945, *FRUS: Berlin*, 2: 1245–1246; Wang Shijie, *Wang Shijie Riji*, 5: 136.

[38] Minutes of Chiang–Petrov conversation, 4 August 1945, ZZSC, 3(2): 640–642.

[39] Hurley to Byrnes, 5 August 1945, *FRUS, 1945*, 7: 954–955.

failed, Chongqing decided to make a new concession over the Liaodong Peninsula: the Russians could establish a military zone in the region, excluding the port of Dalian and the connecting railroads.[40] But when the Chinese delegates met with Soviet leaders on the same evening, they learned that the Russians' appetite had grown during the past four weeks. Stalin agreed that the municipality of Dalian could be administered by China but insisted on a Russian supervisor for the port. Soong's argument about the integrity of China's sovereignty only invited Stalin's acid remark: "As to sovereignty of China we are going to fight and shed blood for it, what [sic] you never did." This military logic rendered the Chinese speechless. Another embarrassment for the Chinese delegation occurred when Soong presented a Chinese map of Outer Mongolia to show its identity with a map allegedly produced by the Soviets in the 1920s. Stalin suggested that the so-called Soviet map might be a copy of Japanese forgeries. Soong could neither rebut Stalin's accusation nor demand a genuine Soviet map. This performance disappointed even other members of the Chinese delegation.[41]

In other matters, Stalin showed a moderate degree of leniency. Soong suggested a formula for Port Arthur that would "entrust" the defense of that port to Russia but also allow the Chinese government theoretically to share responsibility through a joint military commission. Soong explained that this arrangement would not interfere with Soviet power at Port Arthur but could save the Chinese government from disgrace in the eyes of the Chinese people. Stalin granted this hope. For the moment, Stalin also did not challenge a Chinese "principle of parity" with regard to the two countries' responsibilities for the management of the two railroads in Manchuria. Pursuant to a special instruction from Chiang Kai-shek, Soong raised a new subject, demanding that Japanese government and private properties in Manchuria be regarded as part of Japanese reparations to China. This "war booty" question would cause serious controversy in the postwar years between the Chinese and Soviet governments. But this evening, Stalin assured Soong that "we will not wrong China," and meanwhile suggested a special discussion.[42]

After his meeting with Stalin, Soong routinely reported the contents of the discussion to Ambassador Harriman. Harriman was especially interested in the issue of war booty in Manchuria. In his report to Secretary Byrnes, Harriman mistakenly attributed the subject to Stalin, seeing it as "another case where Stalin has increased his appetite." When he spoke with Soong, Harriman was also shocked by the low morale of the frustrated Chinese and by their readiness to make further concessions to the

[40] Harriman to Byrnes, 7 August 1945, ibid., 957.
[41] "Moscow Notes," 7 August 1945, *VHP*, box 2; Soong and Wang Shijie to Chiang, 7 August 1945, *ZZSC*, 3(2): 643; *RWK*, 5(E): 879.
[42] "Moscow Notes," 7 August 1945, *VHP*, box 2; Chiang to Soong, 7 August 1945, *ZZSC*, 3(2): 642.

Russians. He felt compelled to intervene.[43] In fact, Harriman had received authorization to do so from Washington three days before. Based on Harriman's own recommendation, the interference was aimed at safeguarding American interests in Dalian as a free port and in the integrity of the open door principle in Manchuria. Compared with the general concern about Dalian expressed by President Truman and Secretary Byrnes at Potsdam, Harriman's representation would be concrete. He would ask the Moscow conferees to support definitive Chinese administration of Dalian or, as an alternative, an international management team including representatives from the Big Four.[44]

Belatedly, Truman and Byrnes came to realize that the KMT regime would be unable to hold the door open in Manchuria by itself. If at Potsdam they had still calculated their steps to avoid taking direct diplomatic action in the Sino–Soviet talks, now Harriman convinced them that a bolder stand must be taken by the American government. The sluggish progress of the Moscow negotiations also began to tax Truman's patience. He now became "not too hopeful about the renewed talks between Soong and Stalin."[45] Always seeing Soviet intervention in the Pacific war as inevitable, American policymakers in the last moment of the war finally gave up the Rooseveltian confidence that the Russians could be both contented and contained in Manchuria with a Chongqing–Moscow compromise. Washington's direct request for a definite commitment by Soviet leaders to the open door principle seemed the last resort to safeguard American interests.

Harriman talked to Stalin on 8 August. But this intervention came too late and was too measured to impress either the Russians or the Chinese. It came just two days after the Americans deployed the first atomic bomb on Hiroshima, yet the nuclear element did not seem to assist Harriman's diplomacy in any discernible way. Instead, on the same day, the Soviet government decided to send the Red Army into Manchuria, honoring Stalin's promise to Harry Hopkins made in May. Predictably, in his conversation with Harriman, Stalin denied that the Soviet scheme for Dalian would be contradictory to the free port or the open door idea. He also advised Ambassador Harriman against trusting the Chinese point of view too much. Afterward, in reporting his failure to the president, the disheartened Harriman stated that given the intransigence of the Soviet government, the United States should no longer feel obliged to support any arrangement with Moscow that would put a nominally "free" Dalian under the control of Soviet secret police.[46]

The last week before the Japanese surrender was a period of psychological

[43] Harriman to Byrnes, 8 August 1945, *FRUS, 1945*, 7: 958–959.
[44] Byrnes to Harriman, 5 August 1945, ibid., 953–956; Byrnes, *All in One Lifetime*, 304.
[45] Truman, *Memoirs*, 1: 467.
[46] Memorandum of conversation between Harriman and Stalin, 8 August 1945, *FRUS, 1945*, 7: 960–965; Harriman to Truman, 8 August 1945, ibid., 965.

testing for the Chinese as well as for the Japanese. The military presence of the Soviet Union in Manchuria brought pressure on Chongqing as much as on Tokyo. At 5:00 p.m., on 8 August, Soviet Foreign Minister Molotov, in his typically cold manner, read to Japanese Ambassador Naotake Sato the Soviet declaration of war against Japan. Two and a half hours later, Molotov read the same document to Wang Shijie and Chinese Ambassador Fu Bingchang. This time, he warmly shook hands with the Chinese. Although the atmospheres of the two occasions differed, the Chinese and the Japanese must have felt similar anguish.[47]

The next day, Wang Shijie and T. V. Soong cabled Chiang Kai-shek that due to the Soviet declaration of war against Japan, the conclusion of a treaty with the Soviet Union could no longer be delayed. They were contemplating further concessions to the Soviet demand concerning Dalian. Obviously, between the new American rhetorical effort in Moscow and the Russian military presence in Manchuria, the Chinese delegation made its judgment as to which weighed more heavily. Harriman was apprised of the Chinese intention but did not feel capable of altering it. He only told Soong that "as a matter of record," any further concessions to the Russians made by the Chinese government should no longer be interpreted as steps toward fulfilling the Yalta agreement but rather as Chongqing's own actions for "obtaining Soviet support in other directions," meaning Chiang Kai-shek's political needs at home.[48] It is interesting to note that during the first round of the Moscow negotiations and the Potsdam Conference, the Russians and the Chinese competed in using the American influence to their own advantage. Now competition began between the Russians and the Americans over who could gain greater influence on the Chinese stand in the negotiations. In both contests the Kremlin prevailed.

Before meeting with the Soviet leaders again on the evening of 10 August, the Chinese delegates heard the news broadcast of the British Broadcasting Corporation about Japan's decision to accept the Potsdam Proclamation. T. V. Soong became convinced that the treaty with the Russians must be concluded before Japan surrendered formally. Otherwise, the Chinese government would have a very difficult task in justifying to the Chinese people its concessions to the Soviet government.[49] The Russians did not have this anxiety; more to the point, they inflated their prices and made the negotiations increasingly difficult. Now Soviet leaders insisted that Dalian be included in the Soviet military zone in the Liaodong Peninsula; that Russia have definitive control over Port Arthur, without interference from a so-called joint commission; that Soviet preeminent interests

---

[47] Robert J. C. Butow, *Japan's Decision to Surrender* (Stanford, CA: Stanford University Press, 1954), 153; Soong and Wang to Chiang, 8 August 1945, *ZZSC*, 3(2): 643–644.

[48] Soong and Wang to Chiang, 9 August 1945, *ZZSC*, 3(2): 644; Harriman to Truman and Byrnes, 10 August 1945, *FRUS, 1945*, 7: 966–967.

[49] "Haisang ji," 3: 7, *HSP*, box 2; Garver, *Chinese–Soviet Relations*, 225.

in the railroads be guaranteed by Russian domination in their management; and that the "existing" Chinese–Mongolian borders be accepted according to the Soviet version. To remind the Chinese that he was holding the trump card, at one point in the discussion Stalin suddenly inserted a remark: "It's now five o'clock in [the] Far East and our troops will continue movement." By the same token, Stalin suggested making Soviet support of Chiang Kai-shek's government conditional: the projected Sino–Soviet treaty should include a clause providing for the KMT's commitment to national unity and "democratization of China." When Soong and Wang argued that such a regulation would not be "suitable," Stalin expressed doubt that the Soviet government would be able to support the KMT regime if the latter continued to beat the Communists. But Stalin was only plaguing his negotiation partners and he soon gave up the "democratization" proposal, showing that he was willing to make "concessions" even at the risk of being "cursed" by the CCP.[50]

In their report to Chiang Kai-shek, Soong and Wang proposed that a Russian chief of the Dalian port might be acceptable in exchange for Stalin's giving up his demand to include Dalian in the military zone. As for Port Arthur, the railroads, and the Mongolian border, they could not see how the differences between the two sides could be resolved unless Chiang Kai-shek was willing to make further concessions. In the next two days, the negotiations continued between Molotov and the Chinese. But without Stalin present and with no new instructions from Chongqing, the conferees did not achieve a breakthrough.[51]

In the meantime, Soong made another effort to enlist American support. On 11 August, Soong talked to Harriman and expressed his gratitude for the ambassador's earlier intervention on the issue of Dalian. Despite the fact that the Russians had raised their demand regarding Dalian, Soong asserted that the American interference "had materially assisted" the Chinese delegation. Now he asked the American government to back him up in the controversies over Mongolia, Port Arthur, and the railroads. To impress Harriman with his predicament, Soong said that at the previous day's meeting, Stalin had plainly threatened that a delay in signing the agreement would result in the CCP's marching into Manchuria. According to the Chinese minutes of that meeting, Stalin made no such threat. Soong must have been desperate to fabricate the story for Harriman. Yet Harriman was not much stirred. In his report to Washington, Harriman's concern still focused on Dalian. He did not believe the railroads were important enough to concern the American government. As for the Sino–Soviet disagreements over the Mongolian border and the joint use of Port Arthur,

---

[50] "Moscow Notes," 10 August 1945, *VHP*, box 2.
[51] Soong and Wang to Chiang, 10 August 1945, *ZZSC*, 3(2): 645; "Moscow Notes," 11 and 12 August 1945, *VHP*, box 2.

Harriman did not even care to make any comment. Aware that no assistance was forthcoming, Soong and Wang cabled Chiang again on 12 August, saying that if they did not receive any new instructions from Chongqing by the next day, they would go ahead and accept all the Russian demands and sign the treaty.[52]

For some unknown reason, from 10 to 12 August, a communication gap between Chongqing and the Chinese delegation occurred. During this period, Chiang and the Chinese delegation could not communicate with each other, and both became extremely uneasy about the situation. On the 11th and the 12th Chiang despatched three instructions successively to his envoys in Moscow, which were sent without knowledge of the meeting on 10 August. The first was sent after Chiang received President Truman's inquiry about his opinion on the procedure of the Japanese surrender. Chiang believed that the Japanese intention to surrender had changed the whole situation "drastically"; he was therefore ready to accept Soviet administration of the port of Dalian as long as it would be a free port "nominally." In this matter, Chiang indicated that Soong could take action "expediently" (*quanyi banli*) and that he himself did not want to apply control from afar. This was the first time the Chinese delegation was allowed some freedom of action. But immediately Chiang began to apply control from afar again. In his second message to Soong, Chiang qualified the earlier one, saying that the concession over Dalian must not be made unless the Russians accepted the parity principle concerning the railroads' management. In the third instruction, addressed to both Soong and Wang, Chiang adopted an intransigent stand on the issue of the Mongolian boundary. If the Russians continued to refuse to work with the Chinese delegation to define the Chinese–Mongolian boundary, Chiang predicted, China's recognition of Mongolian independence would only create further troubles in the future. In that case, Chiang commanded his envoys, the Chinese delegation should not hesitate to break off the negotiations.[53] The latter two telegrams proved to be Chiang's last stand against a complete capitulation at Moscow, a stand he would not maintain for long.

After agreeing to renounce China's sovereignty over Outer Mongolia, why did Chiang Kai-shek become adamant on a seemingly minor issue like the Mongolian border? The Chinese–Soviet disagreement in this matter involved a region called Altai between Xinjiang and Outer Mongolia. From the beginning of the Moscow negotiations, Chiang had insisted that the Altai region be regarded as part of Xinjiang.[54] The background of this attitude was a continual ethnic disturbance in Xinjiang involving the

---

[52] Harriman to Truman and Byrnes, 11 August 1945, *FRUS, 1945*, 7: 967–969; "Moscow Notes," 10 August 1945, VHP, box 2; Soong and Wang to Chiang, 12 August 1945, ZZSC, 3(2): 648.

[53] Four cables from Chiang to Soong, 11 and 12 August 1945, ZZSC, 3(2): 646–648.

[54] Chiang to Soong, 7 July 1945, ibid., 2: 596.

Kazakhs, who had their bases in the Altai region. In 1944 there had been
a riot in Xinjiang, followed by a dispute between Chongqing and the
Soviet–Mongolian alliance on whether the Altai region was a Chinese
territory in which Chinese troops could conduct pacification operations.
Therefore, to Chiang Kai-shek, what was at stake was not merely China's
ownership of the Altai region of some 83,000 square miles, but also China's
right to maintain order in Xinjiang without Soviet interference.[55]

But this concern alone did not fully explain Chiang's willingness to
break off the Moscow negotiations and to risk allowing Soviet troops'
entry into Manchuria without any treaty restriction. Chiang's momentary
toughness was also based on a presumed improvement in Chongqing's
military position due to the Japanese decision to surrender. On 11 August,
the KMT Central Committee and the Supreme Council of National Defense
approved a resolution to implement a comprehensive program for receiving the Japanese surrender in China. A corollary to the resolution was
Chiang's order issued on the same day to the government's "underground
army" – the Chinese puppet troops in the Japanese areas. In the order
Chiang commanded these forces to assume responsibility for maintaining
order in their own regions. A wartime rumor seemed to be confirmed that
earlier, the KMT government had purposely allowed a large number of its
troops to become Japan's puppet forces in order to preserve them for use
at the war's end. After reconverting these troops into a loyal force, Chiang
Kai-shek might feel in touch with North China again.[56]

A more important factor enhancing Chiang's morale was his success in
committing the Americans to helping him reoccupy North China and
Manchuria. In the first few days of August, Chiang's and General Wedemeyer's staffs worked closely on a plan for deploying government forces
to take control of key points in these areas. General Wedemeyer was no
less concerned than Chiang with preventing the CCP from entering these
areas. On 11 August, Chiang requested Wedemeyer to despatch some
American units to land on the southern and northern Chinese coasts. He
demanded that the United States continue its assistance to his regime "at
least until Japan has complied to the Potsdam proclamation in its application not only to the Japanese Archipelago but to all of China." Wedemeyer
agreed. Two days later, Wedemeyer reassured Chiang that his plan in
China was to "make certain that Chinese and American forces and resources
are disposed to insure a strong unified Central Government." Delighted,

[55] Henry Wei, *China and Soviet Russia* (Princeton, NJ: Van Nostrand, 1956), 158–159; Garver, *Chinese–Soviet Relations*, 226; David J. Dallin, *Soviet Russia and the Far East* (New Haven, CT: Yale University Press, 1948), 364–365.
[56] Joint resolution by the standing council of the KMT Central Committee and the Supreme Council of National Defense, 11 August 1945, ZZSC, 7(4): 9–10; CSYZ, 37: 308; Joseph W. Esherick, ed., *Lost Chance in China: The World War II Despatches of John W. Service* (New York: Random House, 1974), 49–56.

Chiang called this plan "the plan for the joint American–Chinese acceptance of the capitulation of Japan."[57] Along with the other developments
mentioned before, General Wedemeyer's promise of support helped convince Chiang that he was now in a better position to deal with the Communists even without an understanding with Moscow.

Chiang's momentary confidence was paralleled by a drastic yet short-
lived reorientation in Washington's military planning with regard to
Manchuria. On 10 August, irritated by Stalin's ever-increasing demands in
his talks with the Chinese, Ambassador Harriman recommended to President Truman that American troops be landed at Dalian and Korea if
Japan surrendered before Soviet occupation of these areas.[58] This led to an
urgent assignment for the Joint War Plans Committee of the Joint Chiefs
of Staff (JWPC). According to the JWPC, the proposed landings in Dalian
and Korea would involve important changes of an earlier Joint Chiefs
policy. The earlier plan for American troops' landings on the Asian mainland assigned the highest priority to Shanghai, followed by Pushan in Korea
and some port cities in southern Manchuria. The plan was aimed at facilitating swift and direct aid to the KMT regime in South China and assumed
that Manchuria would be principally a Soviet responsibility. Now this
order of priority had to be reversed in preparation for the race for Dalian.
Dalian would be captured first; and then American troops would need to
secure the Beiping (Beijing)–Tianjin area to "complement our advanced
position at Dairen." Shanghai consequently lost its prominence in the new
plan. The JWPC proposed that two American Marine divisions be shipped
from Okinawa and Guam on 22 August and land in Dalian on 30 August.
Thus, after Harriman's diplomatic representation failed to impress Stalin,
the American policy in Northeast Asia was theoretically heading toward
military containment. But it was too late for the American government to
change its Pacific strategy against Japan and too early to start a cold war
against the Soviet Union in Asia. The swift progress of the Soviet Red
Army in Manchuria overtook the Joint Chiefs' timetable. On 30 August,
the projected date for the Marines' landing in Dalian, the Joint Chiefs
cancelled the landing.[59]

The new direction of Washington's military policy had no impact on
the Moscow negotiations. Soong and his colleagues had no way of knowing the secret military planning in Washington, and therefore they had no
reason to stiffen their stand in their negotiations with the Russians. They
were also puzzled and disturbed by Chiang Kai-shek's sudden unyielding

---

[57] Schaller, *U.S. Crusade in China*, 263–264; Wedemeyer to Marshall, 11 August 1945,
RCT, box 1539; minutes of [American–Chinese] combined staff meetings, no. 17, 13
August 1945, ibid., box 1550.

[58] Harriman to Truman, 10 August 1945, *FRUS, 1945*, 7: 967.

[59] SWNCC 67: JCS SM-3149, 30 August 1945, *SWNCCF*, reel 9; Louis Allen, *The End of
the War in Asia* (London: Hart-Davis, MacGibbon, 1976), 162–166, 193–200.

attitude in his latest instruction. Before receiving Chiang's instruction on 12 August, the Chinese delegation had scheduled a final session with Stalin that night. But now they had to cancel the appointment and became engaged in a vehement dispute among themselves. T. V. Soong and Jiang Jingguo argued for acceding to Soviet demands and signing the treaty and other agreements. Wang Shijie and Xiong Shihui, both of whom joined in the delegation during the second round of the negotiations, insisted that no action should be taken without giving another explanation to Chiang Kai-shek. For the moment, Soong conceded. He and Wang together despatched a telegram to Chiang, trying to convince him that the Russians seemed to have no intention of using the issue of the Mongolian border to create trouble in the future. They pleaded:

> We and our colleagues here unanimously believe it necessary to conclude the Sino–Soviet treaty. Any further delay may cause unexpected developments. We earnestly request your swift decision and hope to be authorized to dispose the Mongolian and other undecided issues expediently.[60]

The next day was a time of tortuous waiting by the Chinese in Moscow. Soong lost his patience again. Believing that Chiang's authorization would not come soon, Soong suggested that a choice between his and Wang's positions be made immediately by Ambassador Fu Bingchang's tossing a coin. Wang Shijie refused to handle so grave a matter in this trifling manner. However, he agreed to take the responsibility for sending one more cable that day appealing to Chiang for action. In the telegram, aside from reassuring Chiang that the Soviet leaders were sincere in their desire to improve relations with China, Wang emphasized two conditions vital to China's stability in the postwar years that could not be gained without a treaty with the Russians: (1) clarification of the Soviet–KMT relationship, which would have the effect of containing the Chinese Communists, and (2) a definite agreement that would limit Soviet influence in Manchuria and guarantee final Soviet withdrawal from that area.[61]

Wang's telegram proved unnecessary. Chiang had already changed his mind after receiving the earlier Soong–Wang message. His new instruction arrived in Moscow at 10:00 p.m. on 13 August, early enough for the Chinese delegation to arrange a midnight session with the Russians. In this

[60] "Haisang ji," 3: 7, *HSP*, box 2; Soong and Wang to Chiang, 12 August 1945, *ZZSC*, 3(2): 649.
[61] "Haisang ji," 3: 7, *HSP*, box 2; Wang to Chiang, 13 August 1945, *ZZSC*, 3(2): 650. In his postwar memoirs, Wellington Koo suggested that at Moscow, T. V. Soong wanted to play for time, but Wang Shijie was more anxious to carry out Chiang's wish to conclude a treaty with the Russians. Soong may have wanted to delay the signing during the first round in order to wait for support from Washington, but in the wake of the Soviet entry into the Pacific war, he saw no point in delaying. In the episode delineated here, Soong and Wang disagreed on their authority to take diplomatic initiatives but not on policy. See *RWK*, 5(E): 884.

one-sentence message, Chiang gave Soong and Wang what they had asked for: "With regard to Outer Mongolia and other unsettled problems, I authorize you to dispose them expediently."[62] Without solid documentation, we can only speculate how the Soong–Wang telegram persuaded Chiang to give up his intransigent stand of the previous day. Perhaps he again became uncertain about his ability to deal with the "unexpected developments" predicted by his envoys in Moscow, or perhaps he was moved by their assertion that the Russians had no evil purposes regarding his government. Chiang Kai-shek's capricious stand in the last few days of the Moscow negotiations indicated that aside from a predominant concern about enhancing its ability to deal with the CCP, the KMT regime typically lacked a well-defined position on China's sovereignty to uphold in the negotiations with the Russians.

The meeting that started at midnight on 13 August and ended at 1:30 the next morning was the last important session of the Moscow Conference. The Chinese delegation yielded to the Soviet stand on the "current boundaries" of Outer Mongolia, gave up the parity principle regarding the management of the railroads, agreed to lease the port installation of Dalian to the Soviets without charge, and accepted a Russian port master in Dalian. To console the Chinese, who were anxious to embellish the final agreements with an appearance of equality, the Soviet leaders agreed to accept a Chinese chairman for a powerless board of directors for the railroads, to desist from demanding joint ownership of the port of Dalian, and to tolerate a Chinese–Soviet joint military commission for Port Arthur that had no power to interfere with the Soviet military authority in that port. But the Russians would not let the Chinese off the hook easily. Molotov made a new demand: a financial agreement be concluded calling for Chinese payment to the Russian troops in Manchuria. He warned that unless these troops were provided with Chinese currency to buy goods, they would take what they needed. Soong and Wang pleaded for Russians' generosity to war-torn China. They also cited America as an example that gave China lend-lease aid but demanded nothing in return. To this the Russians retorted that the Americans had not liberated any Chinese town and that about 1 million Soviet troops would be engaged in liberating Manchuria by the end of the war. In the end, the two sides agreed to leave the problem for further discussion in the future.[63]

On the evening of 14 August, the formal ceremony was held for signing the Sino–Soviet Treaty of Friendship and Alliance and the other four agreements on the railroads, Dalian, Port Arthur, and the administration of Manchuria. Soong washed his hands of the outcome and did not affix his

---

[62] "Haisang ji," 3: 7, HSP, box 2; Chiang to Soong and Wang, 13 August 1945, ZZSC, 3(2): 649; Garver, *Chinese–Soviet Relations*, 227.
[63] "Moscow Notes," 13 August 1945, VHP, box 2.

name to these documents. Wang Shijie and Molotov signed the documents on behalf of their governments. Ten days later, the Chinese Legislative Yuan held an extraordinary session to decide its ratification of the treaty. At the beginning of the meeting, the representatives were told that the Supreme Council of National Defense, or Chiang Kai-shek, had already approved the results of the Moscow negotiations. Consequently, it took only two hours for the legislators to conclude their debate and reach a unanimous decision for ratification.[64]

The next day, the treaty and its supplementary agreements were made public. Despite the swift ratification of the Moscow agreements by the Legislative Yuan, Wang Shijie later had to endure a prolonged attack within the Chinese government for his signing of the treaty. At one point, the attack became so severe that Chiang Kai-shek felt obliged to take personal responsibility for the treaty at a meeting of the Standing Committee of the KMT Central Committee. After the Moscow negotiations concluded, T. V. Soong expressed to Ambassador Harriman his satisfaction with the final result of the Moscow negotiations. Soong had more reasons to congratulate himself for surviving the Moscow ordeal than for Chongqing's diplomatic performance. To save both his relations with Chiang and his name in Chinese history, Soong made the deal for Chiang with Stalin but affixed Wang Shijie's name, not his, to these humiliating agreements. The absurdity and deceptiveness of the new alliance between Chongqing and Moscow clearly resided in the fact that it was intended as a wartime alliance against Japan but was concluded only four days after Japan declared its surrender. Much as Chongqing needed the treaty for its postwar purposes, Chiang himself admitted that the treaty for Russia's "friendship and alliance" had a degrading effect on China.[65]

The Sino–Soviet treaty was a step toward the completion of a larger international system initiated earlier at Yalta. The full meaning of the agreements concluded at Moscow cannot be evaluated properly without seeing them as part of a "Yalta–Moscow system." This system dealt with three sets of problems. The first and most immediate issue was a military one: Soviet belligerency in the Pacific war. This issue had urgency at Yalta but only questionable relevance at Moscow. The Americans needed Soviet participation in the war against Japan at the beginning of 1945. But at the time of the Moscow negotiations and at the Potsdam Conference, the American policy on this matter was concerned mainly with not breaking the previous commitment to a no longer desired Soviet entry. The Russians never doubted that at an opportune time they would enter the war against

[64] Aitchen K. Wu, *China and the Soviet Union: A Study of Sino–Soviet Relations* (New York: John Day, 1950), 289–290.
[65] *RWK*, 5(E): 884; Harriman to Truman and Byrnes, 14 August 1945, *FRUS, 1945*, 7: 972; *CZM*, 13: 193.

Japan in order to enhance their strategic and economic interests in postwar East Asia. Whether the entry should take place under international agreements was only a matter of convenience. At Yalta, Soviet leaders saw the advantage of promising Soviet participation in the Pacific war to obtain the Western Allies' endorsement of their schemes for Manchuria and other Asian territories. But later, they were cynical and pragmatic enough to send troops into Manchuria without waiting for the conclusion of a Sino–Soviet treaty, which was supposed to complete the Yalta deal. The Chinese never had a chance to exert any influence in this matter. The Yalta agreement imposed the Soviet entry as an established matter on the Chinese government, and in Moscow the Chinese were only allowed to discuss with the Russians the aftermath of such a military development. Therefore, the Sino–Soviet alliance for the war against Japan was merely an awkward cover for a deal concerning the two sides' postwar interests.

The second category of problems involved the American, Soviet, and Chinese interests in Manchuria. In this respect, all three governments retreated respectively to certain points in history. At Yalta, Stalin's scheme for Manchuria had a clear precedent in tsarist policies. Consenting to the Russian demands, President Roosevelt modified his great-power China policy significantly and allowed the American policy to return to the open door era so far as Manchuria was concerned. During the Moscow negotiations, under pressure from both Moscow and Washington, the KMT regime let itself be satisfied by Moscow's abstract pledge to respect China's sovereignty in Manchuria, but in practice it capitulated to Soviet policies in Manchuria and Outer Mongolia. In doing so, the KMT leadership compromised one of its principal war aims: the recovery of China's full sovereignty in the northeast provinces and other peripheral regions.[66]

But it would be a mistake to suggest that only the Soviets gained from the Yalta–Moscow bargaining. The bargain was made over Manchuria but the deal was made for something bigger: a new equilibrium in East Asia. This was the third level of the Yalta–Moscow system, which contained the basic compromise made by the three parties concerned. It was strange that this system was completed in Asia at a time when Western–Soviet relations in Europe were collapsing. If at Yalta President Roosevelt was still committed to Big Four harmony based on readjustment of these powers' interests, the Moscow negotiations continued his work but were consummated with a very different structure. Now the United States and the Soviet Union no longer regarded each other as partners. Although the Yalta bargain on Asia was largely maintained at Moscow, the Moscow agreements became part of the new balance of power between the two competing superpowers. They gave recognition to the Soviet predominance in Northeast Asia balanced by America's control of Japan and its strong

---

[66] The text of the treaty and appendixes are in *ZZSC*, 3(2): 652–668.

political and economic influence in China. Chongqing was an unqualified player in the game of the giants, and it kept getting hurt regardless whether the two superpowers flirted with or competed against each other. Yet there was something for it as well in the Yalta–Moscow system. To Chongqing, nothing was more important than Moscow's promise, which was written into one of the Moscow agreements, that the Soviet government would offer its "moral, military, and other material assistance" only to the "Nationalist Government" of China. Moscow's pledge not to make further encroachments in Manchuria and Xinjiang was also greatly valued by the KMT regime. Thus, the Yalta–Moscow arrangements at once supplemented the Cairo decisions by completing the international endorsement of the KMT regime's right to rule China and modified those decisions by reducing China's territories and external sovereignty.

A question yet to be answered was what would be the impact of the new international system on China's domestic politics. Wellington Koo once talked about what he believed was the canon for Chinese diplomacy: "When one is engaged in important negotiations, he must concern himself only with national interests, but not with partisan or political interests, still less with personal gains or losses in politics. Otherwise, his diplomacy cannot be successful in terms of national interests."[67] During the Moscow negotiations, Chiang Kai-shek and T. V. Soong vacillated between these different concerns. This did not escape the American officials in Washington. When the Chinese and the Russians were about to conclude their talks, Secretary of State Byrnes told Ambassador Harriman: "We feel that the only compensatory advantage which the Chinese Government is being given in return for the concessions which it is asked to make is an unequivocal commitment on the part of the Soviet Government to withhold support from dissidents within China." Officials in the Office of the Far Eastern Affairs had serious doubts about this "advantage." Aside from seeing the Moscow agreements as a retreat from the spirit and letter of the Yalta accord in respect to Dalian, Port Arthur, and the Manchurian railroads, they worried about the consequence of Moscow's endorsement of the KMT regime. The concern was that afterward the KMT government might become less willing to restrain itself in dealing with the CCP and more inclined to seek a military solution of China's domestic problems.[68]

Such a thought was ironic in light of Washington's own support for the KMT. By the end of the war, the Yalta formula for East Asia had become a paradox in America's foreign policy: the consummation of the Yalta arrangement in the Moscow agreements prepared the formula's dissolution.

---

[67] Gu Weijun (Wellington Koo), *Gu Weijun Huiyilu* (Memoirs of Gu Weijun), 12 vols. (Beijing: Zhonghua Shuju, 1983–1993), 1: 397.
[68] Byrnes to Harriman, 11 August 1945, *FRUS, 1945*, 7: 969–970; Ballantine to Byrnes, 15 August 1945, ibid., 975–976.

This was not because China and the KMT regime were physically weakened by the consequences of the American–Soviet understandings concerning Chinese territories, but rather because the KMT leadership was mentally intoxicated by the Washington–Moscow pledge of diplomatic support for its rule in China.

12

Epilogue: The crisis of peace

At noon, on 15 August 1945, the Japanese people listened to Emperor Hirohito's voice over the radio announcing Japan's acceptance of the Potsdam Proclamation. Japan's military defeat was complete. Nevertheless, Tokyo's decision to surrender in mid-August fixed the timing of peace and the balance of military power in East Asia under which peace would unfold. For policymakers in Washington and Chongqing, Japan's surrender came either too late or too soon: Japan stumbled too long in the Pacific war to prevent the Soviet Red Army from pouring into Manchuria and Korea, yet its resistance against the Russians in these areas collapsed too rapidly to allow the American and Chinese military forces to play a role.

On Victory in Japan day in East Asia, while most people were intoxicated by the coming of peace, Harry Truman and Chiang Kai-shek were filled with anxieties about the future. On 14 August, after receiving the news that Emperor Hirohito had decided to surrender, President Truman talked to a cheering crowd through a loudspeaker on the north portico of the White House. Aside from hailing the triumph of the United Nations coalition over the Axis powers, the president exhorted his audience to complete the task of implementing free government in the world, referring to an "emergency . . . as great as it was on December 7, 1941."[1] Across the Pacific, Chiang Kai-shek's "victory broadcast" to the Chinese people was no more optimistic. Predicting "stupendous and difficult tasks" ahead, Chiang warned the Chinese people that "at times we may feel that the problems of peace that descend upon us are more trying even than those we met during the war."[2] Average people listening to Truman or Chiang could sense the magnitude of the monumental task of peace, but they did not necessarily

[1] *New York Times*, 15 August 1945.
[2] Chinese Ministry of Information, *The Collected Wartime Messages of Generalissimo Chiang Kai-shek, 1937–1945* (New York: John Day, 1946), 851–852.

comprehend exactly why their leaders considered the beginning of peace to be as much a crisis as the beginning of war. They did not realize that although peace was a condition of life irrefutably preferable to war, it was not always more congenial than war to their leaders' policy objectives.

Aftermath

President Roosevelt had never shared his postwar foreign policy designs with his vice-president, Harry Truman. It should not be surprising that President Truman, presiding over the execution of U.S. foreign policy in the postwar years, willing as he was to continue his predecessor's policies, had to improvise his own course. In doing so, Truman relied heavily on his advisers in the State and War departments, as well as on the Joint Chiefs of Staff.[3] But Truman also had some concerns of his own. In a letter to his wife, "dear Bess," in early 1942, Truman was up against "all that old isolation fever." His internationalism was based on power: "We must take this one [the war against the Axis powers] to its conclusion and *dictate* peace terms from Berlin and Tokyo. Then we'll have Russia and China to settle with afterwards [original emphasis]."[4] Yet Senator Truman's resolution at the beginning of the war could not be implemented by President Truman at the onset of peace. The United States was indeed in Berlin and Tokyo, but it could not dictate peace for either Europe or Asia.

At war's end, Chiang Kai-shek was a survivor. Although World War II had elevated him to the same rank as other Big Four leaders, with the arrival of peace the KMT government faced a domestic situation far worse than the one existing before the war with Japan. In August 1945, Chiang again had to deal with his old but much stronger adversary, the CCP. He resolved in his diary that the CCP issue must be "settled once and for all politically and militarily."[5] In time, however, Chiang would be overcome by his problems, not solve them.

The peace after World War II proved lukewarm, a settlement that would soon freeze into an armed truce in Europe and, even worse, flare up into new wars in Asia. To cope with the urgent task of making peace in Asia, the American and Chinese governments were equipped with a paper Yalta–Moscow system that they had pasted together with the Russians during the final months of the war. As it stood in August 1945, the Yalta–Moscow system included a continental and an oceanic segment involving, respectively, China and Japan, leaving in between an ambiguous Korean situation for which Roosevelt and Stalin had reached only an oral understanding on

---

[3] Melvyn P. Leffler, *A Preponderance of Power: National Security, the Truman Administration, and the Cold War* (Stanford, CA: Stanford University Press, 1992), 26–27.

[4] Robert H. Ferrell, ed., *Dear Bess: The Letters from Harry to Bess Truman, 1910–1959* (New York: W. W. Norton, 1983), 474.

[5] *CZM*, 14: 18.

trusteeship. The assumptions underlying that system were no different from those applying to Europe, namely, a peace settlement based on readjustment and accommodation of each others' interests among the Big Four. Yet the vacuum in the Yalta–Moscow system with regard to Korea would soon be filled by what one historian called the "first act of postwar containment," and the continental component of the system would eventually be consumed by a protracted civil war in China.[6]

It is a well-known fact that near the end of the Pacific war, the U.S. government took the initiative in dividing Korea along the 38th parallel, and Stalin acquiesced in the act. Despite its arbitrary and contentious character, the division of Korea completed the big-power arrangement for East Asia. But when the Chinese Civil War resumed, the Yalta–Moscow system also began to erode. Eventually, the flames of war would engulf the Korean Peninsula and later the Indochinese Peninsula. These new wars would eventually cause long-term, if not permanent, internal divisions of the Asian nations involved. When the 1950s arrived, only the oceanic section of the wartime inter-Allied understanding remained intact. This concerned U.S. control over Japan, Soviet annexation of the Kurile and Sakhalin islands, and Moscow's treaty-making rights involving Japan. Indeed, if the phrase "cold war" is used to characterize the postwar international history of both Europe and Asia, "cold" was for Europe but "war" was, for Asia, hot and bloody.

Even in defeat, Japan maintained its uniqueness among East Asian countries, for unlike the others, it did not suffer from serious civil violence or upheaval during the postwar years. This helps explain the exceptional success of the U.S. government's wartime foreign policy planning. America's postwar policy in Japan was officially proclaimed in the form of a "Basic Initial Post-Surrender Directive" for General Douglas MacArthur, the designated Supreme Commander of the Allied Powers for the Occupation and Control of Japan.[7] As the wartime planning indicated, the American government sought a predominant role in postwar Japan for the dual purpose of placing the former enemy under close surveillance and controlling Japan as the most important strategic territory in the western Pacific. Control of Japan at once ensured America's military and economic security in the Pacific and vindicated its newly achieved leading position in the international life of the Asian–Pacific region.

In the war years, American control of Japan had also been contemplated as a measure to counter the Soviet influence in Northeast Asia. Despite all the pious talk about international cooperation, U.S. leaders were convinced that

[6] Bruce Cumings, *The Origins of the Korean War: Liberation and the Emergence of Separate Regimes, 1945–1947* (Princeton, NJ: Princeton University Press, 1981), 117.
[7] Supreme Commander for the Allied Powers, *Political Reorientation of Japan, September 1945 to September 1948* (Washington, DC: G.P.O., 1949), 2: 423–426.

a manageable relationship with the Soviets had to be based on a balance
of power. By controlling Japan, the only industrialized country of Asia, the
United States would possess a valuable asset in either co-operation or confrontation with the Soviet Union, depending on how the U.S.–Soviet relations evolved. Conventional wisdom holds that around 1947 and 1948 the
American government softened its reform policies toward Japan in order
to meet the conditions of the cold war. But moderation had always been
advocated by most of the participants in the U.S. government's wartime
planning for Japan, though their reasoning did not bear a cold war emblem.[8]

   The KMT regime buried the hatchet with Japan sooner than its American ally. In his moody "victory broadcast" on 15 August 1945, Chiang
Kai-shek asked the Chinese people to practice the lofty virtues of "our
sages," "remembering not evil against others" but "doing good to all
men" in their attitude toward Japan.[9] Chiang Kai-shek's conciliatory attitude toward the recent enemy should be understood in the context of the
political climate confronting his government at the end of the war. To the
KMT leadership, the immediate roots of the rapprochement policy lay
within China. When the Americans were asserting their victor's preroga-
tive in occupying Japan, the KMT government had already begun to utilize
Japanese troops to stabilize conditions in China. When victory suddenly
occurred, the KMT regime was not yet ready to supplant surrendering
Japanese forces in many regions in eastern and northern China. Fearing
that the CCP would take advantage of the military weakness of his government in these areas, Chiang urged his compatriots to practice leniency
toward the former enemy in order to gain support from Japanese troops
in the already ongoing contest for territories with the CCP. The Japanese
military command in China proved responsive to Chiang's call for reconciliation. Soon after Chiang's speech, General Okamura Neiji, commander-
in-chief of the China Expeditionary Force, adopted a surrender program,
objectives of which included turning over weapons and equipment only
to the KMT in order to "contribute to the strengthening of the Central
Government's armed forces." During the civil war that ensued in China,
much to Washington's chagrin, the KMT government used tens of thousands of Japanese military and civilian personnel in its own operations.[10]

[8] Michael Schaller's *The American Occupation of Japan: The Origins of the Cold War in
   Asia* (New York: Oxford University Press, 1985) is a popular treatment of its subject. John
   W. Dower's *Empire and Aftermath: Yoshida Shigeru and the Japanese Experience, 1878–
   1954* (Cambridge, MA: Council on East Asian Studies, Harvard University, 1979) offers
   an authoritative discussion of the Japanese aspect that Schaller's study skips.
[9] *Messages of Chiang Kai-shek*, 851–852.
[10] *Gangcun Ningci Huiyilu* (Memoirs of Okamura Neiji), trans. Committee of Compilation
   and Translation of the Political Council of Tianjin (Beijing: Zhonghua Shuju, 1981), 45,
   98–99, 110–111; Donald G. Gillin and Charles Etter, "Staying On: Japanese Soldiers and
   Civilians in China, 1945–1949," *Journal of Asian Studies*, 42 (May 1983): 497–517.

In the meantime, the KMT regime dodged its responsibility for participating in the Allied occupation of Japan. After establishing his headquarters in Japan, General MacArthur urged the Chinese government to send troops to join in the occupation. The KMT leadership saw no need to rush. Not until May 1946 did the Chinese government work out some arrangements with MacArthur's headquarters for sending Chinese forces to Japan. This, however, proved a hollow gesture. Eventually, not a single Chinese soldier would cross the seas and arrive in Japan for occupation service.[11] The KMT regime had higher priorities for its troops at home.

Neither Washington nor Moscow wanted a civil war in China. Given the highly volatile political and social conditions in China at the end of the Pacific war, the leaders in Washington and Moscow still believed that the Yalta–Moscow structure could best serve their respective interests in China. For the arrangement to work, the key was to stabilize Chiang Kai-shek's government. Therefore, as the two superpowers waged a cold war in Europe, they worked along parallel lines to promote a coalition government between the KMT and the CCP in China. In Chongqing, U.S. Ambassador Patrick Hurley had worked for some time to bring the two rivals together. On 14 August 1945, the day that the KMT government signed its treaty with the Soviet government, Chiang Kai-shek seized the opportunity to send Mao Zedong an invitation for peace negotiations. Soon Stalin made his move to implement the Yalta–Moscow system. In a cable to Yan'an, Stalin exhorted: "Mao Zedong ought to negotiate with Chiang Kai-shek and seek an agreement on preserving peace in China. If a civil war breaks out, the Chinese nation will be destroyed."[12]

Yet, the chances for peace in China were slim. Mao Zedong indeed went to Chongqing in late August to discuss peace with Chiang. The negotiations lasted into October, but neither side made any meaningful concessions. At one point during the negotiations, Chiang challenged Mao either to accept his conditions or return to Yan'an to prepare for war. Mao responded: "If we fight now, I cannot beat you. But I can deal with you with the same method that I used to deal with the Japanese. You can seize [strategic] points and [transportation and communication] lines, and I shall occupy their sides and rural areas to surround cities. What do you

---

[11] The correspondence between the KMT government and the U.S. government and General MacArthur's headquarters on this matter can be found in SWNCC 70/13, 24 October 1945, SWNCC 70/17, 21 January 1946, SWNCC 70/20, 18 June 1946, and SWNCC 70/22, 10 October 1946, *SWNCCF*, reel 9.

[12] Zhonggong Chongqing Shiwei Dangshi Gongzuo Weiyuanhui, *Chongqing Tanpan Jishi* (Records of the Chongqing Negotiations) (Chongqing: Chongqing Chubanshe, 1983), 21; Sun Qiming, *Hetan, Neizhan Jiaoxiangqu–Mao Zedong he Chiang Kai-shek zai Kangzhan Shengli Chuqi* (A Symphony of Peace Negotiation and Civil War: Mao Zedong and Chiang Kai-shek during the Early Days of Victory of the War of Resistance) (Shanghai: Renmin Chubanshe, 1992), 25.

think?"[13] Later, the KMT–CCP scramble for Manchuria would unfold exactly as Mao described.

Manchuria's strategic importance could be learned from history. Three hundred years before, from Manchuria, the Manchu banner troops had launched a successful conquest of the entire Chinese territory. Then, in the 1920s, from Guangdong, the KMT and the CCP embarked north on a joint military expedition to unify China. The capture of Manchuria would have consummated the victory had the two parties' mutual antagonism not interfered with the national cause. For the failure of the northern expedition, China paid dearly in its lengthy and arduous conflict with Japan, which, following in the Manchu banner troops' footsteps, began its invasion of China from Manchuria. Therefore, when the KMT–CCP rivalry for Manchuria began in late 1945, both parties viewed the contest as a resumption of their unfinished struggle for national unification in the 1920s.[14]

But in the 1940s, the two parties' northern expeditions were against each other. The KMT's and the CCP's advances toward Manchuria took different forms that were indicative of their divergent social backgrounds. The KMT government's political and military operations for taking over Manchuria bore the regime's stamp of bureaucratic ineptitude and foreign reliance. The KMT's efforts to resume political rule in the cities of Manchuria were similar to its corrupt and unwieldy operations in the rest of China. From August 1945 to April 1946, KMT officials failed to create a single solid local government in Manchuria. Afterward, when large-scale fighting broke out in the region, the KMT's political apparatus had to flee across the Soviet border under the protection of the Soviet Red Army.[15]

The political takeover was only a prelude. Chiang Kai-shek's real hope was that the U.S. government would help transport his trusted elite troops from southern China to Manchuria in time to accomplish a military reconquest. In September 1945, when Chiang's troops destined for Manchuria were receiving smallpox immunizations and waiting for warm winter clothing to be shipped from Alaska, throngs of CCP forces, hungry, shabbily dressed, poorly armed, and marching on foot, poured into Manchuria. Before the year's end, the CCP troops in Manchuria numbered 200,000, half of whom were seasoned regulars.[16] CCP cadres and soldiers

---

[13] Sun Qiming, *Hetan*, 55.

[14] Sun Qiming, *Hetan*, 120; *Messages of Chiang Kai-shek*, 855.

[15] "Dongbei zhengwu jieshou baogao" (Report on the Administrative Takeover of the Northeast) March 1947, ZZSC, 7(1): 78–88; Suzanne Pepper, *Civil War in China: The Political Struggle 1945–1949* (Berkeley, CA: University of California Press, 1978), 175–180.

[16] Tang Tsou, *America's Failure in China, 1941–1950* (Chicago: University of Chicago Press, 1963), 328–329; Albert C. Wedemeyer, *Wedemeyer Reports!* (New York: Henry Holt, 1958), 349; Sun Qiming, *Hetan*, 158.

wittily dubbed their arduous expedition *chuang Guandong*, or "brave the journey to the Northeast." Invoking the restive folk tradition of North China, the CCP troops appropriately defined their mission as not only resisting the KMT regime but also defying the Yalta–Moscow system that bestowed Manchuria on that regime.[17]

In competing for influence in China but avoiding direct involvement in China's civil strife, both the United States and the Soviet Union played double games. In November 1945, President Truman chose to believe that in China, the United States was "merely winding up the war" against Japan but "not mixing in China's internal affairs."[18] Yet, during the ensuing civil war in China, the U.S. government actively sought ways to salvage the KMT regime, the linchpin of the Yalta–Moscow structure. In 1946, Truman sent General George Marshall to China on a mission to mediate between the warring sides. Meanwhile, Washington put its economic and financial power behind Chiang Kai-shek's military effort to overcome his adversary. Although, in private, Chiang complained about Marshall's "connivance with the Communists," he never suffered from a shortage of military supplies.[19]

From their own associations with the two Chinese parties in the past, Soviet leaders knew better than the Americans that neither the KMT nor the CCP was amenable to foreign influence. Anchoring his China policy to Russia's new treaty rights and military superiority in Northeast Asia, Stalin waited patiently for the winning side to emerge from the Chinese Civil War. In the postwar political context of China, Stalin proved less a revolutionary than a calculated player of power politics. He never allowed his pragmatic sense of China's position in Moscow's global strategy to be obscured by his ideological sympathy toward the Chinese Communists. To his formal ally, the KMT government, Stalin was guilty not so much of breaking the Sino–Soviet treaty of August 1945 as of utilizing

---

[17] Sun Qiming, *Hetan*, 150–152; Zhang Zhenglong, *Xue Bai Xue Hong: Liao Shen Zhanyi Juan* (White Snow, Red Blood: The Volume on the Liao Shen Campaign) (Beijing: Jiefangjun Chubanshe, 1989), 36–37. *Chuang Guandong* was a spontaneous migration to the Northeast practiced by poor peasants from northern Chinese provinces during the first two or three decades of the twentieth century. The move often occurred during social turmoil caused by natural disasters or civil wars.

[18] Robert Ferrell, ed., *Off the Record: The Private Papers of Harry S. Truman* (New York: Penguin Books, 1980), 74.

[19] CZM, 14: 67, 73; Lloyd E. Eastman, "Who Lost China? Chiang Kai-shek Testifies," *The China Quarterly*, No. 88 (December 1981): 658–668. According to *The China White Paper, August 1949; Originally Issued as United States Relations with China with Special Reference to the Period 1944–1949* (Stanford, CA: Stanford University, 1967), 1042, between V-J Day and the spring of 1949, during a period of less than four years, American aid to the KMT government reached a total of $2 billion. In contrast, during China's eight-year war of resistance against Japan, American aid to Chongqing had totalled just $1.5 billion.

the CCP's situation in Manchuria to press Chiang Kai-shek to make further concessions.[20]

Without question, before its withdrawal from Manchuria in May 1946, the Soviet Red Army was a significant force in the initial stage of the KMT–CCP competition for control of the provinces. More important, however, was the CCP forces' vigorous and ingenious expansion in the Northeast despite their difficulties with the Soviet occupation troops there. In contrast, the KMT's "takeover" operations were sluggish, and KMT leaders' attitude toward their treaty with the Soviet Union indicated a high level of complacency.[21] In this struggle, the Chinese were the principal players and the superpowers adjusted their policies according to the military fortunes of the two warring parties. Toward the end of 1947, when the CCP's predominance in Manchuria was beyond question, both Washington and Moscow were compelled to make important policy changes. Whereas the Truman administration shifted to a policy of limited assistance to Chiang's hopeless regime, Stalin "opted to throw in his lot with Mao."[22] In early November 1948, when the CCP forces captured Shenyang (Mukden), the struggle for Manchuria concluded. Having lost 300,000 of his best troops in the northward drive, Chiang was denied control of Manchuria. Although the war in the rest of China would continue for

[20] Donald G. Gillin and Ramon H. Myers, ed., *Last Chance in Manchuria: The Diary of Chang Kia-ngau* (Stanford, CA: Hoover Institution Press, 1989), and *ZZSC*, 7(1): 371–453, contains documents on the Sino–Soviet negotiations for "economic cooperations" in Manchuria in late 1945 and early 1946.

[21] Sun Qiming, *Hetan*, 145–146, 156; Zhang Zhenglong, *Xue Bai Xue Hong*, 30, 82–83, 91–92; Zhou Wenqi and Chu Liangru, *Teshu er Fuzai de Keti: Gongchan Guoji, Sulian he Zhongguo Gongchandang Guanxi Biannianshi, 1919–1991* (A Peculiar and Complex subject: The Chronicle of the Relations between the Comintern, the Soviet Union and the Chinese Communist Party, 1919–1991) (Wuhan: Hubei Renmin Chubanshe, 1993), 433–443. Steven I. Levine's *Anvil of Victory: The Chinese Communist Revolution in Manchuria, 1945–1948* (New York: Columbia University Press, 1987) is an authoritative study of the subject. The collaborative work by Sergei N. Goncharov, John W. Lewis, and Xue Litai, *Uncertain Partners: Stalin, Mao, and the Korean War* (Stanford, CA: Stanford University Press, 1993) contains a valuable chapter on the Soviet–CCP–KMT relations from 1945 to 1948 based on new Chinese and Russian materials. Pepper's *Civil War in China* offers an insightful and vivid discussion of the KMT's political catastrophe of its own making in the civil war period.

[22] Tang Tsou, *America's Failure*, 462–477; Leffler, *A Preponderance of Power*, 246–251; Goncharov, Lewis, and Xue, *Uncertain Partners*, 12–14. The issue of Stalin's military aid to the CCP troops in Manchuria has recently been clarified. In the fall of 1945, certain CCP units indeed obtained weapons and supplies from some abandoned Japanese depots in Manchuria. Yet, soon the Soviet Red Army tightened its control over matériel left by the Japanese Guandong Army and denied the CCP troops access. Both the CCP and the KMT sources agree that not until October 1947 did the Russians begin to provide large-scale military aid to the CCP. See Goncharov, Lewis, and Xue, *Uncertain Partners*, 14, 301 notes 88 and 89; "Ejun gongji gongfei junhuo shishi diaochabiao" (Table on the Findings Regarding the Russian Army's Supply of Weapons to the Communist Bandits), n.d., *ZZSC*, 7(1): 599–606.

another year, the KMT regime's defeat in Manchuria foreshadowed its ultimate fate.

The struggle for Manchuria had serious implications for Korea, its immediate neighbor in the east. Well in line with the traditional Russian policy in Northeast Asia, at the time of the Yalta Conference Stalin was interested in Manchuria, not Korea.[23] Besides having struck the deal over Manchuria with the Western Allies, he might having preferred to postpone the Korea issue until military developments in the war propelled the Russians into a stronger bargaining position. Stalin's tactic worked well due to either the indifference of American officials toward Korea or their preoccupation with the campaign against Japan. When the war in Asia ended, the Red Army's presence seemed dominant in Korea. Nonetheless, Stalin opted to trade the unilateral short-term advantage for Washington's acceptance of Soviet occupation limited to the northern half of the peninsula. In doing so, Stalin showed the Americans that he was still willing to work with the West.[24]

Both the wartime trusteeship formula and the postwar arrangement to divide Korea violated the will of the Korean people. After Japan surrendered, "people's committees" mushroomed throughout Korea. These committees might not qualify for self-government by American officials' standards, but they were serious about establishing Korea's own independent government. History does not disclose what would have emerged in Korea from this popular movement for independence. What really took place, in historian Bruce Cumings's words, was that "the Korean leap to Rhodes was caught in midair... with the entries of the American and Soviet troops."[25]

The Chinese government was truly interested in Korea. Yet, in 1945 and afterward, its ability to influence developments there was almost nil. A month after Japan's defeat, Chiang Kai-shek tried in vain to convince the U.S. government that the return of the Korean Provisional Government to Korea would be necessary to prevent the spread of Communism in that country. The American military authorities in Korea agreed to allow members of the KPG to enter its occupation zone only as individuals.[26] At one time during the struggle for Manchuria, Chiang Kai-shek hoped that by controlling the 3 million Korean nationals in the northeastern and other Chinese provinces, the Chinese government would be able to act from

[23] Hilary Conroy's *The Japanese Seizure of Korea, 1868–1910* (Philadelphia: University of Pennsylvania Press, 1974) is an effective treatment of the earlier international intrigues concerning Korea.
[24] Cumings, *The Origins of the Korean War: Liberation*, 117–122; William W. Stueck, Jr., *The Road to Confrontation: American Policy toward China and Korea, 1947–1950* (Chapel Hill: University of North Carolina Press, 1981), 19–22.
[25] Cumings, *Origins of the Korean War: Liberation*, 429.
[26] CSYZ, 37: 321; Shao Yulin, *Shi Han Huiyilu* (My Mission to Korea) (Taipei: Zhuanji Wenxue Chubanshe, 1980), 71–72.

Manchuria as the holder of the balance wheel between the Americans and the Russians in Korea. But Chiang's defeat in Manchuria deprived him of the geopolitical advantage. When the KMT government fled to Taiwan in 1949, it was separated from Korea by the seas. The old "lips and teeth" allegory lost relevance to the KMT's relations with Korea. Later, however, a different kind of common interest would emerge between the KMT government and South Korea: the extent of Washington's willingness to defend South Korea would be used by KMT officials to measure Taiwan's own chance of survival.[27]

Where the KMT had failed, the CCP succeeded. During the struggle for Manchuria, the CCP and their Korean comrades in North Korea were indeed as closely related as lips and teeth. Unlike the KMT, CCP leaders at this time did not see their Korean connection in the context of the superpowers' maneuvering in Korea. Their focus was on the struggle in China. Between 1946 and 1949, the CCP's Northeastern Bureau had set up an office in Pyongyang, which eventually concluded more than twenty agreements with Kim Il Sung's government for facilitating the CCP's military activities in Manchuria. These understandings allowed the CCP forces to use North Korea as a safe passage for transportation of matériel and personnel, as well as a rear area for attending their sick and wounded. During 1946 and 1947, North Korea even assisted the CCP with 2,000 carriages of war matériel left by Japanese troops. Given the situation between the United States and the Soviet Union in Korea, the CCP had to disguise its agency in Pyongyang as a business company.[28] In these years, the CCP's camouflaged presence in Korea was minor compared to the superpowers' influence. But it represented the beginning of a renovated geopolitical relationship between China and Korea, the relevance of which would be fully appreciated by the rest of the world only in late 1950, when China, now unified under the CCP, intervened in the Korean War.

---

[27] Shao Yulin, *Shi Han Huiyilu*, 75, 105.

[28] "Huiyi Dongbei jiefang zhanzheng qijian Dongbeiju zhu Bei Chaoxian banshichu" (Reminiscences on the Office of the Northeastern Bureau in North Korea during the War for Liberating the Northeast), no author, in *Zhonggong Dangshi Ziliao* (Materials on the history of the Chinese Communist Party), 17 (1986): 197–210. Bruce Cumings, *The Origins of the Korean War, Volume II: The Roaring of the Cataract, 1947–1950* (Princeton, NJ: Princeton University Press, 1990), 358, suggests that after 1947, Kim Il Sung also despatched "tens of thousands" of Korean troops to China to fight on the CCP's side. This allegation is based entirely on contemporary Western and KMT intelligence information and still needs to be verified with CCP and North Korean sources. The KMT intelligence information tended to exaggerate. For instance, an undated KMT report in ZZSC, 7(1): 616, asserted that by March 1947 there were 190,000 Korean communist troops in Manchuria. Yet, according to Goncharov, Lewis, and Xue, *Uncertain Partners*, 140–141, and 329, note 56, available CCP sources have indicated some 40,000 ethnic Koreans in the 4th Field Army that was the CCP force in the Northeast. And it is not clear how many of these were Korean nationals and how many were Chinese Koreans.

Regarding the wartime American–Chinese partnership for a peaceful order in Asia, the most ironic turn of events occurred in Taiwan. Unlike Manchuria and Korea, Taiwan in 1945 did not figure at all in the Allied diplomatic maneuvering at Yalta and Moscow. After Japan's surrender, in pursuance of the Cairo decision on Taiwan, the Chinese government returned peacefully to the island as a liberator. But soon, when the Yalta–Moscow structure on the mainland collapsed under the CCP's devastating offensive against the KMT regime, the status of Taiwan changed from a relatively simple issue of peace settlement to one of the thorniest problems in postwar East Asian international politics. Prior to this development, however, the relationship between the KMT government and the populace of Taiwan had deteriorated rapidly.

In late October 1946, visiting Taiwan for the first time, Chiang Kai-shek described the island in his diary as "a stretch of pure land," in contrast to Manchuria, which had been penetrated by the CCP influence.[29] Chiang wrote his remark at a time when the "pure land" was being adulterated by the KMT's own catastrophic occupation. Early in the year, the Central Executive Committee of the KMT transmitted to the Executive Yuan a report on the current situation in Taiwan. According to the report, since Japan's surrender, the Taiwanese people's attitude toward the Chinese government had changed from one of "warm welcome" to one of "cold aloofness." The reasons for the change were many, but all had their basis in the KMT's takeover policies. For instance, the Taiwanese bitterly resented the Chinese authorities' reliance on Japanese personnel and *Taijian* (Taiwanese who had collaborated with Japan) in administering and even in policing the island. The KMT's postwar financial policy in Taiwan actually served to maintain Japanese nationals' interests while forcing the Taiwanese people "to live in dire poverty." The Taiwanese began to feel that "exploitation by China is even worse than that by Japan," and they could not understand why, when living under a government of their own "mother land," they had even less freedom than under Japan's rule. The alarmed authors of the report concurred with a widely shared opinion on the island that if the KMT government did not readjust its ways at once, "China will lose Taiwan for the second time."[30]

The ministries of the KMT government in charge of policies in Taiwan

---

[29] *CZM*, 14: 68.

[30] "Kuomintang zhongzhihui mishuchu wei chaosong 'Taiwan xianzhuang baogaoshu' zhi Xingzhengyuan han ji ge bu fuhe qingxing" (The "Report on the Current Situation in Taiwan," Transmitted by the Secretariat of the KMT Central Executive Committee to the Executive Yuan, and Reactions from the Ministries Concerned), 16 January 1946, GRN 2(2) (Executive Yuan): file 6523, *TG*, 2: 552–561; "Taiwan chujiantuan tuanzhang Qiu Xia cheng Chiang Kai-shek hanjian" (A Letter from Head of the Taiwanese League for Eliminating Traitors, Qiu Xia, to Chiang Kai-shek), 7 July 1946, GRN 1(2) (Nationalist Government): file 7023, *TG*, 2: 564–571.

responded to the report either by evading responsibility or by disputing its findings. Four months after Chiang Kai-shek praised the "purity" of Taiwan, widespread discontent on the island exploded into a serious crisis. At the end of February 1947, as a peaceful mass demonstration in Taipei protested against the brutality of some customs officers, the crowd was confronted by KMT authorities with machine guns. Thousands were killed at the scene. During the next two weeks, popular anti-government uprisings spread throughout the island. Eventually the KMT government was able to suppress the rebellion but only by sending additional troops into Taiwan.[31] To the nearly 30,000 Taiwanese who had been on the mainland during the war and had cooperated with Chongqing in restoring Taiwan's proper place in China, the developments on the island from the time of Japan's surrender to the February event constituted a tragedy full of bitter ironies. Under the KMT rule, Taiwan's "liberation" quickly turned into suppression. The open conflict in Taiwan in the spring of 1947 at last persuaded the KMT government to adopt some overdue policy changes in order to return stability to the island. Yet, one year after the violent confrontation, some KMT officials in Taiwan admitted that the "deep and awesome wound" in the regime's relationship with the Taiwanese could not be healed easily.[32]

Beginning in late 1948, the issue of Taiwan took another turn. Unable to reverse the military debacle on the mainland, Chiang Kai-shek chose Taiwan as his new base for recuperation, hoping to repeat his wartime experience in Chongqing. Obviously, Chiang preferred Taiwan to other possible locations because the CCP influence on the island was weak and the Taiwan Strait constituted a natural barrier against a CCP attack. Moreover, at a time when Chiang had lost much credibility with the Americans but had also become more than ever reliant on American support, Chiang could only hope to capitalize on Washington's strategic interest in the island of Taiwan to salvage his government. From December 1948, Chiang began to take measures to reinforce his control of the island. On 7 December 1949, the KMT government formally decided to move to Taiwan, hoping that another event of epochal proportions like Japan's attack on Pearl Harbor would soon occur and start World War III between the two superpowers.[33]

[31] Yang Lianggong to Yu Youren, 12 March 1947, GRN 8(2) (Control Yuan): file 21, *TG*, 2: 589; "Chuli Taiwan shibian yijianshu" (Suggestion on How to Settle the Incident in Taiwan), 14 March 1947, GRN 8(2): file 22, ibid., 590–593.

[32] Yang Lianggong to Yu Youren, 27 March 1948, GRN 8(2): file 20, *TG*, 1: 352–353; Gu Weijun, *Gu Weijun Huiyilu* (Memoirs of Gu Weijun) (Beijing: Zhonghua Shuju, 1983–1993), 7: 630–633.

[33] Chen Dunde, *Mao Zedong yu Chiang Kai-shek, 1949–1976: Shangwei Zuihou Shixian de Wuoshou* (Mao Zedong and Chiang Kai-shek, 1949–1976: The Last Handshake Yet to Be Done) (Beijing: Bayi Chubanshe, 1993), 8–11; Gu Weijun, *Huiyilu*, 7: 474–475; CZM, 14: 99.

By this time, postwar developments in China had drastically altered the context of U.S. policy in East Asia. The KMT's rout deprived the U.S. government of its means for influencing events on the mainland through an indigenous ally. U.S. policymakers could only hope that a policy might be devised to drive a wedge into the presumed CCP–Moscow monolith. Under these circumstances, Washington began to reestimate the importance of Taiwan against the U.S. position in Japan. In the late 1940s, the Cairo decision on China's sovereignty over Taiwan increasingly became a liability for U.S. policymakers. Although both the KMT and the CCP regarded the matter as settled, U.S. officials abhorred the prospect of Taiwan's becoming entangled in the Chinese Civil War lest it eventually fall under the CCP's control. Such an eventuality was believed detrimental to Japan's economic recovery and security. Yet, not prepared to become involved in Taiwan militarily, the U.S. government in 1948 and 1949 contemplated various schemes for separating Taiwan from China by giving support either to a non-KMT Chinese regime or to an indigenous government in the island. Only after the Korean War began were Chiang Kai-shek and the U.S. government able to identify a new basis for their cooperation. At that time, the United States acquiesced in Chiang's rule on the island as a necessary, if not ideal, condition for protecting Taiwan. Chiang Kai-shek would have to settle for America's support for his government's theoretical, though not actual, sovereignty over China in order to retain U.S. assistance. In response to the Korean War, President Truman despatched the U.S. Seventh Fleet to the Taiwan Strait to prevent the spread of the war. Truman's doubled-edged interference contained both the KMT and the CCP. The Chinese Civil War was thereby frozen across the strait, but the KMT–CCP confrontation would continue.[34]

Conclusion

In March 1946, Winston Churchill delivered his famous "iron curtain" speech in Fulton, Missouri. Although Churchill emphasized his contemporaries' apprehension of the West–East confrontation along political and ideological lines in central Europe, in retrospect he really announced the beginning of a half-century of peace in that part of the world.[35] Despite the

[34] Gu Weijun, *Huiyilu*, vol. 7, chapter 10, describes the KMT government's diplomatic effort in the late 1940s to gain U.S. commitment to Taiwan and KMT officials' stubbornness in expecting a new world war between the United States and the Soviet Union to happen soon. For U.S. policy toward Taiwan in the late 1940s, see Ronald McGlothlen, *Controlling the Waves: Dean Acheson and U.S. Foreign Policy in Asia* (New York: W. W. Norton, 1993), 86–134; Leffler, *A Preponderance of Power*, 291–298, 333–341, 347–383; Cumings, *Origins of the Korean War, Volume II*, 508–544.

[35] This irony has been captured in the title of John L. Gaddis's study of the cold war, *The Long Peace: Inquiries into the History of the Cold War* (New York: Oxford University Press, 1987).

crisis-ridden conditions of Europe in the following decades, the postwar status quo on that continent would prove exceedingly stable. The stability in Europe was due as much to the Allied military victory over the Axis powers as to the political maneuvering among the members of the United Nations coalition. The iron curtain reflected a stalemate that had been reached by the wartime inter-Allied diplomacy. In contrast, no political leader could perform a service for Asia analogous to what Churchill did for Europe. In postwar East Asia, the superpowers were unable to identify a plausible geopolitical line for defining the balance of power between them. At different times, the boundary between Manchuria and China proper, the Yangtze River, the 38th parallel in Korea, and the 17th parallel in Vietnam might be considered such lines. But, one after another, these lines proved merely "wooden curtains" that could be easily demolished by wars beyond the superpowers' control.

It is in this context that the CCP's success in Manchuria between 1946 and 1948 should be understood. Recognizing their completely different political connotations, one can compare the development in Manchuria in these years with the Mukden Incident of September 1931. In 1931, Japanese military forces had made the first move in Manchuria to break the legal armor of the interwar peace system in East Asia. In the late 1940s, the CCP's daring advance in the same region inflicted the first devastating blow on the international order in Asia that the wartime Allies had so painstakingly put together. Why, then, was the peace structure in Asia so fragile that it collapsed at the first instance of the postwar civil wars?

The question is posed not to imply that the U.S.–Chinese cooperation in World War II in constructing a new international order in East Asia produced no lasting results. An obvious consequence was the changed political map of the Asian–Pacific region that grew out of the Allied policy to demolish the Japanese Empire. Japan's loss of its empire-based economy decisively set it on a new course of peaceful national development. It would not be too long before the rest of the world felt Japan's impact as an ascending trading power. Another result of the wartime inter-Allied diplomacy was to abrogate the old treaty system in China, which opened opportunities for a new type of Chinese foreign relations to grow. Furthermore, China's recovery of its lost territories from Japan marked the beginning of the Western powers' accommodation to the irredentism in China's foreign policy. Simply put, the military and diplomatic endeavors of the Allies in East Asia during World War II created a revolution in the international politics of the region.

But the revolutionary changes affecting China's and Japan's relative positions in East Asian politics did not ensure a lasting peace. They only offered the necessary conditions for wartime leaders to pursue their particular visions of a new international order. A status quo power in prewar East Asia, the United States in World War II nevertheless realized that the

era of Western empires dominating Asia was over. The problem facing
U.S. policymakers was to devise a new framework for postwar international relations in Asia that would secure U.S. leadership in the region but
would also be compatible with America's global economic and political
interests.

American officials found three cornerstones on which to construct the
U.S. foreign policy in postwar East Asia. Based on a pure calculation of
power, American leaders first were determined to achieve a monopolizing
position in Japan to guarantee the physical security of the United States in
the Pacific. And in doing so, the Soviet predomination in northeastern Asia
could also be balanced. They understood, however, that after the war,
Japan would not have much influence elsewhere in Asia. Therefore, the
second cornerstone was a long-term partnership between the United States
and the KMT government in China. This cooperation was necessary not
only to maintain Washington's ability to influence events within China,
but also to use China as a medium of American influence in other Asian
countries. Lastly, the trusteeship formula was developed to maintain Western
influence in the former colonies of Asia, to keep European colonialism at
bay, and to prevent rivalries among the great powers. Generally speaking,
the wartime diplomacy of the United States proved successful in persuading the other three leading members of the UN coalition to support or
acquiesce in Washington's policy suggestions for Asia.

Washington's wartime diplomacy and policy planning for Asia did not
fail because U.S. leaders did not practice power politics well. Just the
opposite: the failure was in their belief that their power politics would be
omnipotent. American officials neglected a potent force in Asian politics –
radical nationalism – which operated too unconventionally to be handled by
ordinary diplomacy. Without a policy to deal with such a force, American
policymakers assumed a general attitude about the Asian peoples. In 1900,
seeing the "apparent impotency" of the Asian peoples for self-regeneration
and self-government, Alfred Thayer Mahan had written: "The condition of
these people is not that of sheep to be owned, although in some respects
it much resembles that of sheep without a shepherd."[36] Despite the passage
of time, Washington's trusteeship formula in World War II for "dependent
peoples" of Asia was essentially in accord with Mahan's "shepherd" conception. It is noteworthy that the trusteeship formula was designed more
to accommodate the concerned big powers' interests in dependent *areas*
than to help the dependent *peoples*. In practice, therefore, Washington's
wartime policy planning for Asia was primarily oriented toward dealing
with other powers in Asia, but not with Asian peoples.

The U.S. government's failure to face Asian nationalism squarely began

[36] A. T. Mahan, *The Problem of Asia and Its Effect upon International Politics* (First published in 1900; reissued Port Washington, NY: Kennikat Press, 1970), 87.

with its wartime perception of China's international identity. Before World War II, basically excluded from Southeast Asian areas by the European empires, the United States had had two foreign policy issues to deal with in East Asia. First, in dealing with a weak and chaotic China, American leaders tended to exercise paternalism. Second, in dealing with a modernized yet aggressive Japan, they practiced power politics. During World War II, a strange new China policy emerged in Washington that contained ingredients of both the prewar China and Japan policies. China was singled out among the emerging Asian states and identified as a new "great power" of Asia. This view was sustained during the war when American leaders needed China as an ally in the war against Japan. The view's other attributes included the American people's sympathy with China's struggle for national rehabilitation and American officials' expectation that China would play an accessory role in dealing with Britain and Russia in international politics. Yet, in the final analysis, the policy reflected American policymakers' inability to contemplate a postwar policy in Asia without resorting to formulas chiefly designed for great-power diplomacy. Once Japan was defeated, American leaders focused their attention on filling in the power vacuum with China's help and on promoting China as a new power in Asia to which the rest of Asia could turn as a model of cooperation with the West. That is why, although State Department planners did not always share President Roosevelt's rosy view of China's role in postwar East Asia, they were aware that, as the only Asian country among the principal members of the UN coalition, China would be a useful partner for America's Asia policy.

This is not to say that American policymakers were blind to the economic and political reality of China. If President Roosevelt was extravagant in suggesting to Chinese officials that he could offer China a "place in the sun" before China became a great power in its own right, he was sober in private in noting that China was in a "period of transition." The problem was that in pursuing their long-term objectives in China, American policymakers did not mold their policies according to the reality of China. Bestowing the title of "great power" on Chiang Kai-shek's government, American leaders tended either to demand that Chongqing shoulder excessive international responsibilities (policing Japan, for instance) or to misconstrue the KMT's foreign policy aspirations regarding China's periphery as expansion (in Korea, for instance). During the greater part of the war, American leaders promoted China's great-power image but then became bewildered by their own artwork. In time, neither their enthusiasm about China's stabilizing role nor their anxiety about China's expansionism in postwar Asia would prove well founded.

Furthermore, by treating China as America's number one client state in Asia that would help promote U.S. interests in the region as a bloc, American leaders spared themselves the responsibility of developing concrete policies for dealing with individual Asian countries. Before all else, America's postwar policy in Asia would founder, as the KMT regime represented only the conservative wing of Chinese nationalism and had no effective influence on the more vigorous nationalist movements in neighboring countries. In the postwar years, it was the Chinese Communists who would lead China to complete its own domestic transformation and to play a new international role. Hopelessly trapped with its super client, Chiang Kai-shek, the U.S. government would be deprived by the KMT defeat in China of any political means to influence events on the Asian continent. Eventually, America's victory in the Pacific war afforded U.S. policymakers their only geopolitical position similar to that of Japanese leaders during the early Meiji years: an insular position based on Japan's home islands. During the years to come, what American policymakers would decide to do about the situation was not radically different from the Meiji leaders' approach to the continent: to use military leverage in place of peaceful variations of political-economic influence.

In the "period of transition," wartime China was neither a great power, as it was promoted in the Rooseveltian rhetoric, nor a fragmentary republic, as it had appeared in the prewar years. Still a country torn apart by foreign aggression and by the KMT–CCP rupture, China nevertheless inhaled a breath of life from one of the most devastating military conflicts of modern times. During the war, the country was actually on the threshold of national revival. The KMT and the CCP shared the view that after the war, China's physical domain would be redefined by rolling back foreign encroachment on Chinese territories; China's international status would be restored to equality with all other countries of the world; and China's regional eminence in Asia would be respected. But the creed of Chinese nationalism could only oblige the two parties to fight the common enemy, Japan. It was unable to amalgamate the two into a coalition at home.

Compared with Washington's global foreign policy planning, the KMT government's wartime diplomacy had a much narrower agenda. Aside from regaining China's lost territories and securing beneficial cooperation from the United States, KMT strategists rarely went beyond China's immediate neighboring areas when contemplating China's postwar foreign relations. Limited by its own weakness and confined by the war conditions, the KMT government's accomplishment in foreign policy was moderate. Although applying irredentism to Chinese territories that had been seized by Japan, the KMT government had to remain largely passive with respect to China's territorial disputes with Britain and Russia. Even worse, on the eve of victory over Japan, the KMT government signed off Outer Mongolia in its treaty with Moscow. In their balance sheet on Chongqing's wartime diplomatic performance, KMT officials might also list Korea, Vietnam, and Japanese reparations as items that registered Chongqing's frustrations. Meanwhile, the KMT diplomacy accomplished much in abrogating the unequal treaties with Western governments and in recovering Manchuria and Taiwan from Japan. In the postwar years, KMT officials tended to blame their American ally for not doing enough to help them stop the Communist opponents at home. By taking such a stand, these officials were unwittingly debasing Chongqing's achievement in making alliances. In the prior history of China, there had been no era in which a Chinese regime had a foreign power committed so tenaciously to its fortune. Even the expensive agreement with Moscow in August 1945 was a success from the KMT's point of view, for it at least created a legal barrier against the Soviet government's open support for the CCP.[37]

Therefore, the most fatal flaw in Chongqing's wartime diplomacy was not its inability during most of the war to persuade Washington to adopt an explicitly anti-Soviet foreign policy in Asia or its reluctant concessions to the Russians in 1945. On the contrary, Chongqing's success in enlisting foreign support intoxicated KMT leaders. Just as U.S. policymakers were overconfident in power politics, KMT leaders were obsessed with the foreign origins of China's problems and their solutions. Chongqing's wartime diplomacy succeeded in redefining China's territorial realm and in creating a generally friendly international environment in which the KMT regime could begin the next round of power struggles with the CCP. Success in foreign policy was one of the reasons why the KMT government stubbornly refused to change its domestic politics.

Soon after the conclusion of the Pacific war, an OSS report pointed out that although the Sino–Soviet treaty might be conducive to a truce between the KMT and the CCP, it provided no definite solution for that conflict. Fundamentally, the Chongqing–Moscow rapprochement did not significantly alter the balance of power within China in favor of the KMT. In a political sense, it might even have weakened Chongqing's position. According to this analysis, because the CCP had always been on its own, the new pledge by Moscow not to give aid to Yan'an did not really enfeeble the Communists. But now the KMT was deprived of a principal excuse for its shortcomings at home based on a so-called Soviet conspiracy in China. The KMT would have to treat the CCP as an indigenous movement.[38] But in the postwar years, the "Soviet conspiracy" theory continued to obscure the KMT policymakers' understanding of the political and social realities in China.

In retrospect, it seems clear that Washington's and Chongqing's peace

[37] The KMT government severed its diplomatic relationship with the Soviet Union right after the latter recognized the CCP government in Beijing in October 1949. But it did not move to nullify the Sino–Soviet treaty of 1945 until 1953, three years after the CCP and the Soviet government concluded their treaty of alliance.

[38] "Implications of the Sino–Soviet Agreements for the Internal Politics of China," 7 September 1945, *OSSR*, reel 2.

schemes foundered on the first day of peace. The American and Chinese governments used the better part of the war to envision a partnership between them in a new international order for postwar Asia. Their cooperation emerging from this effort proved a sham due to its narrow power orientation and its weak link with the reality of revolutionary Asian politics. At the end of the war, the only arrangement in Asia resembling an international security system was the amorphous Yalta–Moscow structure. The Chinese side of the arrangement, however, became irrelevant when civil war resumed in China. Soon the United States and the Soviet Union had to improvise in order to continue their involvement in postwar Asian politics. In postwar Europe, when they turned from wartime allies to peacetime adversaries, the superpowers were still able to set the tempo for events. Asia was an entirely different matter. By the end of World War II, Asian nations, emerging from their colonial and semicolonial past, had grown too vigorous to be manipulated by the superpowers.

Appendix I

Guiding Plan for Helping the Korean Restoration Movement[1]

1. General Program

In pursuance of the teaching of the late Premier [Sun Yat-sen] about Three People's Principles and giving assistance to weak nations, [this party works for] the establishment of permanent peace in East Asia, and actively supports the Korean revolutionary organizations in China in order to strengthen them and to reestablish an independent Korean state.

2. Principles

(1) This party should treat all Korean revolutionary groups in China with friendly spirit and sincere and warm attitudes.

(2) During the anti-Japanese war, Korean revolutionary organizations should coordinate their activities with the need of Chinese military authorities and take practical part in resistant actions to accelerate the collapse of the Japanese imperialism.

(3) The *zongcai* [director-general, i.e., Chiang Kai-shek] will appoint a three-member guiding group responsible for contacting and advising the Korean revolutionary organizations in China; and the financial need of these organizations should be met with loans in the name of the party.

3. Methods

(1) At the proper time, the Chinese government ought to take the lead among the Allies in granting recognition to the Korean Provisional Government; the timing and the procedure of recognition should be decided by the guiding group in accordance with the *zongcai*'s instruction, and then the Waijiaobu should complete necessary steps.

(2) For the present, the Korean Restoration Army should be subject to the direct control of the Chinese National Military Council and be deployed by the chief of staff of the Chinese Army; upon the request of the KRA, Chinese staff officers and political instructors can be assigned to the

KRA to help make operational plans, train military personnel, and develop cultural and propaganda work.

(3) The KPG and other Korean revolutionary groups should cooperate with the Allied strategy and the plans of the Chinese Army, undertaking the following activities:

    a. to penetrate enemy troops and agitate Korean soldiers.

    b. to make contact with Korean people within Korea and overseas Korean nationals.

    c. to enlist and train Korean young people.

    d. to spread frequently statements on the goal of Korean independence in Korea and in enemy's troops.

    e. to collect intelligence information for the Chinese government.

(4) The three-member guiding group should periodically examine the military situation and check the work of the Korean revolutionaries in order to consult proper branches of the Chinese government and provide advice to the Koreans.

(5) Equipment and expenses for military activities [of the Koreans] should be supplied by the National Military Council following regulations and procedures concerned; and expenses for partisan and political activities should be decided by the guiding group and, after informing the Central Executive Committee of the KMT, funded with a particular source.

(6) For antiespionage purposes, the KPG and other Korean revolutionary organizations should undertake detailed investigations into the number, occupations, and locations of all Korean nationals in China and inform the Chinese government.

(7) Korean revolutionaries, who are working in Chinese war zones and in Chinese rear areas, should obey Chinese laws and regulations.

(8) This program is subject to the *zongcai*'s approval; the governmental departments concerned should make concrete plans to implement this program.

APPENDIX II

Two Chinese documents of the Cairo Conference[2]

The Fifth Chinese memorandum

In harmony with the declaration of foreign policy of the United States, which China adheres to, and the assumption that the United States desires to give China such support as will enable her to discharge the responsibilities attaching to her membership of the Four Powers Group, and/or participation in any international covenant, and arising out of her special relations with the United States, there are certain questions to be discussed:

A. International
  1. Chinese participation on [an] equal footing in all deliberations, decisions[,] and machinery of the Four Powers Group acting as such.
B. Armistice Terms with Japan
  1. Deposition of [the] Japanese Imperial House.
  2. Chinese participation in [the] occupation of Japan.
  3. Part compensation by transfer of Japanese industrial plants, shipping, rolling stock, etc.
C. Territorial
  1. Recovery of all Chinese territories (to be specially defined e.f. [sic] Manchuria, Liaotung Peninsula, Formosa, Liu Choo Islands and Hong Kong).
D. Military
  1. Mutual undertakings to come to each other's assistance in case of unprovoked aggression.
  2. Presence of adequate American forces in Pacific bases to share in preventing and opposing aggression.
  3. Assistance and aid to China for equipment of land and air forces for national defence [sic], and for fulfillment of duties arising out of her international obligations.
  4. Furnishing military and naval bases for mutual security.

5. Mutual consultation prior to making decisions affecting the Pacific area and Asiatic mainland.

E. Dependent Areas

   1. Mutual understanding as regards [*sic*] the future of Korea, Indo China [*sic*][,] and other dependent areas.
   2. Chinese participation in any administration of multi-national character in the Pacific zone of which America is a member.

F. Economics

   1. Credits for Chinese Reconstruction [*sic*].

The Chinese summary record

1. On China's International Position. President Roosevelt expressed his view that *China should take her place as one of the Big Four and participate on an equal footing in the machinery of the Big Four Group and in all its decisions.* Generalissimo Chiang responded that China would be glad to take part in all the Big Four machinery and decisions.

2. On the Status of [the] Japanese Imperial House. President Roosevelt enquired [*sic*] of Generalissimo Chiang's views as to whether *the institution of the Emperor of Japan should be abolished after the war.* The Generalissimo said that this would involve the question of the form of government of Japan and should be left for the Japanese people themselves to decide after the war, so as not to precipitate any error which might perpetuate itself in international relations.

3. On Military Occupation of Japan. President Roosevelt was of the opinion that *China should play the leading role in the postwar military occupation of Japan.* Generalissimo Chiang believed, however, that China was not equipped to shoulder this considerable responsibility, that the task should be carried out under the leadership of the United States[,] and that China could participate in the task in a supporting capacity should it prove necessary by that time. The Generalissimo also took the position that the final decision on the matter could await further development of the actual situation.

4. On Reparation in Kind. Generalissimo Chiang proposed that a [*sic*] part of the reparation Japan was to pay China after the war could be paid in the form of actual properties. Much of Japan's industrial machinery and equipment, war and merchant ships, rolling stock, etc., could be transferred to China. President Roosevelt expressed his concurrence in the proposal.

5. On Restoration of Territories. Generalissimo Chiang and President Roosevelt agreed that *the four Northeastern provinces of China, Taiwan[,] and the Penghu Islands [Pescadores] which Japan had taken from China by force must be restored to China after the war, it being understood that the Liaotung Peninsula and its two ports, Lushun (Port of Arthur [sic])*

and Dairen, must be included. The President then referred to the question of the Ryukyu Islands and enquired more than once whether China would want the Ryukyus. The Generalissimo replied that *China would be agreeable to joint occupation of the Ryukyus by China and the United States and, eventually, joint administration by the two countries under the trusteeship of an international organization.* President Roosevelt also raised the question of *Hong Kong.* The Generalissimo suggested that the President discuss the matter with the British authorities before further deliberation.

6. On Matters Concerning Military Cooperation. President Roosevelt proposed that, *after the war, China and the United States should effect certain arrangements under which the two countries could come to each other's assistance in the event of foreign aggression and that the United States should maintain adequate military forces on various bases in the Pacific in order that it could effectively share the responsibility of preventing aggression.* Generalissimo Chiang expressed his agreement to both proposals. The Generalissimo expressed his hope that *the United States would be in the position to extend necessary aid to China for equipping its land, naval[,] and air forces for the purpose of strengthening its national defense and enabling its performance of international obligations.* Generalissimo Chiang also proposed that, *to achieve mutual security, the two countries should arrange for army and naval bases of each to be available for use by the other* and stated that *China would be prepared to place Lushun (Port of Arthur [sic])* at the joint disposal of China and the United States. President Roosevelt, on his part, proposed that *China and the United States should consult with each other before any decision was to be reached on matters concerning Asia.* The Generalissimo indicated agreement.

7. On Korea, Indo-China[,] and Thailand. President Roosevelt advanced the opinion that China and the United States should reach *a mutual understanding on the future status of Korea, Indo-China[,] and other colonial areas as well as Thailand.* Concurring, Generalissimo Chiang stressed on [sic] the necessity of granting independence to Korea. It was also his view that China and the United States should endeavor together to help Indo-China achieve independence after the war and that independent status should be restored to Thailand. The President expressed his agreement.

8. On Economic Aid to China. Generalissimo Chiang pointed out that *China's postwar economic reconstruction would be a tremendously difficult task which would require United States financial aid in the form of loans, etc., and also various types of technical assistance.* President Roosevelt indicated that close and practical consideration would be given to the matter.

9. On Outer Mongolia and Tannu Tuva. President Roosevelt inquired

especially as to the present status of Tannu Tuva and its historical relations with its neighbors. Generalissimo Chiang pointed out that the area had been an integral part of China's Outer Mongolia until it was forcibly taken and annexed by Russia. He said that the question of Tannu Tuva, together with that of Outer Mongolia, must be settled in time to come through negotiations with Soviet Russia.

10. On Unified Command. Generalissimo Chiang proposed the formation of a China–U.S. Joint Council of Chiefs-of-Staff or, as an alternative, China's participation in the existing Britain–U.S. Council of Chiefs-of-Staff. President Roosevelt agreed to consult the chiefs of staff of the United States in order to reach a decision on the matter.

---

[1] This plan was approved by Chiang Kai-shek on 27 December 1942. The translation is based on the Chinese version cited in Hu Chunhui, *Hanguo Duli Yundong zai Zhongguo* (Korean Independence Movement in China) (Taipei: Zhonghua Minguo Shiliao Yanjiu Zhongxin, 1976), 105–107.

[2] The Fifth Chinese memorandum is found in Harry L. Hopkins Papers, Box 331, Book 8: Teheran (a) En Route: First Cairo Meeting. The Chinese summary record is in *FRUS, Cairo and Teheran Conferences*, 323–325. Items in the fifth memorandum can be compared with the parts of the summary record set in italics.

Bibliography

I wish to add some comments on the most important sources for this study. The historical records of the U.S. government's wartime foreign policy planning are not completely unfamiliar to students of the inter-Allied diplomacy of World War II. What I have done in this book is to give full exposure to the planning records on East Asia that have only been dipped into by other researchers for their studies of different concerns. During the war, the Department of State assumed the chief responsibility for the U.S. government's foreign policy preparation. It also provided political advice to military planners who were contemplating the war strategies in the Pacific region. These can be seen from the so-called Notter Files, which contain documents generated by the core operations of the State Department foreign policy planning, and from the State–War–Navy Coordinating Committee Files.

The microfiche publication *The Occupation of Japan: U.S. Planning Documents, 1942–1945*, edited by Makoto Iokibe, includes selections from both sources just mentioned. The concerns of these documents go beyond what is suggested by the title. Although not a substitute for original archival research, the publication nevertheless provides a convenient avenue to gain access to the planning documents. When using the collection, however, researchers should be aware that it does not provide a clear clue to the chief executive's role in the U.S. government's foreign policy planning. Exploration of materials located in the Franklin D. Roosevelt Library and elsewhere, therefore, remains a critical task for serious researchers interested in the origins of U.S. foreign policy in postwar East Asia.

On the Chinese side, an essential source of information is the multivolume *Zhonghua Minguo Zhongyao Shiliao Chubian–Dui Ri Kangzhan Shiqi* (Preliminary Compilation of Important Historical Records of the Republic of China: The Period of the War of Resistance Against Japan), published by the Historical Council of the KMT Central Committee in Taiwan in 1980. In scope and thoroughness, this publication is inferior to the foreign relations series of the U.S. Department of State. Most documents in this collection are minutes of Chiang Kai-shek's meetings and his communications with Chinese officials and foreign governments. Chiang's central position in these volumes is the publication's strength and its weakness.

Users should also be aware that these documents are selected to support the compilers' interpretations expressed in the introduction to each volume. These problems can be solved by consulting other materials that have become available in recent years. One is *Guomin Zhengfu yu Hanguo Duli Yundong Shiliao* (Historical Records on the Nationalist Government and the Korean Independence Movement), published by the Institute of Modern History of the Academia Sinica, Taipei, in 1988. It is based on Zhu Jiahua's official files. These documents reveal the intricate intramural competition that plagued the KMT government's policy making on Korea.

One consequence of the Communist victory in China in 1949 was to slice the official records of the Republic of China into three parts, which appeared separately in Taiwan, mainland China, and the United States. After the KMT regime was defeated in China, numerous KMT officials and diplomats moved to the United States. Some gave their papers to educational or research institutions in this country. For my study, the most useful are the T. V. Soong papers and the Victor Hoo papers at the Hoover Institution and the Wellington Koo papers at Columbia University. All three contain documents in Chinese and in English (the Koo papers also include documents in French). Soong, in my view, emerges from his papers as Chiang's envoy who was versed in maneuvering with the Western Allies but lacked the will or motive to take diplomatic initiatives. Despite Soong's responsibility in the war years for the Waijiaobu, his papers shed little light on how that organization functioned. Part of Soong's personal correspondence remains closed during Meiling Song's (Mrs. Chiang Kai-shek's) lifetime (she was born in 1897). Wellington Koo's constant concern about the domestic operations of Chinese diplomacy resulted in his extensive collection of a variety of documents bearing on Chongqing's foreign policy. These were produced by different branches of the KMT government. Koo's own communications with the Waijiaobu and with Chiang Kai-shek from his overseas posts often proposed alternatives for Chinese diplomacy, which the authorities in Chongqing were not always inclined to adopt. Victor Hoo's name hardly emerged in wartime Chinese diplomacy, even when he was accompanying Soong to the Moscow negotiations in 1945. As Soong's deputy, Hoo was responsible for the routine operations of the Waijiaobu; consequently, his papers contain memoranda and position papers that were circulated within the Waijiaobu or exchanged with other government agencies. Some of these documents disclose the least ornamented aspect of the KMT regime's aspirations in postwar Asia. The Hoo papers also include a complete set of the minutes of the Soong–Stalin negotiations. Because the ZZSC has published only half of these minutes, the Hoo papers become the most authoritative source of information with regard to Moscow diplomacy. It has recently been reported that the Russian government declassified the diplomatic records of the former Soviet Union concerning the Moscow negotiations (see Brian Murry, "Stalin, the Cold War, and the Division of China: A Multi-Archival Mystery," Cold War International History Project Working Paper No. 12. of The Woodrow Wilson Center). Now the Soviet side of the story can be studied.

This study also uses published and unpublished documents from the Second Historical Archives of China, Nanjing, the PRC. The records preserved there account for only a small portion of the pre-1949 archives of the KMT government. For instance, only 9 files of the Committee on Japanese Reparations remain, perhaps by chance, in Nanjing; the committee's other 194,000 files were moved to Taiwan in 1949. This is an extreme case. The records of other agencies have some substance. Still, it can be expected that arguments in my study will likely be corrected in the future by other scholars possessing a wider range of historical records on Chinese diplomacy. Since it was opened in 1980, the Second Archives has made significant progress in making its collections accessible to researchers. A general description of its collections can be found in *Zhongguo Di Er Lishi Dang'anguan Jianming Zhinan* (Brief Guide to the Second Historical Archives of China), edited by Shi Xuanqin et al. (Beijing: Dang'an Chubanshe, 1987). At the Archives, researchers can use registers for the collections as finding aids. These registers are usually informative and easy to use. Because there is still no regular system in the PRC for the declassification of archival materials (even for the Republican period), researchers should expect denial of access to certain records that are deemed sensitive by the Chinese authorities. My general impression is, however, that the Second Archives has not been fully used by either Chinese or overseas researchers.

Manuscript collections and oral histories

The United States

Joseph W. and Stewart Alsop Papers, Library of Congress
Joseph Ballantine Oral History, Butler Library, Columbia University, New York City
Joseph W. Ballantine Papers, Hoover Institution on War, Revolution and Peace, Stanford, CA
Adolf Berle Papers, Franklin D. Roosevelt Library, Hyde Park, NY
Lauchlin Currie Papers, Hoover Institution
Eugene H. Dooman Oral History, Butler Library
Eugene H. Dooman Papers, Hoover Institution
Harry L. Hopkins Papers, Roosevelt Library
Stanley K. Hornbeck Papers, Hoover Institution
Cordell Hull Papers (microfilm), Library of Congress
Institute of Pacific Relations Collections, Butler Library
Philip C. Jessup Papers, Library of Congress
William D. Leahy Papers, Library of Congress
Pacific Relations Collection, Butler Library
Franklin D. Roosevelt Papers, Roosevelt Library
  Map Room File
  Official File
  President's Personal File
  President's Secretary's File
Joseph W. Stilwell Papers, Hoover Institution
Henry L. Stimson Diaries (microfilm), Library of Congress
Arthur N. Young Papers, Hoover Institution

China

Chang Fa-k'uei (Zhang Fakui) Papers, Butler Library
Chang Kia-ngau (Zhang Jia'ao) Papers, Hoover Institution

Ch'en Kuang-fu (Chen Guangfu) Papers, Butler Library
Fu Ping-ch'ang (Fu Bingchang) Oral History, Butler Library
Hoo, Victor Ch'i-ts'a (Hu Shize) Papers, Hoover Institution
Hsiung Shih-hui (Xiong Shihui) Papers, Butler Library
King, Wunsz (Jin Wensi) Papers, Hoover Institution
Koo, V. K. Wellington (Gu Weijun) Oral History, Butler Library
Koo, V. K. Wellington Papers, Butler Library
K'ung Hsiang-hsi (Kong Xiangxi) Papers, Butler Library
Soong, T. V. (Song Ziwen) Papers, Hoover Institution

Unpublished government documents

The United States

National Archives, Washington, DC
General Records of the Department of State Central Files: China, 1937–1945 (Record Group 59)
Records of the Division of Chinese Affairs, 1944–1950 (Record Group 59)
Records of Foreign Service Posts of the Department of State, Embassy in China Files, 1941–1945 (Record Group 84)
Records of Harley A. Notter (Postwar Planning), 1939–1945 (Record Group 59)
Records of the Secretary of State (Edward R. Stettinius, Jr.), December 1944–July 1945 (Record Group 59)
Records of the Special Assistant to the Secretary of State (Leo Pasvolsky), 1938–1945 (Record Group 59)
National Archives and Federal Records Center, Suitland, MD
General Records of Chungking (Chongqing) Embassy, China, 1943–1945
Records of the China Theater of Operations, United States Army (CT): Records of the Office of the Commanding General (Albert C. Wedemeyer)
Top Secret General Records of Chungking Embassy, China, 1945

China

The Second Historical Archives of China, Nanjing, China (records there are listed according to *quan zong hao*, or general record number)
General Record Number 2, Executive Yuan
General Record Number 5, Ministry of Education
General Record Number 18, Waijiaobu
General Record Number 43, Supreme Council of National Defense
General Record Number 171, Central Planning Board
General Record Number 761, National Military Council

Journals and newspapers

China at War, 1937–1945, New York
Da Gong Bao (Grand Public Daily), 1941–1946, Chongqing
Gemingshi Ziliao (Materials on the History of Revolution), Beijing
Jiefang (Liberation), 1937–1941, Yan'an

Jiefang Ribao (Liberation Daily), 1941–1947, Yan'an
Jindai Zhongguo (Modern China), Taipei
Jindaishi Yanjiu (Study of Modern History), Beijing
Xinhua Ribao (New China Daily), Chongqing, 1942–1943
Zhonggong Dangshi Ziliao (Materials on the History of the Chinese Communist
    Party), Beijing
Zhongyang Ribao (Central Daily), 1938–1945, Chongqing
Zhuanji Wenxue (Biographical Literature), Taipei

Published sources and secondary studies

In English

Acheson, Dean. *Present at the Creation; My Years in the State Department.* New
    York: W. W. Norton, 1969.
    Among Friends: Personal Letters of Dean Acheson. Ed. David McLellan and
    David C. Acheson. New York: Dodd, Mead, 1980.
Barrett, David D. *Dixie Mission: The United States Army Observers Group in
    Yenan, 1944.* Berkeley: Center of Chinese Studies, University of California,
    1970.
Berle, Beatrice B., and Jacobs, T. B. *Navigating the Rapids, 1918–1971: From the
    Papers of Adolf A. Berle.* New York: Harcourt Brace Jovanovich, 1973.
Bisson, T. A. *Yenan in June 1937: Talks with the Communist Leaders.* Berkeley:
    Center of Chinese Studies, University of California at Berkeley, 1973.
Blum, John M., ed. *From the Morgenthau Diaries: Years of War, 1941–1945.*
    Boston: Houghton Mifflin, 1959–1967.
    ed. *The Price of Vision: The Diary of Henry A. Wallace, 1942–1946.* Boston:
    Houghton Mifflin, 1973.
Bohlen, Charles E. *Witness to History, 1929–1969.* New York: W. W. Norton,
    1973.
Borton, Hugh. *American Presurrender Planning for Postwar Japan.* New York:
    Columbia University Press, 1967.
Byrnes, James F. *Speaking Frankly.* New York: Harper, 1947.
    All in One Lifetime. New York: Harper, 1958.
Campbell, Thomas M., and Herring, George C., Jr., ed. *The Diaries of Edward R.
    Stettinius, Jr., 1943–1946.* New York: New Viewpoints, 1975.
Carlson, Evans Fordyce. *Twin Stars of China.* New York: Dodd, Mead, 1940.
Chiang Kai-shek. *China's Destiny.* New York: Roy Publishers, 1947.
Chinese Ministry of Information, comp. *The Collected Wartime Messages of Gen-
    eralissimo Chiang Kai-shek, 1937–1945.* New York: John Day, 1946. Reprint
    (2 vols. in 1). New York: Kraus Reprint, 1969.
Churchill, Winston S. *The Second World War.* Boston: Houghton Mifflin, 1948–
    1953.
Council on Foreign Relations. *Studies of American Interests in War and Peace.*
    New York: Council on Foreign Relations, 1941–1944.
Cumings, Bruce. *The Origins of the Korean War: Liberation and the Emergence
    of Separate Regimes, 1945–1947.* Princeton, NJ: Princeton University Press,
    1981.

Dallek, Robert. *Franklin D. Roosevelt and American Foreign Policy, 1932–1945.* Oxford: Oxford University Press, 1979.

Davies, John P., Jr. *Dragon by the Tail: American, British, Japanese and Russian Encounters with China and One Another.* New York: W. W. Norton, 1972.

Dilks, David, ed. *The Diaries of Sir Alexander Cadogan, 1938–1945.* London: Cassell, 1971.

Dower, John W. *War without Mercy: Race and Power in the Pacific War.* New York: Pantheon, 1986.

Emmerson, John K. *The Japanese Thread: A Life in the U.S. Foreign Service.* New York: Holt, Rinehart & Winston, 1978.

Esherick, Joseph W., ed. *Lost Chance in China: The World War II Despatches of John S. Service.* New York: Random House, 1974.

Fairbank, John King. *Chinabound: A Fifty-Year Memoir.* New York: Harper, 1982.
   ed. *The Chinese World Order: Traditional China's Foreign Relations.* Cambridge: Harvard University Press, 1968.

Feis, Herbert. *The China Tangle: The American Effort in China from Pearl Harbor to the Marshall Mission.* Princeton, NJ: Princeton University Press, 1953.

Ferrell, Robert H., ed. *Dear Bess: The Letters from Harry to Bess Truman, 1910–1959.* New York: W. W. Norton, 1983.
   ed. *Off the Record: The Private Papers of Harry S. Truman.* New York: Penguin, 1980.

Garver, John W. *Chinese–Soviet Relations, 1937–1945: The Diplomacy of Chinese Nationalism.* New York: Oxford University Press, 1988.

Gillin, Donald, and Myers, Ramon H., ed. *Last Chance in Manchuria; The Diaries of Chang Kia-ngau.* Stanford, CA: Hoover Institution, 1989.

Grew, Joseph C. *Turbulent Era: A Diplomatic Record of Forty Years, 1904–1945.* Boston: Houghton Mifflin, 1952.

Harriman, W. Averell, and Abel, Elie. *Special Envoy to Churchill and Stalin, 1941–1946.* New York: Random House, 1975.

Hayes, Grace P. *The History of the Joint Chiefs of Staff in World War II: The War Against Japan.* Annapolis, MD: Naval Institute Press, 1982.

Hull, Cordell. *Memoirs of Cordell Hull.* New York: Macmillan, 1948.

Hunt, Michael H. *The Making of a Special Relationship: The United States and China to 1914.* New York: Columbia University Press, 1983.

Institute of Pacific Relations. *War and Peace in the Pacific: A Preliminary Report of the Eighth Conference of the IPR on Wartime and Postwar Cooperation of the United Nations in the Pacific and the Far East.* New York: Institute of Pacific Relations, 1943.
   Security in the Pacific; A Preliminary Report of the Ninth Conference of the IPR. New York: Institute of Pacific Relations, 1945.

Iriye, Akira. *Power and Culture: The Japanese–American War, 1941–1945.* Cambridge, MA: Harvard University Press, 1981.

Kennan, George F. *Memoirs, 1925–1950.* New York: Pantheon, 1983.

Kimball, Warren F., ed. *Churchill and Roosevelt: The Complete Correspondence.* Princeton, NJ: Princeton University Press, 1984.

Kirby, William C. *Germany and Republican China.* Stanford, CA: Stanford University Press, 1984.

Leahy, William D. *I Was There.* New York: McGraw-Hill, 1950.

Lee, Chong-sik. *The Politics of Korean Nationalism.* Berkeley: University of California Press, 1965.

Louis, W. Roger. *Imperialism at Bay: The United States and the Decolonization of the British Empire, 1941–1945.* New York: Oxford University Press, 1978.

MacArthur, Douglas. *Reminiscences.* New York: McGraw-Hill, 1964.

Makoto Iokibe, ed. *The Occupation of Japan: U.S. Planning Documents, 1942–1945.* Bethesda, MD: Congressional Information Service, 1987. Microfiche.

Matray, James I. *The Reluctant Crusade: American Foreign Policy in Korea, 1941–1950.* Honolulu: University of Hawaii Press, 1985.

May, Gary. *China Scapegoat: The Diplomatic Ordeal of John Carter Vincent.* Washington, DC: New Republic Books, 1979.

Notter, Harley. *Postwar Foreign Policy Preparation, 1939–1945.* Washington, DC: G.P.O., 1949.

Reardon-Anderson, James. *Yenan and the Great Powers: The Origins of Chinese Communist Foreign Policy, 1944–1946.* New York: Columbia University Press, 1980.

Romanus, Charles, and Sunderland, Riley. *Stilwell's Mission to China.* Washington, DC: G.P.O., 1953.

Time Runs Out in CBT. Washington, DC: G.P.O., 1959.

Roosevelt, Elliott. *As He Saw It.* New York: Duell, Sloan & Pearce, 1946.

ed. *FDR, His Personal Letters: 1928–1945.* New York: Duell, Sloan & Pearce, 1950.

Roosevelt, Franklin D. *Complete Presidential Press Conferences of Franklin D. Roosevelt, 1933–1945.* New York: Da Capo, 1972.

Rosenman, Samuel I. *Working with Roosevelt.* New York: Harper, 1952.

Sainsbury, Keith. *The Turning Points: Roosevelt, Stalin, Churchill, and Chiang-Kai-Shek [sic], 1943: The Moscow, Cairo, and Teheran Conferences.* New York: Oxford University Press, 1985.

Schaller, Michael. *The U.S. Crusade in China, 1938–1945.* New York: Columbia University Press, 1979.

Schewe, Donald B., ed. *Franklin D. Roosevelt and Foreign Affairs, January 1937–August 1939.* New York: Garland, 1979–1980.

Sherwood, Robert E. *Roosevelt and Hopkins: An Intimate History.* New York: Harper, 1948.

Shewmaker, Kenneth E. *Americans and Chinese Communists, 1927–1945: A Persuading Encounter.* Ithaca, NY: Cornell University Press, 1971.

Sigal, Leon V. *Fighting to a Finish: The Politics of War Termination in the United States and Japan, 1945.* Ithaca: Cornell University Press, 1988.

Snow, Edgar. *Red Star Over China.* New York: Random House, 1938.

Random Notes on Red China, 1936–1945. Cambridge, MA: Harvard University Press, 1957.

Stein, Gunther. *The Challenge of Red China.* New York: McGraw-Hill, 1945.

Stettinius, Edward R., Jr. *Roosevelt and the Russians.* Garden City, NY: Doubleday, 1949.

Suh, Dae-sook. *The Korea Communist Movement, 1918–1948.* Princeton, NJ: Princeton University Press, 1967.

Documents of Korean Communism, 1918–1948. Princeton, NJ: Princeton University Press, 1970.

Sun Yat-sen. *San Min Chu Yi: The Three Principles of the People*. Chongqing: Ministry of Information of the Republic of China, 1943.

Sun, Youli. *China and the Origins of the Pacific War, 1931–1941*. New York: St. Martin's Press, 1993.

Thorne, Christopher. *Allies of a Kind: The United States, Britain and the War Against Japan, 1941–1945*. Oxford: Oxford University Press, 1978.

The Issue of War: States, Societies, and the Far Eastern Conflict of 1941–1945. New York: Oxford University Press, 1985.

Truman, Harry S. *Memoirs by Harry S. Truman*. New York: Doubleday, 1955.

Tsou, Tang. *America's Failure in China, 1941–1950*. Chicago: University of Chicago Press, 1963.

Tung, Hollington K. *Dateline: China: The Beginning of China's Press Relations with the World*. New York: Rockport Press, 1950.

United States Department of Defense. *The Entry of the Soviet Union into the War Against Japan: Military Plans, 1941–1945*. Washington, DC: G.P.O., 1955.

United States Department of State. *The China White Paper, August 1949*. Stanford, CA: Stanford University Press, 1967.

Foreign Relations of the United States: Diplomatic Papers. Washington, DC: G.P.O.:

1937; I–IV (1954)
1938; III–IV (1954–1955)
1939; III–IV (1955)
1940; IV (1955)
1941; IV–V (1956)
China, 1942 (1956)
China, 1943 (1957)
The Conferences at Cairo and Teheran, 1943 (1961)
The Conferences at Malta and Yalta, 1945 (1955)
The Conference of Berlin (1960)
1944; VI (1967)
1945; VII (1969)

O.S.S./State Department Intelligence and Research Reports. Washington, DC: University Publications of America, 1977. Microfilm.

State–War–Navy Coordinating Committee Policy Files, 1944–1947. Wilmington, DE: Scholarly Resources, 1977. Microfilm.

United States Joint Chiefs of Staff. *Records of the Joint Chiefs of Staff*. Frederick, MD: University Publications of America, 1980–1983. Microfilm.

United States Office of Strategic Services. *The Japanese Emperor and the War*. Washington, DC: G.P.O., 1944.

United States Senate, Committee on the Judiciary. *Morgenthau Diary (China)*. Washington, DC: 89th Congress, 1st Session, February 5, 1965.

The Amerasia Papers: A Clue to the Catastrophe of China. Washington, DC: G.P.O., 1970.

United States Strategic Bombing Survey. *Japan's Struggle to End the War*. Washington, DC: G.P.O., 1946.

Vladimirov, Peter. *The Vladimirov Diaries: Yenan, China, 1942–1945*. Garden City, NY: Doubleday, 1975.

Wales, Nym. *Inside Red China*. New York: Doubleday, Doran, 1939.

My Yenan Notebooks. Madison, Conn.: Helen F. Snow, 1961.

Wedemeyer, Albert C. *Wedemeyer Reports!* New York: Henry Holt, 1958.

Welles, Sumner. *The Time for Decision.* New York: Harper, 1944.

Where Are We Heading? New York: Harper, 1946.

Westad, Odd Arne. *Cold War and Revolution: Soviet–American Rivalry and the Origins of the Chinese Civil War, 1944–1946.* New York: Columbia University Press, 1993.

In Chinese

Cao Rulin. *Cao Rulin Yisheng zhi Huiyi* (Memoirs of Cao Rulin). Taipei: Zhuanji Wenxue Chubanshe, 1980.

Chen Bulei. *Chen Bulei Huiyilu* (Memoirs of Chen Bulei). Taipei: Zhuanji Wenxue Chubanshe, 1967.

Chen Bulei Wenji (Collected Works of Chen Bulei). Taipei: Zhongyang Wenwu Gongyingshe, 1984.

Chen Mingzhong and Chen Xingtang, ed. *Taiwan Guangfu he Guangfu hou Wu Nian Shengqing* (The Restoration of Taiwan and the Situation in the Province during the First Five Years). Nanjing: Nanjing Chubanshe, 1989.

Chen Tianxi. *Dai Jitao Xiansheng Biannian Zhuanji* (A Chronological Biography of Mr. Dai Jitao). Taipei: Zhongguo Congshu Weiyuanhui, 1958.

Chiang Zongtong Milu (Secret Records of President Chiang [Kai-shek]). Comp. Furuya Keiji. 14 vols. Taipei: Zhongyang Ribaoshe, 1974–1977.

Dong Xianguang. *Dong Xianguang Zizhuan* (Autobiography of Dong Xianguang). Taipei: Xinsheng Baoshe, 1973.

Dong Yanping. *Su E Ju Dongbei: Di Er Ci Shijie Dazhan Jiesu Shi Su E Qinju Dongbei Zhechong Jiyao* (Soviet Russia Occupies the Northeast: Records of Negotiations with Soviet Russia in the Northeast after World War II). Taipei: Zhonghua Dadian Bianyinhui, 1965.

Gu Weijun. *Gu Weijun Huiyilu* (Memoirs of Gu Weijun). 12 vols. Beijing: Zhonghua Shuju, 1983–1993.

Hu Chunhui. *Hanguo Duli Yundong zai Zhongguo* (The Korean Independence Movement in China). Taipei: Zhonghua Minguo Shiliao Yanjiu Zhongxin, 1976.

Hu Hanmin. *Nanjing de Dui Ri Waijiao* (Nanking's Diplomacy Toward Japan). Guangzhou: Zhongxing Xuehui, 1935.

Yuandong Wenti yu Da Yaxiya Zhuyi (The Far Eastern Problem and Pan-Asianism). Guangzhou: Zhongxing Xuehui, 1935.

Hu Qiaomu. *Hu Qiaomu Huiyi Mao Zedong* (Hu Qiaomu's Reminiscences about Mao Zedong). Beijing: Renmin Chubanshe, 1994.

Hu Songping, ed. *Zhu Jiahua Nianpu* (A Chronicle of Zhu Jiahua's life). Taipei: Zhuanji Wenxue Chubanshe, 1969.

ed. *Hu Shizhi Xiansheng Nianpu Changbian Chugao* (The Preliminary Draft of the Chronicle of Mr. Hu Shi's life). Taipei: Lianjing Chuban Shiye Gongsi, 1984.

Jiang Jingguo. *Fu Zhong Zhi Yuan* (Long Journey with Heavy Burden). Taipei: Youshi Shudian, n.d.

Jiang Tingfu. *Jiang Tingfu Huiyilu* (Memoirs of Jiang Tingfu). Taipei: Zhuanji Wenxue Chubanshe, 1984.

Jiang Yongjing, ed. *Hu Hanmin Xiansheng Nianpu* (A Chronicle of Mr. Hu Hanmin's Life). Taipei: Kuomintang Dangshi Weiyuanhui, 1978.

Jin Jiu (Kim Ku). *Bai Fan Yizhi* (Autobiography of Bai Fan). Taipei: Youshi Shudian, 1969.

Jin Wensi. *Waijiao Gongzuo de Huiyi* (Reminiscences on Diplomatic Missions). Taipei: Zhuanji Wenxue Chubanshe, 1968.

   Cong Bali Hehui dao Guolian (From the Paris Peace Conference to the League of Nations). Taipei: Zhuanji Wenxue Chubanshe, 1983.

Kuomintang Dangshi Weiyuanhui (Historical Council of the Kuomintang). *Geming Wenxian* (Revolutionary documents). Multivolume. Taipei: Kuomintang Dangshi Weiyuanhui, 1976–.

   Zhonghua Minguo Zhongyao Shiliao Chubian–Dui Ri Kangzhan Shiqi (Preliminary Compilation of Important Historical Records of the Republic of China: The Period of the War of Resistance Against Japan). 7 vols. Taipei: Kuomintang Dangshi Weiyuanhui, 1981.

   Xian Zongtong Chiang Gong Sixiang Yanlun Zongji (Complete Works of the Late President Chiang [Kai-shek]). 40 vols. Taipei: Kuomintang Dangshi Weiyuanhui, 1984.

Lin Quan, ed. *Kangzhan Qijian Feichu Bupingdeng Tiaoyue Shiliao* (Documents on the Abrogation of the Unequal Treaties during the Anti-Japanese war). Taipei: Zhengzhong Shuju, 1983.

Mao Zedong. *Mao Zedong Ji* (Works of Mao Zedong). Tokyo: Hokubosha, 1970–1971.

Niu Jun. *Cong Yan'an Zouxiang Shijie: Zhongguo Gongchandang dui Wai Guanxi de Qiyuan* (Approach the World from Yan'an: The Origins of the Foreign Relations of the Chinese Communist Party). Fuzhou: Fujian Renmin Chubanshe, 1992.

Nosaka Sanzo. *Wangming Shiliu Nian* (Sixteen Years in Exile). Hong Kong: Wenjian Chubanshe, 1949.

   Yeban Cansan Xuanji: Zhanshi Pian (Selected works of Nosaka Sanzo: the war years). Beijing: Renmin Chubanshe, 1963.

Pu Xuefeng. "Wo guo dangnian duiyu zhanhou Riben tianhuang zhidu zhi lichang" (Wartime Policy of Our Government Toward the Postwar Status of the Japanese Imperial Institution), *Zhuanji Wenxue*, vol. 28 (1976), no. 6.

   Taixukong li Yi Youchen: Ba Nian Kangzhan Shengya Suibi (Drifting Dust in the Universe: Random Notes from My Experience during the Eight-Year War of Resistance). Taipei: Taiwan Shangwu Yinshuguan, 1979.

Shao Yulin. *Shi Han Huiyilu* (My Mission to Korea). Taipei: Zhuanji Wenxue Chubanshe, 1980.

Shen Yanding. "Dui Ri wangshi zhuiji" (Reminiscences on My Experiences with Japan), *Zhuanji Wenxue*, vol. 25 (1974), nos. 1–3, 5–6; vol. 26 (1975), nos. 1–3, 5–6; vol. 27 (1975), nos. 1, 3–6; vol. 28 (1976), nos. 1, 3, 5–6; and vol. 29 (1976), nos. 2, 4, 6.

Shi Zhe. *Zai Lishi Juren Shenbian: Shi Zhe Huiyilu* (Beside Historical Giants: The Memoirs of Shi Zhe). Beijing: Zhongyang Wenxian Chubanshe, 1991.

Sun Ke. *Zhongguo yu Zhanhou Shijie* (China and the Postwar World). Chongqing: n.p., 1944.

   Zhong Su Guanxi (Sino–Soviet Relations). Shanghai: Zhonghua Shuju, 1946.

Taiwan Wenti Yanlun Ji (Speeches and Writings on the Taiwan Question). Comp. Taiwan Geming Tongmenghui. Chongqing: Guoji Wenti Yanjiusuo, 1943.

Tian Yushi. "Dongbei jieshou san nian zaihuo zuiyan" (Reflection on the Three-Year Catastrophe of Taking Over the Northeast), *Zhuanji Wenxue*, vol. 35 (1979), no. 6; vol. 36 (1980), nos. 1–6; vol. 37 (1980), nos. 1, 3–4, 6; and vol. 38 (1981), nos. 1–4.

Waijiaobu Dang'an Ziliao Chu (Office of Archival Materials of the Ministry of Foreign Affairs). *Zhongguo Waijiao Jiguan Liren Shouzhang Xianming Nianbiao* (A Chronological Table on the Positions and Names of Chief Officials of China's Foreign Affairs Administration). Taipei: Taiwan Shangwu Yinshuguan, 1967.

   Zhongguo Zhuwai Ge Dai Gong Shiguan Liren Guanzhang Xianming Nianbiao (A Chronological Table on the Positions and Names of Heads of China's Overseas Missions). Taipei: Taiwan Shangwu Yinshuguan, 1969.

Waijiao Wenti Yanjiuhui (Research Association on Diplomatic Issues), comp. *Zhong Ri Waijiao Shiliao Congbian* (Documents on the History of Sino–Japanese Diplomatic Relations). 8 vols. Taipei: Waijiao Wenti Yanjiuhui, 1965–1966.

Wang Chonghui. *Kun Xue Zhai Wencun* (Writings at the Kun Xue House). Taipei: Zhonghua Congshu Weiyuanhui, 1957.

   Wang Chonghui Xiansheng Wenji (Writings by Mr. Wang Chonghui). Taipei: Zhongyang Wenwu Gongyingshe, 1981.

Wang Shijie. *Wang Shijie Riji* (The Diaries of Wang Shijie). Taipei: Zhongyang Yenjiuyuan Jindaishi Yenjiusuo, 1990.

Wei Daoming. "Shi Mei huiyilu" (Reminiscences on My Mission to the United States), *Zhuanji Wenxue*, vol. 36 (1980), no. 3.

Wu Huanchang. "Kangzhan shengli hou jieshou Dongbei de huiyi" (Recollections on the Takeover of the Northeast after the Victory of the War of Resistance), *Zhuanji Wenxue*, vol. 24 (1974), nos. 2–3.

Xie Dongmin et al. *Guomin Geming yu Taiwan* (Nationalist Revolution and Taiwan). Taipei: Zhongyang Wenwu Gongyingshe, 1980.

Yan Huiqing. *Yan Huiqing Zizhuan* (Autobiography of Yan Huiqing). Taipei: Zhuanji Wenxue Chubanshe, 1982.

Zhang Qiyun. *Zhonghua Minguo Shigang* (Historical Outline of the Republic of China). Taipei: Zhonghua Wenhua Chuban Shiye Weiyuanhui, 1956.

Zhang Qun. *Wo yu Riben Qishi Nian* (I and Japan for Seventy Years). Taipei: Zhong Ri Guanxi Yanjiuhui, 1980.

Zhang Zhongfu. *Miwang Ji* (A Perplexed Reminiscence). Taipei: Wenhai Chubanshe, 1978.

Zhonggong Zhongyang Wenjian Xuanji (Selected Documents of the Central Committee of the Chinese Communist Party). Comp. Zhongyan Dang'anguan (Central Archives). 18 vols. Beijing: Zhonggong Zhongyang Dangxiao Chubanshe, 1989–1992.

Zhonggong Zhongyang Wenxian Yanjiushi (Office of Documentary Research of the Central Committee of the Chinese Communist Party). *Zhou Enlai Nianpu, 1898–1949* (A Chronicle of Zhou Enlai's Life, 1898–1949). Beijing: Zhongyang Wenxian Chubanshe, 1989.

Zhongyang Yanjiuyuan Jindaishi Yanjiusuo (Institute of Modern History of the Academia Sinica). *Guomin Zhengfu yu Hanguo Duli Yundong Shiliao* (Historical Records on the Nationalist Government and the Korean Independence Movement). Taipei: Zhongyang Yanjiuyuan Jindaishi Yanjiusuo, 1988.

Index

Japan (*cont.*)
 postwar disposition of, at Cairo
  Conference, 131–6, 146, 154
 postwar strength of, 59–60
 postwar treatment of, 27, 28, 120, 129,
  176, 179–88
 reform of, 213, 214–15, 217
 reintegrating into community of
  nations, 218
 responsibility for policing of, postwar,
  51, 52
 rule in China's lost territories, 80
 in secret diplomacy (World War I), 2
 seized Manchuria, 86, 232
 struggle on racial front, 23–4
 Taiwan ceded to, 64
 total defeat of, 214
 unconditional victory over, 119
 U.S. dealings with, 302
 U.S. joined China in war against, 19–20
 war guilt, 38
"Japan hands" (CCP), 169
Japan policy (U.S.), 48, 50
Japanese–American relations, 6, 59
Japanese Army, 171–2, 173, 203–4
 proposed destruction of, 40–1
Japanese Communist Party (JCP), 161,
 168, 174
Japanese emperor
 CCP attitude toward, 169–70, 173
 policy regarding, 181
 proposed removal of, 131, 132, 133
 proposals on punishment/treatment of,
  42–5, 49, 182
 retention of, 217
Japanese Empire, 8, 60, 64, 231
 demolished, 300
 Korea detached from, 102
 militarist foundation of, 41
 postwar dissolution of (proposed), 37,
  46, 55, 101, 126, 127
 Taiwan's economic integration with, 74
Japanese expansionism, 12, 39, 46, 59, 72,
 83, 85
Japanese home islands, 220, 227, 303
Japanese imperialism, 22
Japanese Mandated Islands, 46, 72, 79,
 125, 224
 international administration of
  (proposed), 45
 postwar disposition of, 188, 194, 210
 as strategic base, 219
Japanese Navy, 42
Japanese people: anti-war front among, 172
Japanese People's Emancipation League
 (JPEL), 171, 172–3, 216
Japanese soldiers: captured, reeducated,
 and sent back, 171–2
Japanese sovereignty: over Taiwan, 73–4

Japanese surrender, 187, 232, 278, 279,
 280, 283, 287
 terms of (proposed), 29, 42
Japanese territories: geographic criterion
 for disposal of, 219
 postwar disposition of (proposed), 52
Japanese Workers' and Peasants' School,
 171
Java islands, 13
Jehol, 158
Jiefang Ribao (Liberation Daily), 153, 154,
 159, 163, 164, 170, 172, 173
Johnson, Nelson T., 18
Joint Chiefs of Staff (U.S.), 32, 124, 140,
 219, 227, 248
 Joint intelligence Committee, 204
 Joint Psychological Warfare Committee,
  20–1
 Joint War Plans Committee, 212, 280
 and Korea policy, 228–9
 and occupation of Japan, 211, 212
 and postwar foreign policy, 288
 and Soviet participation in Pacific war,
  238

Kailuo Huiyi (The Cairo Conference)
 (Liang Jingtong), 130*n*12
Kamchatka Peninsula, 212
Kang Ze, 162
Ke Taishan, 192
Kennan, George, 228, 248
Kerr, George H., 76*n*55
Kim Il Sung, 296
Kim Ku (aka Jin Jiu; Bai Fan), 86, 87, 88,
 89, 90, 92, 94–5, 99, 166, 195, 196
Kim Won-bong (aka Chen Guobin; Jin
 Roshan), 87, 91, 93, 97, 165, 166, 196
King, Ernest J., 124, 220
"kingly way" culture, 39
Kirk, Grayson, 59*n*11
KMT; *see* Kuomintang (KMT, National
 People's Party)
Koo, Wellington (Gu Weijun), 26, 44, 83,
 132, 178, 184–5, 233, 235, 247, 253
 on Chinese foreign policy, 177–8
 at Dumbarton Oaks, 194
 on Korea policy, 195, 200
 and reparations policy, 187
 and Sino–Soviet relations, 253–4,
  256–7
 and Yalta accord, 245–6
Korea, 14, 46, 62, 64, 65, 78, 79, 139,
 212, 220, 233, 280, 302, 303
 CCP and recovery of, 160, 173
 China's relationship with, 13
 discussed at Cairo Conference, 114,
  141–3, 146
 divided at 38th parallel, 289, 300
 liberation of, 168

"On the Coalition Government"
(Mao Zedong), 168, 174
One World (Willkie), 110
"Open Door," 240
open door policy, 263, 266, 269, 270,
275, 284
"Our Victory Is Imminent" (Sun Ke), 41
Outer Mongolia, 62, 114, 212
autonomy for, 251
border incidents, 234
CCP attitude toward status of, 160–1
China's claims in/recovery of, 58, 124
China's concession to Soviet demands
in, 258, 259, 260–7, 268, 270–1,
273, 277, 278, 282, 284
discussed at Cairo Conference, 144
maintenance of status quo regarding,
242, 243–4, 255
Sino–Soviet negotiations over, 256, 303
Soviet interests in, 239, 243
"Outline of the Plan for Taking Over
Taiwan," 189–90

"Pacific Charter," 82
Pacific islands: disposition of, 193–4
U.S. interest in, 72, 78
Pacific Ocean, 64, 71
Pacific: strategic bases in, 124, 219–20,
223
Pacific territories: multinational
administration of, 141
Pacific war, 8, 17, 42, 56, 65, 82
American troops in, 204–5
CCP and, 154–5
China's passivity in, 20
Chinese–American cooperation in,
106
Chinese government and Korean
nationalists during, 85–6
Chinese–Korean–U.S. triangular
relationship in, 96
and Chinese lost territories, 65, 66
countries entering at end of, 233
effect on international relations, 10
end of, 174, 192, 212, 217, 229
Korea in/and, 87, 92–3
as race war, 23–4
Soviet entry into, 29, 63, 145, 158,
188, 225, 226, 227, 231, 233–4,
237, 238, 239, 241–2, 248,
249–50, 271, 272, 275, 283–4
Soviet neutrality in, 103
Taiwan and, 64–5, 70, 162–3
Pacific War Council, 32, 72, 100, 101,
111, 112, 115, 131, 202
pan-Asianism, 39–40
Paris Peace Conference, 11–12
paternalism, 230
U.S., 97–8, 302

peace: crisis of, 287–305
partnership for waging, 24–36
peace with Japan: principles for, 59
severe, 214
peace settlement (East Asia), 3–4, 8–9,
129, 176
CCP and, 149
peace settlement of 1919, 46
peace structure in Asia, 300–5
peace terms for Japan, 169
Pearl Harbor attack, 10, 15, 16, 17, 20,
25, 37, 56, 59, 73, 91, 116
Peffer, Nathaniel, 60
Pence, H. L., 51
People's Political Council (China), 37, 181,
182
People's Republic of China, 5, 159
Pescadores, 66, 120, 125, 136
Petrov, Appolon A., 255, 267–8, 273
phased revolutionary strategy (CCP),
159–60, 161, 170, 173
Philippines, 51, 84, 220, 223
"Plan for Assisting the Independence of
Korea," 199
Poland, 61, 201, 248
policy planners (U.S.): and postwar reform
of Japan, 213–14
"Policy with Respect to China," 205–6
Polish government, issue of, 197
political objectives: in Korea policy, 225,
226–7
political planning
China, for Manchuria, 232
for postwar Japan, 50, 53
political revolution: in Japan (proposed),
41, 43, 132
political situation (China), 23
political strategy: CCP, 159
in Yalta accord, 243
politics, international; *see* international
politics; power politics
Port Arthur, 120, 238, 242, 244, 246
bases in (proposed), 109, 115
in Moscow negotiations, 264, 265,
266, 276, 277–8, 282, 285
Soviet interest in, 239, 247, 255, 260
port privileges, 145–6
postwar issues: continuity in U.S. thought
about, 34–5
postwar objectives: of CCP, 155
postwar objectives in Asia
divergent U.S./China, 8, 10–11, 24,
35, 36, 37, 39, 46–7, 49, 53–4,
106, 107–11, 112, 131, 146–7,
230
divergent U.S./China: lost territories,
55, 79–80
postwar settlement: East Asia, 110, 121,
122, 126, 140–1, 202, 239